P9-ECJ-993

Albrecht Dürer

MASTER ARTISTS LIBRARY

Series directed by
Antonio Paolucci

GIVEN TO LEON H. BOYER
BY
RODNEY LEON BOYER
&
JULIEANNE BOYER
DEC. 1998

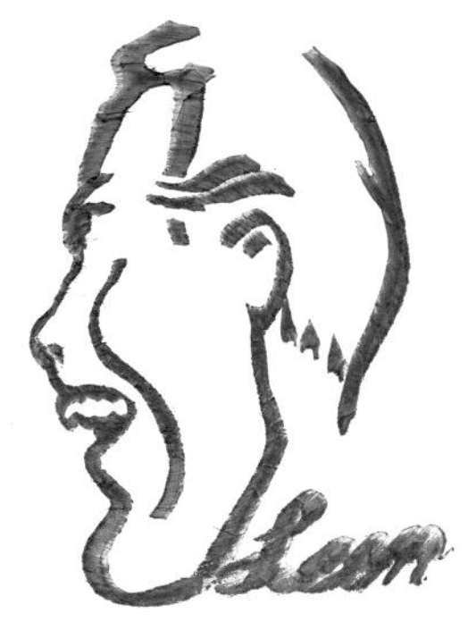

This edition published in 1998 by SMITHMARK Publishers,
a division of U.S. Media Holdings, Inc.,
115 West 18th Street, New York, NY 10011.

SMITHMARK books are available for bulk purchase for sales promotion and premium use.
For details write or call the manager of special sales,
SMITHMARK Publishers, 115 West 18th Street, New York, NY 10011.

Library of Congress Cataloging-In-Publication Data Is Available
ISBN: 0-7651-0864-X

Printed in Italy

10 9 8 7 6 5 4 3 2 1

Graphic design: Auro Lecci
Layout: Nina Peci
Prepress: Alfacolor, Bluprint
Printed by: Baioni Stampa

Dürer

Wolfram Prinz

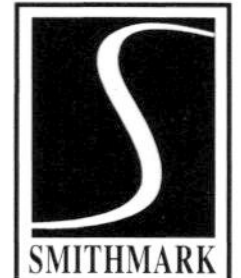

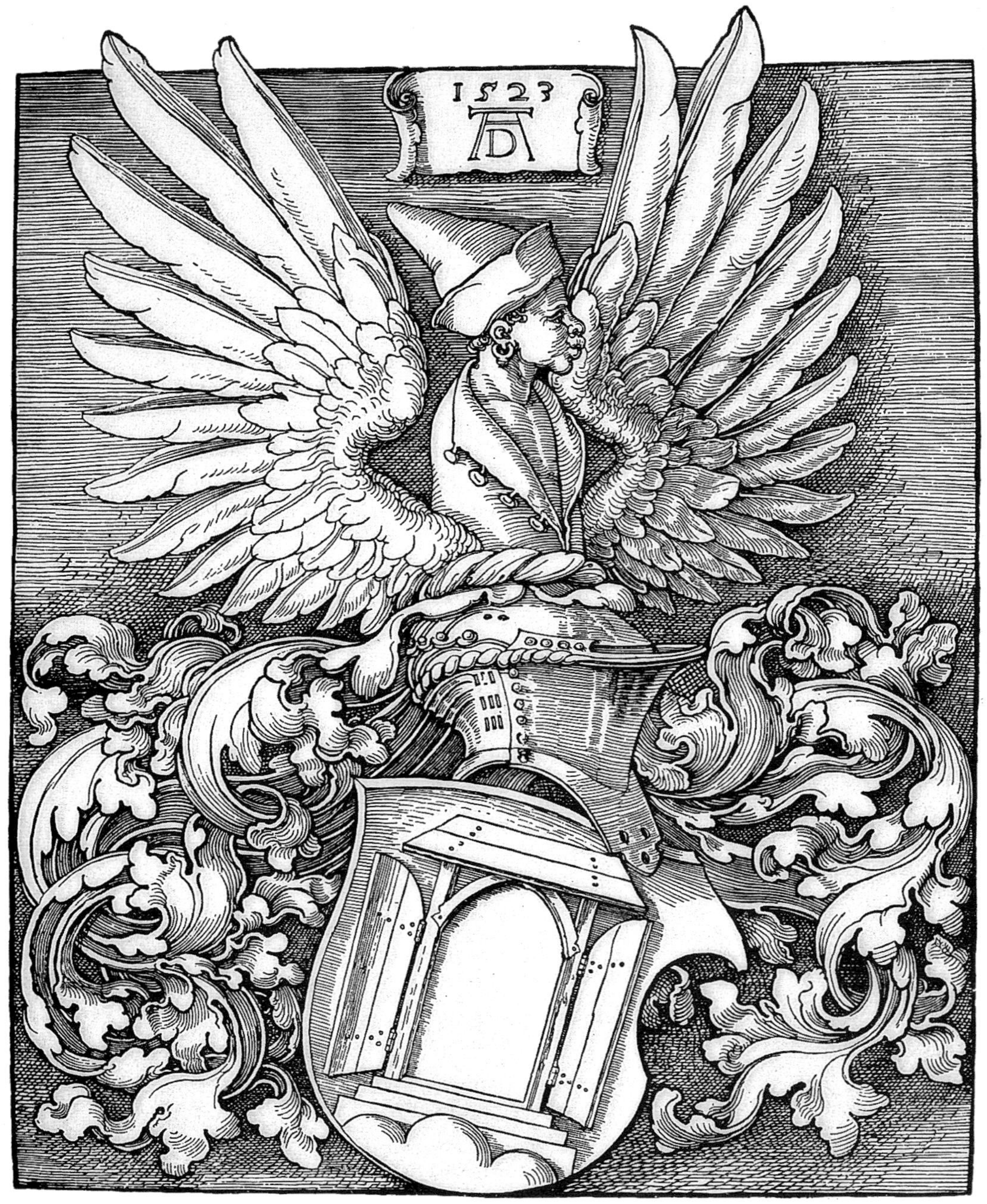

Fig. 1 *Coat of Arms of the House of Dürer*, 1593, woodcut.

Albrecht Dürer 1471-1528

Formative Years: The First Journeys, 1483–1494

All the great painters of the German Renaissance, including Mathis Grünewald (ca. 1470/75–1528), Lucas Cranach the Elder (1472–1553), and Albrecht Altdorfer (ca. 1490–1535), had remarkable artistic personalities. This was partly conditioned by their environment, where they were quite rooted. The fact that they often held positions in government, as did Cranach and Altdorfer, also contributed to this geographic stability. Dürer stands out among them not only for his artistic value, but because he was the only one who, without ever interrupting his own artistic activity, traveled to Italy and the Netherlands to search for new stimuli and experiences. Hans Holbein the Younger (1492–1543) also traveled: he went to France, Lombardy, and England. In England, he entered into the service of Henry VIII, where he remained until his death. However, he is an exception among German painters, and, in any case, he is younger than the artists mentioned, coming almost a generation after Dürer.

Dürer was born in Nuremberg, 21 May 1471. His artistic formation and his travel routes were affected by different circumstances, though they were largely determined by two factors: the central geographical position of his city—which favored commercial, cultural, and artistic relationships; and his family. His father, whose name was also Albrecht, was a respected goldsmith of Hungarian origin who, after having traveled and worked for a certain period in the Netherlands, settled in Nuremberg in 1455. Here he began to work in the workshop of the goldsmith Hieronymus Holper, and married his fifteen-year-old daughter, Barbara. He inherited the workshop after Holper's death, following custom (see the portraits of Dürer's parents, *cat. 1, 2*).

The third of eighteen children, Dürer discovered, early on, his first artistic inclinations while training at his father's workshop for a three-year apprenticeship. He then entered, at age sixteen, the workshop of Michael Wolgemut, the painter and woodcutter; like other great artists, Dürer was first a goldsmith and then a painter. At Wolgemut's workshop, altar polyptychs consisting of sculptures and large painted panels were executed. However, many were also done, which were then printed by Anton Koberger, Dürer's godfather, a famous printer and editor of the time. It was the apprenticeship in wood engraving that was to leave a mark on the artistic development of Albrecht.

At the end of this three-year apprenticeship, the nineteen-year-old Dürer, unable to tolerate the limitations of Wolgemut's workshop, and determined to widen his horizons, set out *auf Wanderschaft*. At that time, and for a long time after, these so-called *Wanderjahre* (years spent wandering) were, in Germany, the "journeying" apprenticeship of every reputable artisan. And it was so in Dürer's Germany, even for an artist from the artisan class. The *Lehrling* (apprentice) would pass to *Geselle* (worker), then to become *Meister*, that is, master, and thus, proprietor and owner of a workshop. Dürer did this, setting out along the upper Rhine. Certainly on his father's advice—who, in that period, had much influence on his decisions and artistic development in general—Dürer made a stop in Colmar, in the workshop of Martin Schongauer, one of the most respected German painters and engravers of the age, who was also a gold-

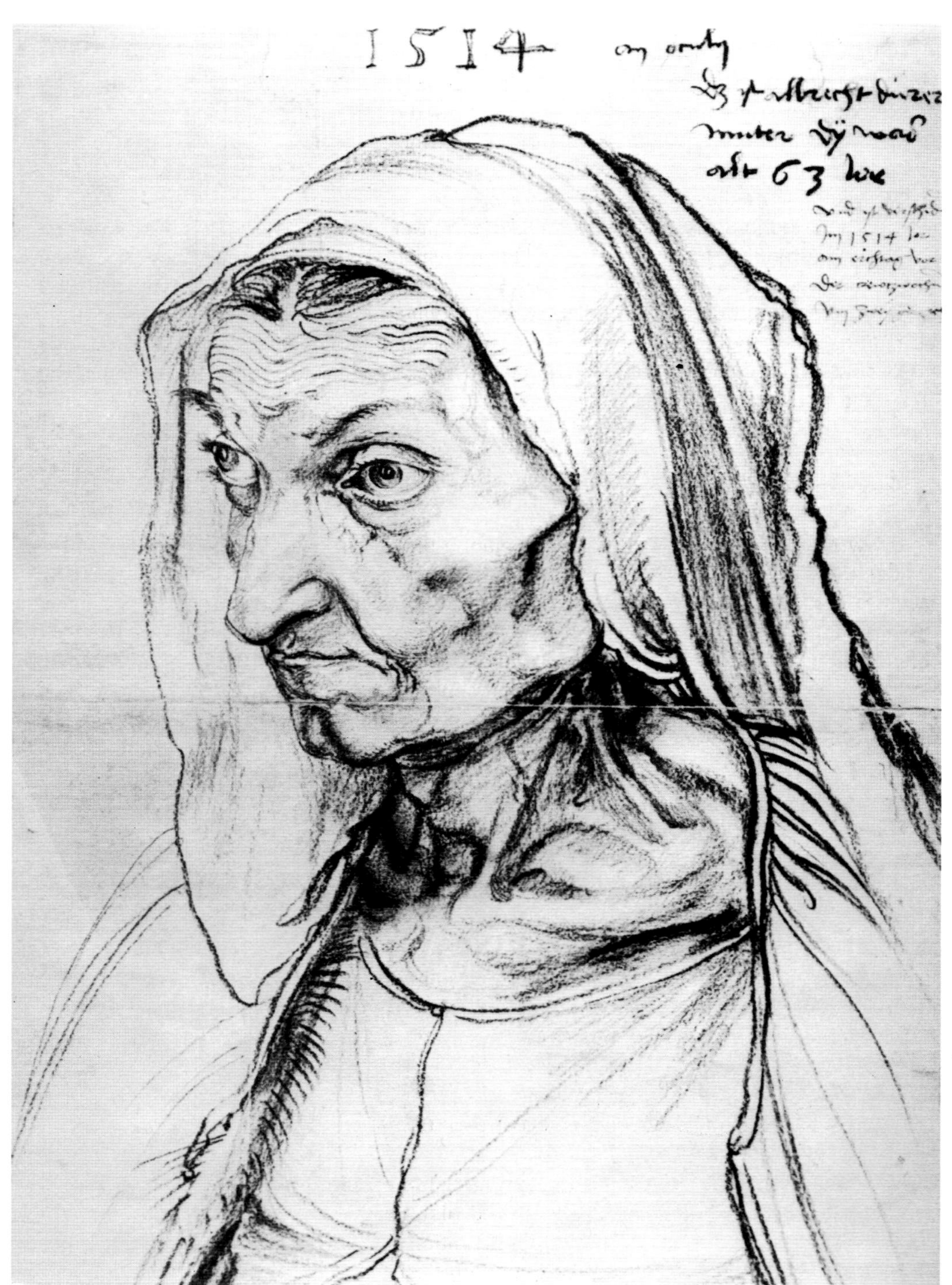

Fig. 2 *Portrait of Dürer's Mother*, 1514, charcoal. Berlin, Staatliche Museen.

smith's son. Here he was to have stayed for another period of apprenticeship.

Unfortunately, Schongauer died shortly before Dürer's arrival; however, his brothers allowed the young artist access to his works, particularly to his drawings, a certain number of which he kept for some time afterward. He proceeded on, arriving in Basel in 1492, which at that time was an important publishing center. Here he could put to use his experience as a woodcutter, contributing with illustrations to Sebastian Brant's edition of *Narrenschiff* (*stultifera navis*), Terence's comedies and *Ritter vom Turm*.

After a period in Strasbourg (see the *Self-Portrait* of Strasbourg, *cat. 7*), toward the end of 1494, Dürer returned to Nuremberg. He had been away from home for four years. Unfortunately, we do not know if his *Wanderschaft* took him to the Netherlands as well, where his father had been as a young boy. It is very likely that he was in Cologne and Mainz. His return just three months away, the twenty-four-year-old Albrecht took, along with the conspicuous dowry of 200 florins, the hand of Agnes, the daughter of the artisan Hans Frey. She belonged to the well-to-do Nuremberg bourgeois and was an acclaimed harpist.

First Trip to Italy, 1494–95

A few months after his wedding, the plague broke out in Nuremberg. Following doctors' advice, Dürer left the city as a precaution. He crossed the Alps, passing Augsburg, Innsbruck, and Trent, to reach Venice, which was then an important trading center; the German merchants had their own flourishing colony and owned the "Fondaco dei Tedeschi." During his trips, Dürer painted numerous and very beautiful watercolors with landscape and architectural themes (*figs. 3-5*), watercolors that—thanks to his technique (which was adopted, before Dürer, only by a Wolfgang Katzheimer the Elder in his scenes of Bamberg, as far as we know) and their exquisite execution—can be considered among the most beautiful works by the artist.

Presumably, the German merchants of Venice introduced Dürer into the artistic circles of the city. He naturally frequented Gentile Bellini's workshop, while the latter worked on the *Procession of the Relics of the Cross in Saint Mark's Square*. This is demonstrated by a drawing with three Turks and one Moor, evidently taken from that painting, which was not yet completed. In Venice, he painted devotional images and contemporaneously executed copies of some of Mantegna's and Antonio Pollaiolo's engravings and of Lorenzo di Credi's drawings. In the meantime, he carefully observed all that surrounded him—people, animals, and things—as the drawings of the clothes of Venetian ladies, the costumes of the Turkish figures, and the famous *Sea Crab* (*eriphia spinifrons*), besides the portraits, all bear witness.

Dürer's Workshop in Nuremberg, 1495–1505

Upon his return from Venice, in the spring of 1495, Dürer opened his own workshop in Nuremberg. In the beginning, he concentrated his energy on the profitable production of woodcuts, which were also devoted to the illustration of entire series, like the *Great Passion* and the *Apocalypse*, and a great deal of engravings. For the engravings, he was not lacking subjects of classical character from the moment in which he regularly started mixing with the humanist circles of the city. In those years, his relationship with Frederick the Wise began, which, in the course of his life, brought him quite a few commissions. He also had a lot of other kinds of work, including portraits, devotional images, and altarpieces, in which his treasured Venetian experience is often reflected (see the *Haller Madonna, cat. 14*). In addition, his theoretical studies had begun, especially those on human proportions, studies that had a great influence on his work. From time to time, he depicted himself, almost as if to measure how his ability and sensibility were being refined with time. The peak was reached with his famous *Self-Portrait with Fur Coat* of 1500 (pl. 26).

Second Trip to Italy, 1505–7

In the autumn of 1505, Dürer left his city as he had eleven years before, because of a plague epidemic. Without delay, he set out for his beloved Venice. The most important work that he painted during this second sojourn in the Serenissima was the *Feast of the Rose Garlands* (pl. 39), an altarpiece that won admiration and enthusiasm even from the Venetian artists who previously had seriously opposed him, criticizing his method of using color. Even the doge Lorenzo Loredan and the patriarch Antonio Suriano wanted to see his work and went to his workshop. It is said that the doge offered Dürer a salary of 200 florins per year to stay in Venice. Dürer felt at ease in Venice, since he enjoyed much more consideration there than at home. It is worth remembering that artists in Italy represented a class unto themselves—good or bad—while in the same period in Germany, an artist was always part of, however much respected, the artisan world. Dürer writes: "Oh, how much more I will endure the cold, breathing this sun! Here I feel like a gentleman; at home I am a parasite."

The following event, related by Joachim Camerarius in the preface to the edition of books on human proportion of 1532, demonstrates how much the Venetian painters must have admired the refined technique of Dürer's painting: It seems that one day, Giovanni Bellini begged Dürer to lend him one of his brushes for painting hair and, to his great surprise, Dürer handed over some brushes that were identical to his own.

In Venice, in addition to the important commission by the German merchants for the altarpiece the *Feast of the Rose Garlands*, Dürer had many other commissions—above all, portraits of Italian and German personages. We know that he managed to sell the six works that he had brought with him from Nuremberg. One work that was probably not painted on commission was the *Madonna with the Siskin* (*cat. 42*), which he brought back with him to Nuremberg.

Vasari tells us that, during his Venetian sojourn, Dürer wanted to denounce to the city's law court the Bolognese engraver Marcantonio Raimondi, an artist who—it should not be forgotten—contributed, by the spread of his own engravings, much to the reception of Raphael's works. The accusation was that he had copied Dürer's works and signed them with the famous monogram. It should be remembered that Dürer's idea to embed his initials, one inside the other, was a big success and was adopted by German painters such as Altdorfer and Aldegrever. This is one of the first trials defending the rights of the author. It seems that the denunciation had an effect. Though, even without Raimondi's contribution, Dürer's graphic work was renowned and recognized throughout Italy. That Vasari knew him and that most Italian artists, including Vasari himself, drew on his work for their own themes, surely proves his fame throughout Italy.

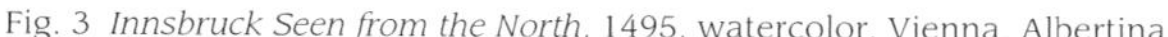
Fig. 3 *Innsbruck Seen from the North*, 1495, watercolor. Vienna, Albertina.

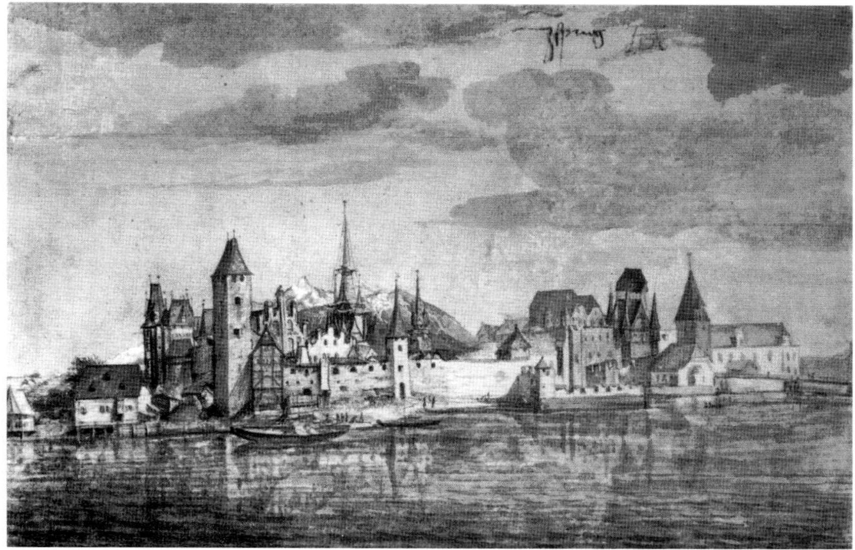

Fig. 4 *View of Arco*, 1495, watercolor. Paris, Louvre.

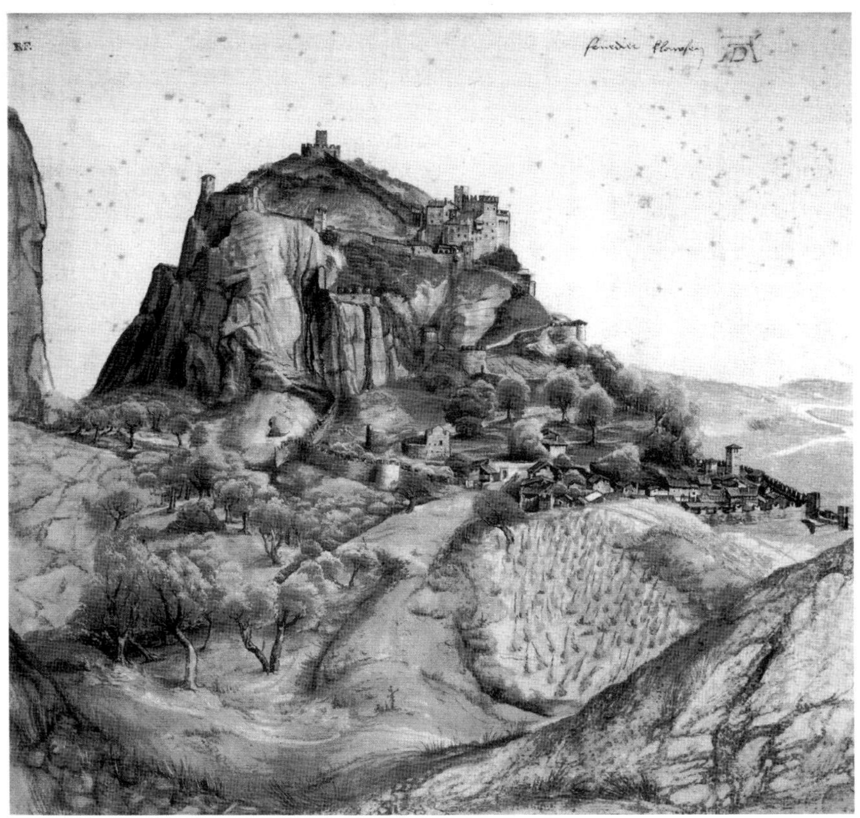

The second sojourn in Venice was very important to the artist, especially in establishing his character and his artistic personality. A detailed chronicle remains from this period in the many interesting letters that he wrote to his friend Willibald Pirckheimer, who wanted to be, in addition to other matters, informed about his acquisitions, which Dürer looked after, of Oriental rugs, precious gems, original editions of Greek books, and other items.

From Venice, Dürer went by horseback to Bologna, where he was welcomed triumphantly as a "second Apelles." His friend Christoph Scheurl, a humanist and judge in Nuremberg, who attended his graduation at that university, introduced him to some Bolognese artists. He did not, unfortunately, have a chance to meet Luca Pacioli, whom Dürer had wanted to meet so as to develop his ideas on the laws of central perspective. The famous mathematician, however, had moved to Florence.

Dürer's supposed sojourns in Florence and Rome are not documented. Nevertheless, his drawings modeled on Leonardo's works and his sketches for *Christ among the Doctors*, signed "Romae 1506" (*cat. 43*), traced from Leonardesque studies on physiognomy (see also *Heller Altar, cat. 48*), lead one to the conclusion that he stayed in Florence at the workshop of the Tuscan painter, twelve years his junior. The master, however, was certainly not there, since he was away in Milan. In addition, Dürer must have at least seen Raphael's *Coronation of the Virgin,* of 1503, whose reflection is unmistakable in his impressive altarpiece, painted in 1508–9, and commissioned from Jakob Heller for the Dominican Church in Frankfurt (compare with the *Heller Altar, cat. 48*).

As for Rome, we know that Dürer wanted to go there from Venice, as part of Maximilian's retinue. Maximilian was proceeding there to be crowned emperor by the pope, but the Republic of Venice did not allow him to cross her territories with his army. Dürer must have begun his journey alone. He probably had urgent cause to go to Rome because his commercial agent in charge of his engravings had died there, incurring a sizable economic loss for him. However, Dürer must have stayed in Florence and Rome rather briefly, as only very few of his art works reveal signs of these cities. On the other hand, the influence of Bramante, Raphael, and Michelangelo on Roman art began only after his visit of 1506.

Nuremberg, 1507–20

In early 1507, Dürer was again in Venice, and at the beginning of February—the middle of winter—he again took the difficult trip to return to Nuremberg. In the period that followed, he produced several masterpieces: the two very beautiful panels of *Adam* and *Eve* (*cat. 44*), tangible and immediate reflection of his studies on human proportion; great altarpieces (*cat. 48, 50*); and important works of graphic art.

The first thing he set about doing was to translate, with the help of his friend Willibald Pirckheimer, Euclid's *Perspectiva naturalis,* which he had acquired in Venice. During the same time, he was dedicated to the plan for a treatise on the theoretical elements of painting, which he had already outlined during his trip to Italy. Following this came a treatise on human proportion (see *fig. 12*) and one on horses and architecture. A third treatise was to concern perspective in general, light and color. Having developed the ideas of Italian artists and theoreticians—Vitruvio, Alberti, and Leonardo—in 1508–9, Dürer finally began to write and lay out his own concepts, demonstrating once again that he was not only a great artist, but a serious scholar of theoretical problems concerning art.

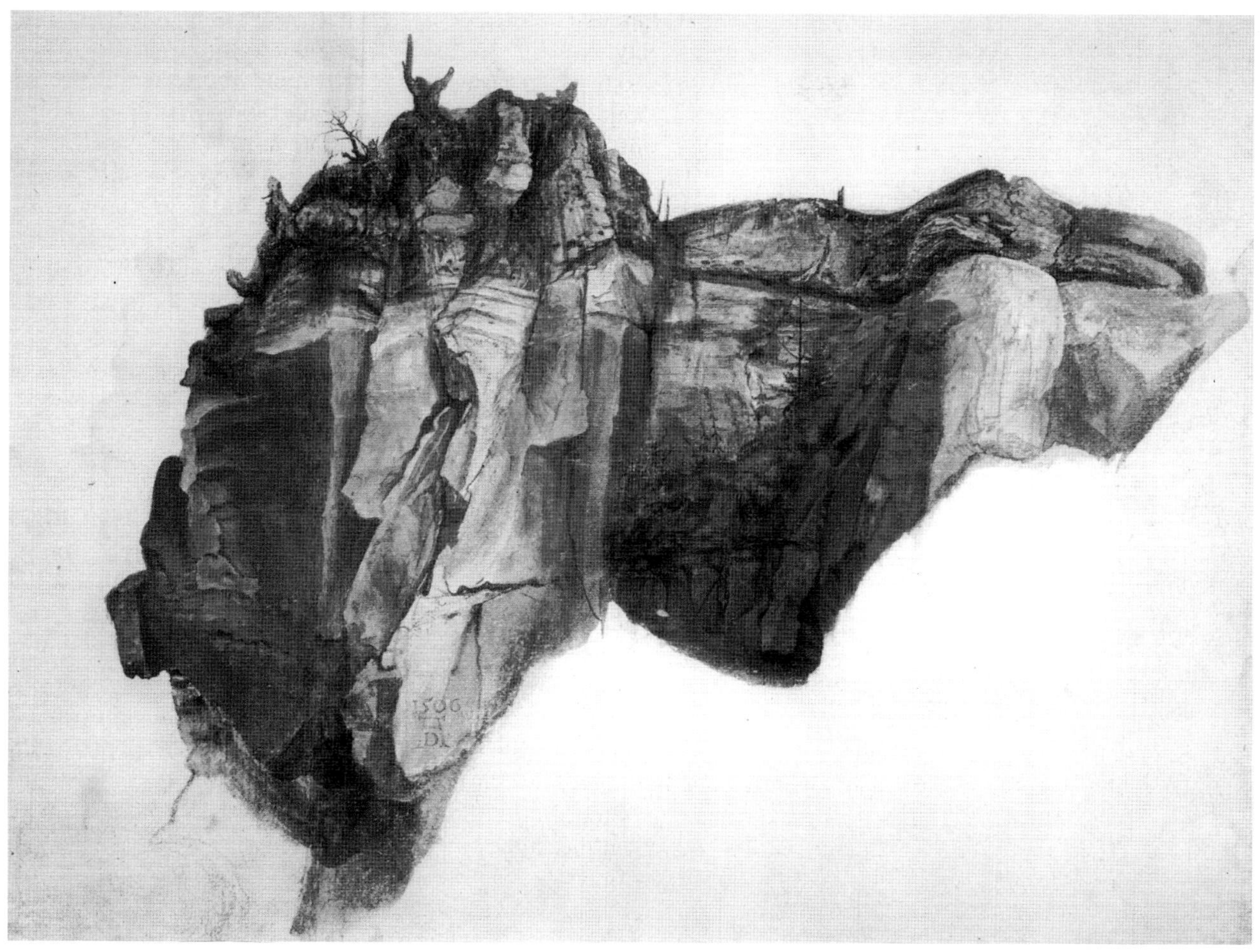

Fig. 5 *The Quarry*, 1495, watercolor. London, British Museum.

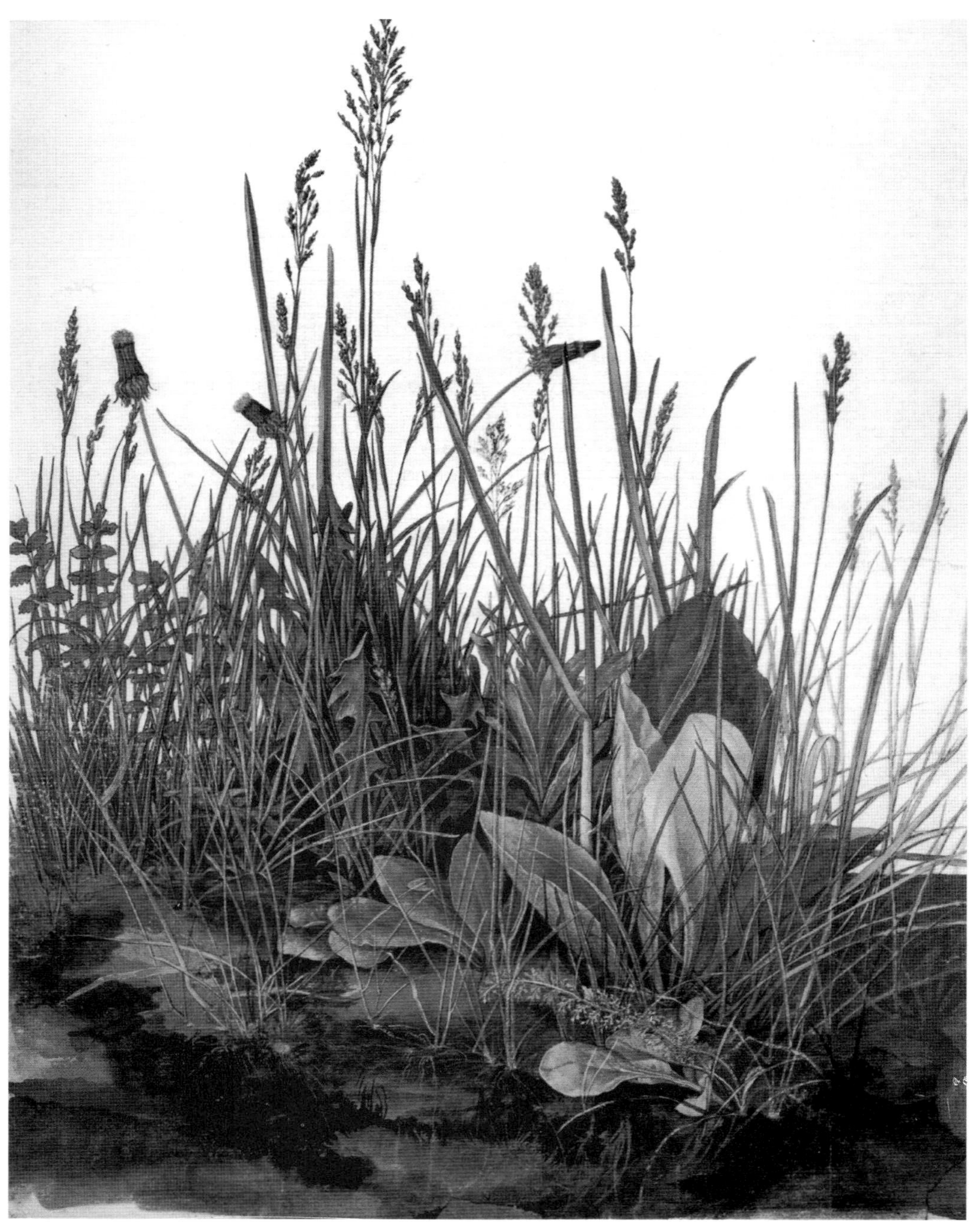

Fig. 6 *The Great Piece of Turf*, 1503, watercolor and gouache. Vienna, Albertina.

Journey to the Netherlands, 1520-1521

In that epoch, the Netherlands represented, after Italy, the second place of great art. The opportunity to go there presented itself to Dürer with the coronation of Charles V in Aachen. The artist needed to have him confirm the lifelong annuity granted by his predecessor, Maximilian.

Dürer, this time accompanied by his wife and his maidservant, Susanna, set off 12 July 1520. He arrived first in Bamberg, where he was the guest of the bishop; Dürer gave him a Madonna painting, among other things, receiving in turn valuable letters of recommendation and customs admittances that allowed him to continue his journey with greater ease. Traveling along the Main and the Rhine, passing through Frankfurt, Mainz, and Cologne, he arrived in Antwerp, a big metropolis and, at that time, a capital center of commerce (*fig. 7*). We have a meticulous and interesting account of the long trip from the artist's diary.

In Aachen, where he went from Antwerp, Dürer joined the delegation of the town council of Nuremberg, which was bringing the imperial insignia, kept in the city for the coronation of Charles V. He was its guest for the duration of his stay, which lasted several weeks, and on 23 October he attended the coronation. Once back in Antwerp, the artist was able to attend the triumphant entrance of Charles V into that city.

Wherever his travels took him—to Antwerp, Bruges, or Brussels—Dürer had an enthusiastic welcome: the artists organized lavish festivities in his honor, and the city authorities invited him to processions and banquets. King Christian of Denmark, whose portrait he painted, had him as his guest at a banquet he organized in honor of Margaret, the daughter of Maximilian I. The city of Antwerp offered him an annual salary of 500 florins plus accommodation to entice him to take up permanent residence there, according to accounts in his diary.

Dürer's portrait-painting activity continued without pause, as the twenty oil portraits and roughly one hundred drawings prove. He gave away and sold his paintings and graphic art, which enabled him to pay his travel expenses. It was in that period that he developed and polished his characteristic style of portraiture, distinct in being both imposing and psychologically acute. Unfortunately, many of the paintings that were executed in those years have been lost, as, for example, the one from Antwerp of King Christian II of Denmark. From the portrait of a ninety-three-year-old man, which he writes about in his diary without mentioning his name, came *The Portrait of Saint Jerome* (*cat. 68*). Several drawings of cityscapes (e.g., *fig. 7*) and animals demonstrate his unwavering curiosity and creativity, qualities that led him to Zeeland where he had wanted to go to view from up close a beached whale. He didn't see the whale, but caught a serious strain of fever—possibly malaria—that brought him terrible, prolonged suffering.

During his stay in the Netherlands, Dürer was able to see churches and city halls and works of important artists, including the paintings of Jan van Eyck and Rogier van der Weyden, and in Bruges, Michelangelo's *Madonna*. He was received by Margaret of Austria, daughter of Maximilian I, at her residence in Malines, where he had the opportunity to admire her important art collection. In Brussels, he was able to see how much had been brought over to Charles V from the "New Country of Gold." Wherever he was, he tried to acquire or receive little curiosities, including objects from the Indies, which were fashionable to collect at that time. He met with many artists, including Joos van Cleve, Lukas van Leyden, and Joachim Patinier, the last whose wedding he attended. In Antwerp, he met Erasmus of Rotterdam and drew his portrait.

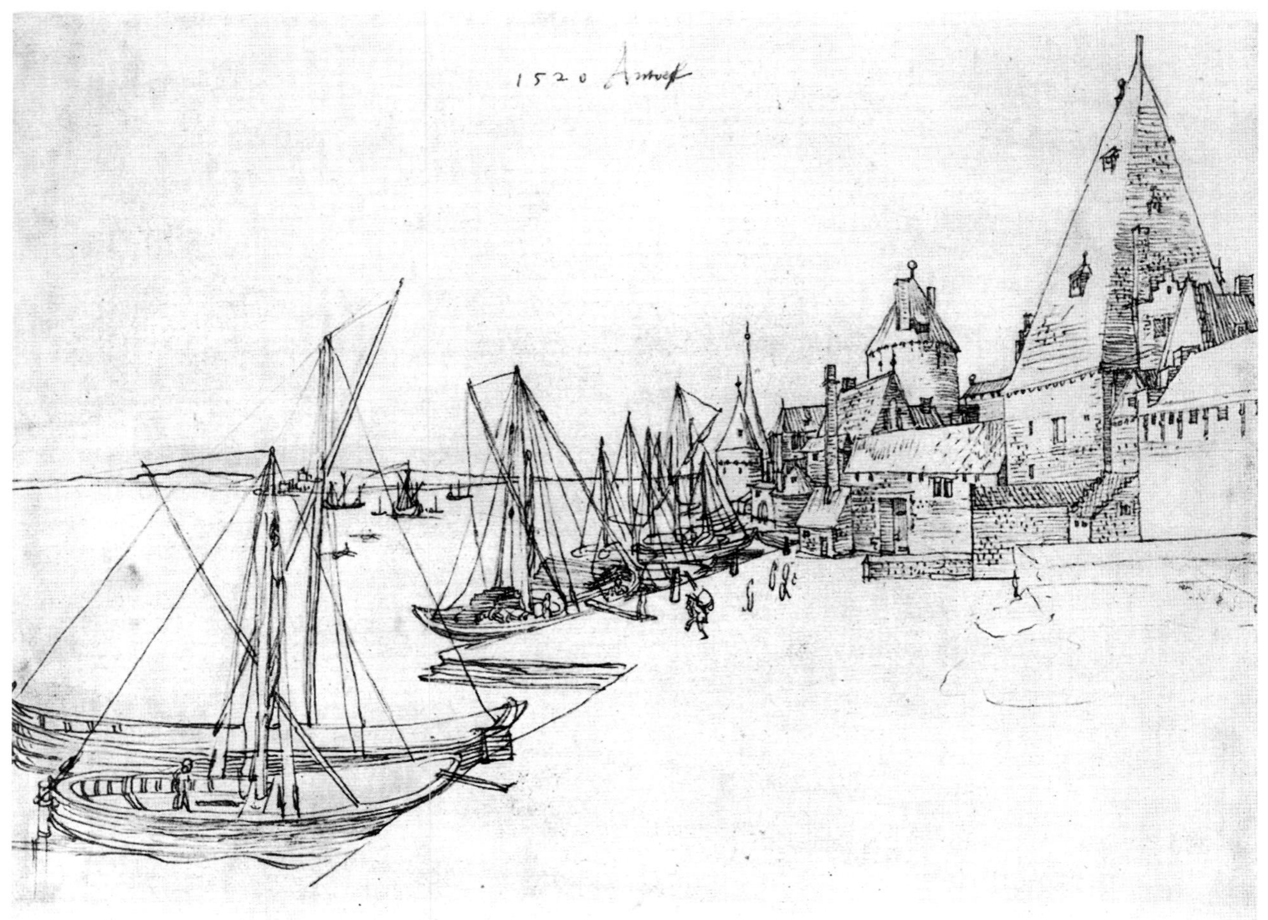

Fig. 7 *Antwerp Harbor*, 1520, drawing from the sketchbook of his trip to the Netherlands. Vienna, Albertina.

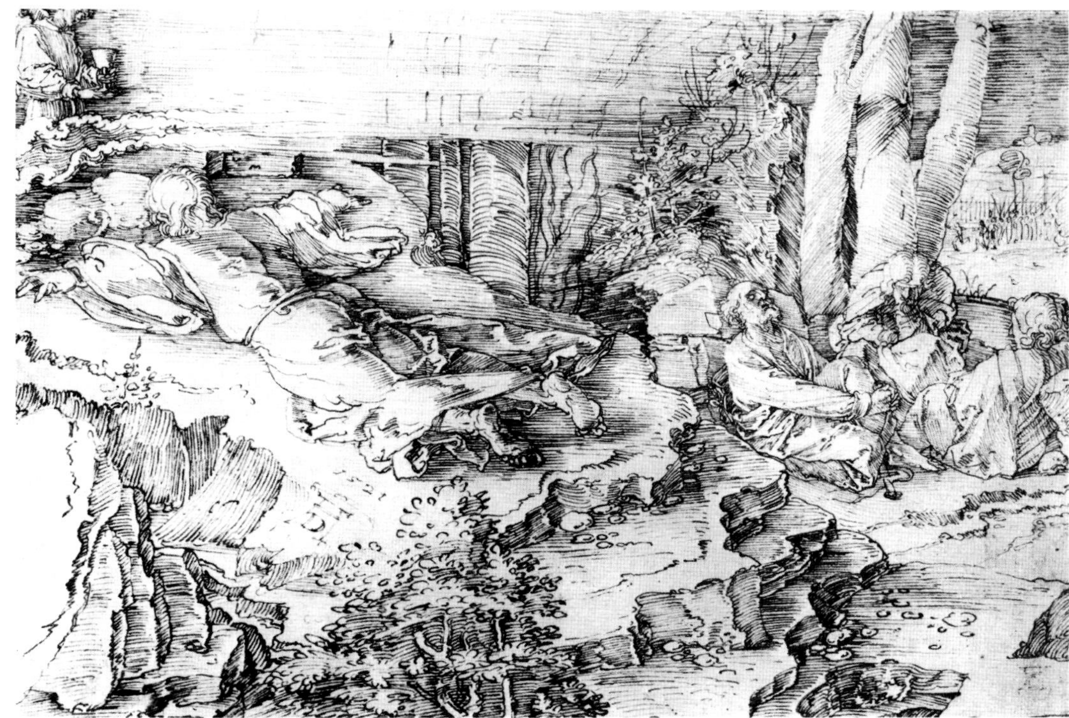

Fig. 8 *Agony in the Garden*, 1521, ink. Frankfurt, Städelsches Kunstinstitut.

Final Years in Nuremberg, 1521–28

Upon Dürer's return to Nuremberg, the city assigned him to prepare some projects to renew the decoration of the city hall; at least one of the preparatory drawings had a classical theme, which represents the *Slander of Apelles*. However, his work for the city never went beyond the initial project. At the same time, he was executing various drawings for an impressive altarpiece, for which work never even began. The main enterprise of this final period of his life was the completion of various theoretical texts: a treatise on geometry, 1525; a treatise on fortification, 1527; and the treatise on human proportions, 1528 (*fig. 12*), which was published posthumously. In any case, there were many noteworthy portraits, mainly in the form of woodcuts and engravings, but also oil paintings: from that of Jakob Muffel (*cat. 72*) to that of Johannes Kleberger (*cat. 74*). Last, he painted the *Four Apostles* (*cat. 75*), which he wanted to leave to the city as a spiritual inheritance.

The Self-Portraits

Dürer had never participated, in a substantial way, in the vast production of altarpieces in vogue in the workshops of his contemporaries, including his master, Michael Wolgemut. Altar

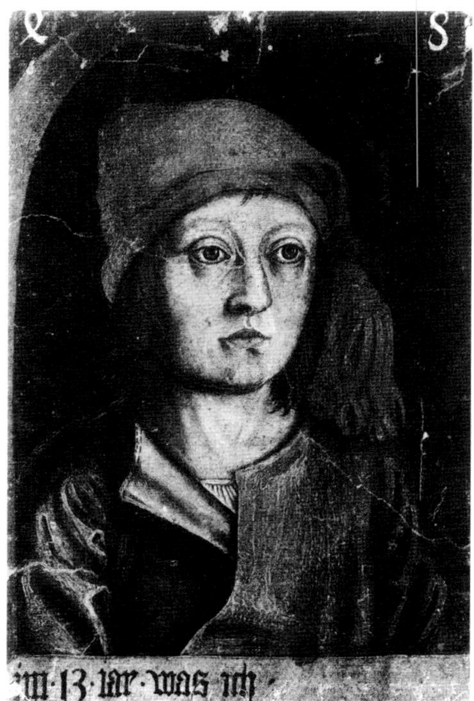

Fig. 9 *Self-Portrait at Thirteen Years Old*, 1484, oil on parchment, copy from a manuscript (original lost). Stettino.

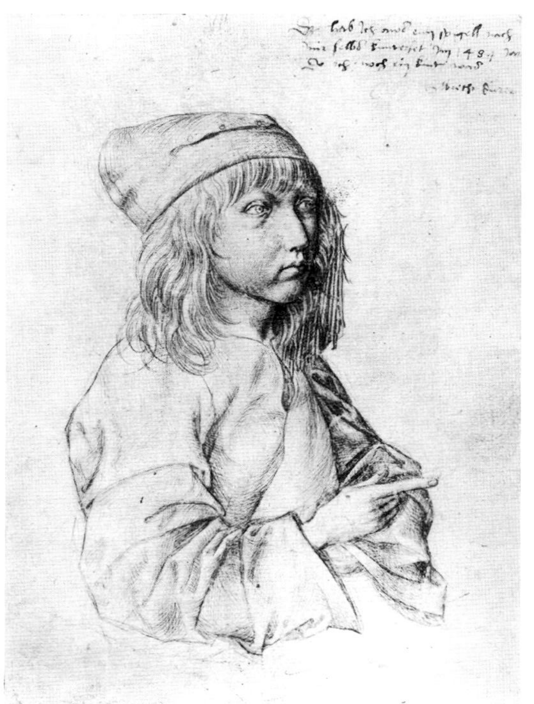

Fig. 10 *Self-Portrait at Thirteen Years Old*, 1484, silverpoint. Vienna, Albertina.

panels by him are rare, while his devotional images abound, especially the Madonnas. The most important part of his work is represented by his portraits.

No other artist of his time made as many self-portraits as Dürer. In Italy, the first "autonomous" self-portrait—that is, unto itself—that we know of is by Leon Battista Alberti, which has only survived in a copy. One must also ask oneself if the portrait by Raphael in the Uffizi is really an autonomous self-portrait, or rather, if it has been modeled on the one in the *School of Athens*, where the Raphael figures together with Sodoma. Neither Leonardo nor Michelangelo is known to have done self-portraits on panels. As for the self-portraits of the German artists of that era, one cannot even comment. With Dürer, we actually have two images he made of himself at thirteen: one silverpoint from 1484 (*fig. 10*) and a miniature oil on parchment (*fig. 9*), dated 1484 with the inscription *im 13. Iar was ich* (I was like this at thirteen), which is probably the copy of a missing self-portrait.

Other portraits by him show him at twenty and at twenty-two: they are not official portraits, but introspective images, studies of his actual character and his own destiny, as shown by the clear difference between being melancholic (*fig. 11*) and being ill.

Out of the paintings of self-portraits of which we are aware, three have survived: the self-portrait of 1493 "with sea holly" at the Louvre (*cat. 7*); the one "with gloves," of 1498 (*cat. 19*) at the Prado; and the famous one *en face* of 1500, at the Alte Pinakothek in Munich (*cat. 26*). How much importance Dürer gave self-portraits as representing one's own personality is further

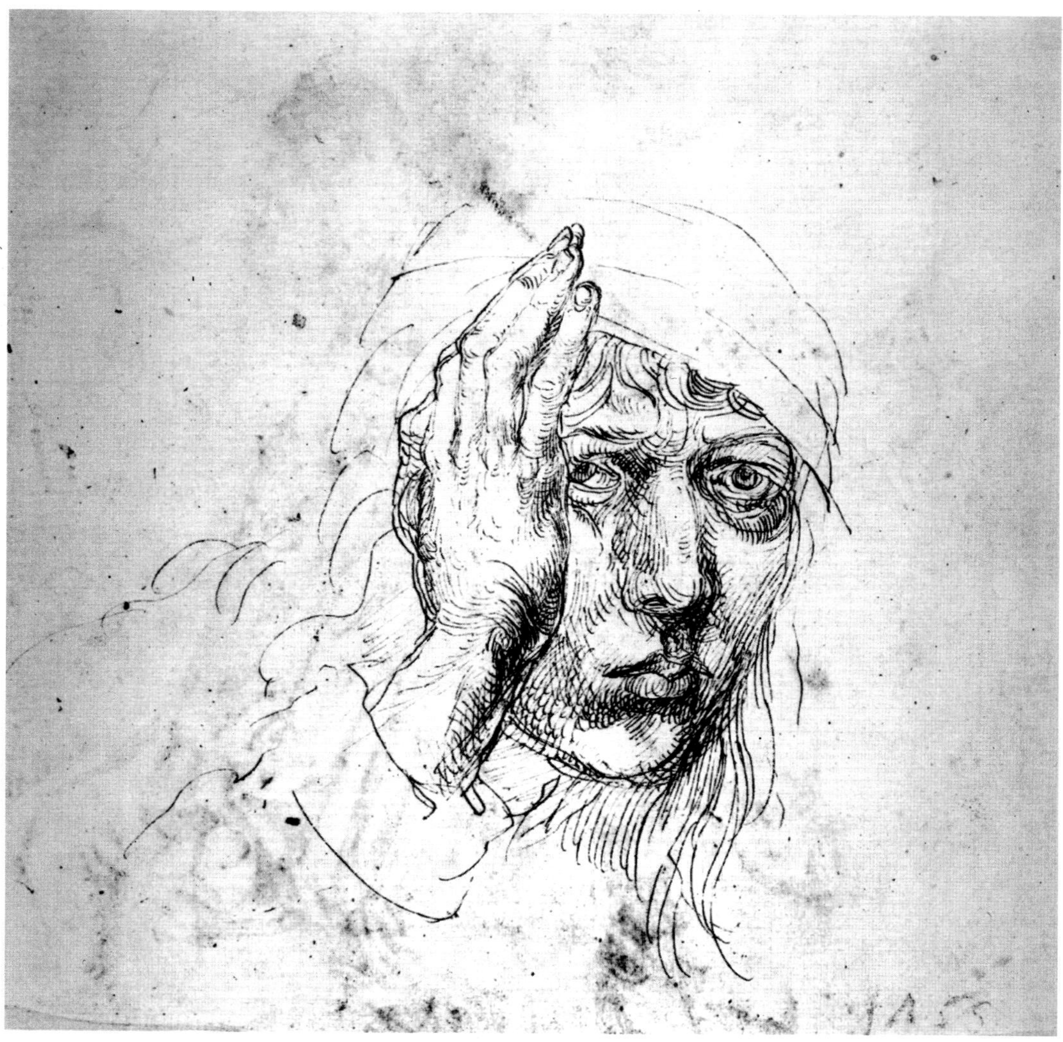

Fig. 11 *Self-Portrait at Twenty Years Old*, pen and ink. Erlangen, University Library.

demonstrated by the news surrounding the lost portrait: Vasari tells us that he saw it in Mantua, at the house of Giulio Romano, who had inherited it from Raphael, to whom, in turn, it had been given by Dürer in exchange for the nude drawings for the *Battle of Ostia* in the "Stanze" in the Vatican. This exchange of different gifts clearly shows the difference between Nordic and Italian art regarding the value of the subject as an expression of the personality of the artist: for the one, the self-portrait; for the other, a nude study.

According to Vasari, the self-portrait of Dürer was painted with watercolor on particularly delicate canvas, so that it could be observed both from the anterior and posterior side. It is an obvious display of true talent that, besides eternalizing the features of the artist, was to demonstrate his pictorial ability. It is presumed that Dürer painted it between 1510 and 1515. Given that Raphael wanted to depict Dürer, in the Eliodoro Stanza in the back sedan bearer of the pope, and supposing that it acted as a gift for a model, the date of this self-portrait can be narrowed to approximately 1514.

Conclusion

Out of the 189 paintings listed in the complete catalog by Fedja Anzelewsky (1991), which includes the missing paintings, provided that they are documented by copies or by written works, only the pictorial works that are definitely, if not entirely, by Dürer himself are presented here.

To these, more than a thousand drawings, about 350 woodcuts and around 130 engravings and etchings should be added. This would mean that the artist Dürer should not be understood or appreciated only through his painting. Let us not forget another important part of his work, which represents an exceptional artistic expression for his era: the watercolors, about sixty of which survive. If we also consider his numerous treatises, finished and unfinished, we will manage to grasp the importance of one of the most impressive artists of his time in all his complexity. Alongside, naturally, are Leonardo, Michelangelo, and Raphael. In Germany, furthermore, Dürer is an exceptional figure, being the first artist to be interested in the theoretical problems of art.

He discovered and adopted new pictorial techniques, like that of the watercolor; he developed and brought graphic art to the peak of refinement, from a technical and compositional standpoint. He also elaborated some artistic concepts that Italian artists and scholars had proposed and outlined: more specifically, the geometrical construction of the Roman alphabet (fig. 13) and of the illustrated reconstruction, and subsequently elaborated the so-called screen, a kind of grid destined to grasp more precisely the reality of nature, which Alberti had proposed and described but never depicted (*fig. 14*).

Outside artistic circles, Dürer enjoyed close relationships with humanists—in particular, Willibald Pirckheimer, his lifelong friend, who, having studied in Italy for six years, first at Padua and then at Pavia, introduced him to the world of the Florentine Neoplatonists. Dürer owned a rich library, in which appeared works like the *Hypnerotomachia Poliphili* and Alberti's *De pictura*. He was an artist and a man of universal culture. At the same time, thanks to his manners of a "grand seigneur," his facility of speech, his charm, and his spirit in leading conversation, he certainly approached the ideal figure, as postulated by Baldassar Castiglione, of the "courtier." This is a position, however, he never actually had, unlike many of his Italian contemporaries. One can perhaps conclude, as Jacob Burckhardt affirms, that the characteristic of the Renaissance was the discovery of man and the universe, Dürer, more than any on else, personifies it.

Fig. 12 *Studies on the Proportions of the Female Body.*

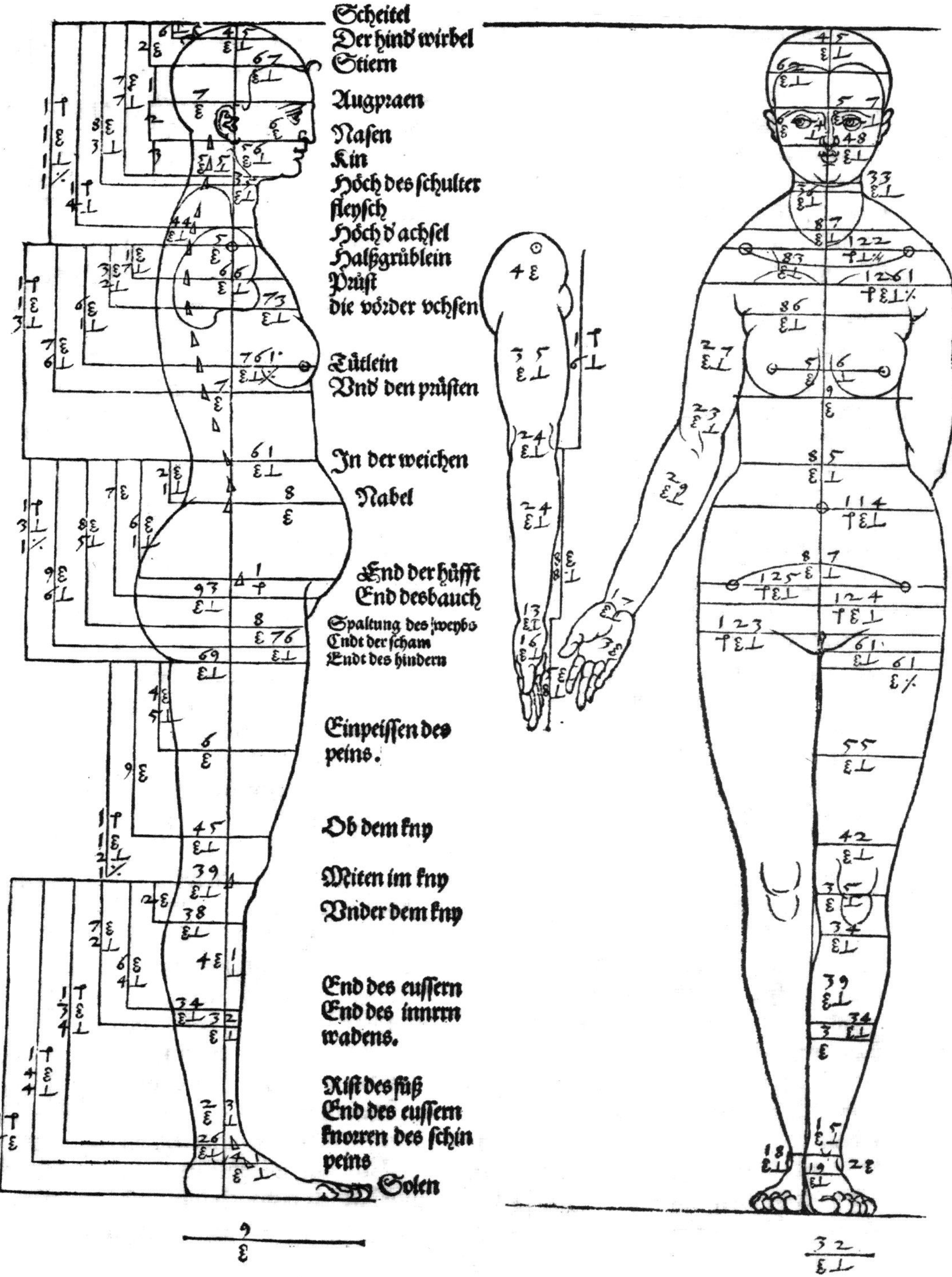

Fig. 13 *Construction of the Letter A.*

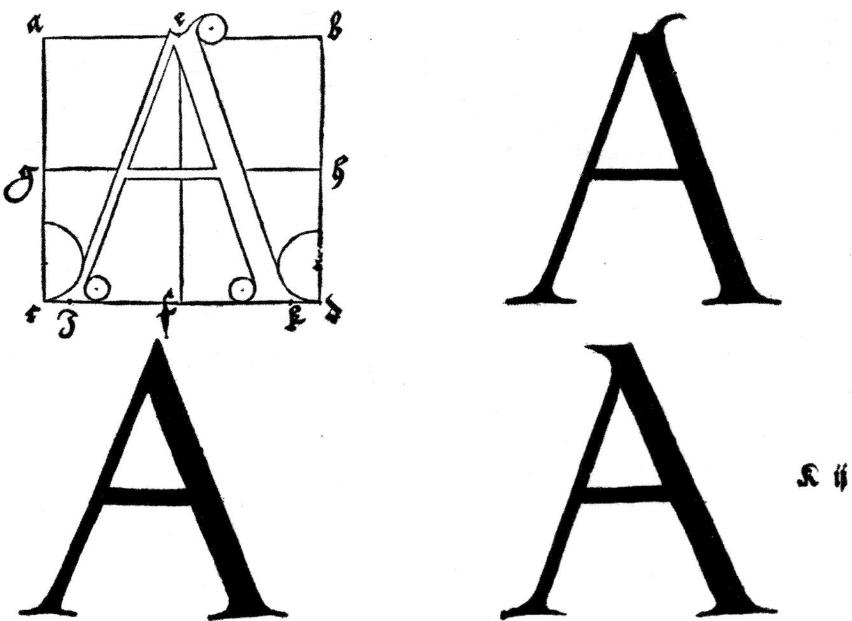

Fig. 14 *Draftsman Drawing a Vase.* Construction by Leon Battista Alberti.

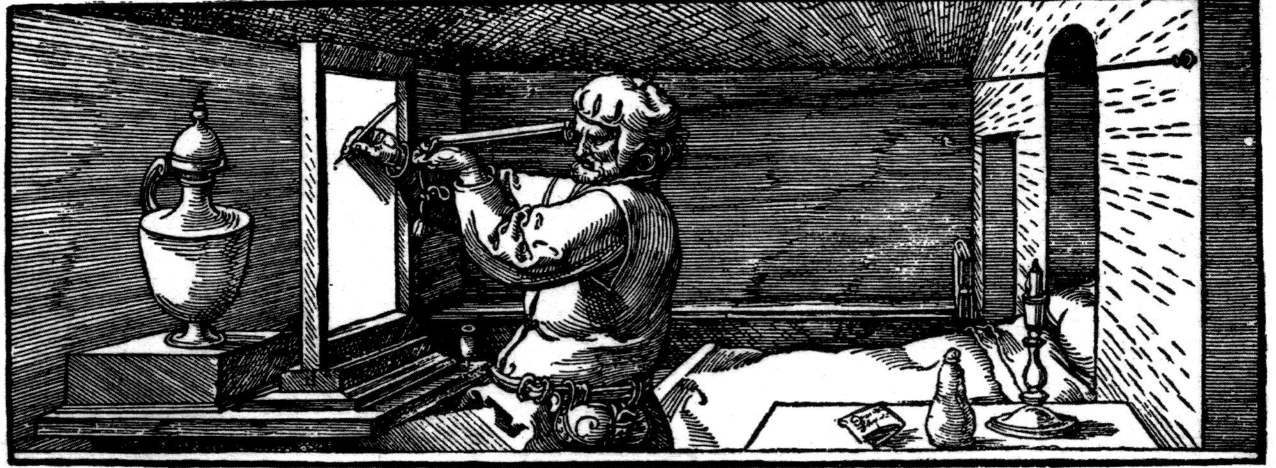

Color Plates

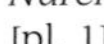

Portrait of Barbara Holper (Dürer's Mother)
Nuremberg, Germanisches Nationalmuseum
[pl. 1]

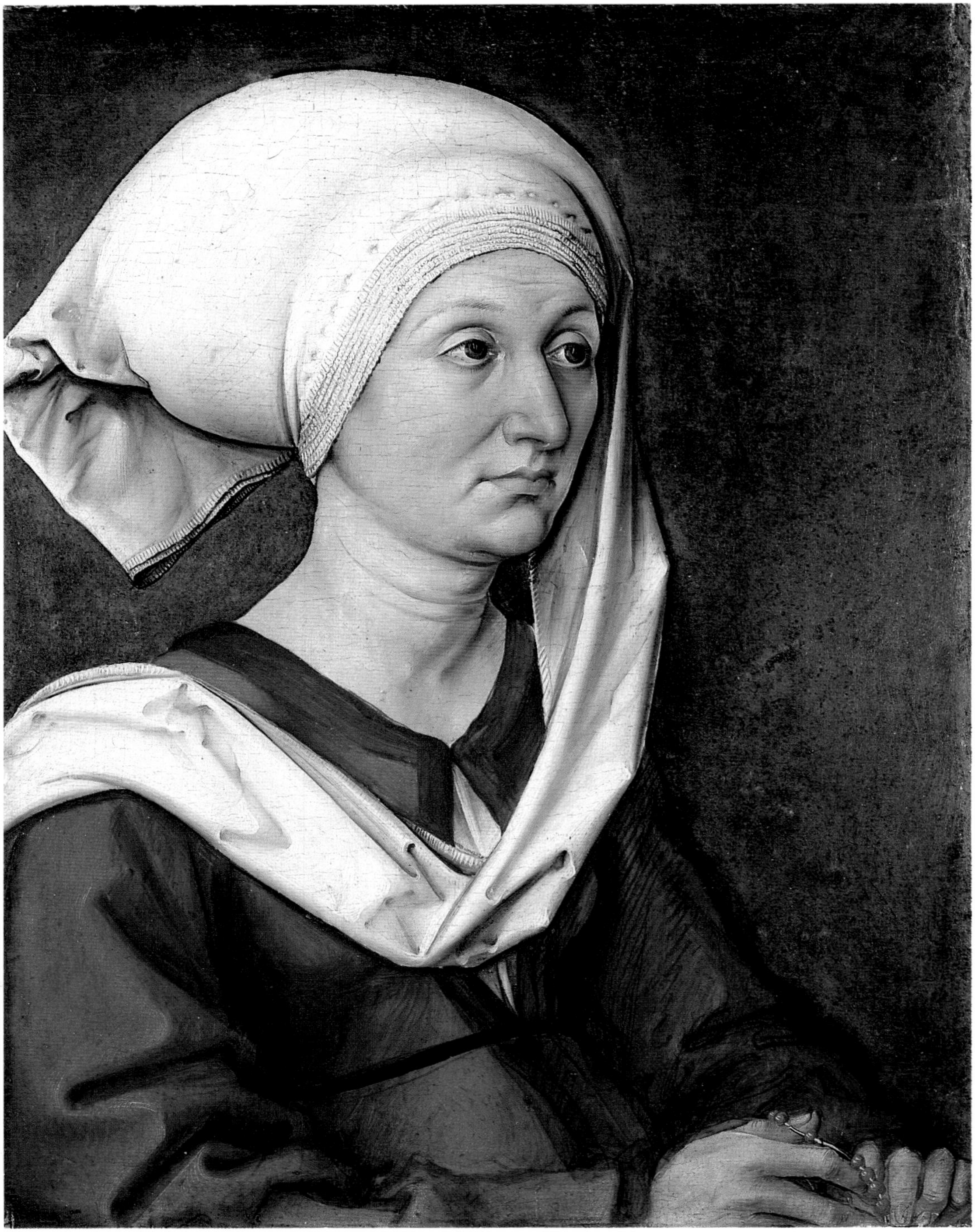

Portrait of Albrecht Dürer the Elder with the Rosary
Florence, Galleria degli Uffizi
[pl. 2]

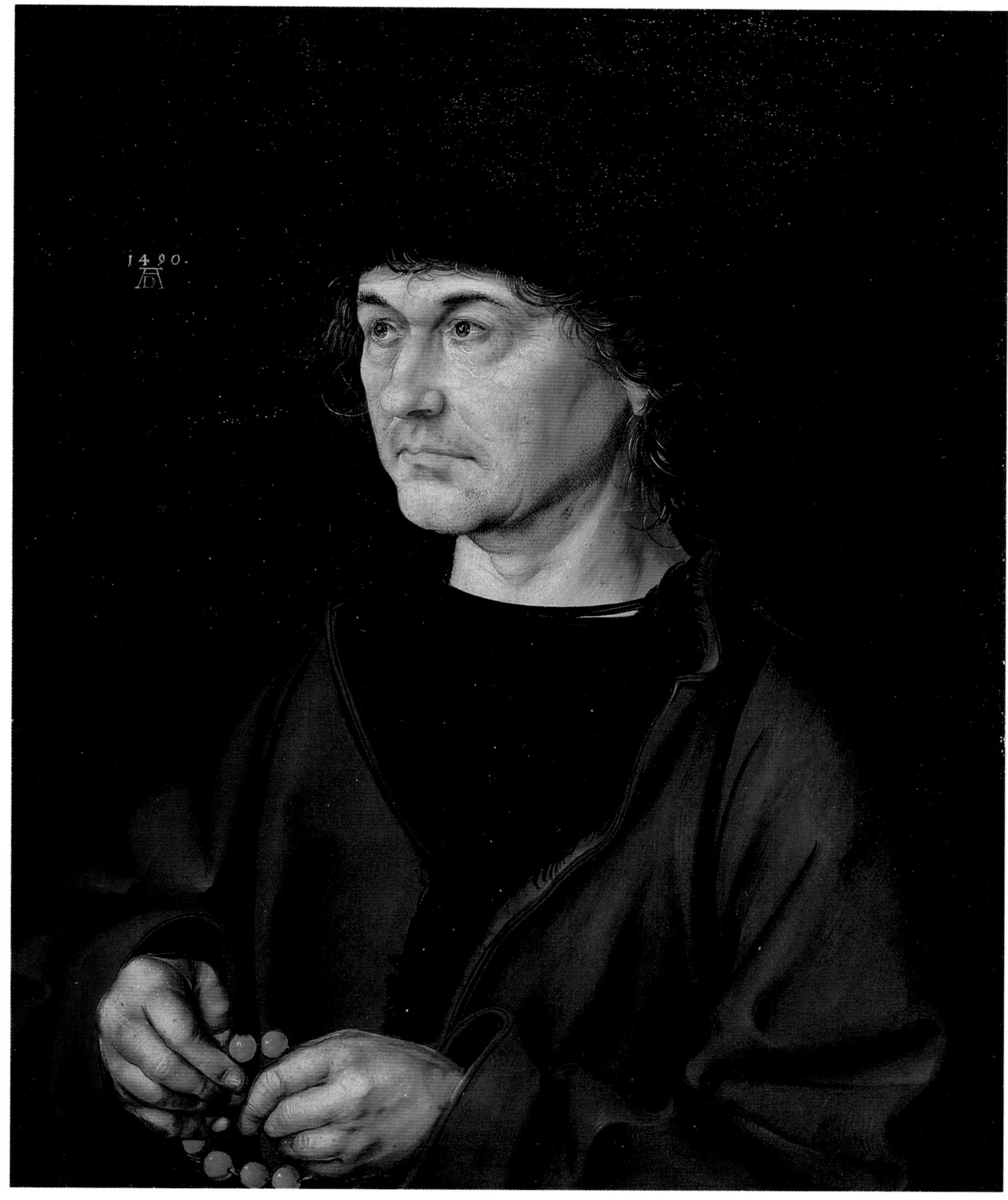

Coats of Arms of the Dürer and Holper Families
verso of [pl. 2]

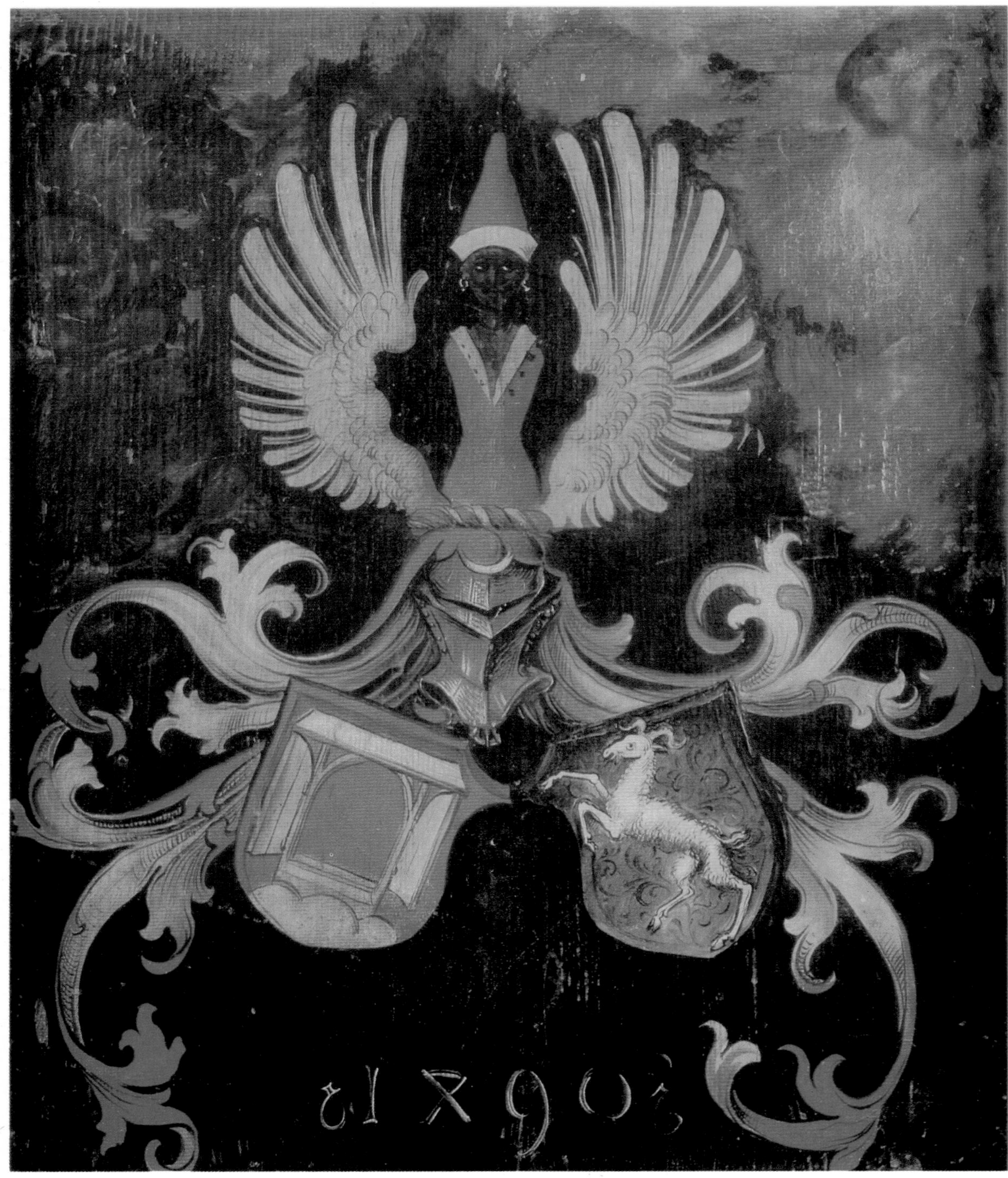

Self-Portrait
Paris, Musée du Louvre
[pl. 7]

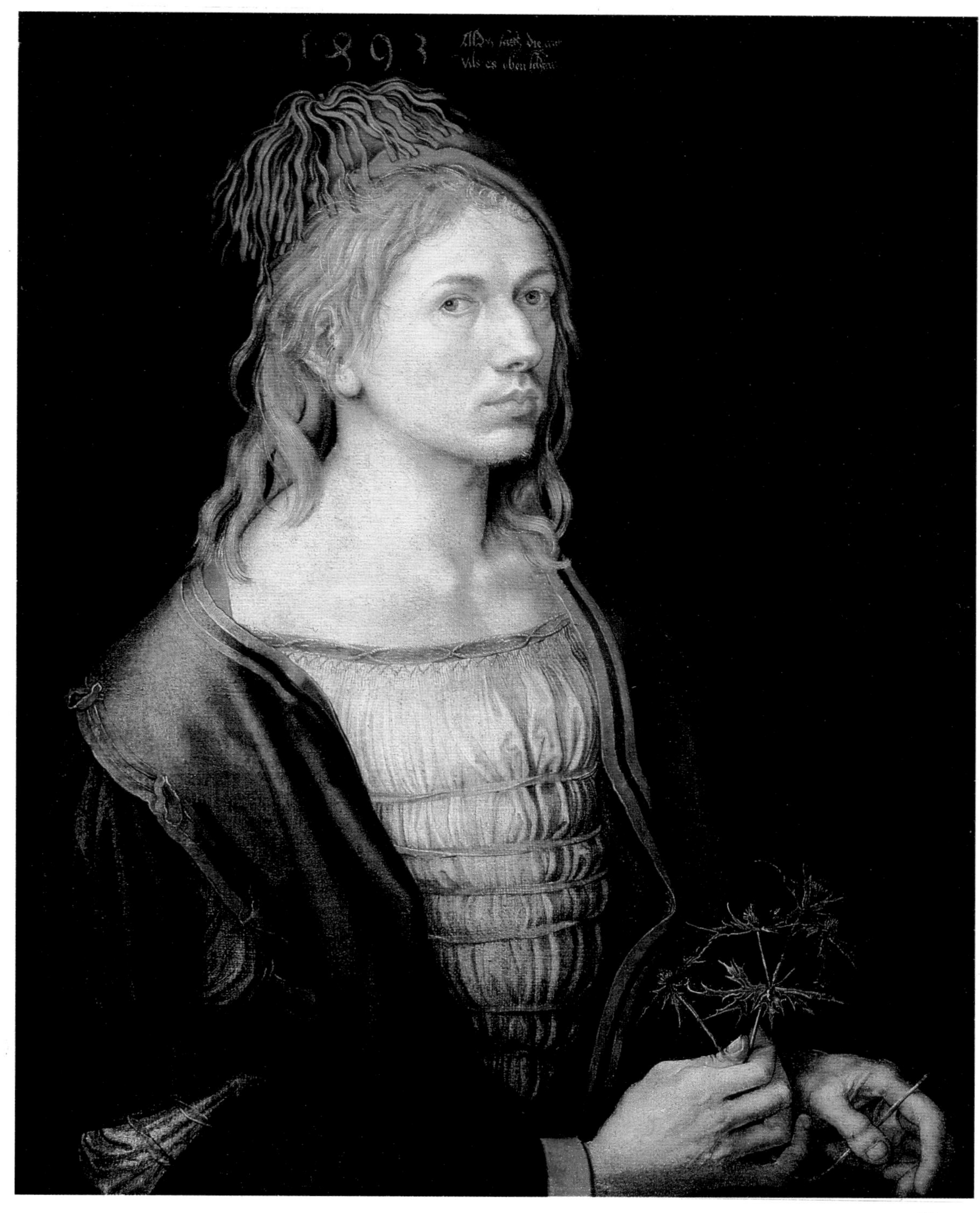

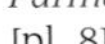

Madonna and Child
Parma, Fondazione Magnani-Rocca
[pl. 8]

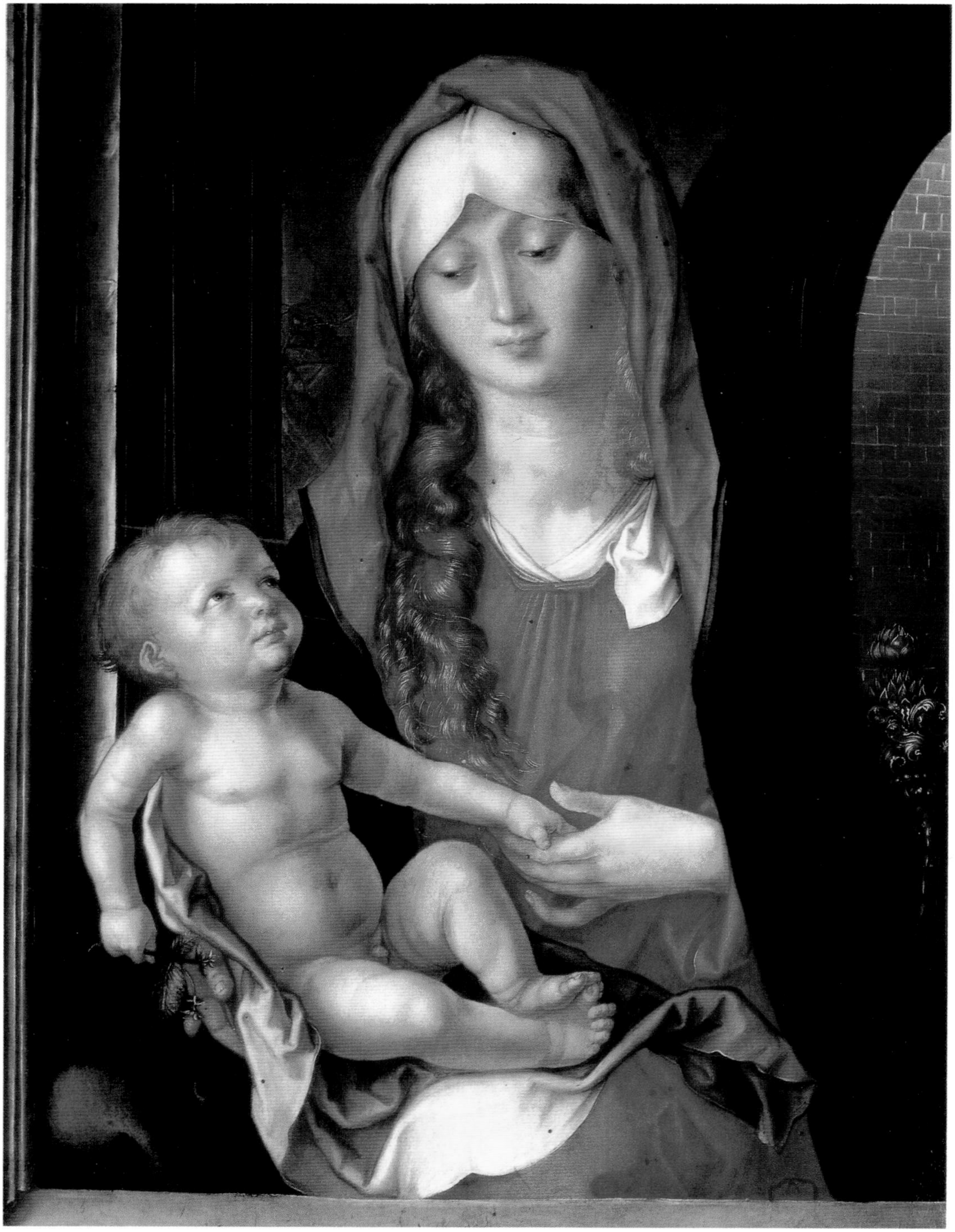

Saint Jerome in the Wilderness
Cambridge, Fitzwilliam Museum
[pl. 9]

on the following page: [pl. 9] *detail*

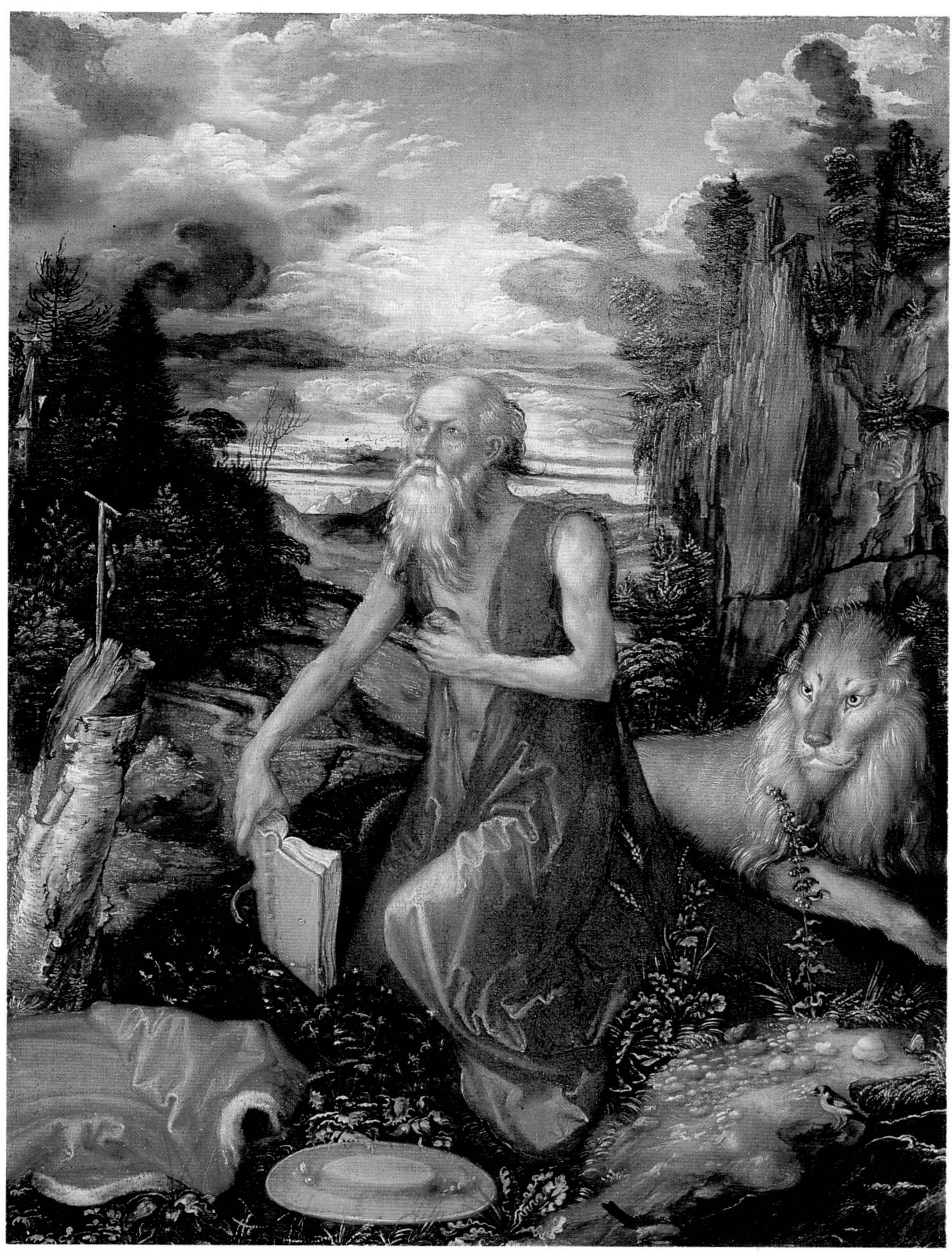

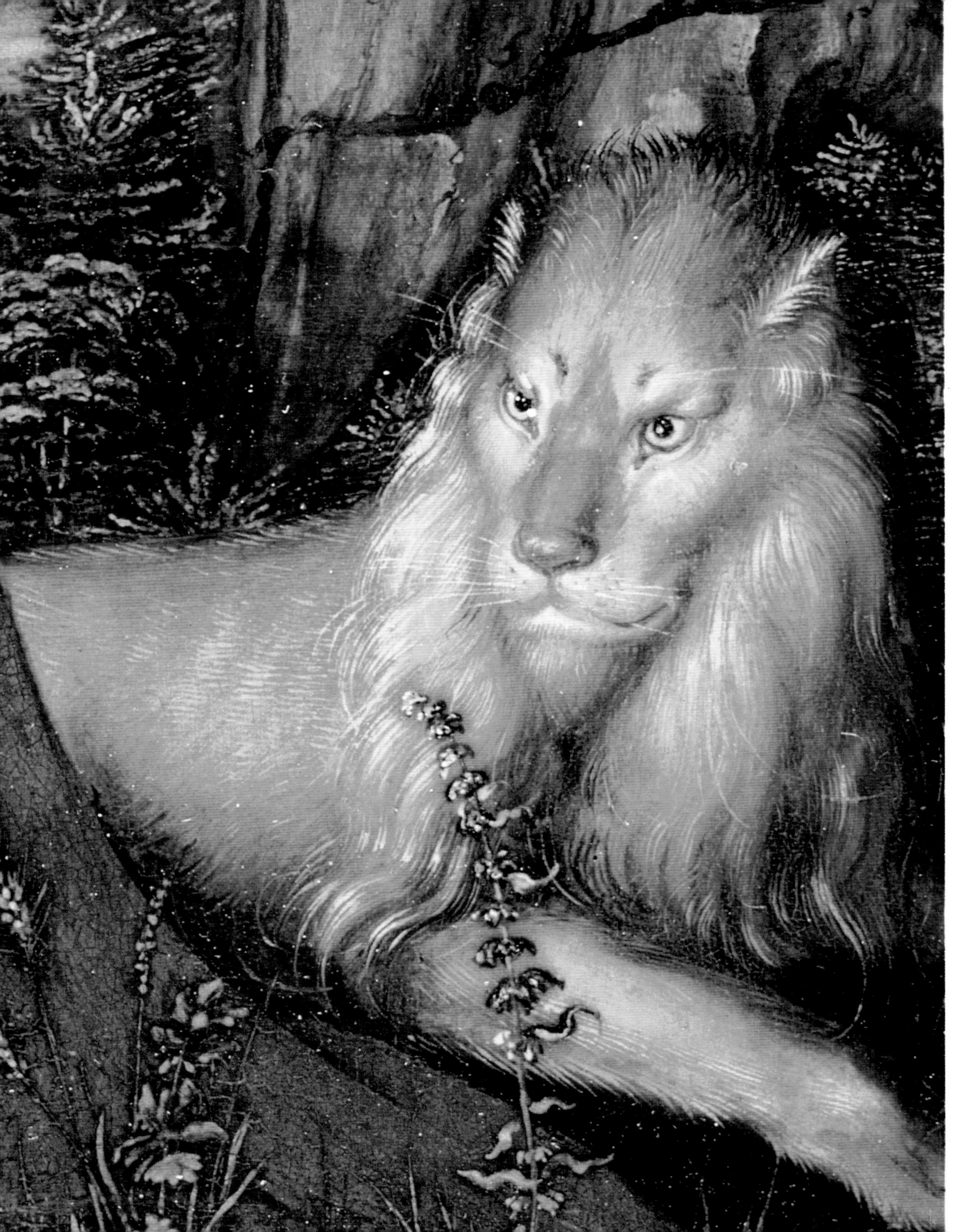

Frederick the Wise of Saxony
Berlin, Staatliche Museen, Gemäldegalerie
[pl. 11]

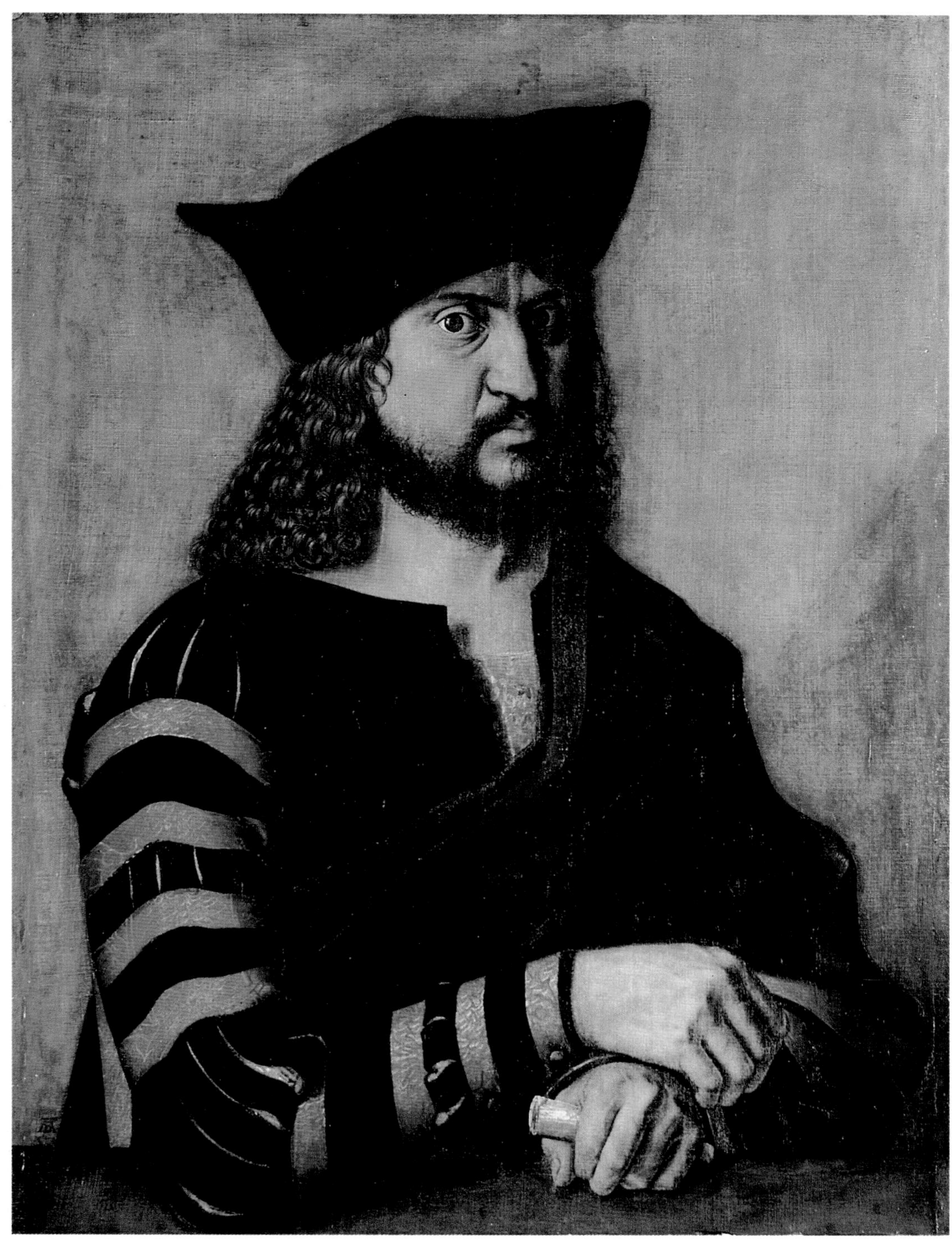

Madonna and Child (Haller Madonna)
Washington, National Gallery of Art
[pl. 14]

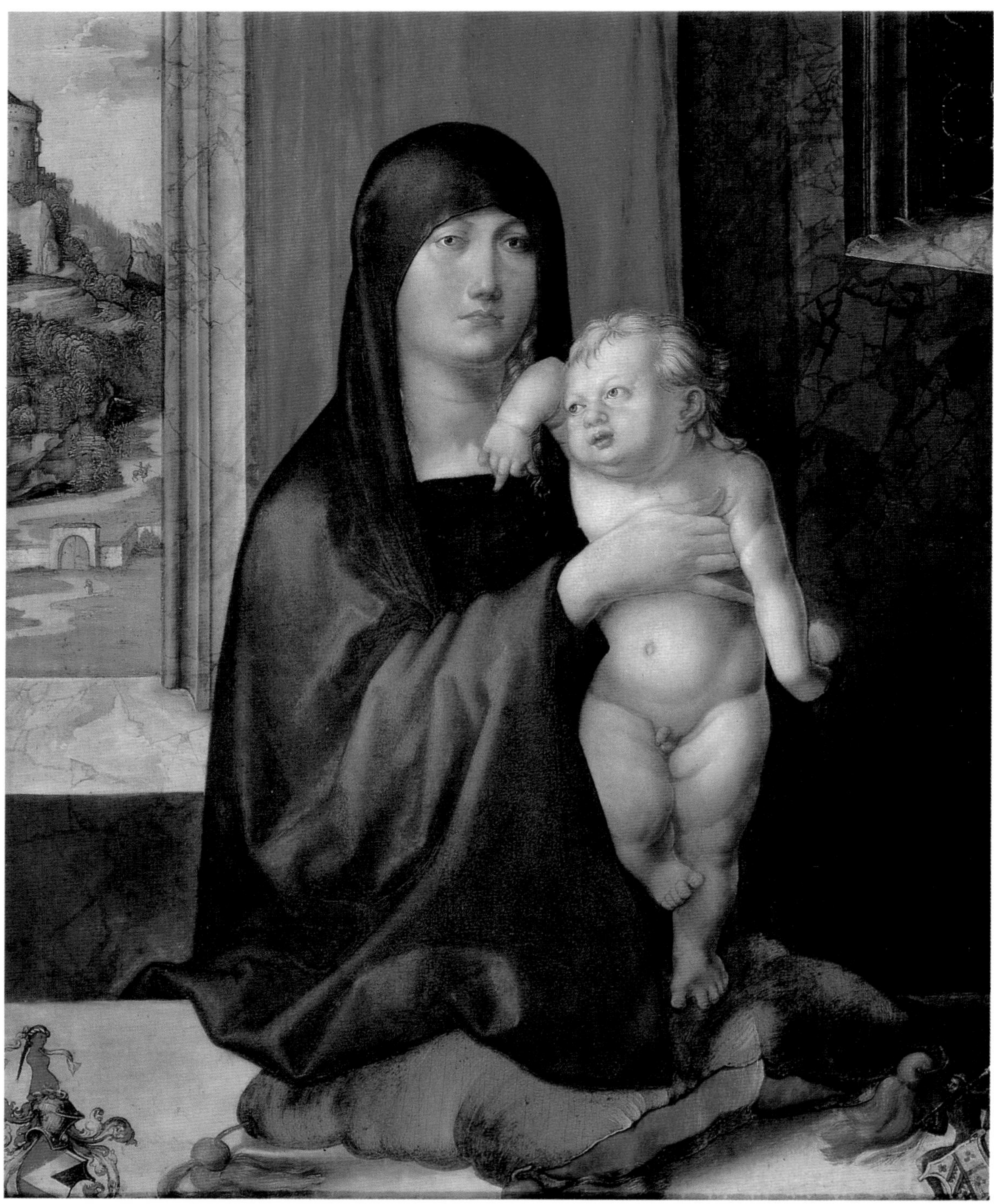

Dürer's Father
London, National Gallery
[pl. 15]

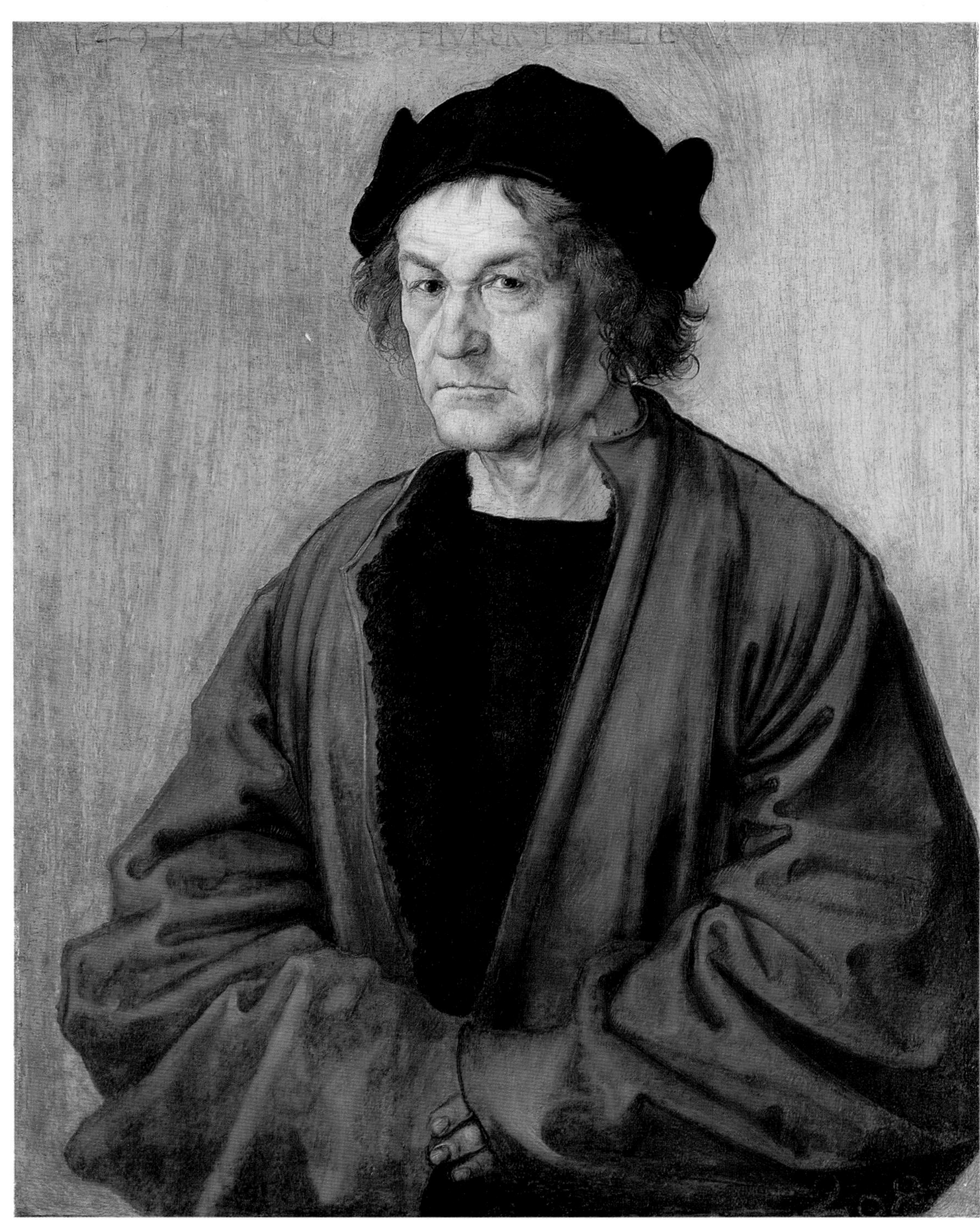

Portrait of a Young Fürleger with Loose Hair
Frankfurt, Städelsches Kunstinstitut
[pl. 16]

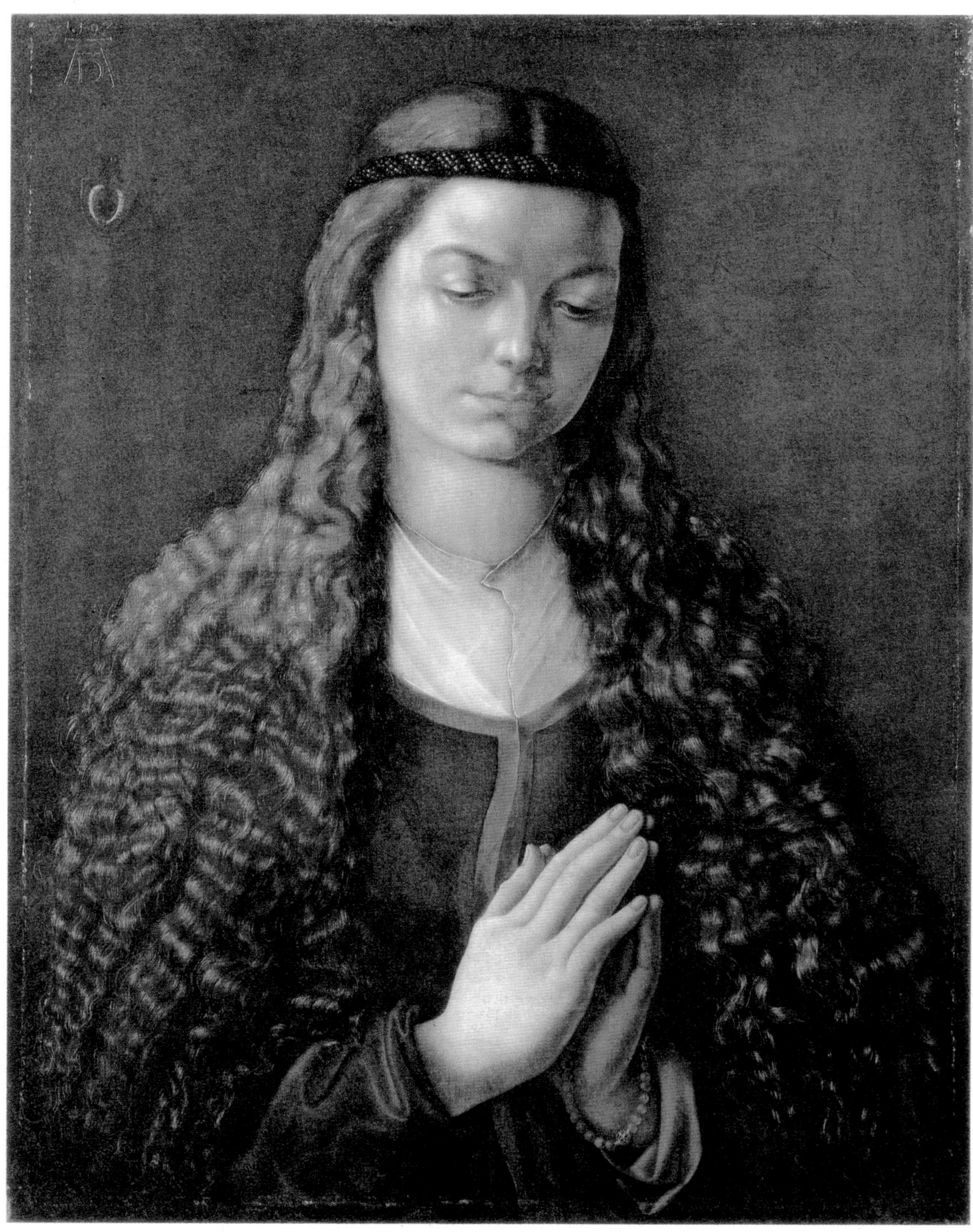

Portrait of a Man
Kreuzlingen, Switzerland, Kisters collection
[pl. 18]

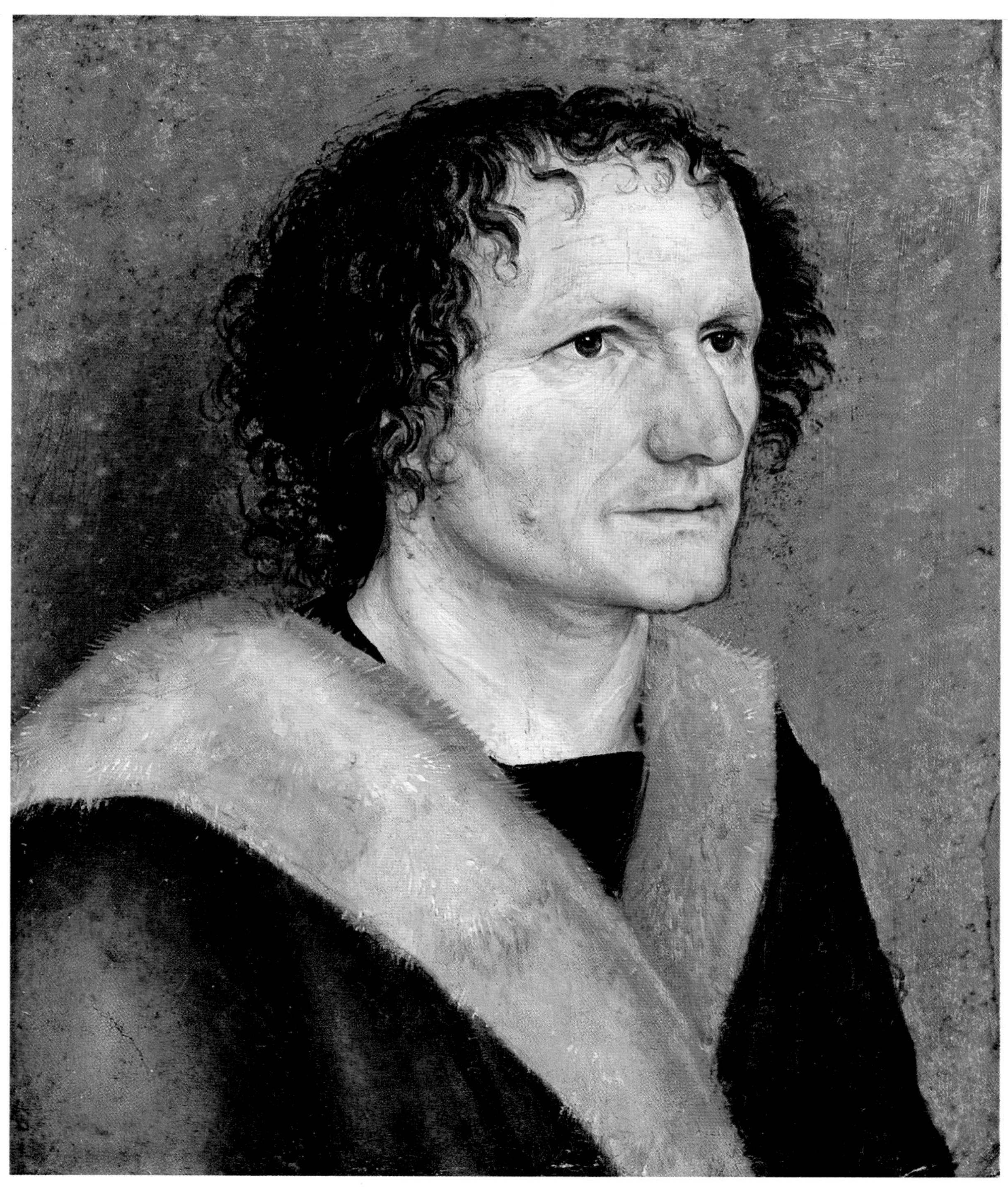

Self-Portrait with Gloves
Madrid, Museo del Prado
[pl. 19]

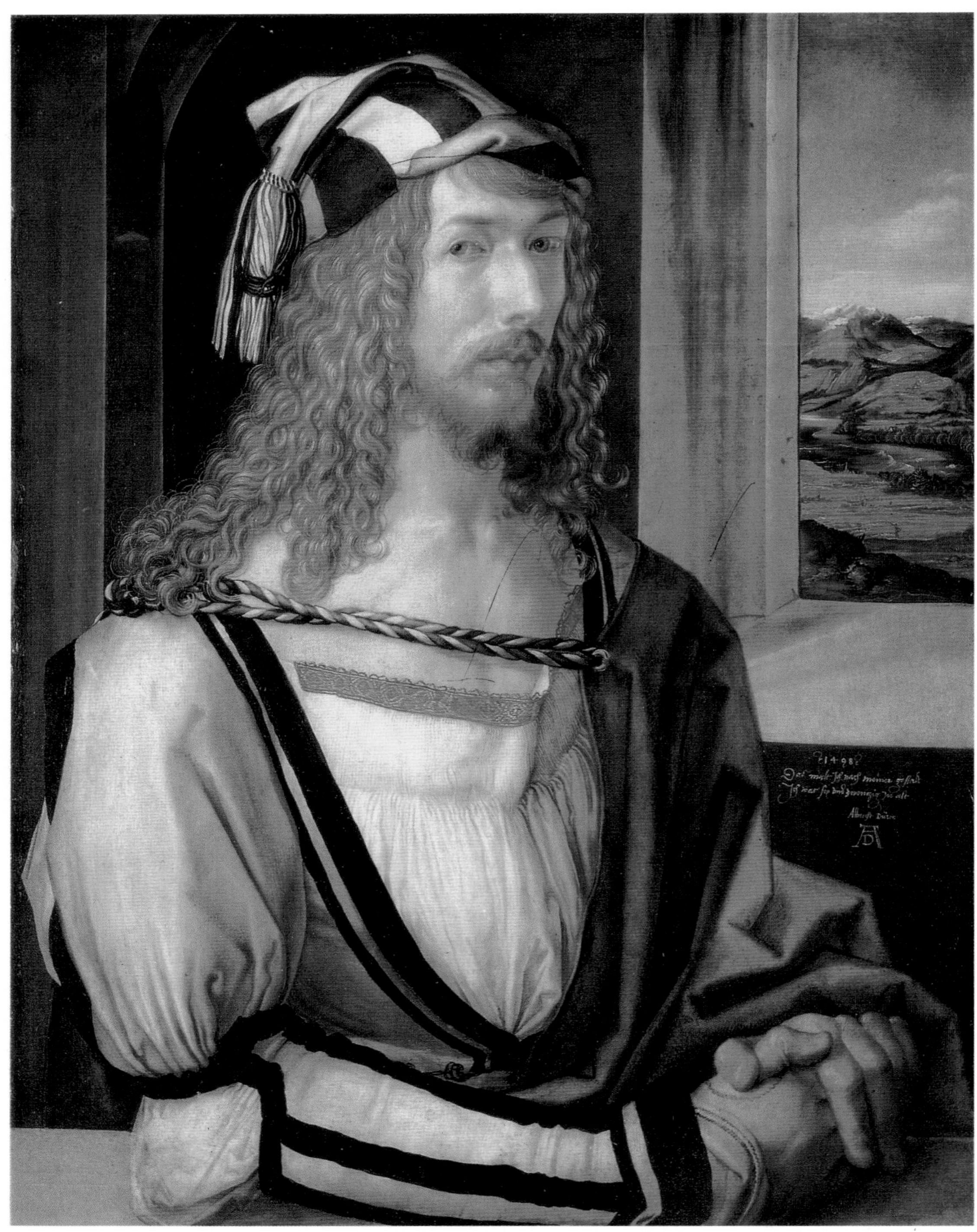

Hans Tucher
Weimar, Schlossmuseum
[pl. 20]

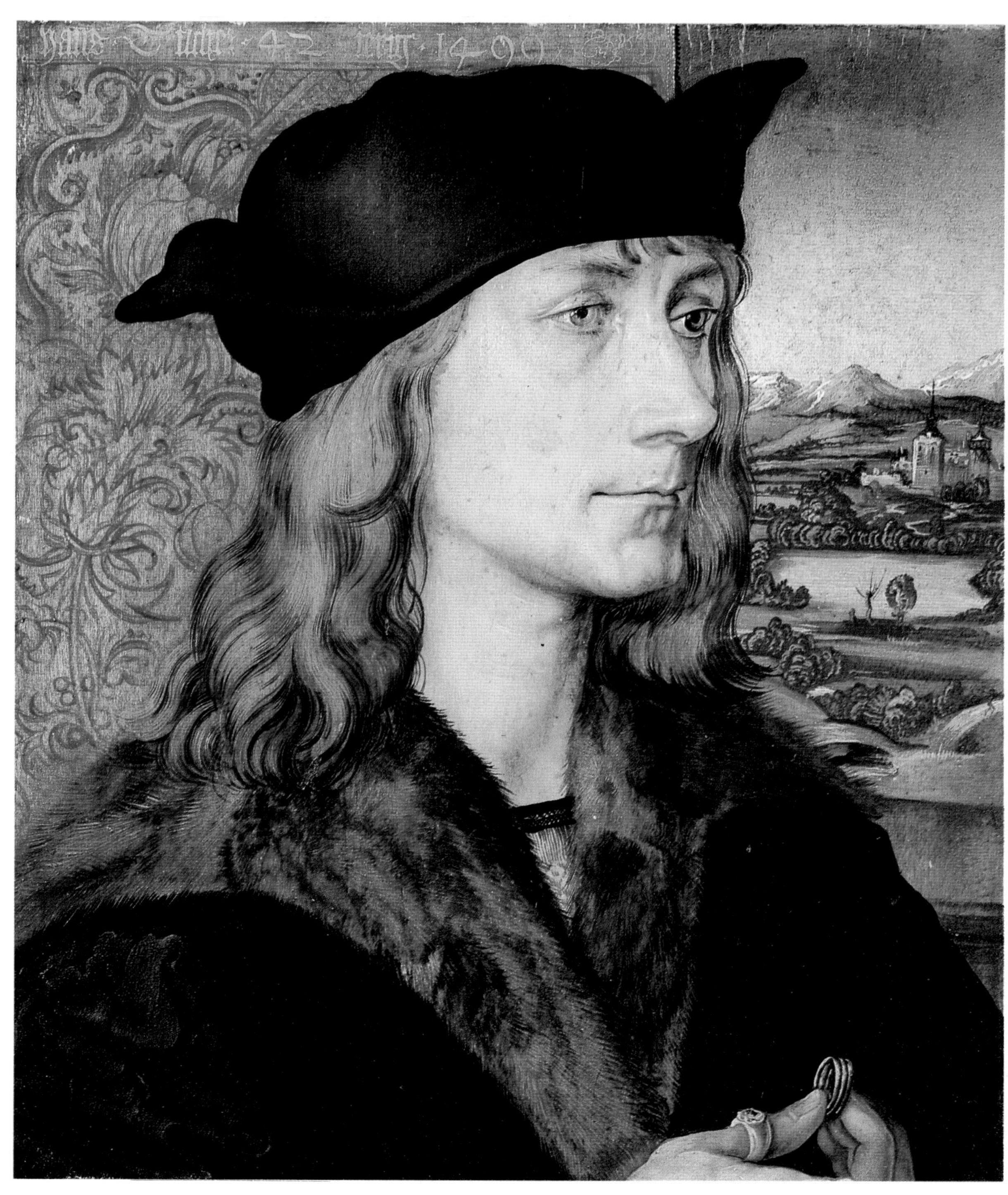

Coats of Arms of the Tucher and Rieter Families
verso of [pl. 20]

Felicitas Tucher, née Rieter
Weimar, Schlossmuseum
[pl. 21]

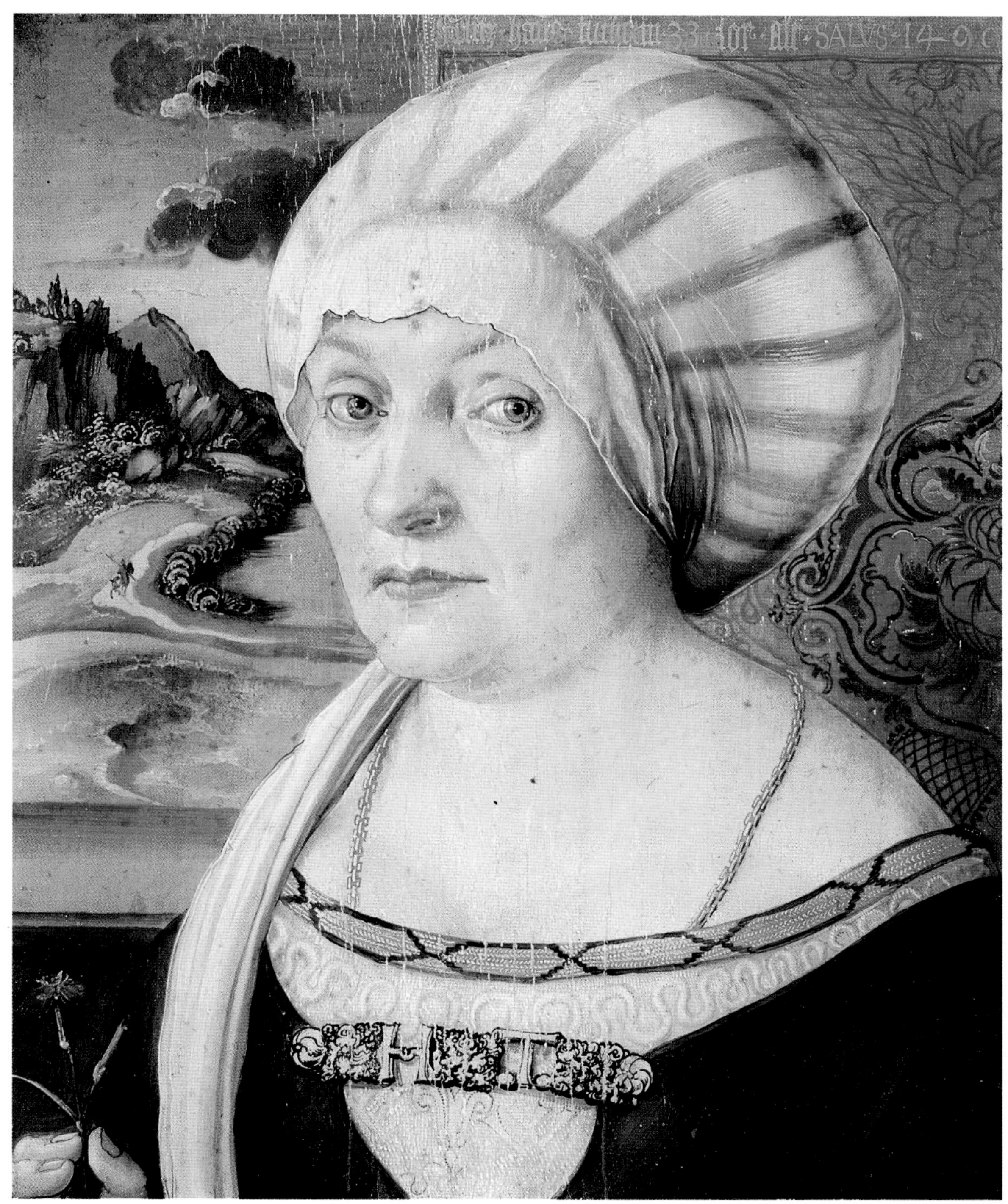

Elsbeth Tucher, née Pusch
Kassel, Staatliche Kunstammlungen
[pl. 22]

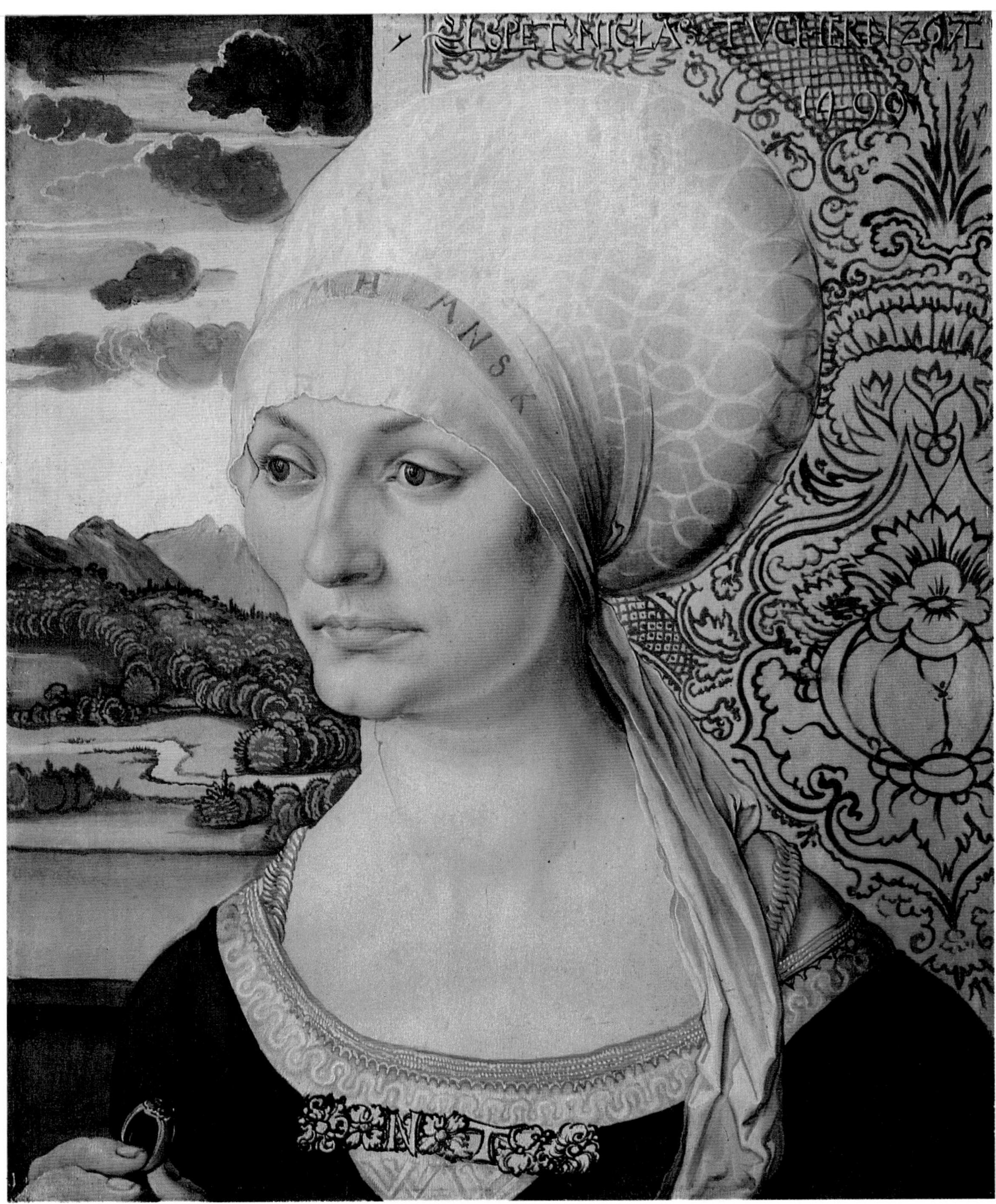

Portrait of Oswolt Krell
Munich, Alte Pinakothek
[pl. 23]

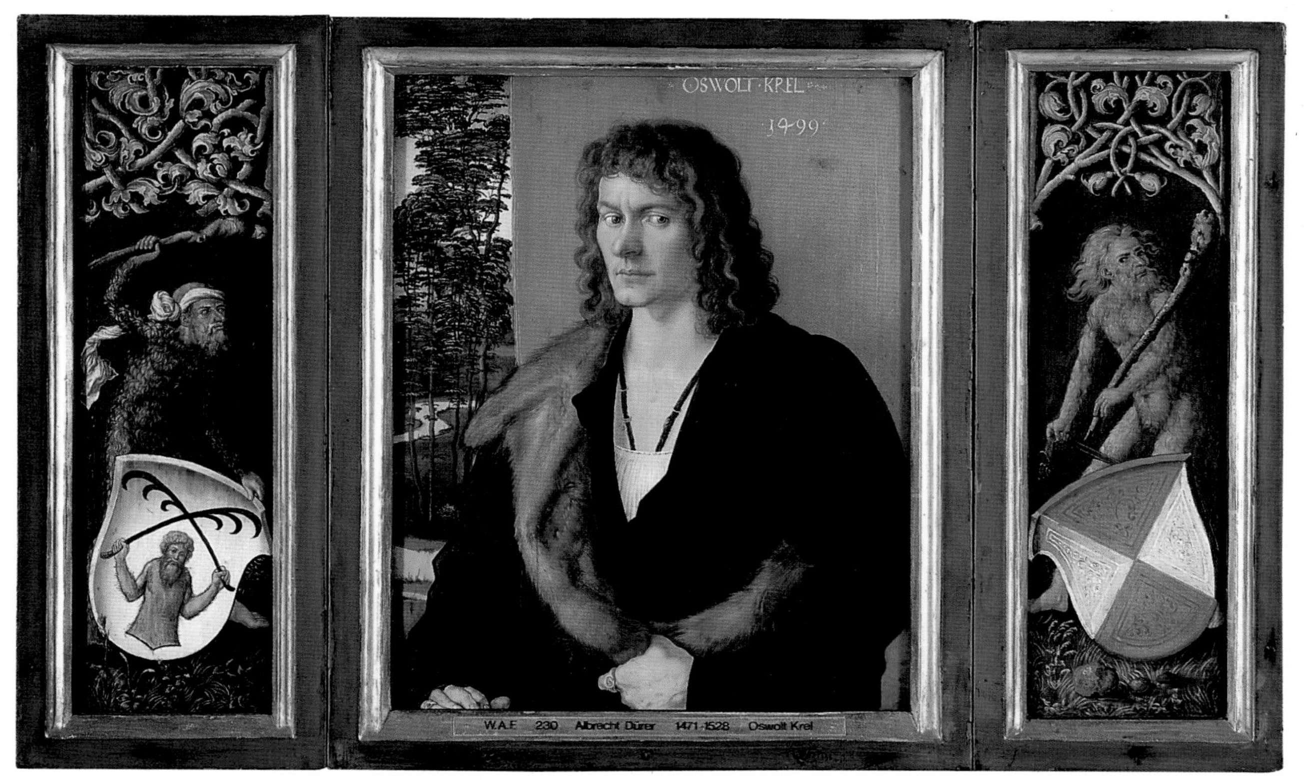

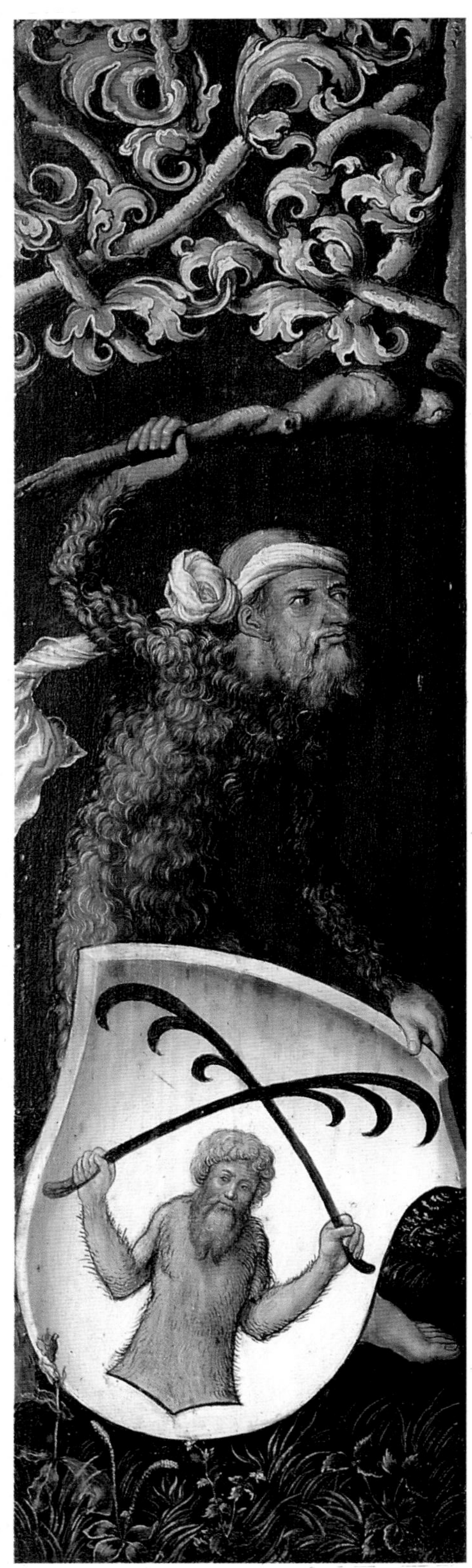

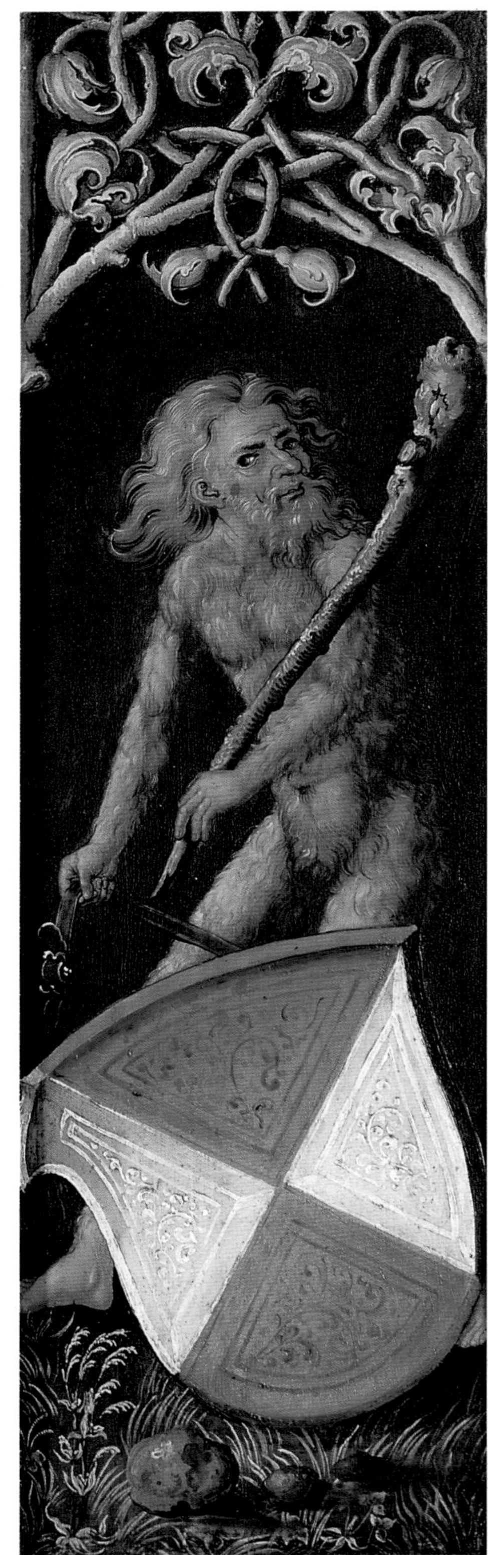

on the side and facing page: [pl. 23] *details*

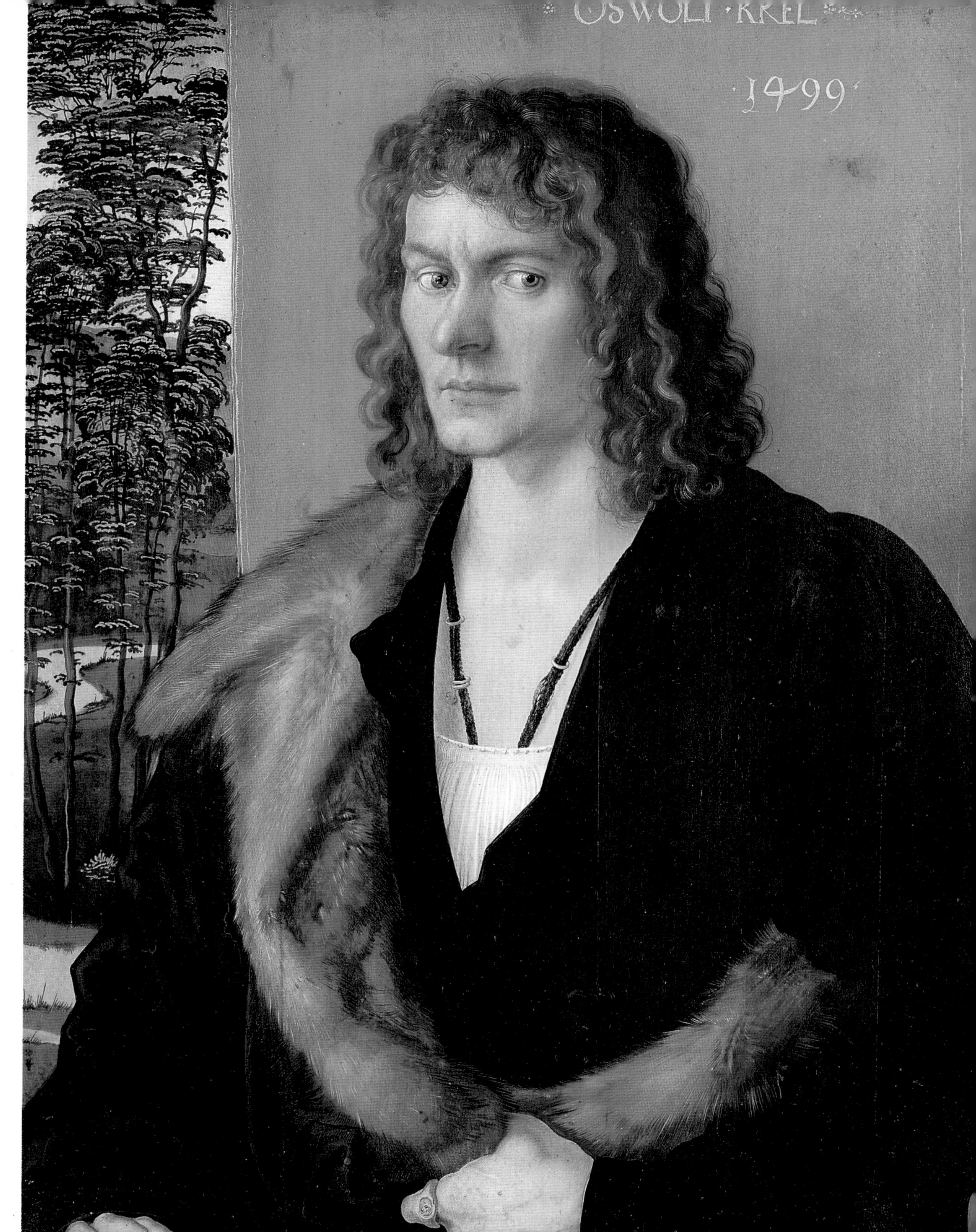
OSWOLT·KREL
·1499·

Portrait of Saint Sebastian with an Arrow
Bergamo, Accademia Carrara
[pl. 24]

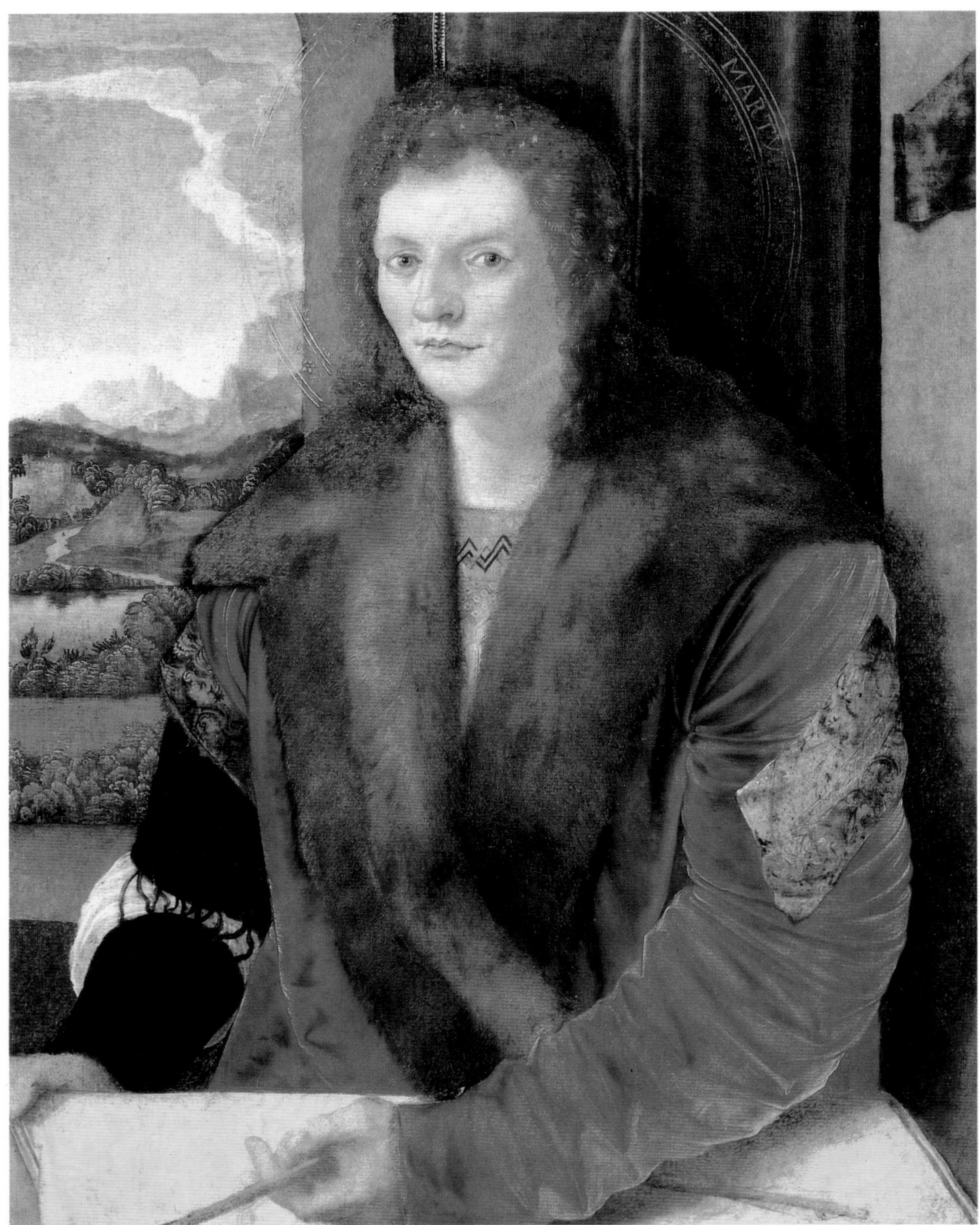

Lamentation over the Dead Christ
Munich, Alte Pinakothek
[pl. 25]

on the following pages: [pl. 25] *details*

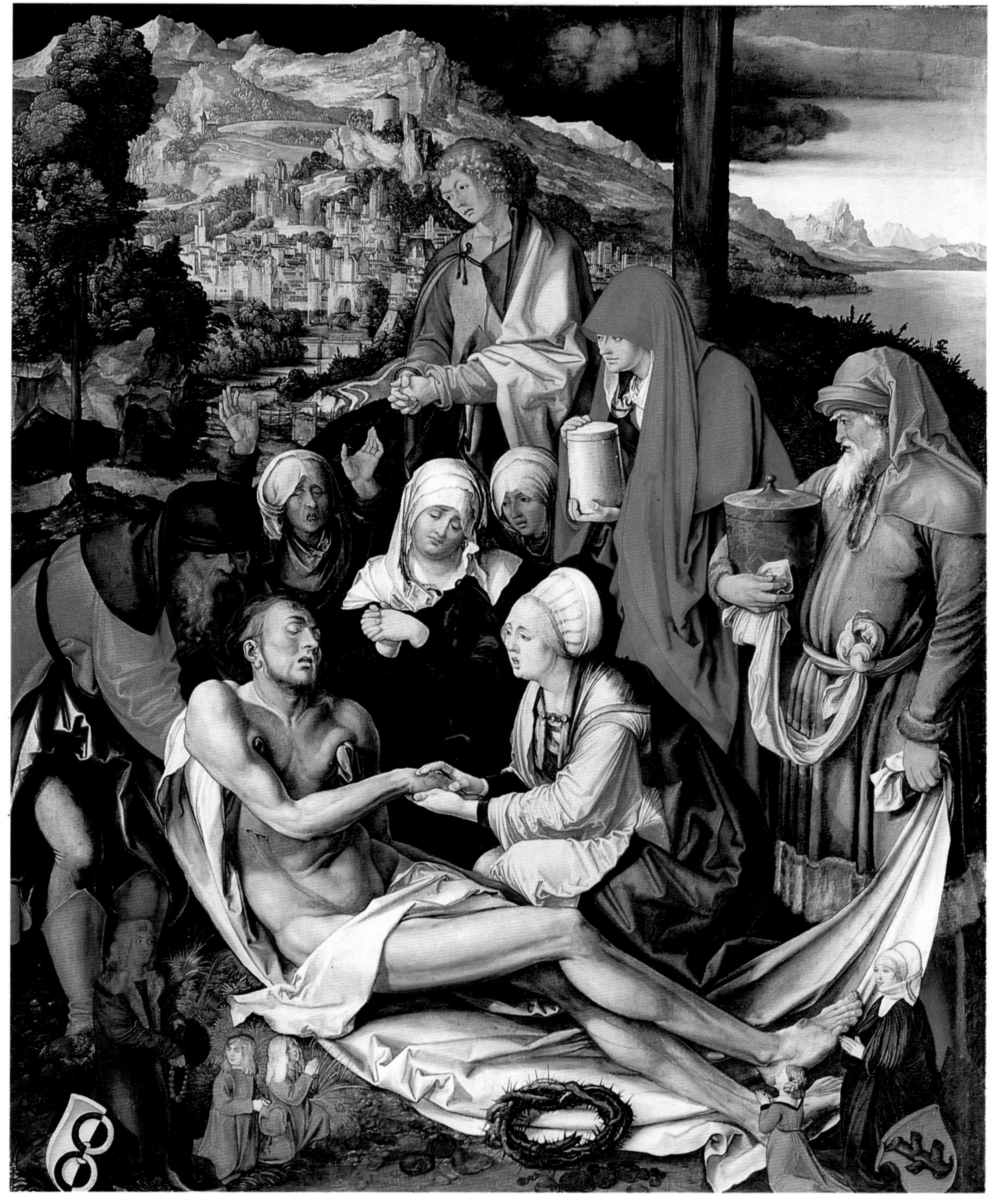

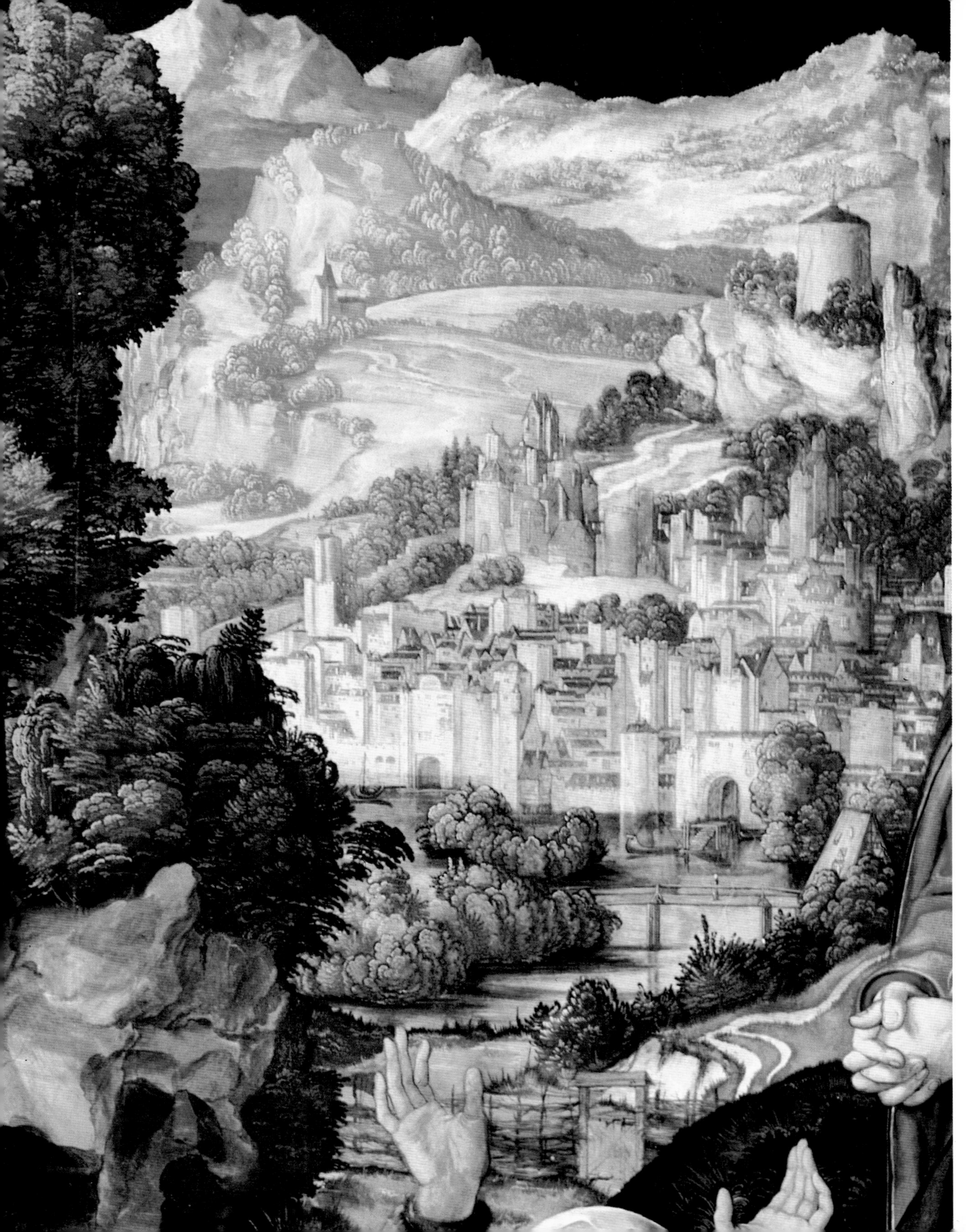

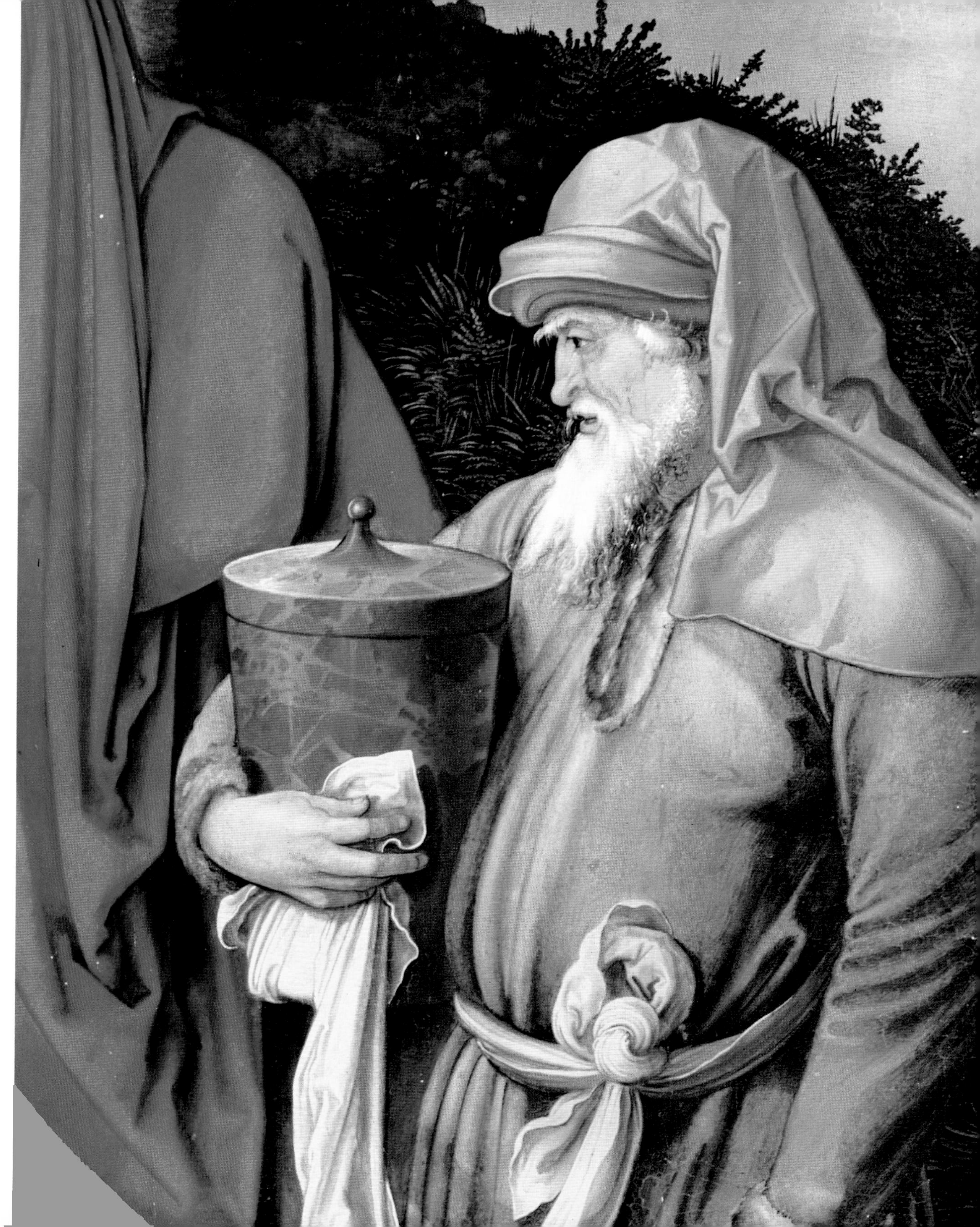

Self-Portrait with Fur Coat
Munich, Alte Pinakothek
[pl. 26]

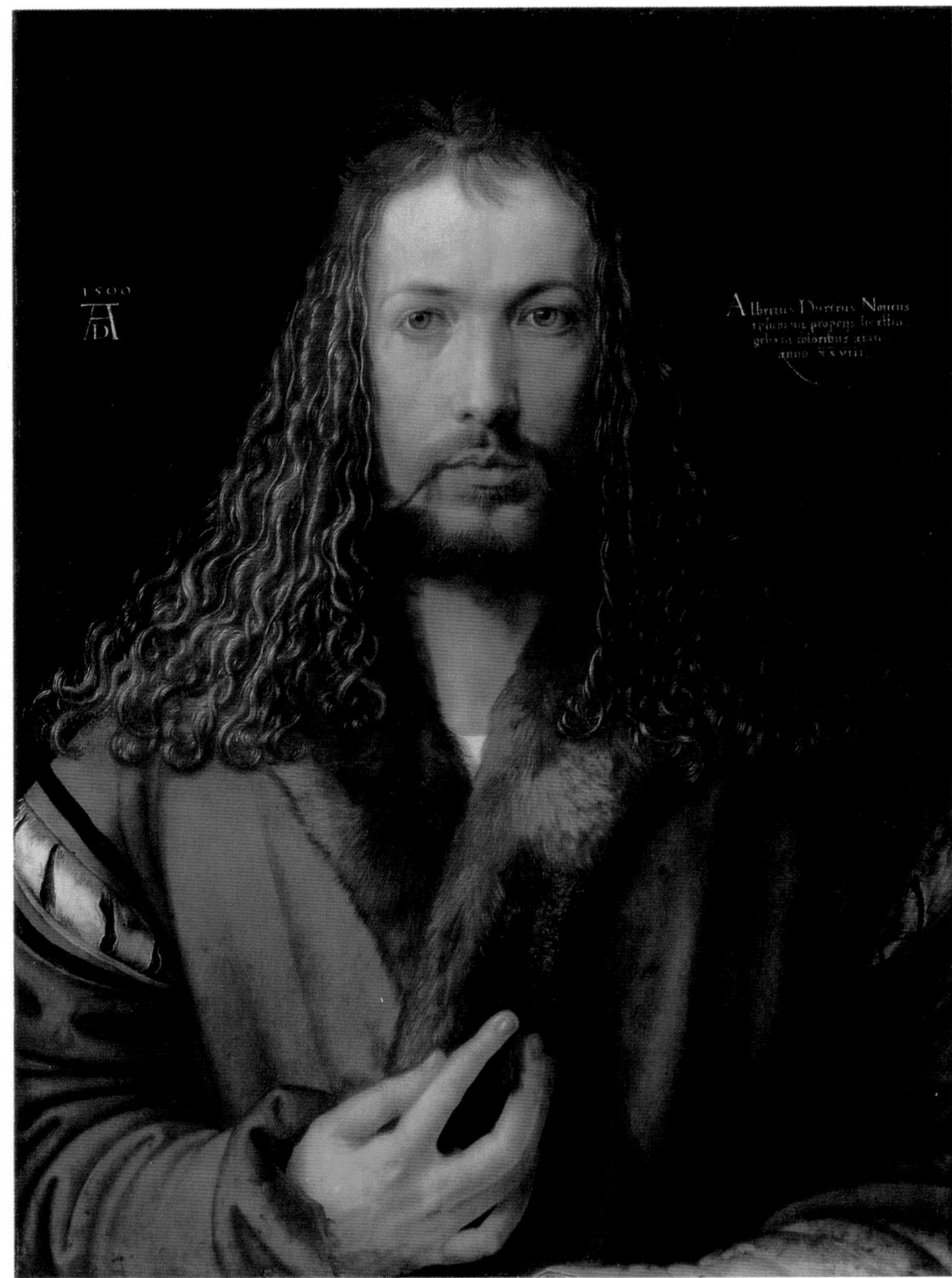

Paumgärtner Altar
Munich, Alte Pinakothek
[pl. 28]

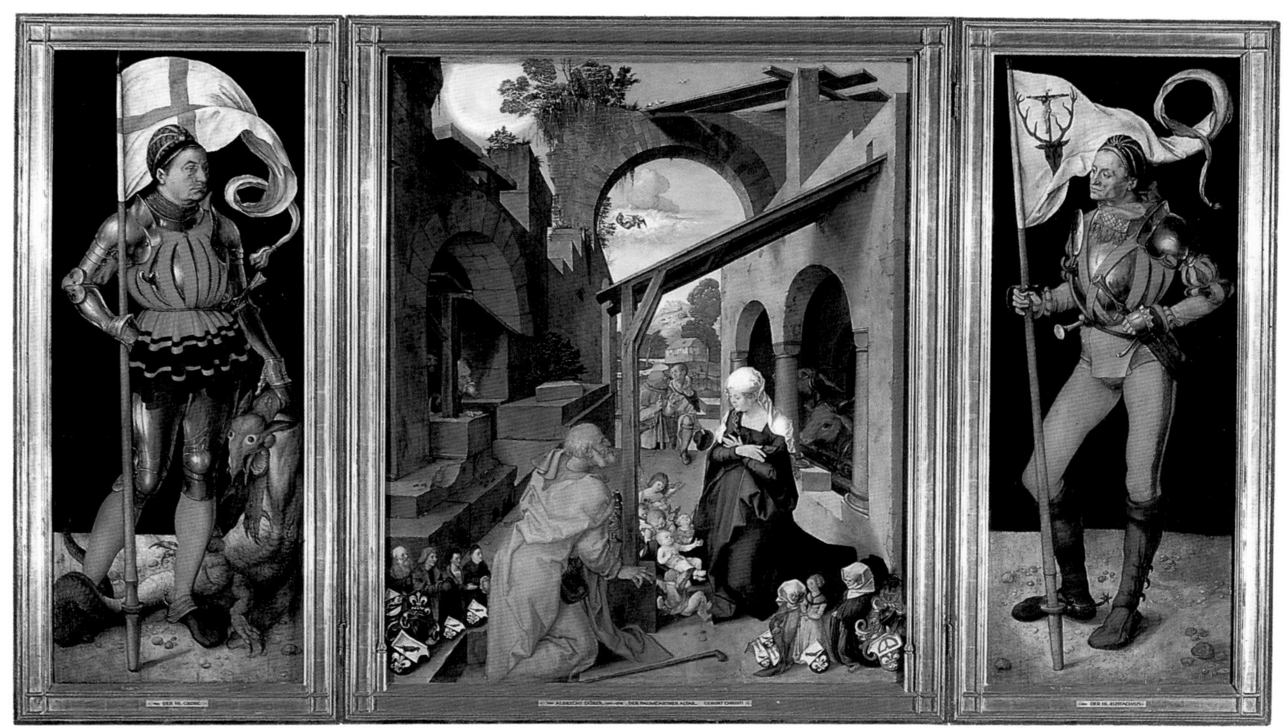

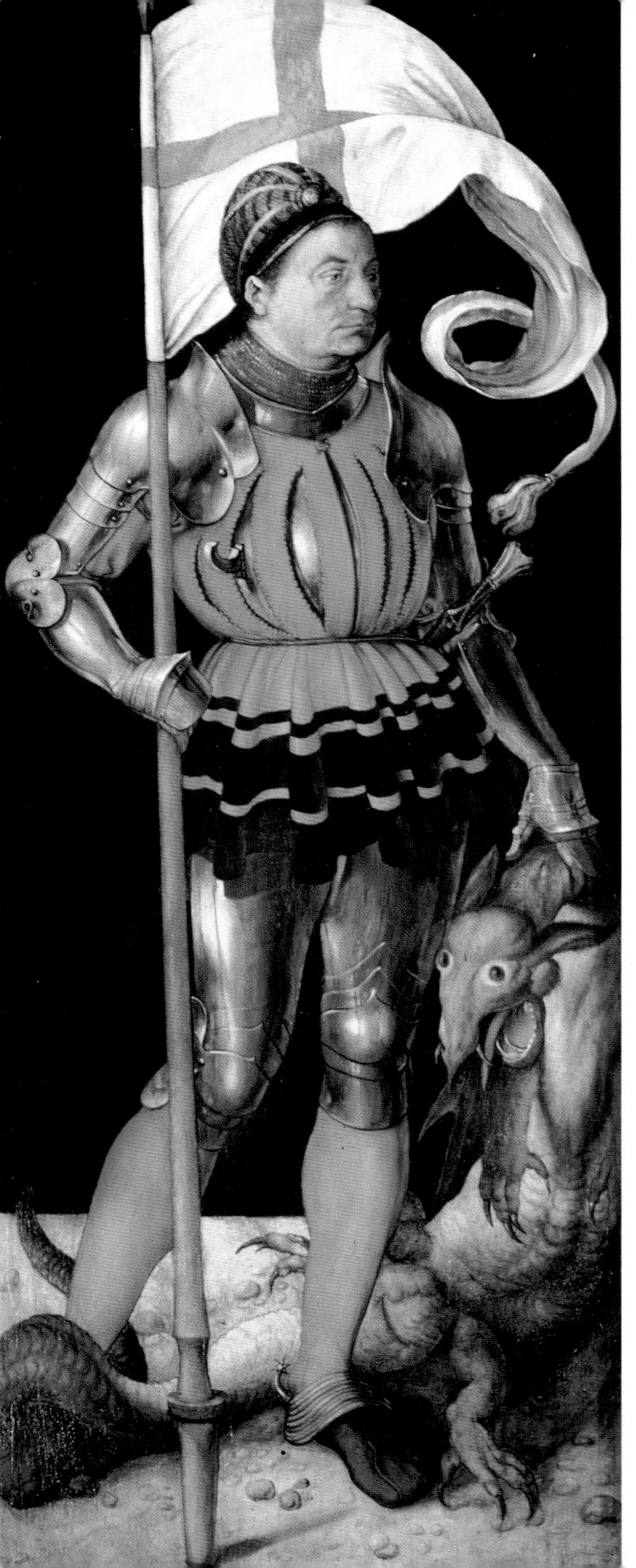

on this, and the following two pages:
[pl. 28] *details*

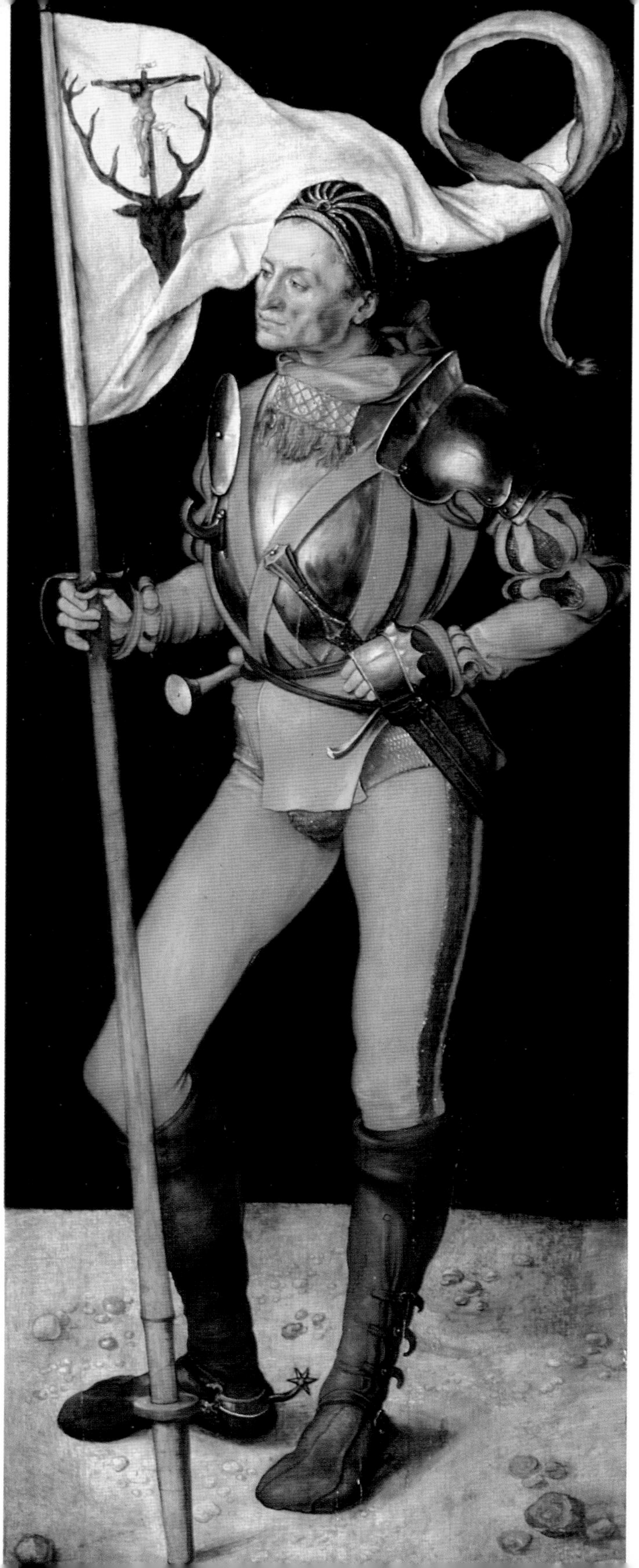

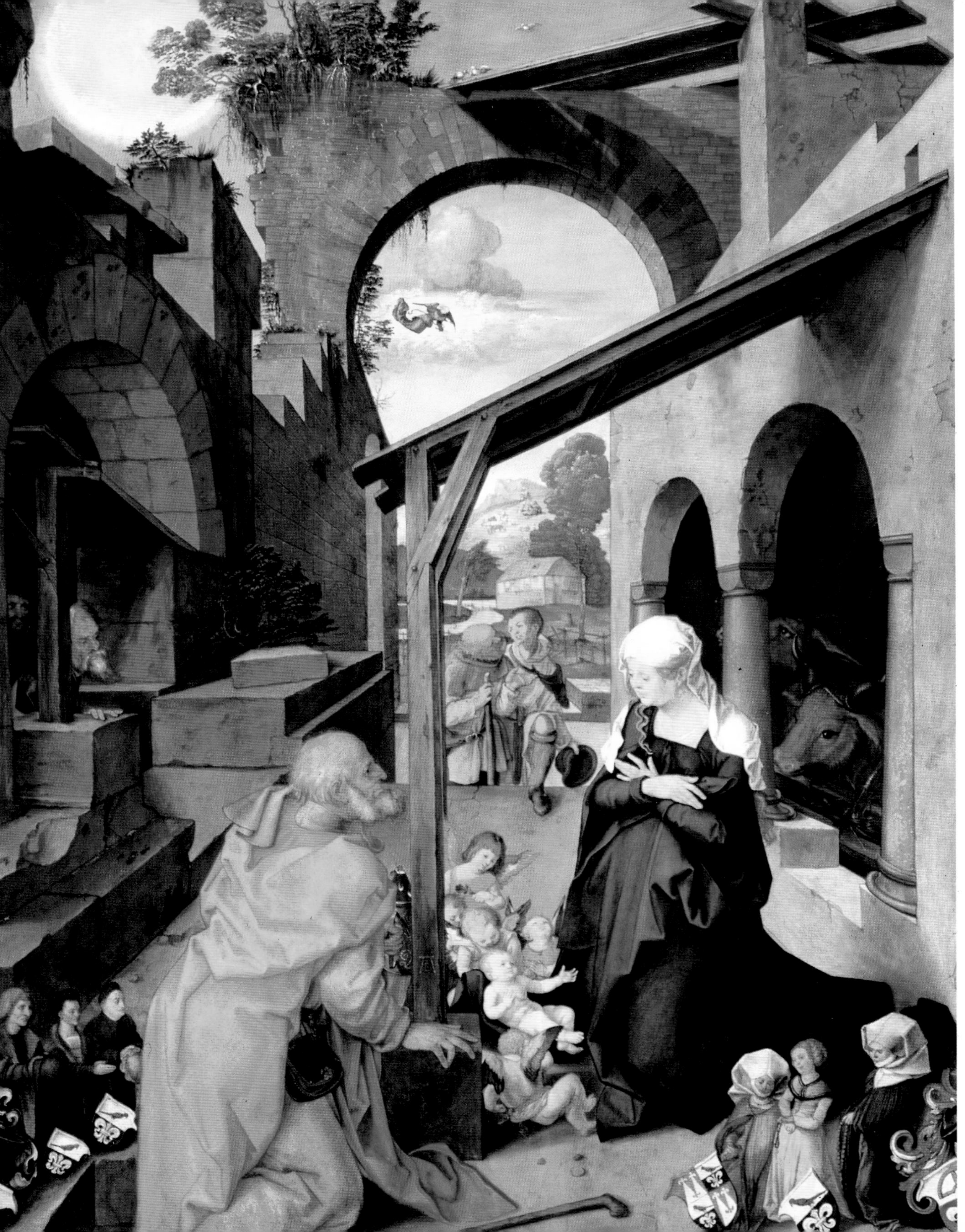

Jabach Altar

Job and His Wife
Frankfurt, Städelsches Kunstinstitut
[pl. 34]

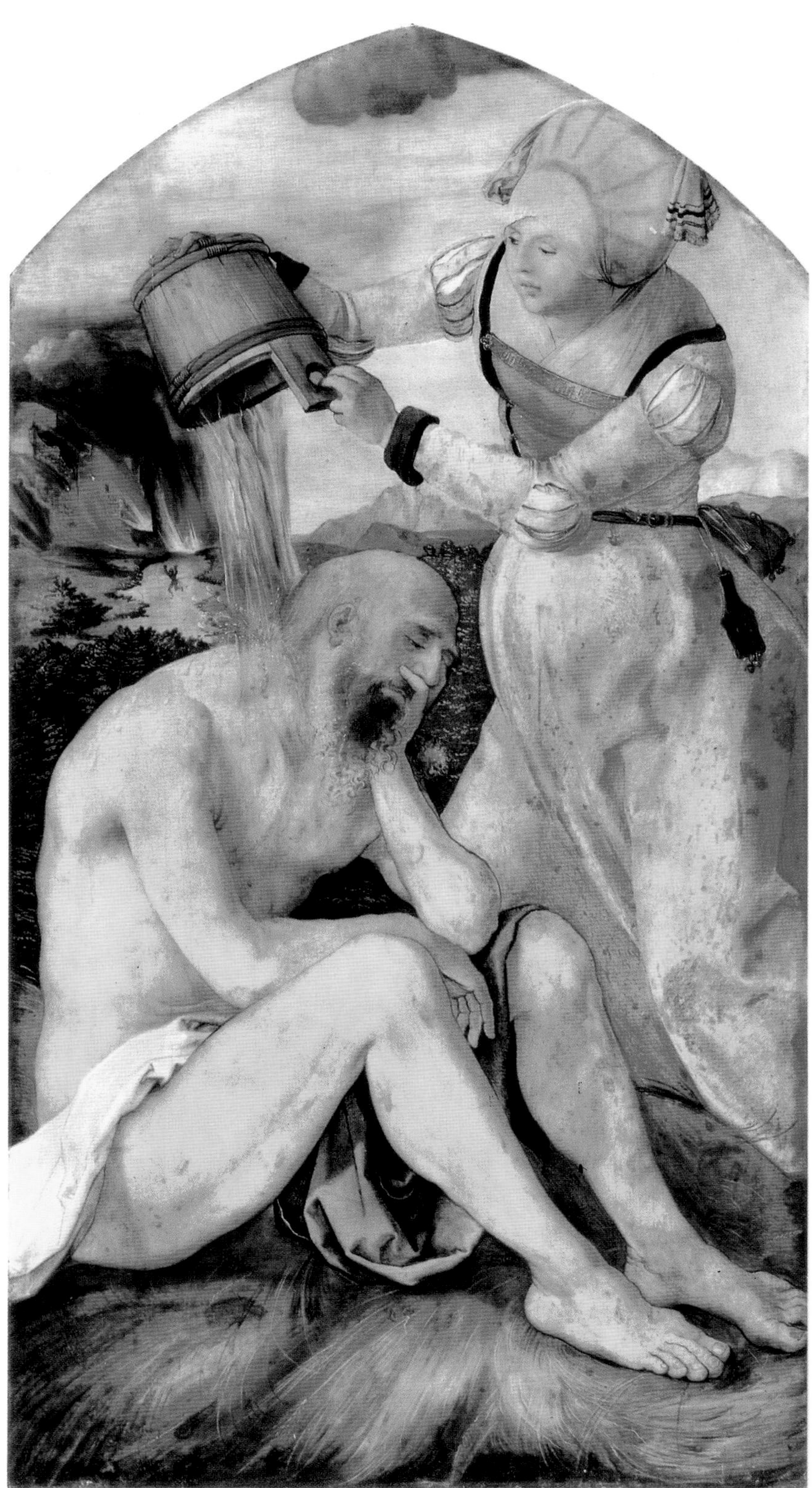

Jabach Altar

Two Musicians
Cologne, Wallraf-Richartz-Museum
[pl. 34]

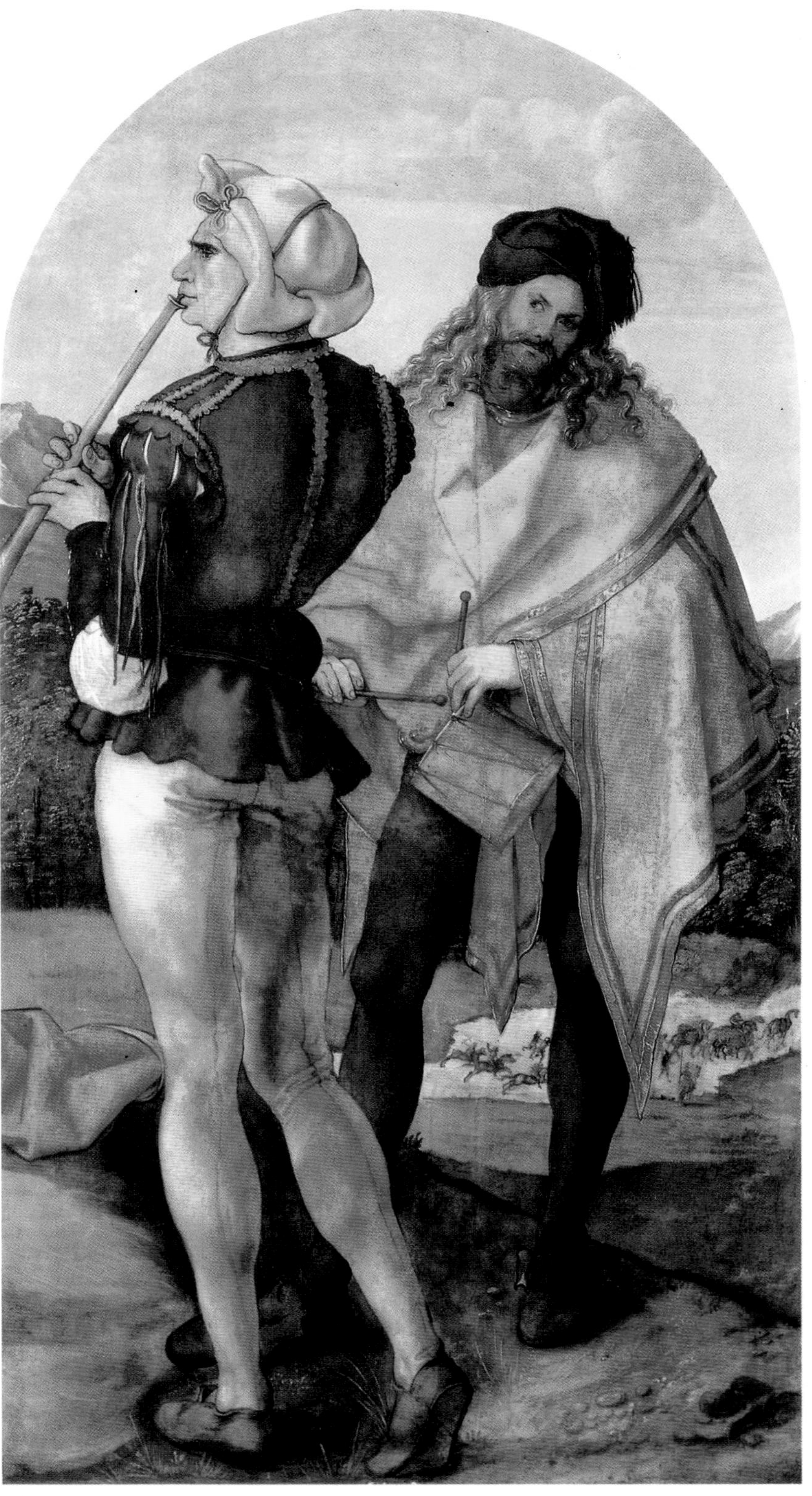

The Adoration of the Magi
Florence, Galleria degli Uffizi
[pl. 35]

on the following pages: [pl. 36] *details*

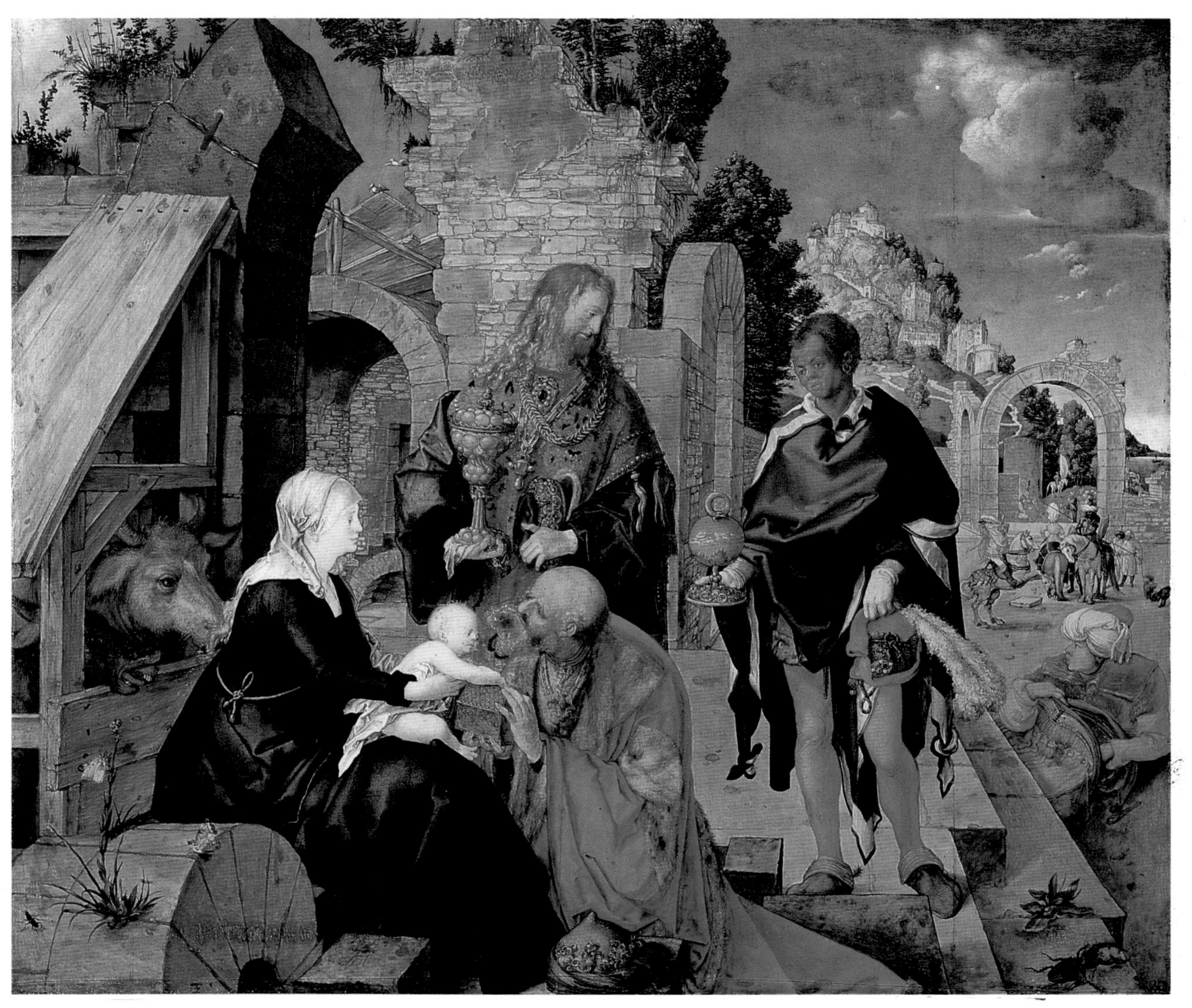

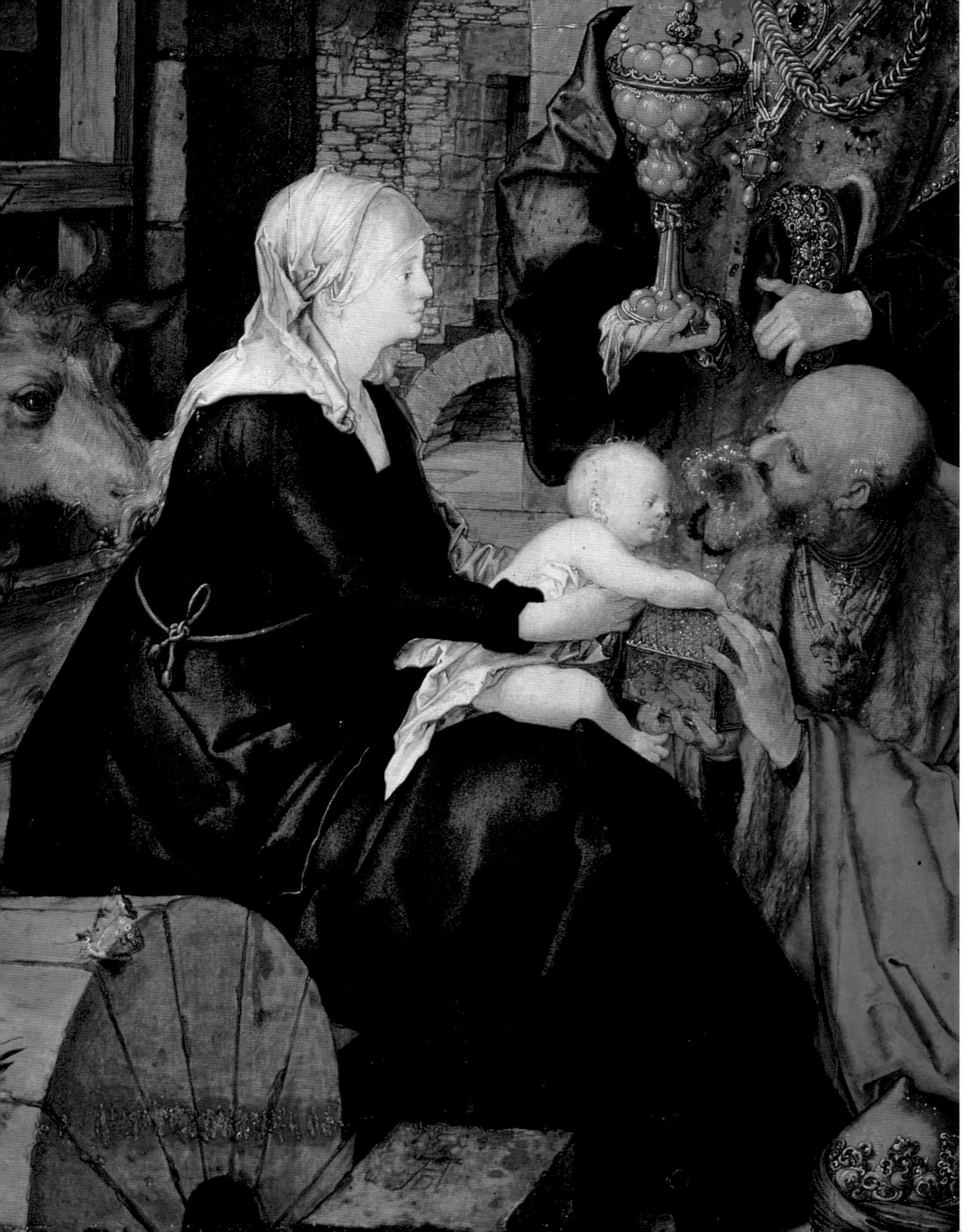

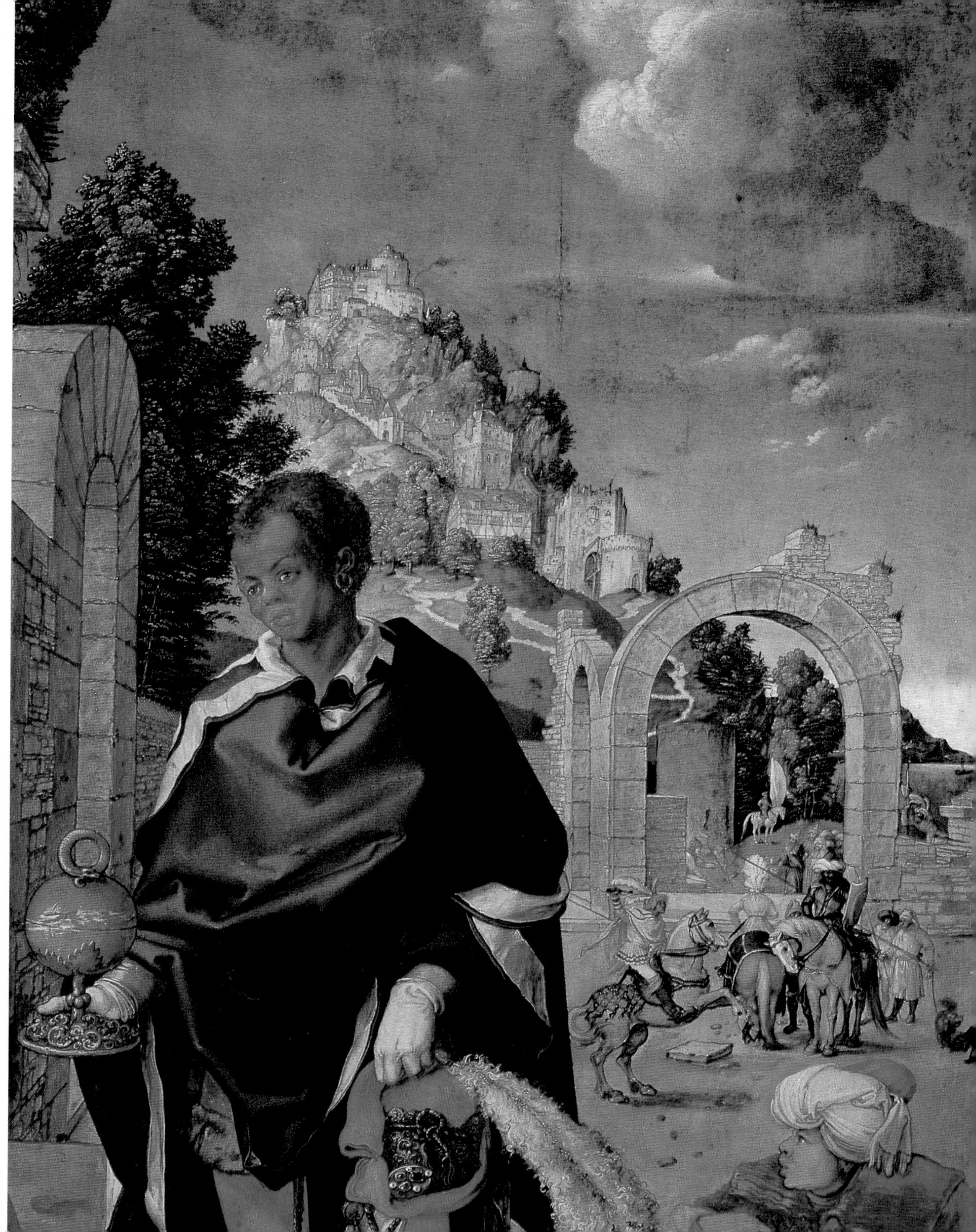

Portrait of a Young Venetian Woman
Vienna, Kunsthistorisches Museum
[pl. 37]

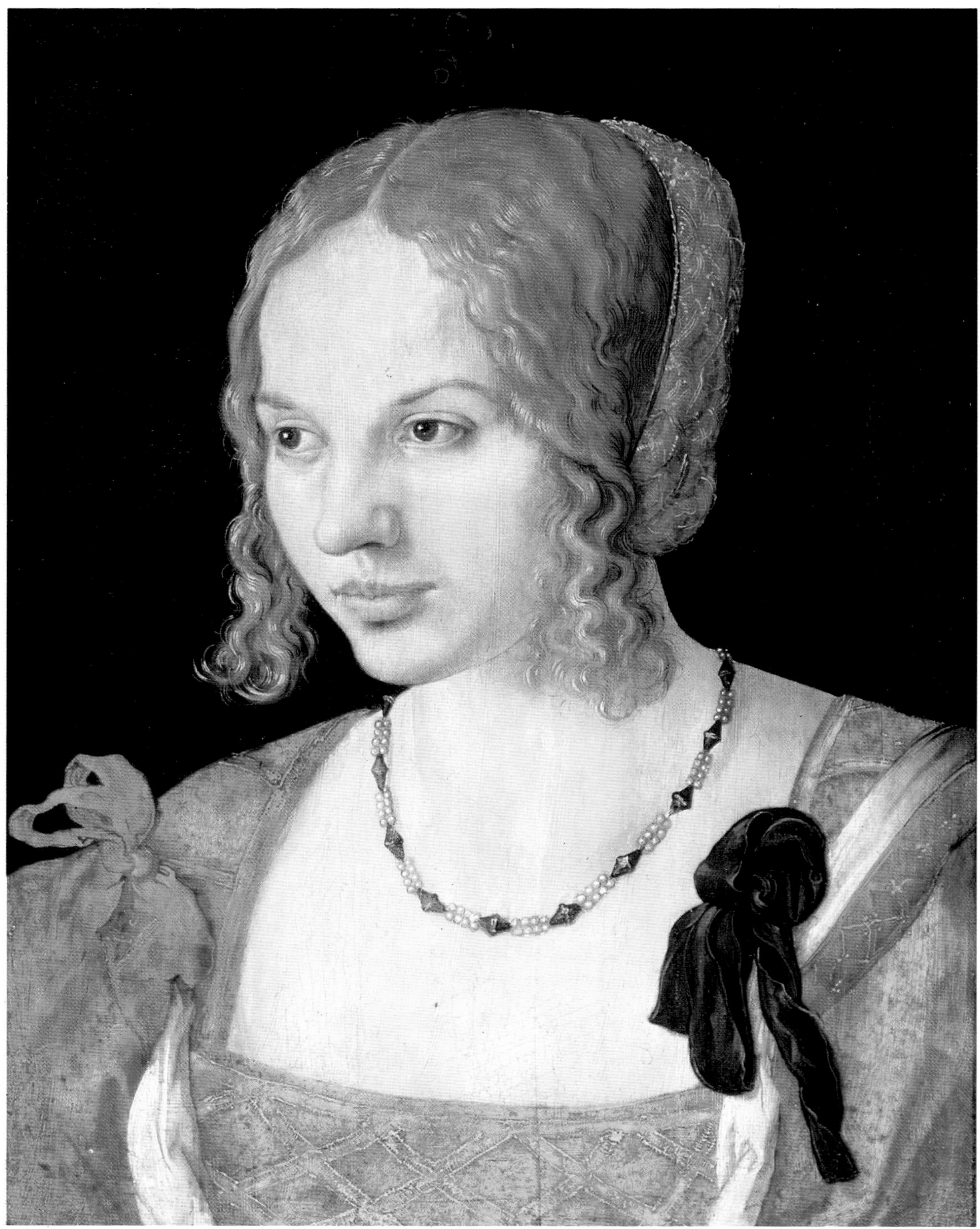

Portrait of a Venetian Woman
Berlin, Staatliche Museen, Gemäldegalerie
[pl. 38]

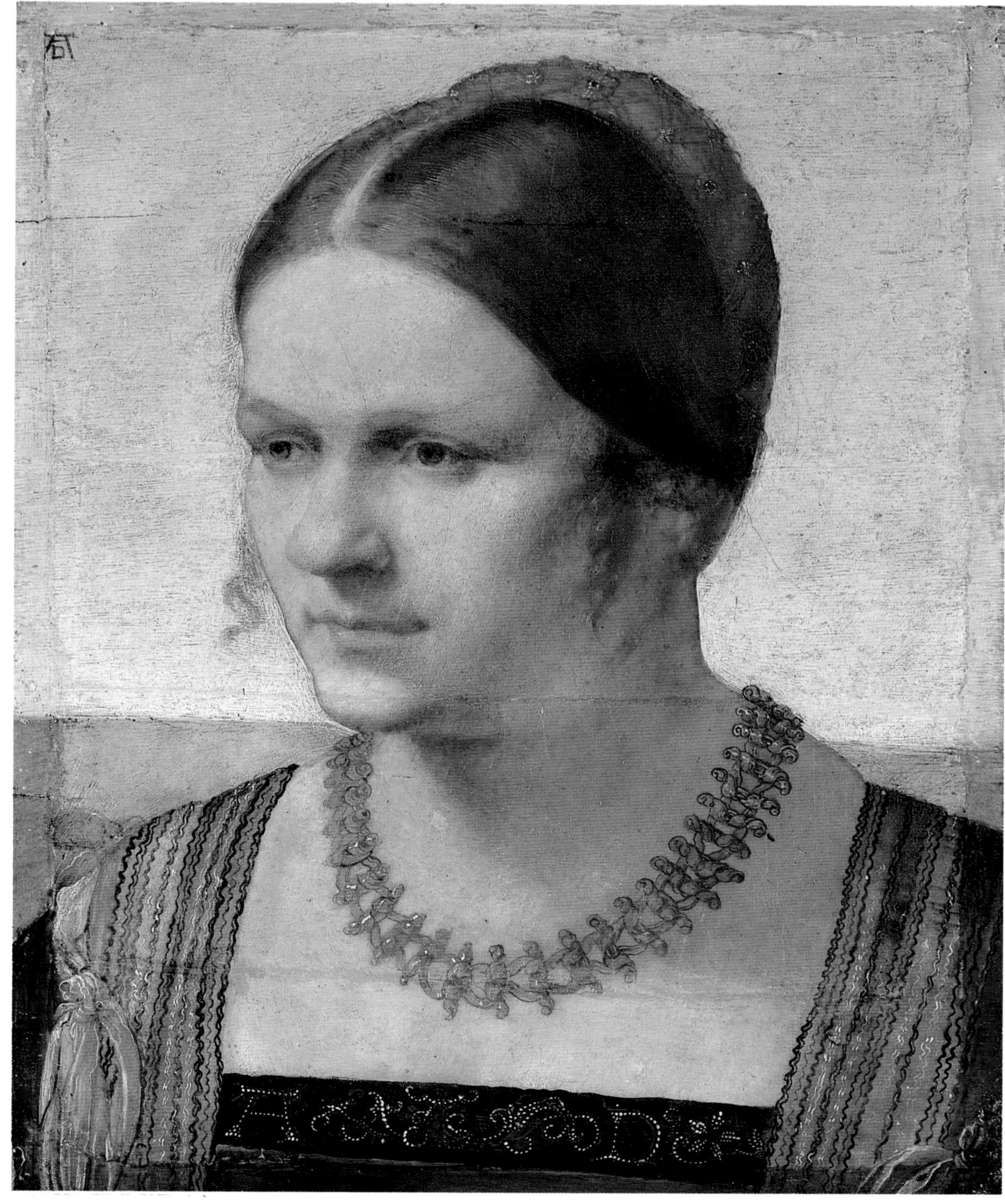

The Feast of the Rose Garlands
Prague, Nàrodni Galerie
[pl. 39]

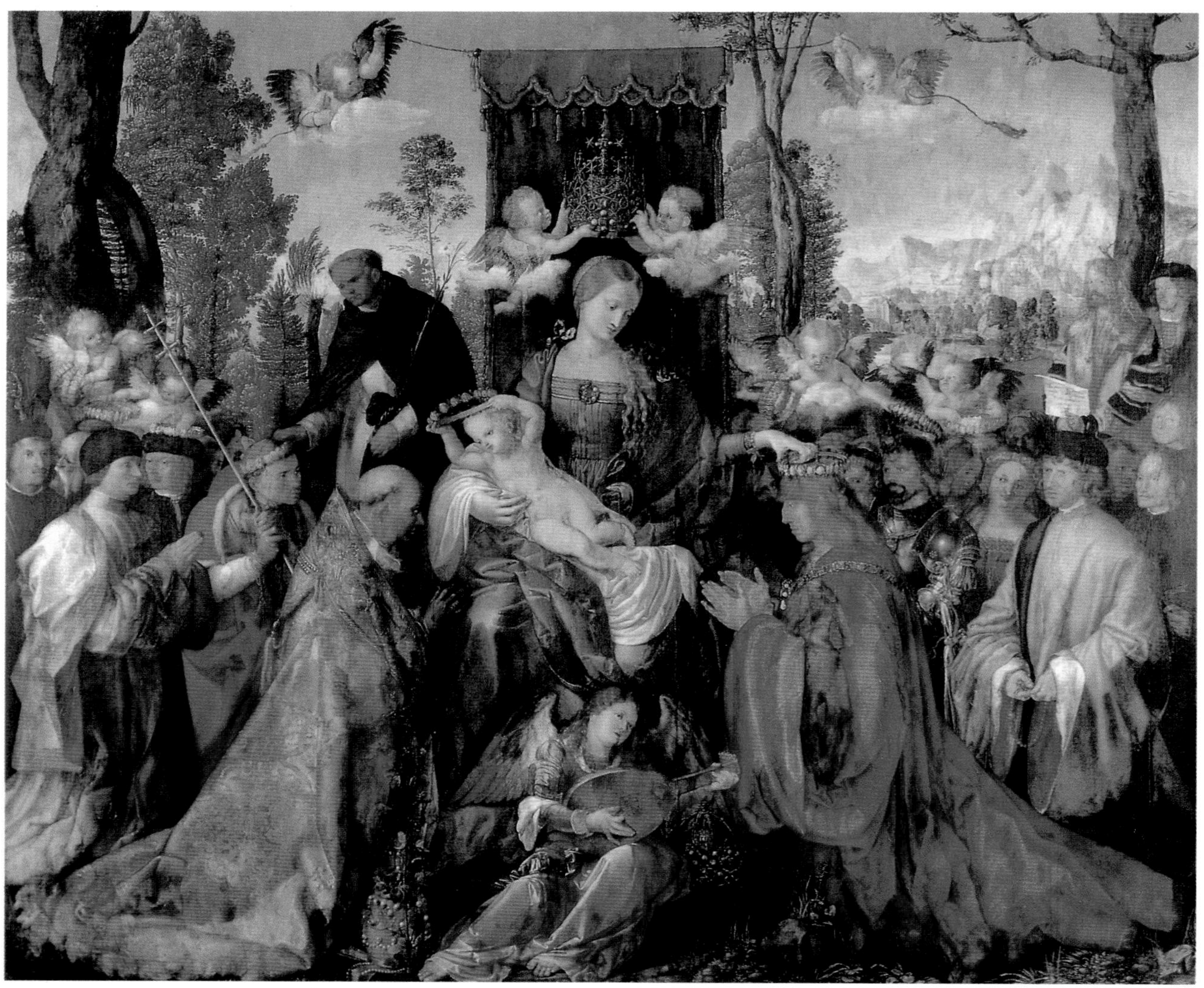

Burkhard von Speyer
Windsor Castle, coll. of H. M. the Queen
[pl. 40]

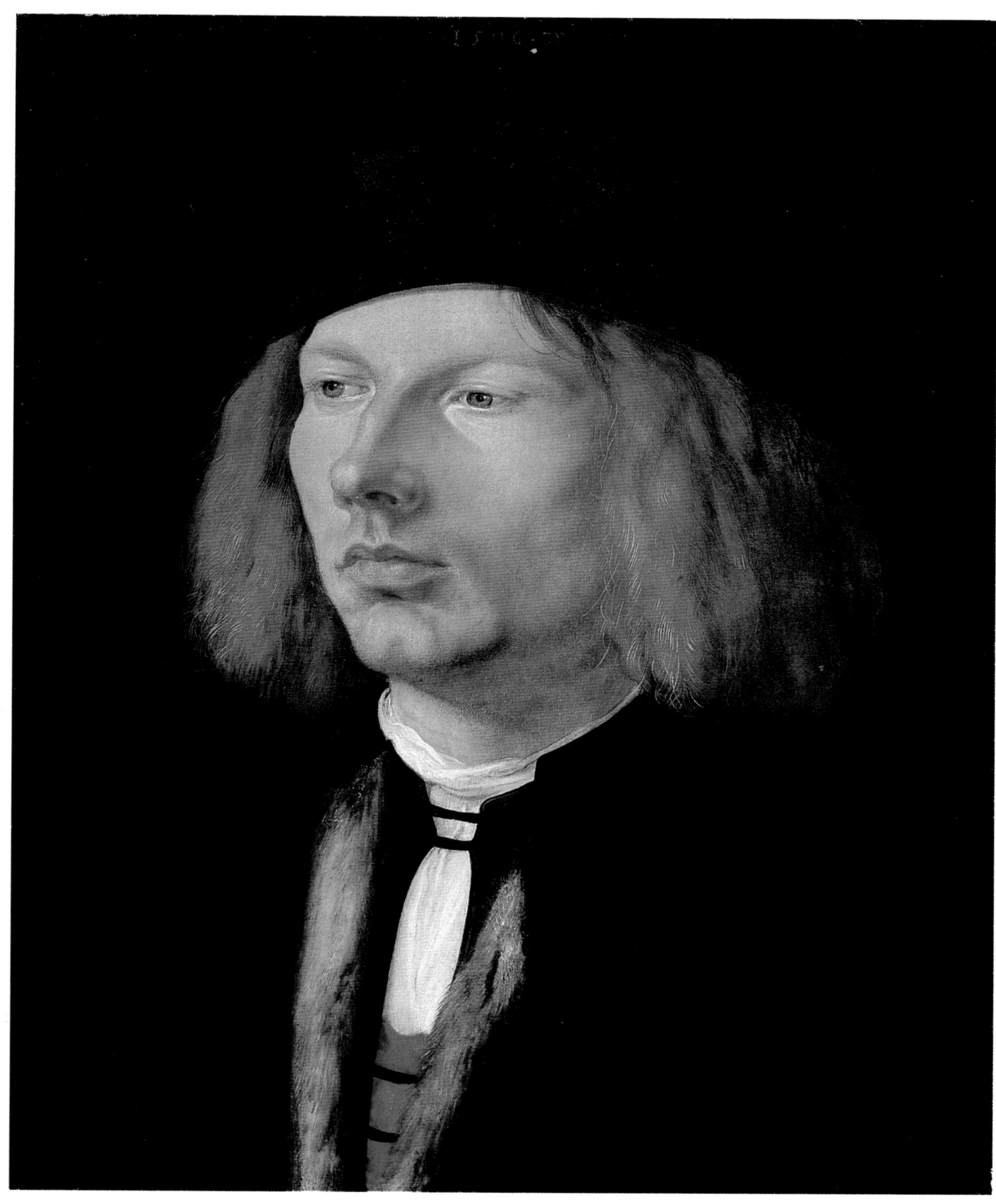

Portrait of a Young Man
Genoa, Palazzo Rosso
[pl. 41]

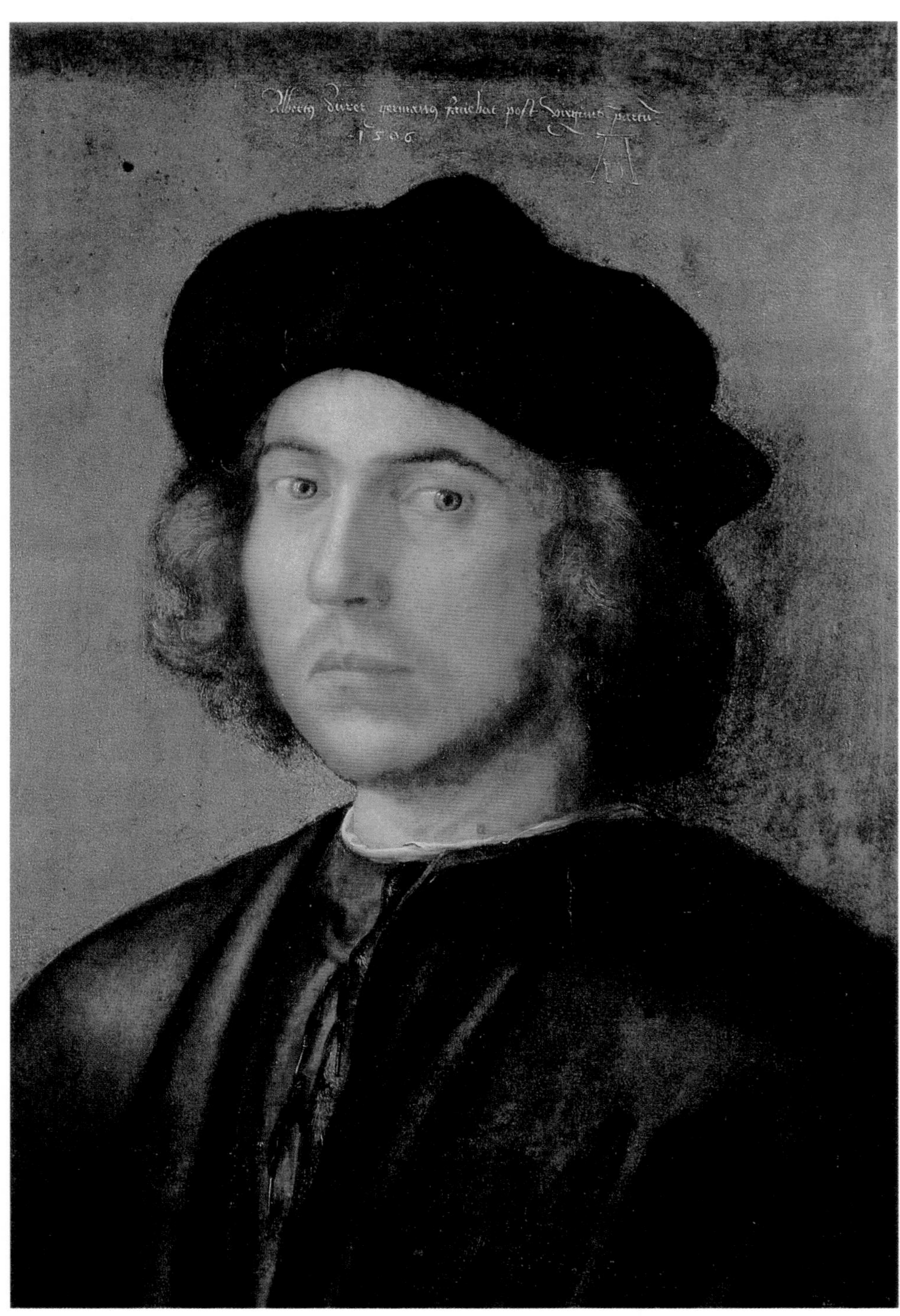

Madonna with the Siskin
Berlin, Staatliche Museen, Gemäldegalerie
[pl. 42]

on the following pages: [pl. 42] *details*

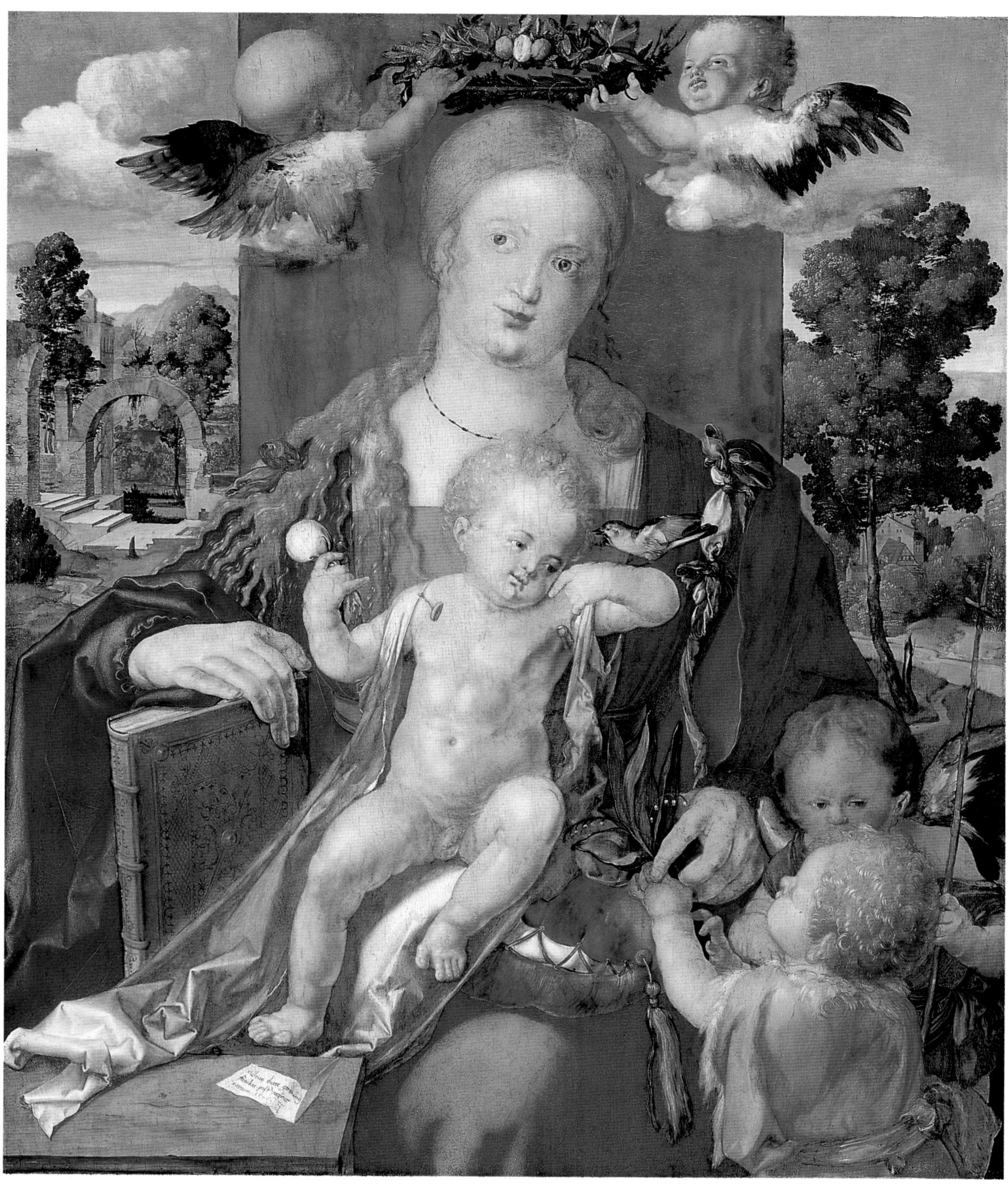

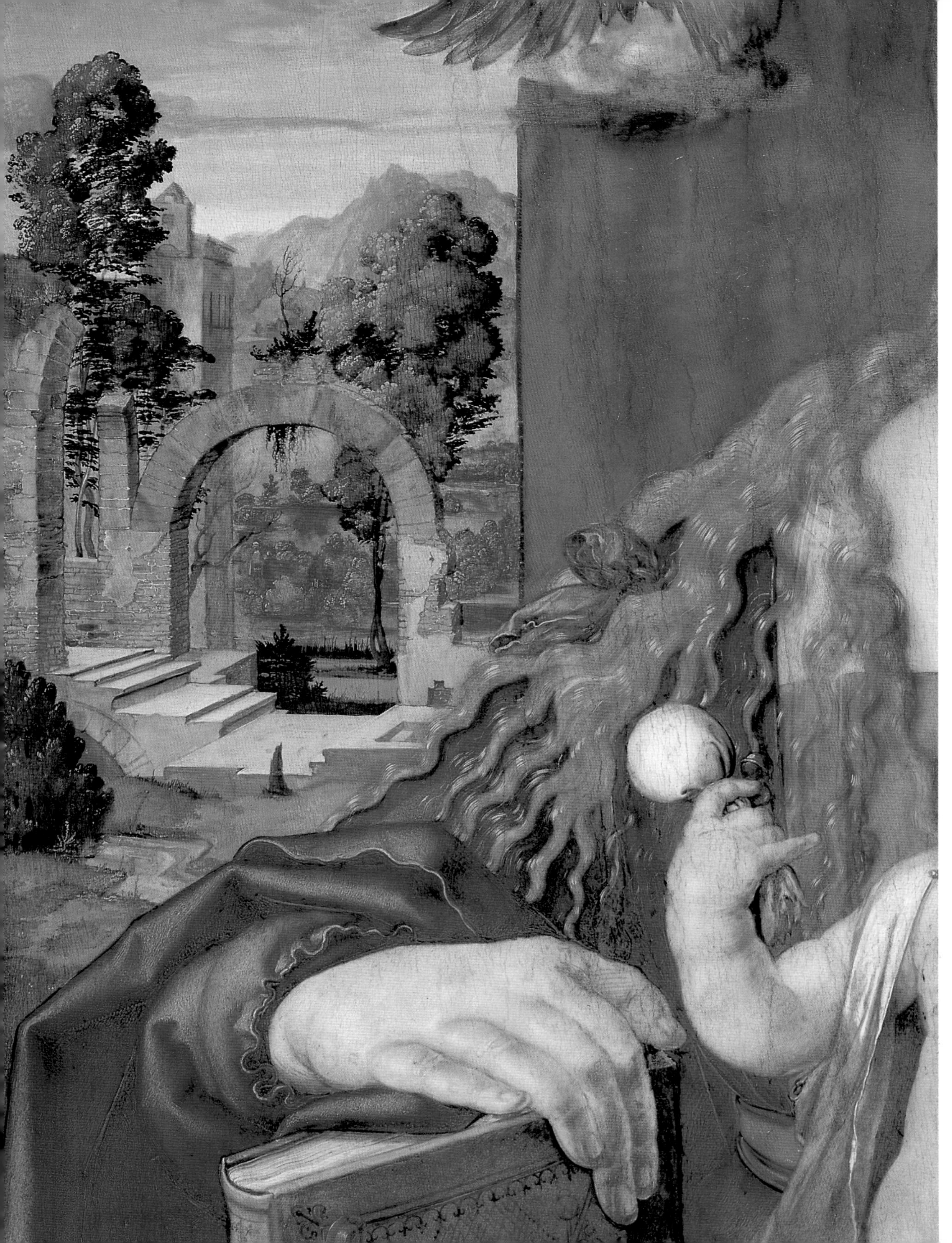

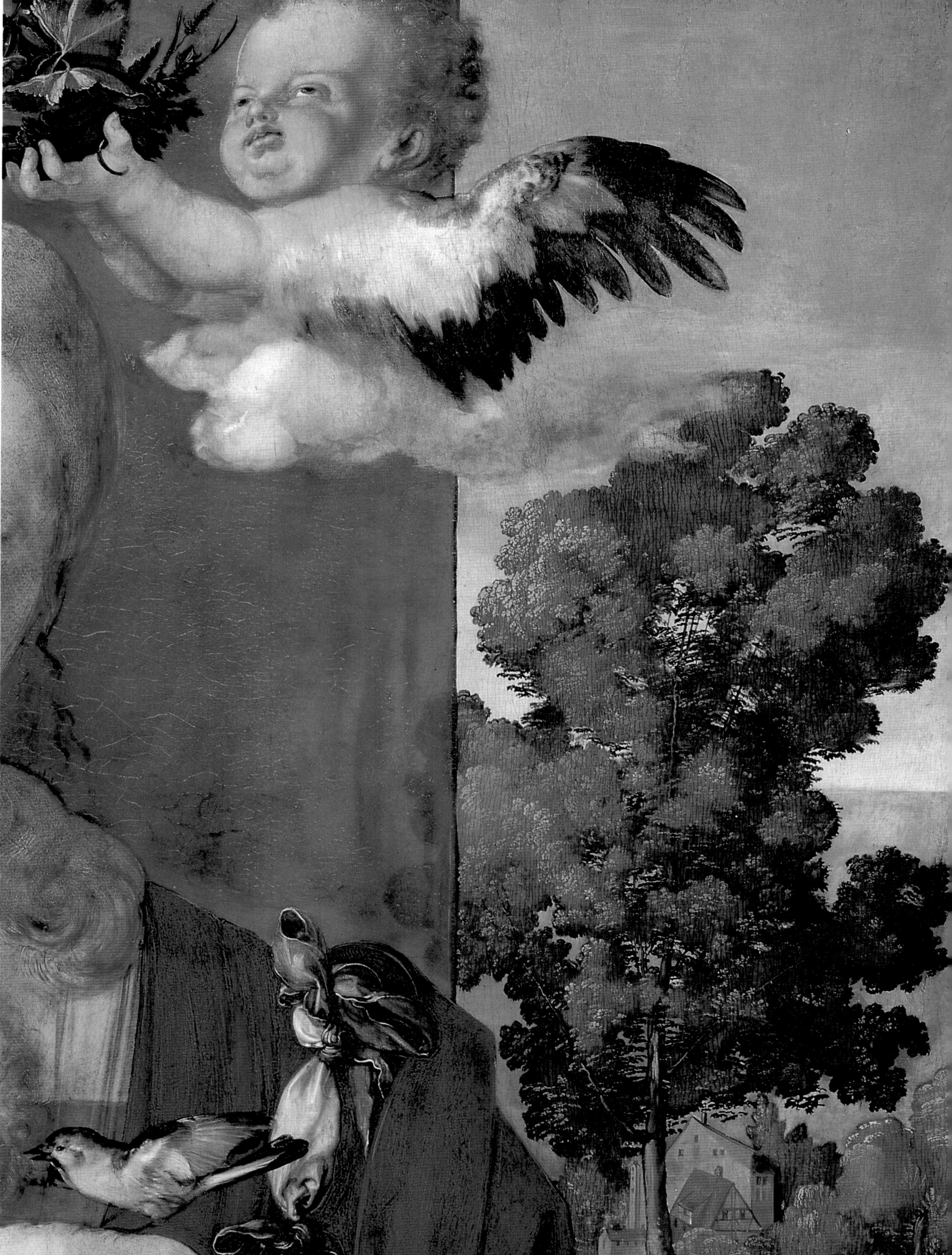

Adam
Madrid, Museo del Prado
[pl. 44]

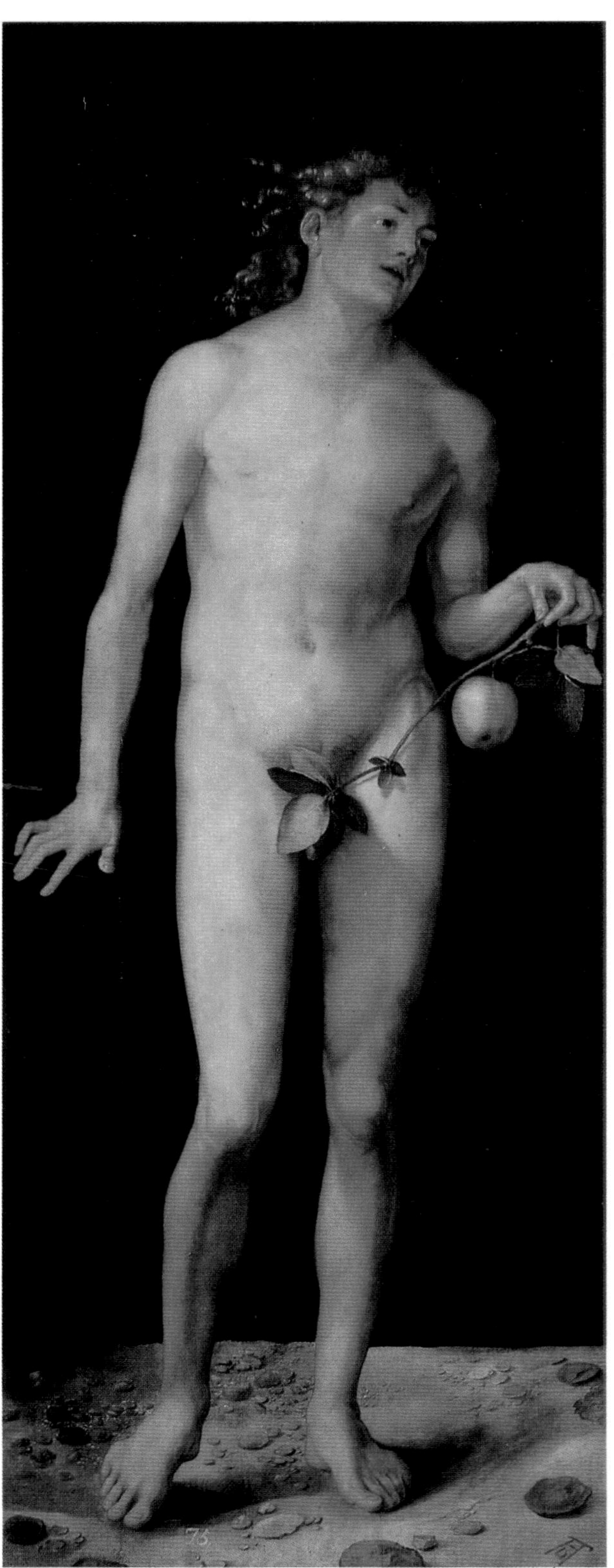

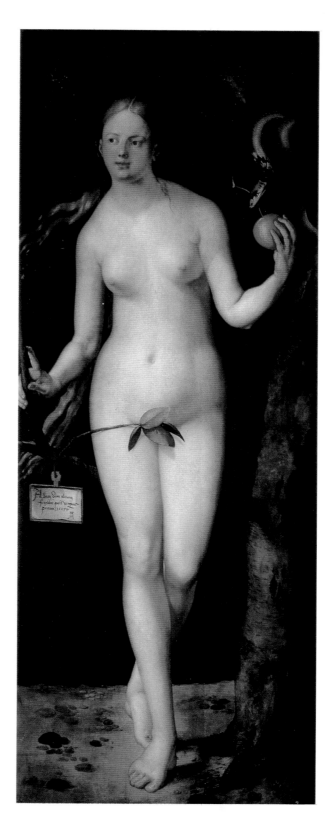

Eve
Madrid, Museo del Prado
[pl. 44]

Portrait of a Young Man
Vienna, Kunsthistorisches Museum
[pl. 45]

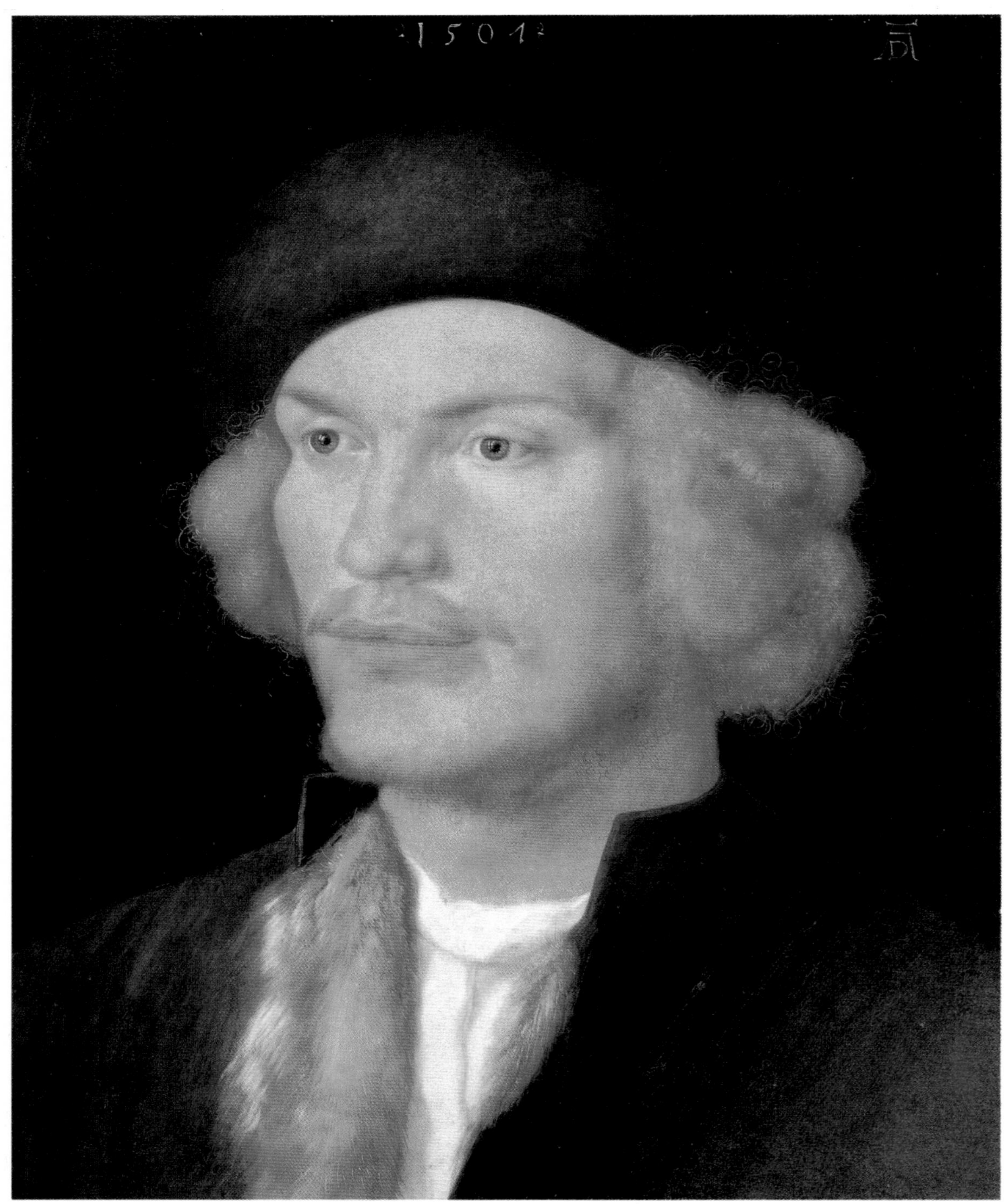

Portrait of a Young Girl
Berlin, Staatliche Museen, Gemäldegalerie
[pl. 46]

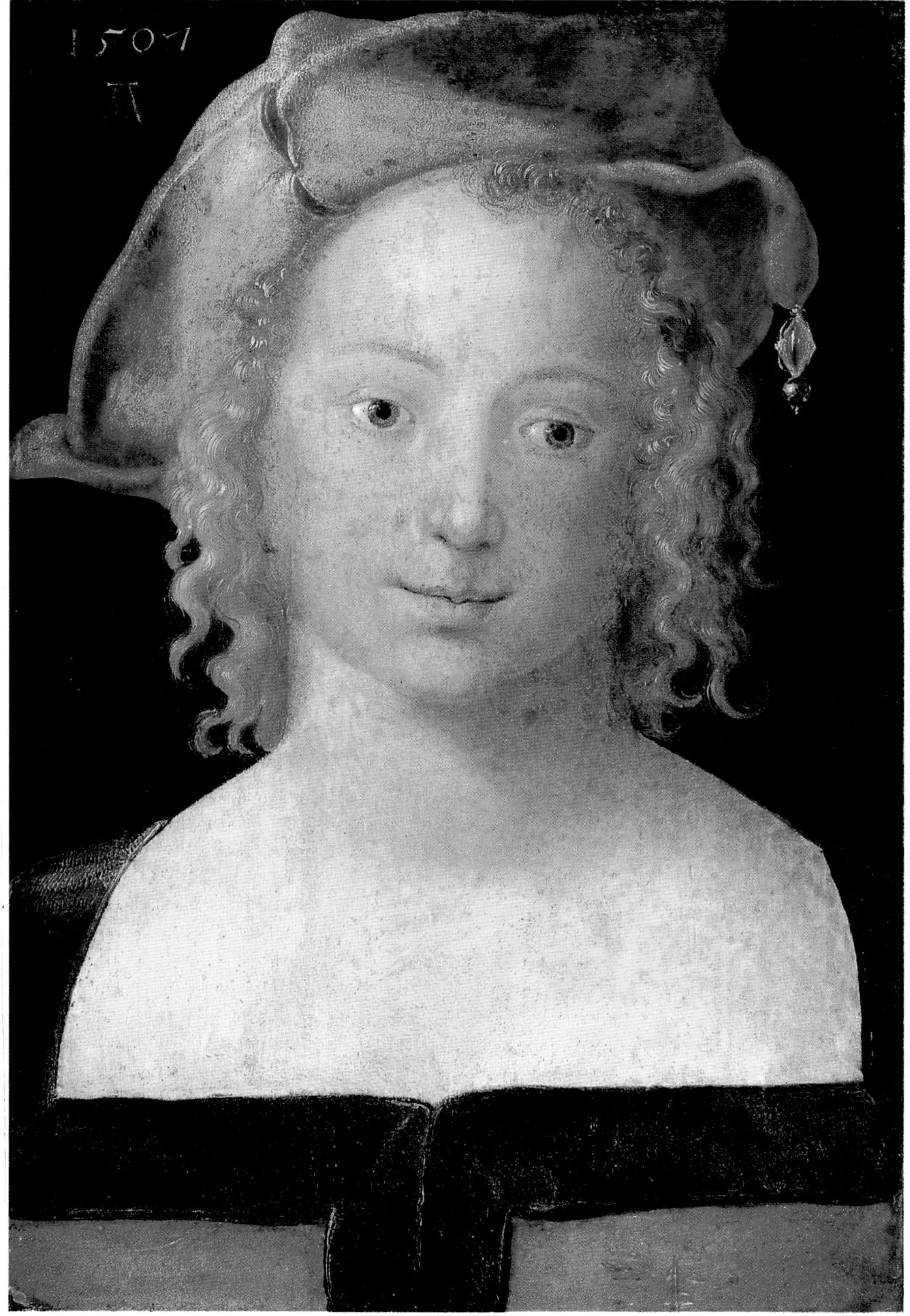

The Martyrdom of the Ten Thousand
Vienna, Kunsthistorisches Museum
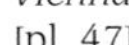
[pl. 47]

on the following pages: [pl. 47] *details*

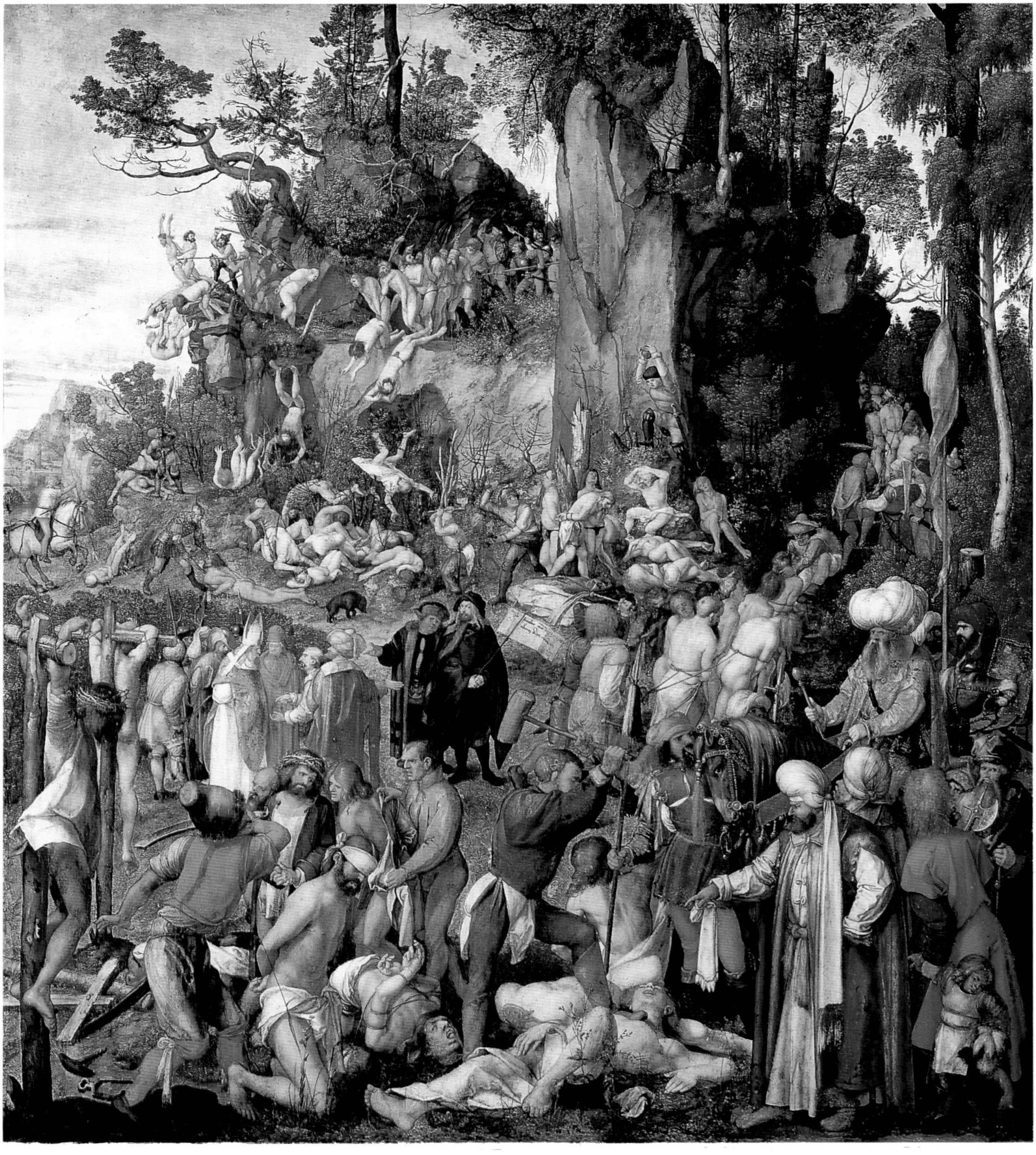

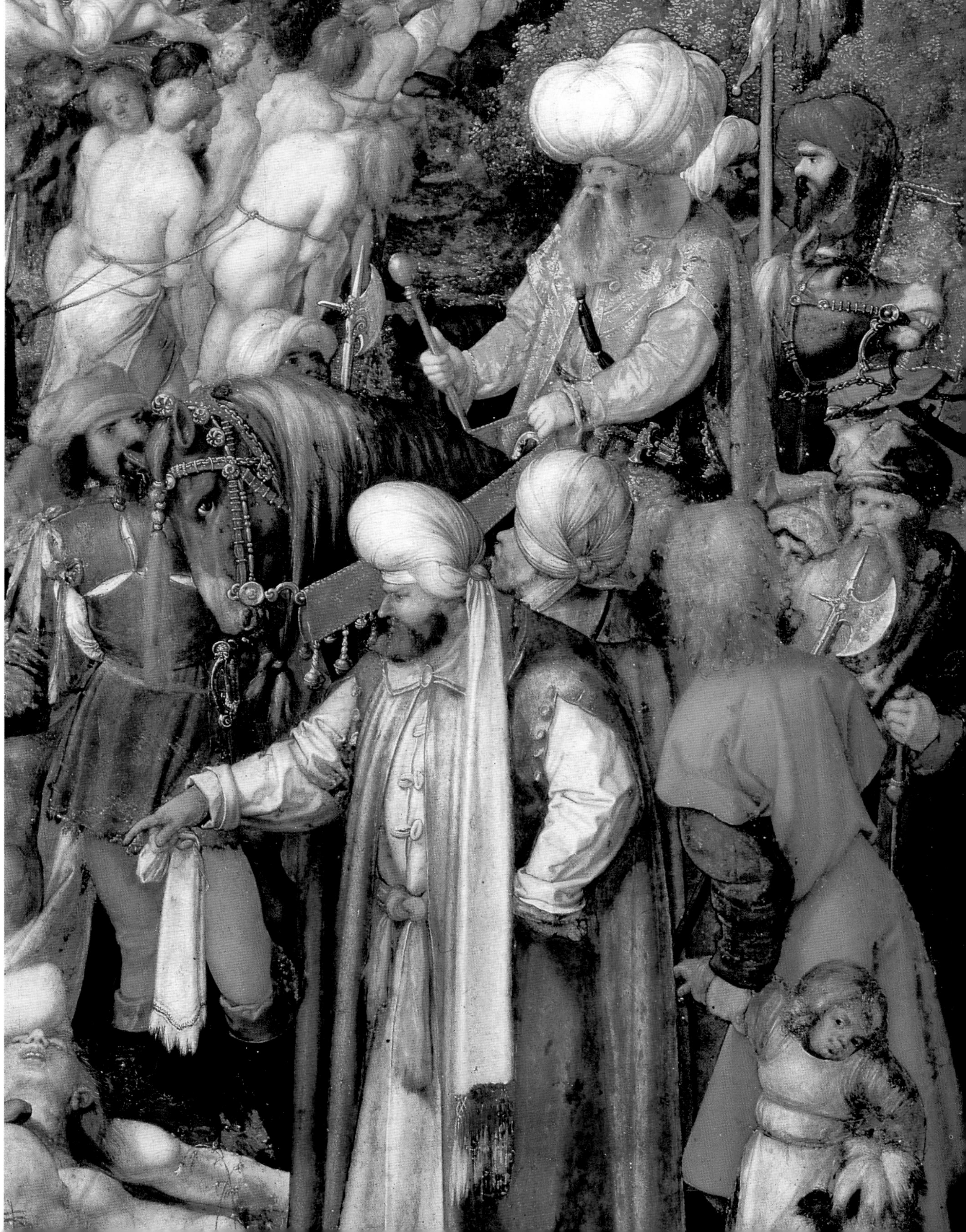

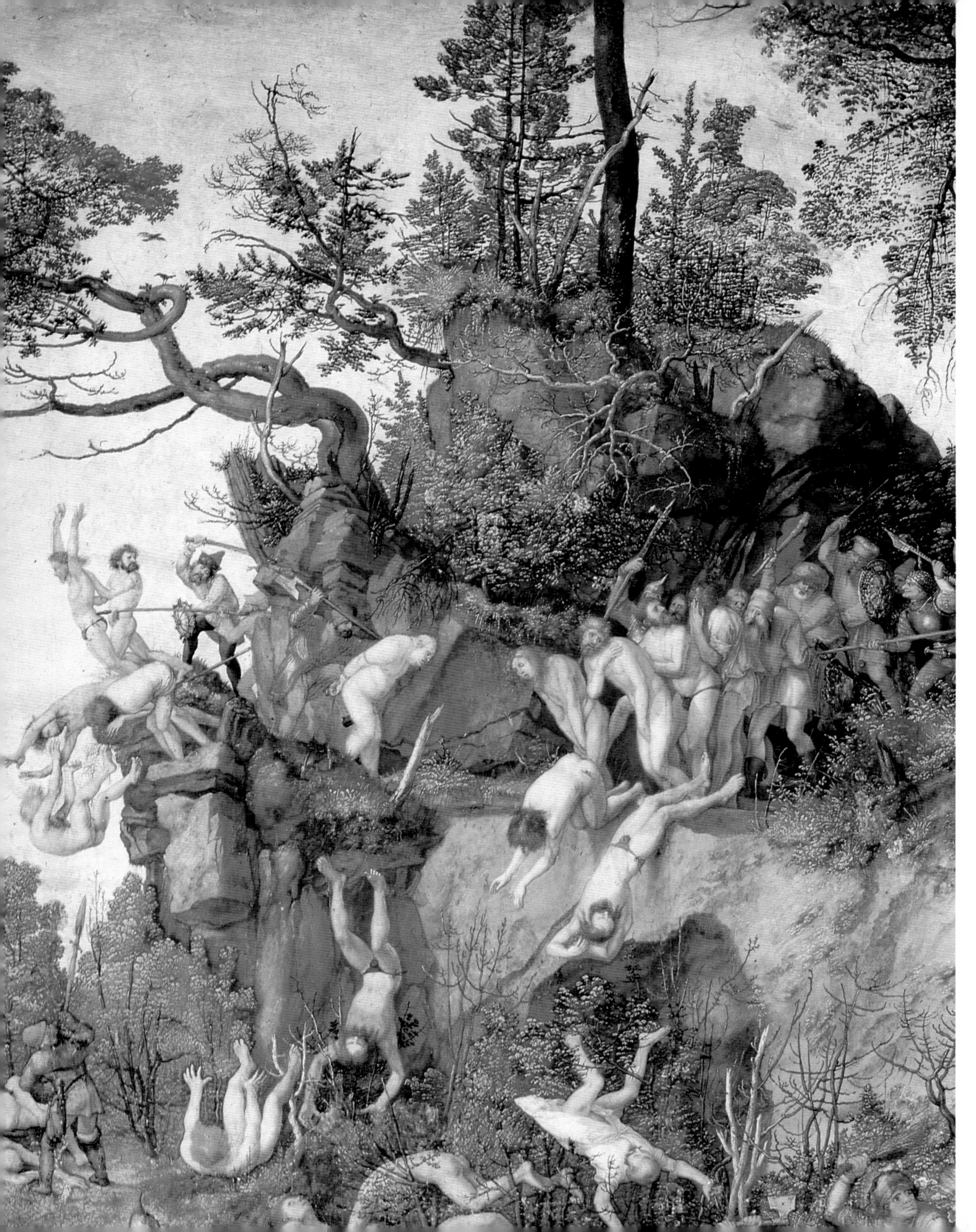

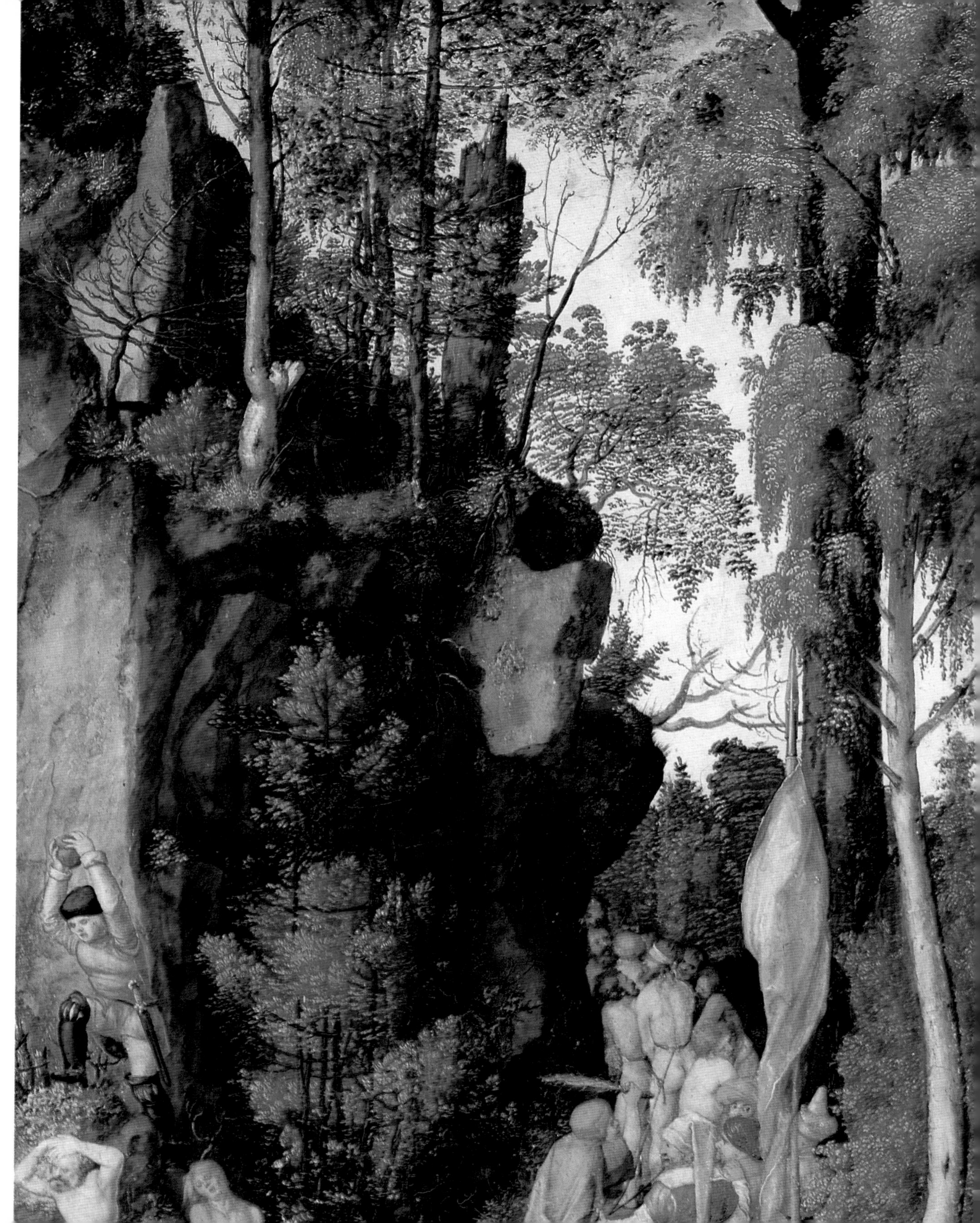

Heller Altar
Frankfurt, Historisches Museum
[pl. 48]

side page: [pl. 48] *detail*

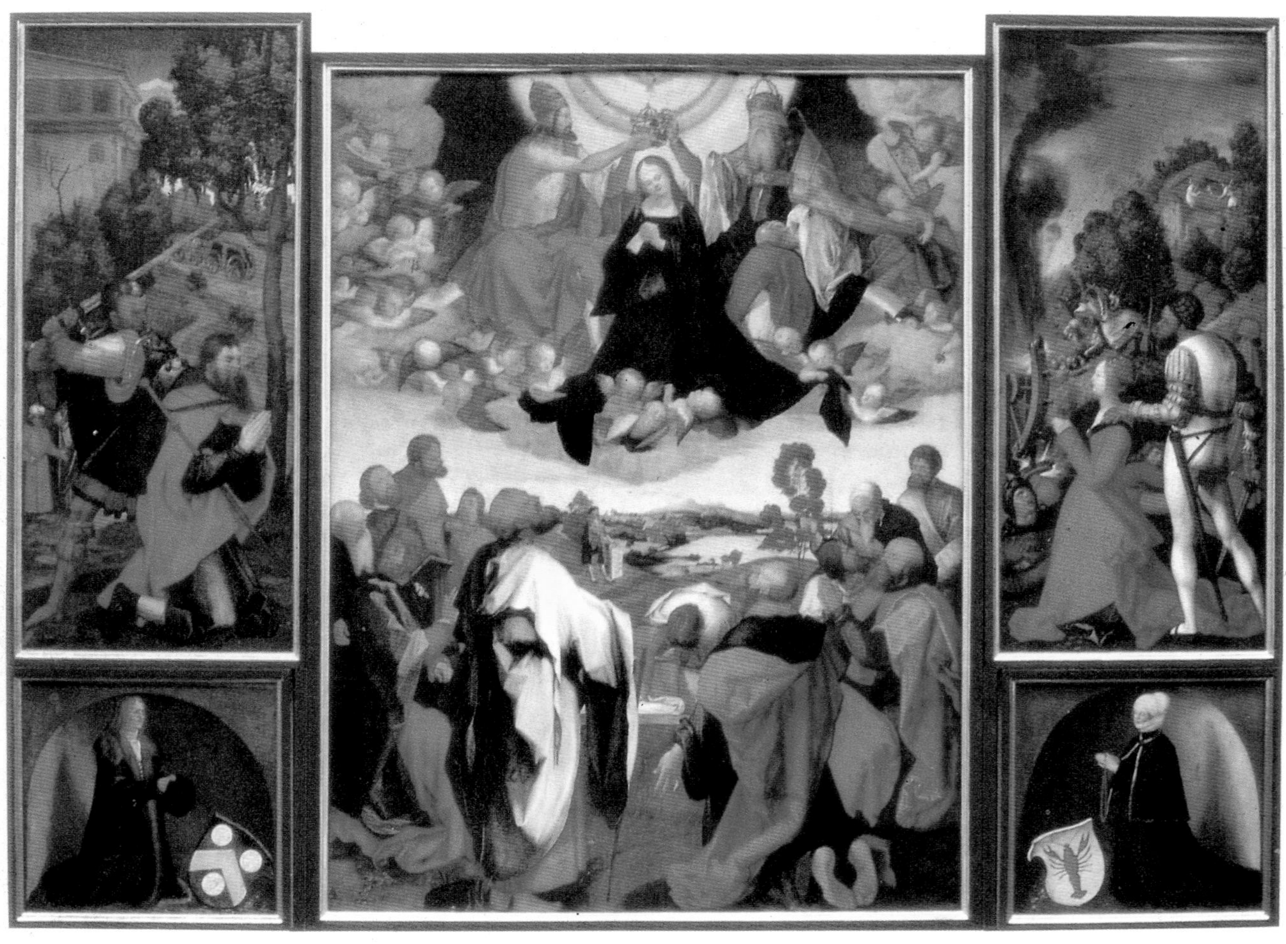

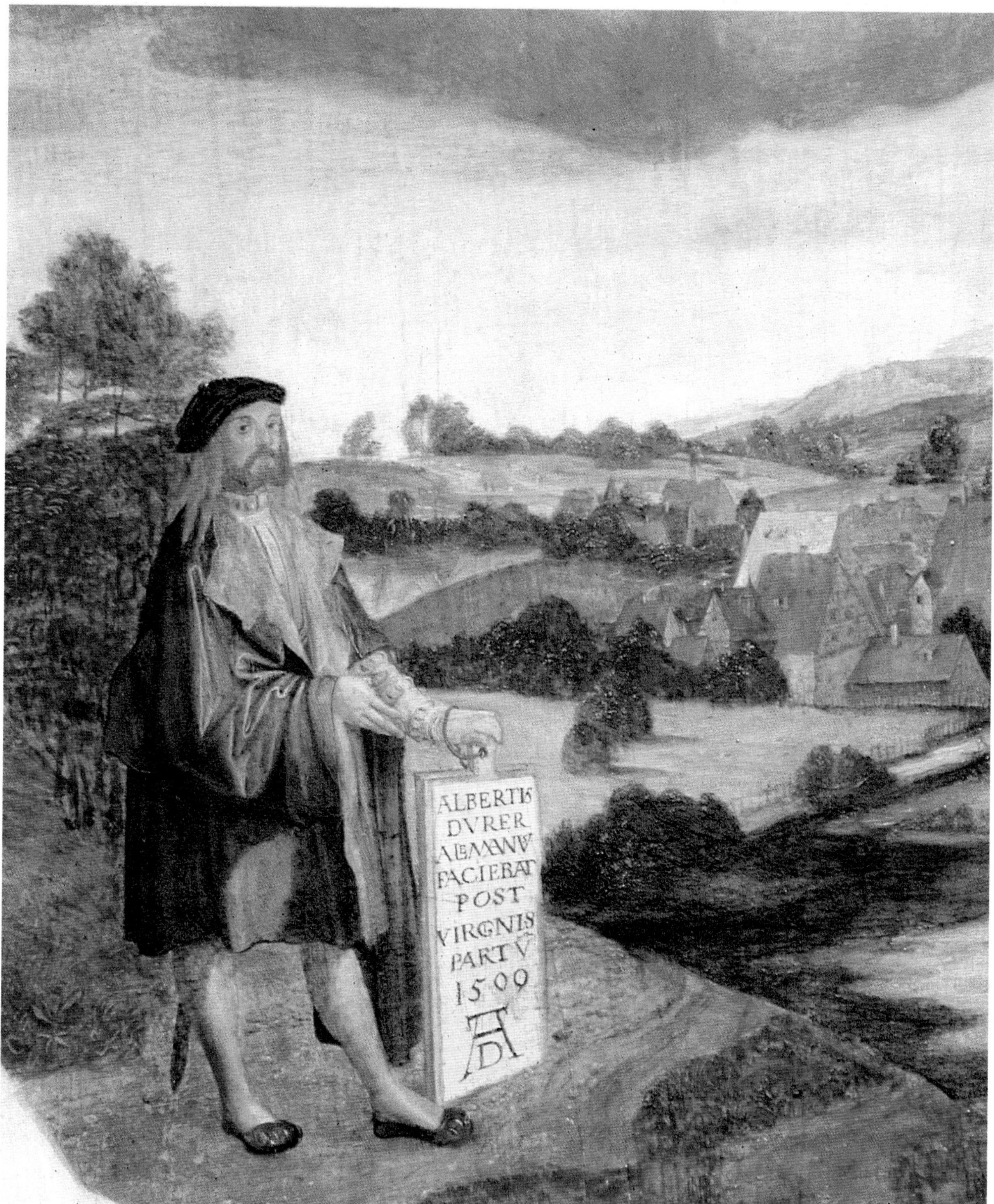
DVRER
FACIEBAT
POST
PARTV
1509

Landauer Altar

The Adoration of the Holy Trinity
Vienna, Kunsthistorisches Museum
[pl. 50]

on the side and following pages: [pl. 50] *details*

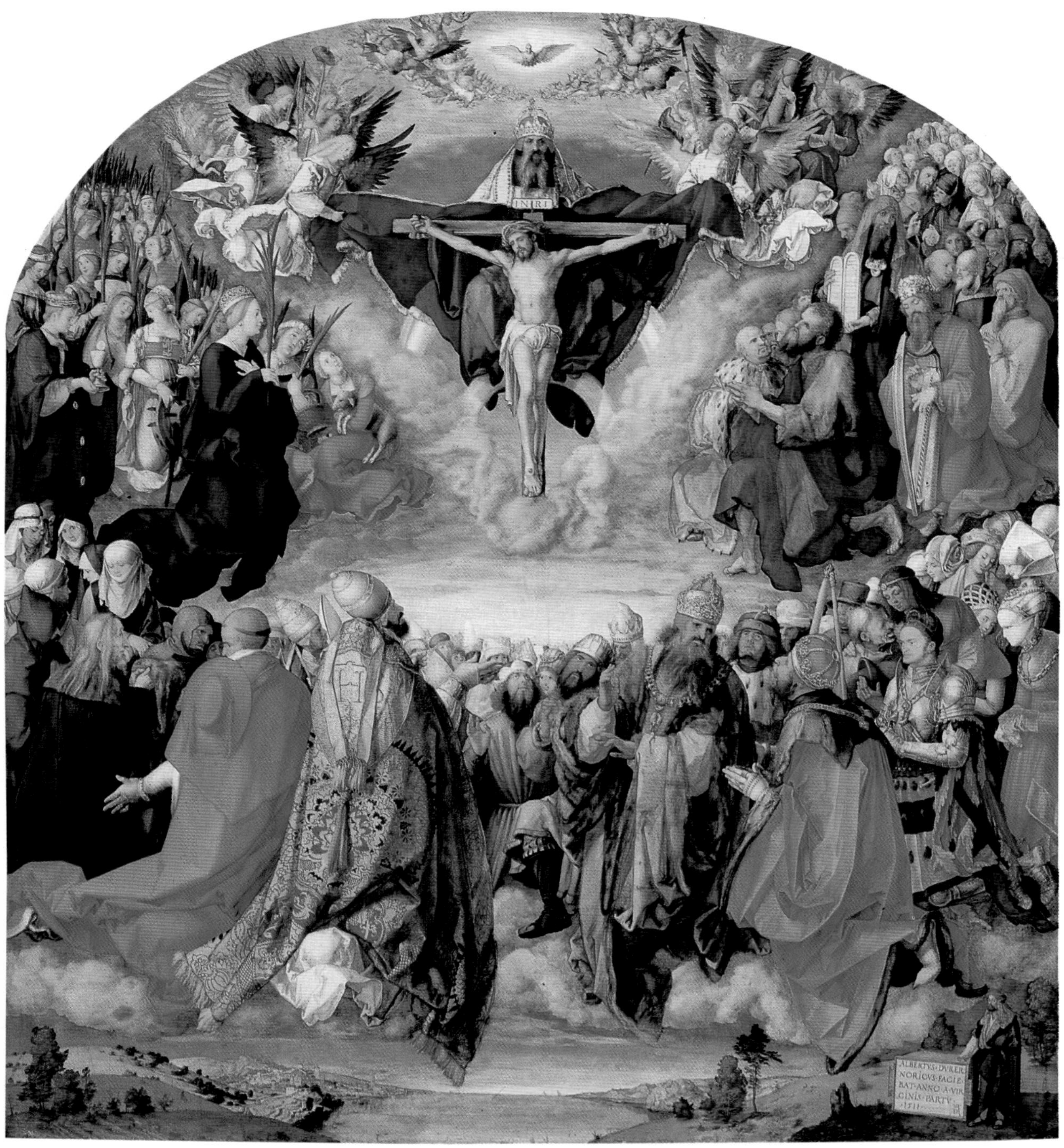

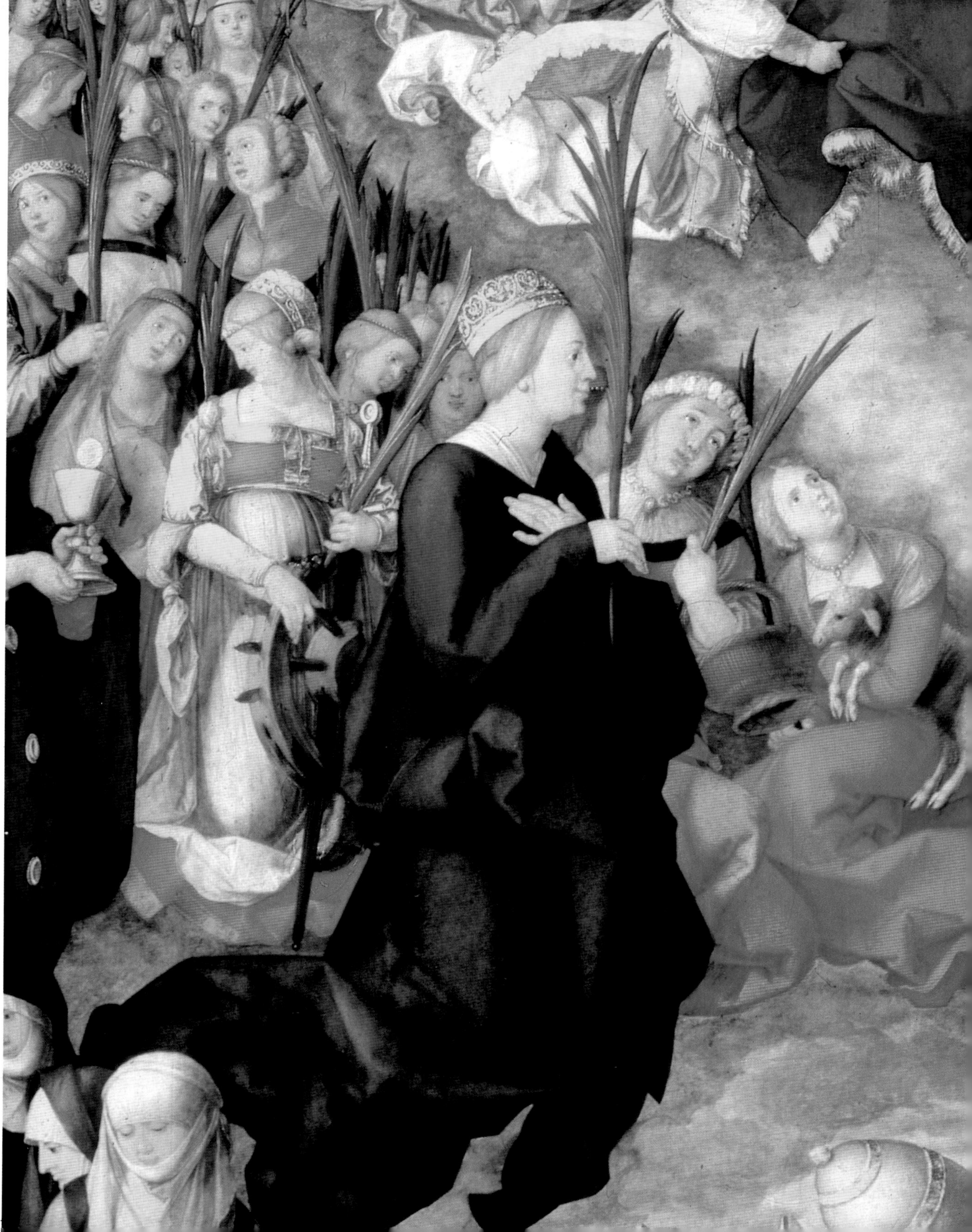

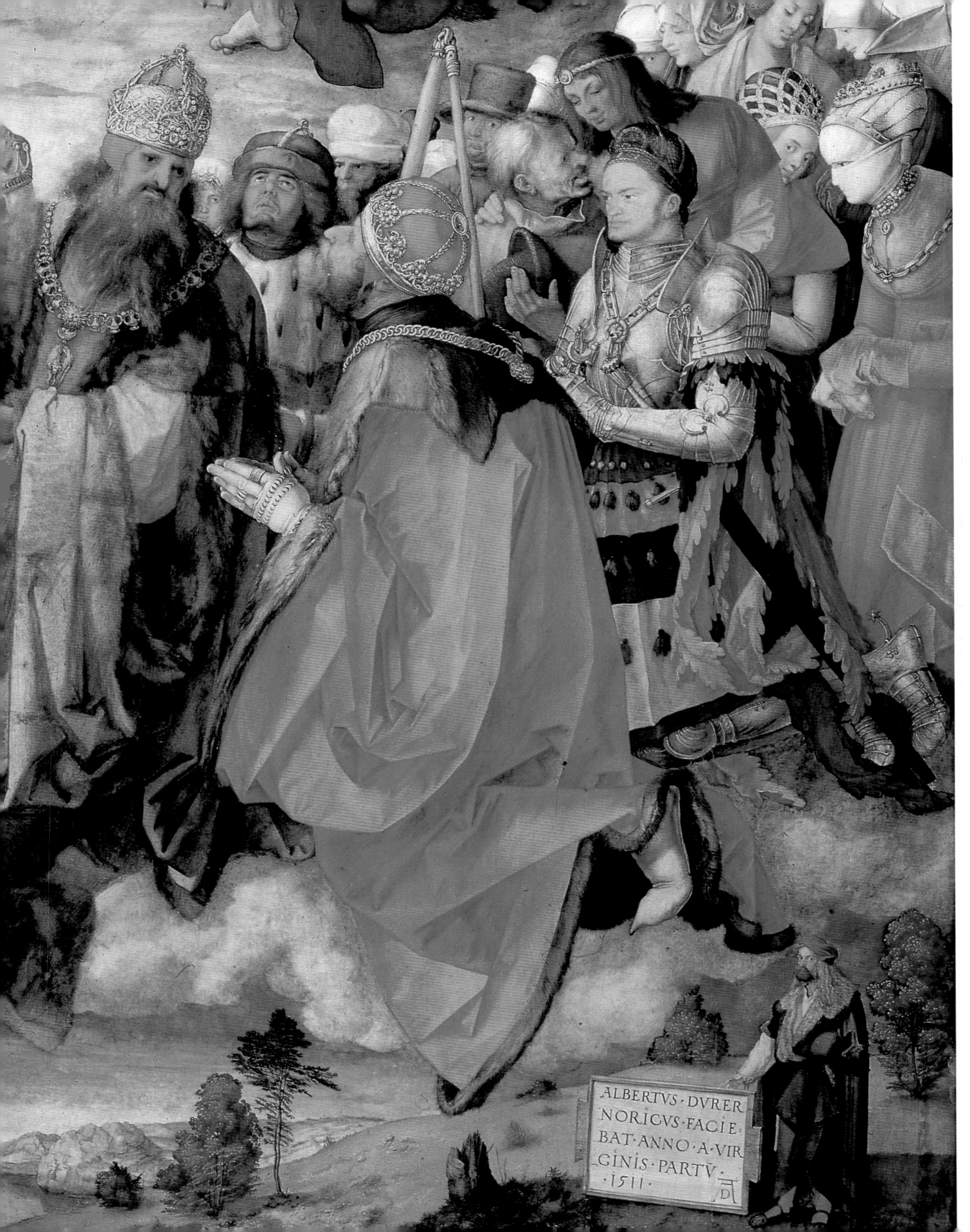
ALBERTVS·DVRER
NORICVS·FACIE
BAT·ANNO·A·VIR
GINIS·PARTV
·1511·

Madonna and Child (Madonna of the Pear)
Vienna, Kunsthistorisches Museum
[pl. 53]

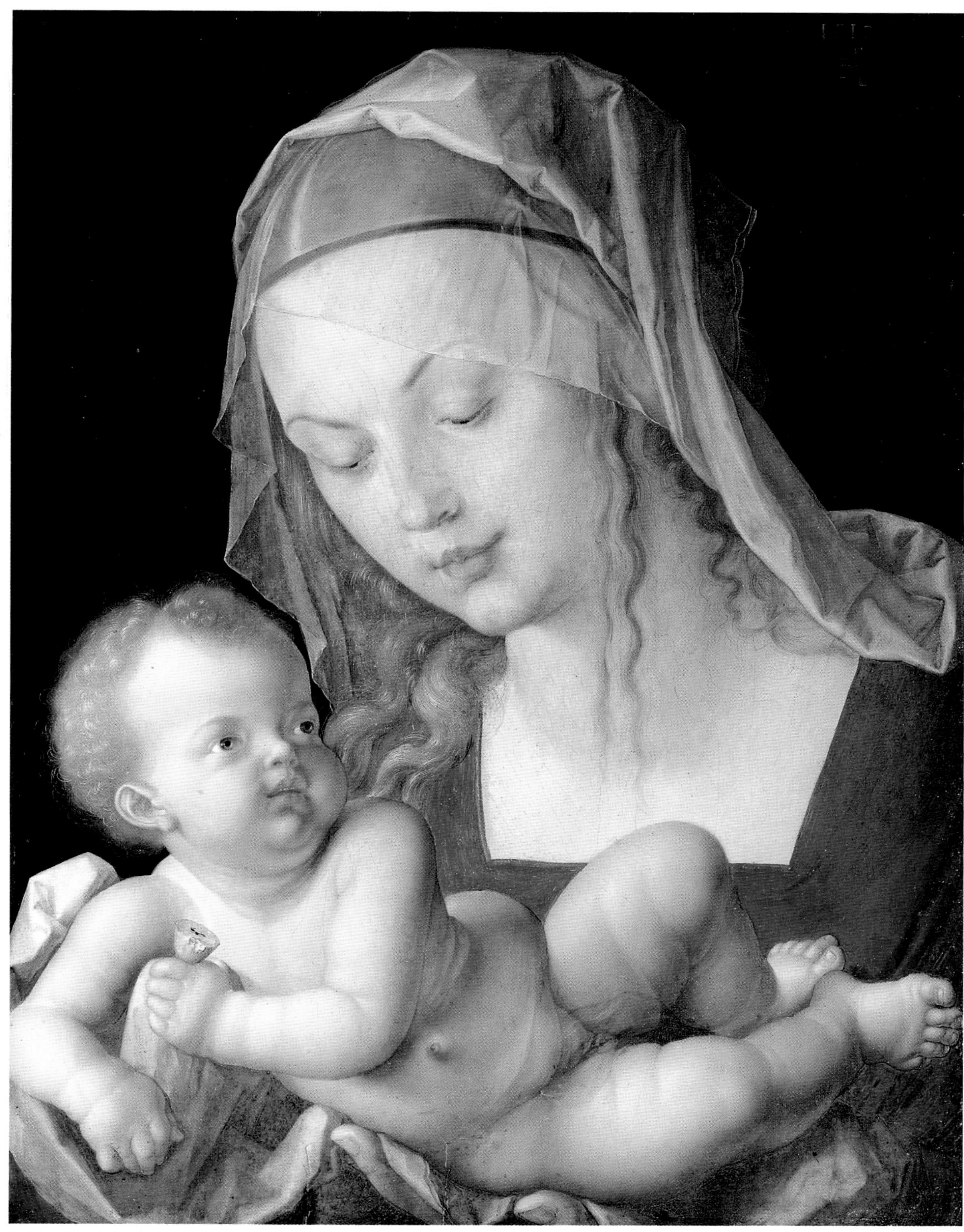

Portrait of Michael Wolgemut Nuremberg,
Germanisches Nationalmuseum
[pl. 55]

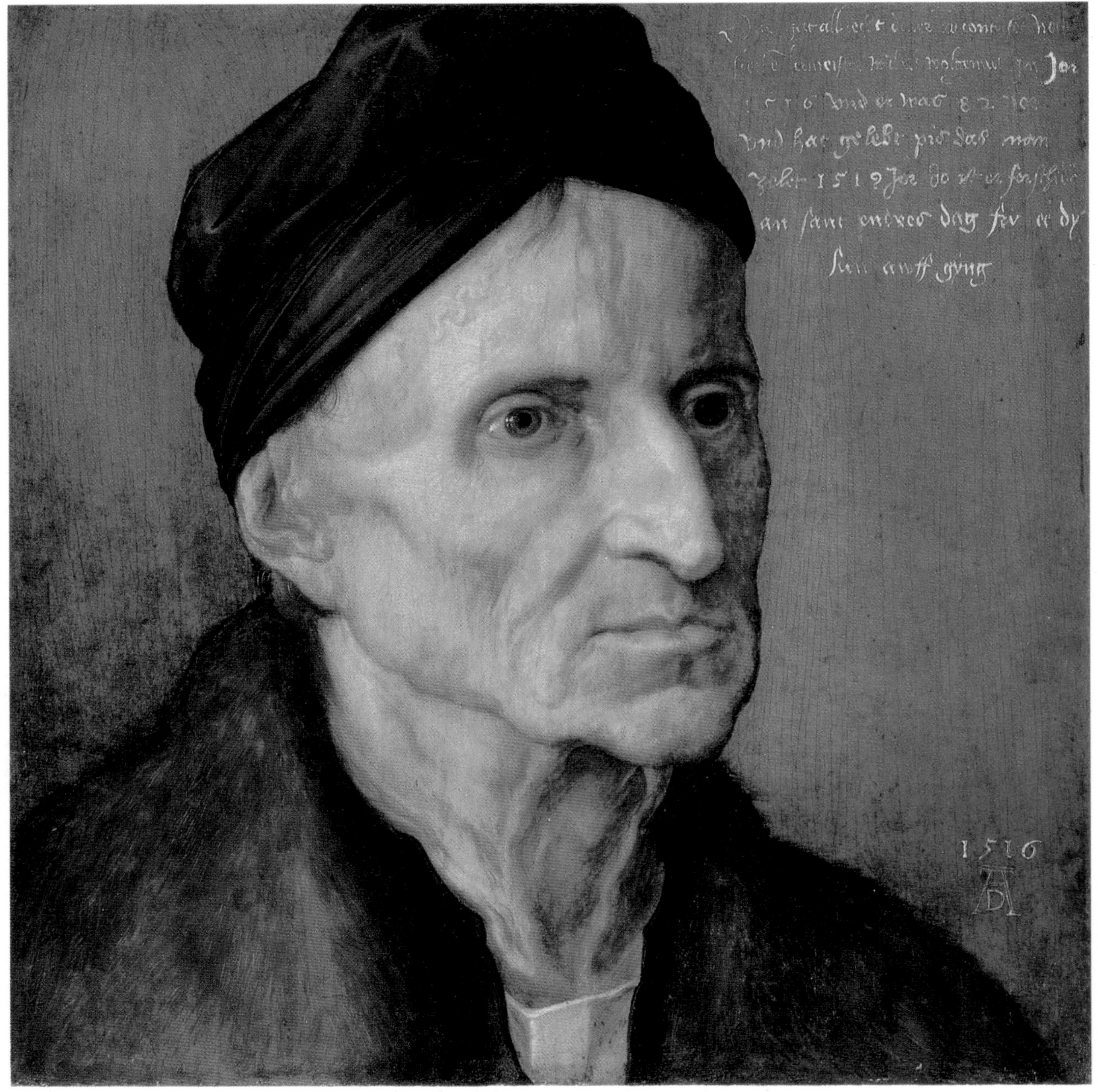

Portrait of a Cleric
Washington, National Gallery, Kress collection
[pl. 58]

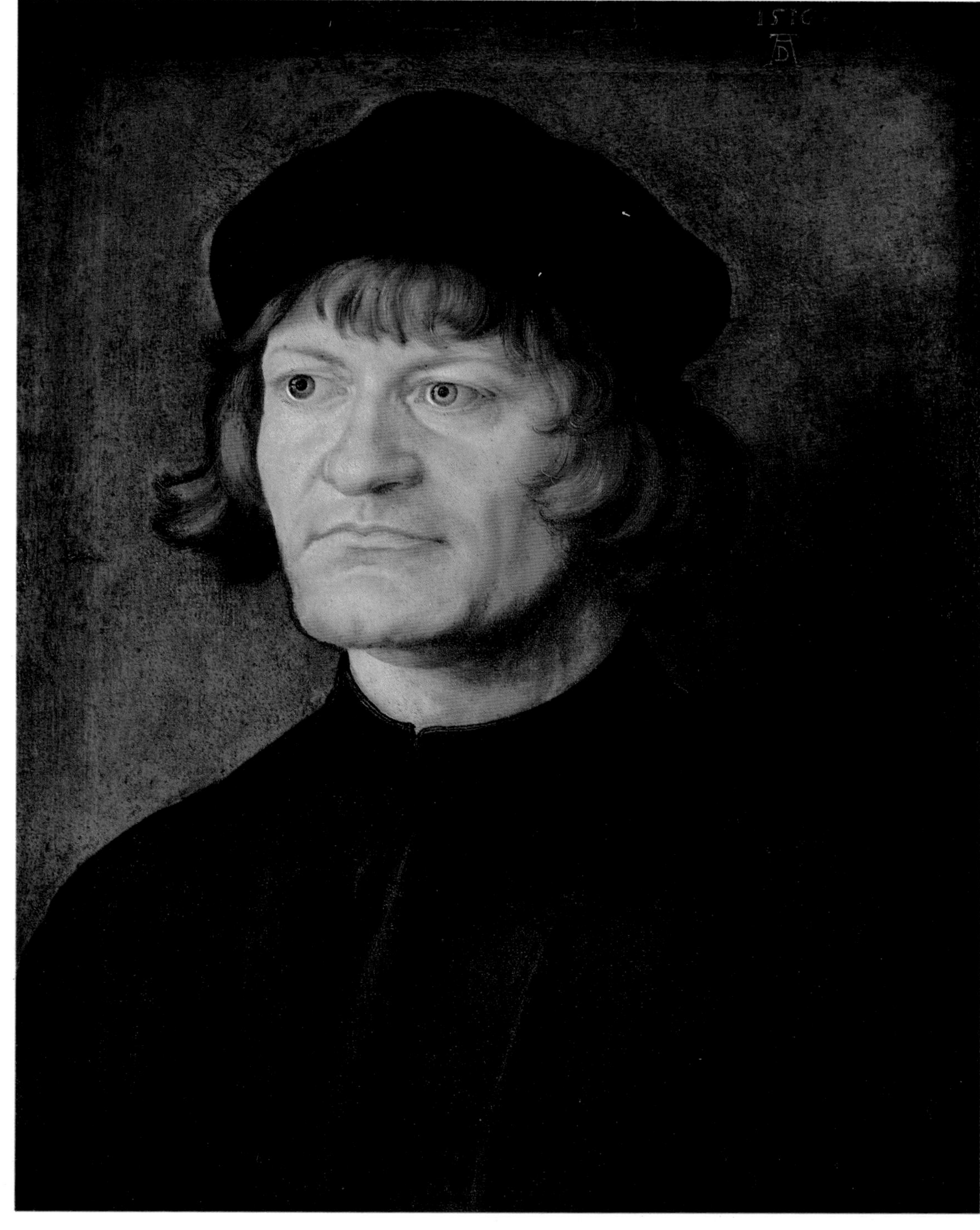

The Virgin Mary in Prayer
Berlin, Staatliche Museen, Gemäldegalerie
[pl. 60]

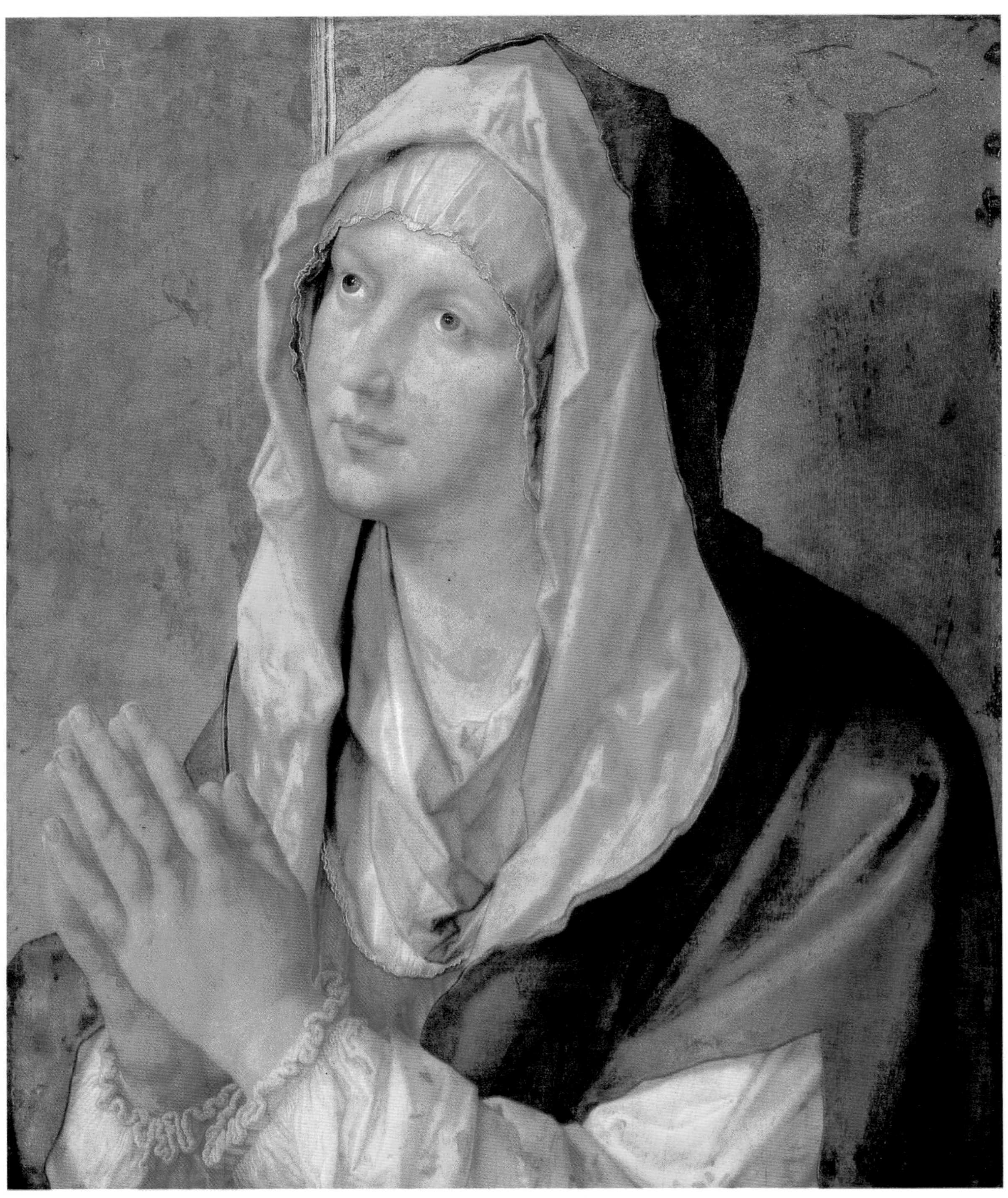

Jakob Fugger, the Wealthy
Augsburg, Staatsgalerie
[pl. 62]

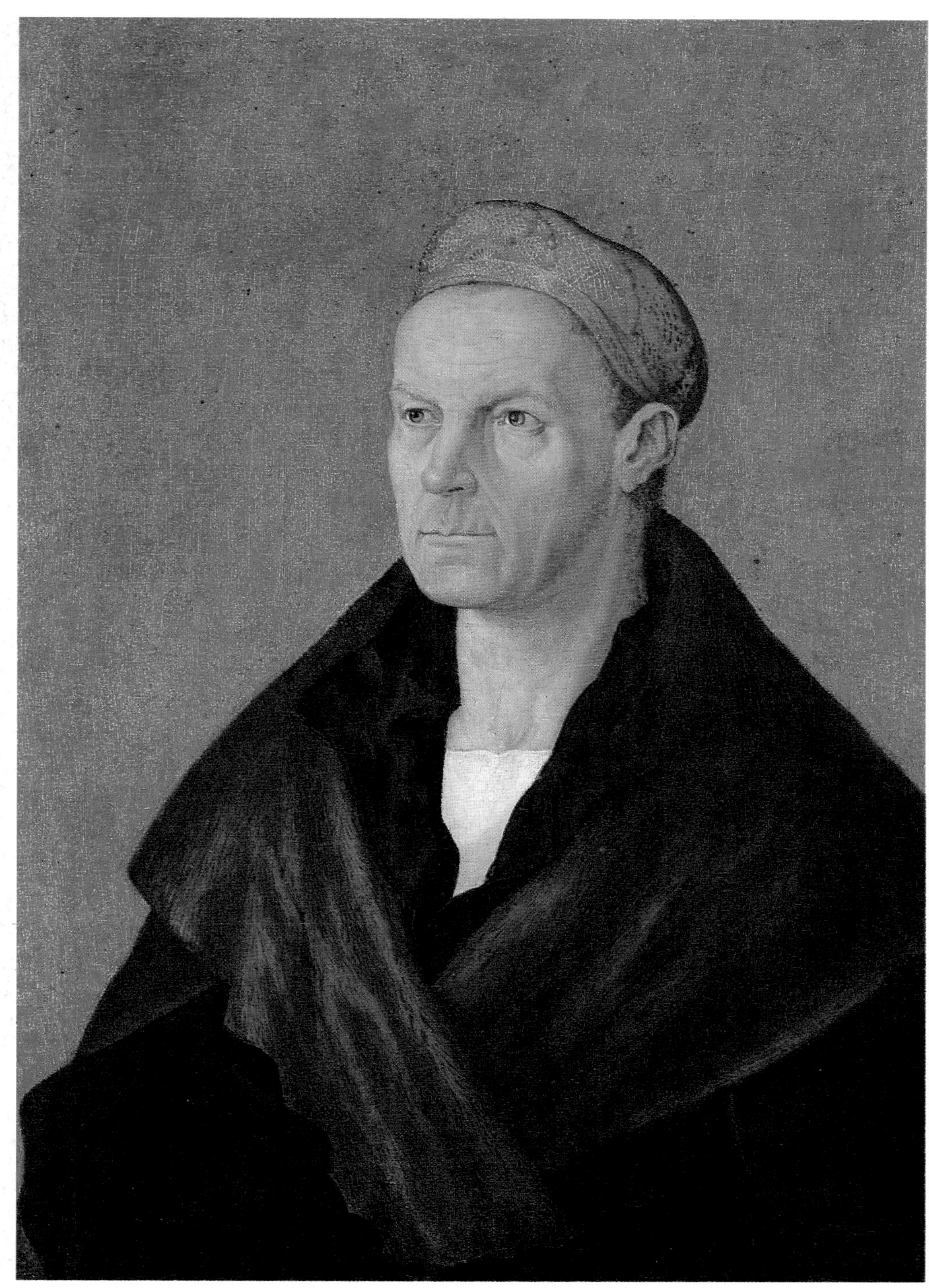

The Emperor Maximilian I
Vienna, Kunsthistorisches Museum
[pl. 64]

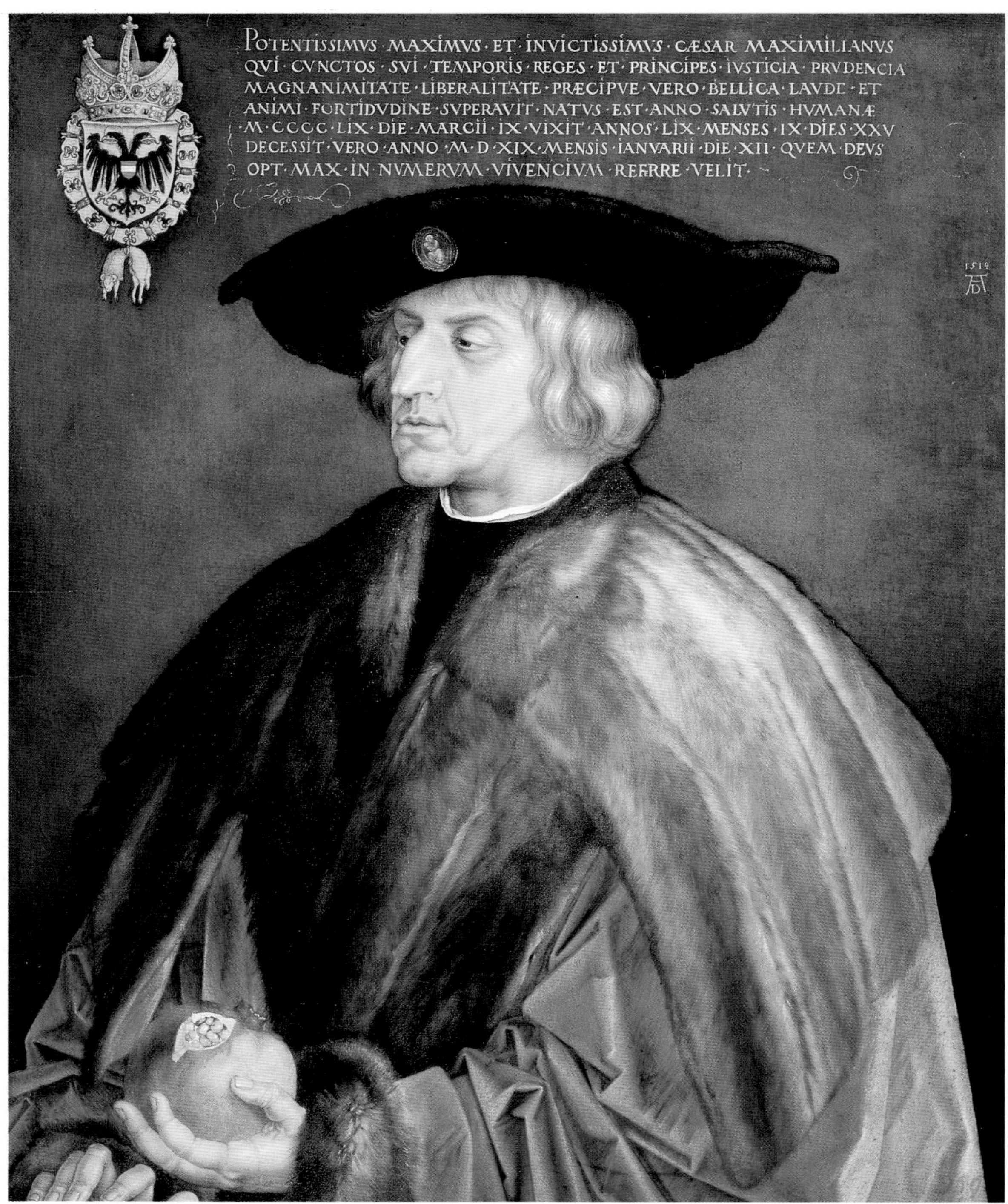

POTENTISSIMVS · MAXIMVS · ET · INVICTISSIMVS · CÆSAR · MAXIMILIANVS
QVI · CVNCTOS · SVI · TEMPORIS · REGES · ET · PRINCIPES · IVSTICIA · PRVDENCIA
MAGNANIMITATE · LIBERALITATE · PRÆCIPVE · VERO · BELLICA · LAVDE · ET
ANIMI · FORTIDVDINE · SVPERAVIT · NATVS · EST · ANNO · SALVTIS · HVMANÆ
· M · CCCC · LIX · DIE · MARCII · IX · VIXIT · ANNOS · LIX · MENSES · IX · DIES · XXV
DECESSIT · VERO · ANNO · M · D · XIX · MENSIS · IANVARII · DIE · XII · QVEM · DEVS
OPT · MAX · IN · NVMERVM · VIVENCIVM · REFRRE · VELIT ·
1519

The Emperor Maximilian I
Nuremberg, Germanisches Nationalmuseum
[pl. 65]

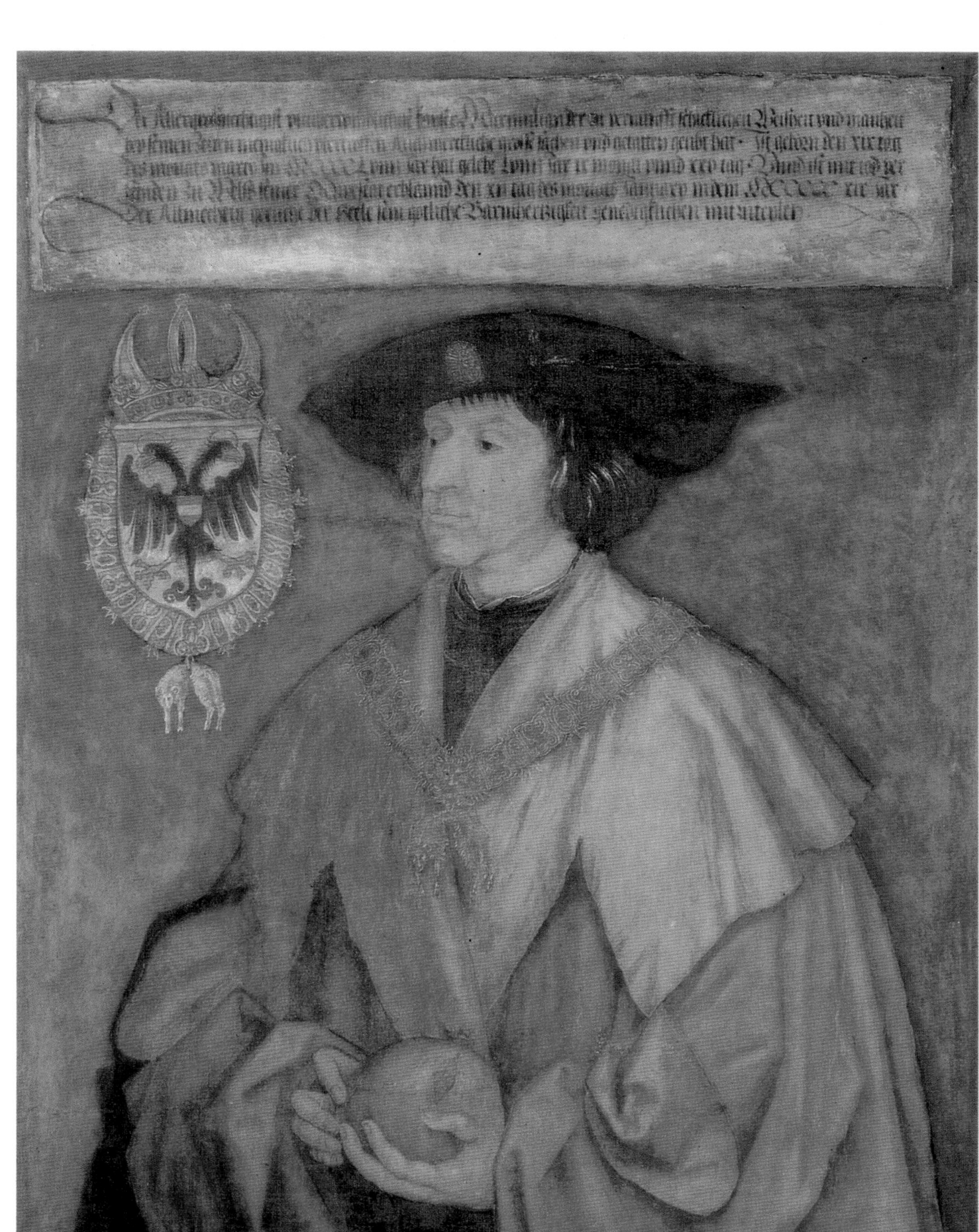

Saint Jerome
Lisbon, Museo Nacional de Arte Antiga
[pl. 68]

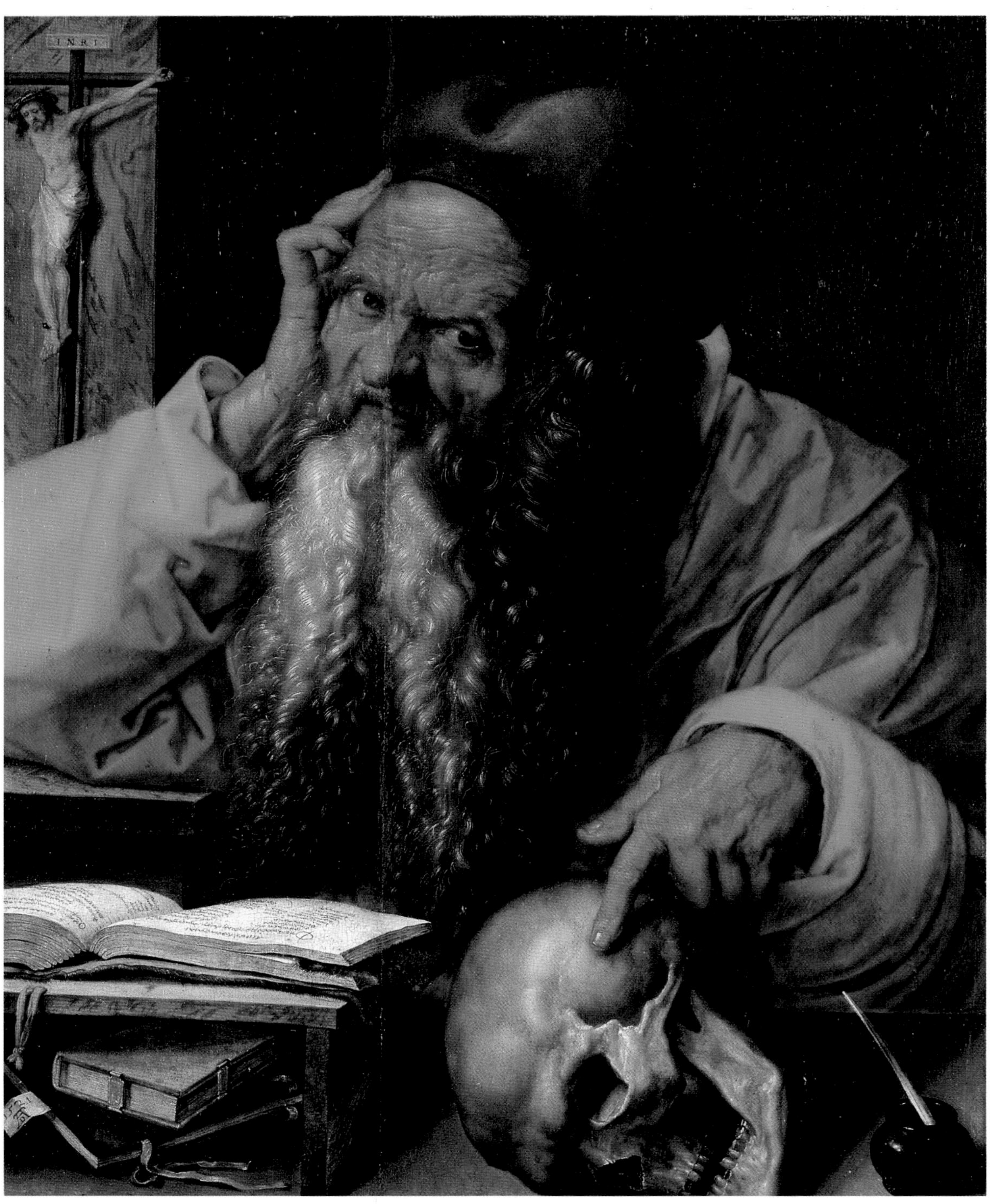

Portrait of an Unknown Man
Madrid, Museo del Prado
[pl. 69]

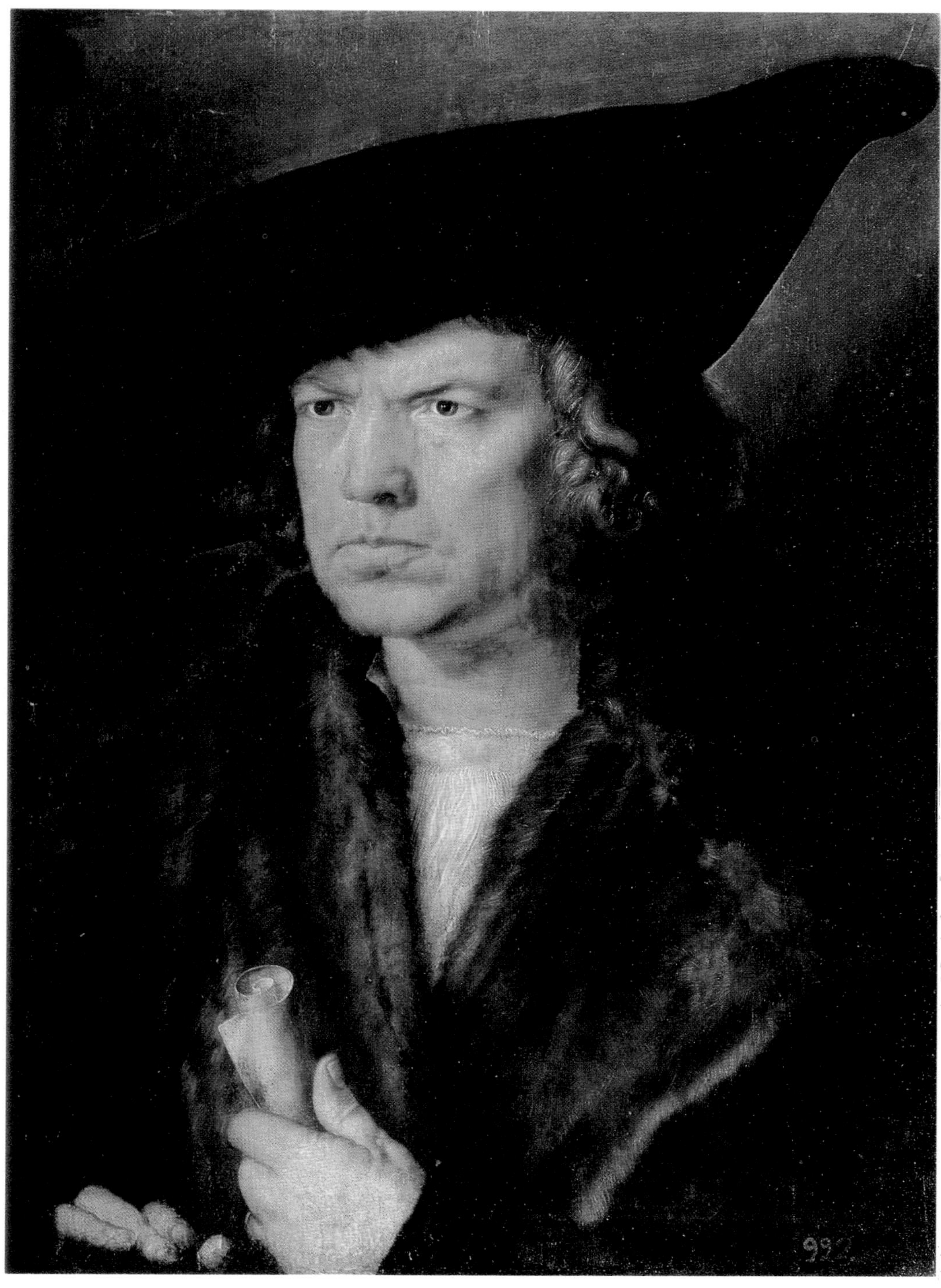

Portrait of Bernhard von Reesen
Dresden, Staatliche Kunstsammlungen
[pl. 70]

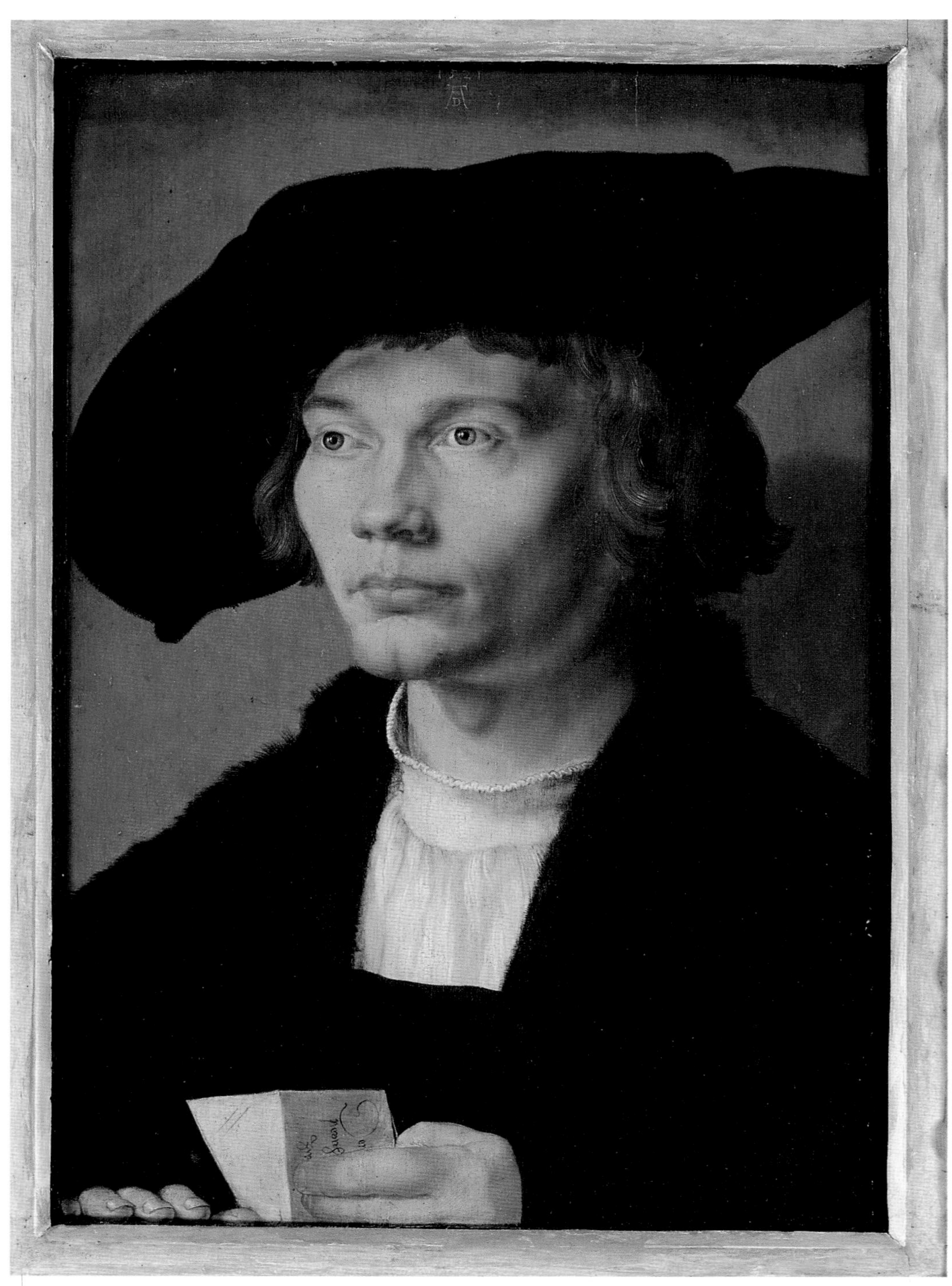

Portrait of Jakob Muffel
Berlin, Staatliche Museen, Gemäldegalerie
[pl. 72]

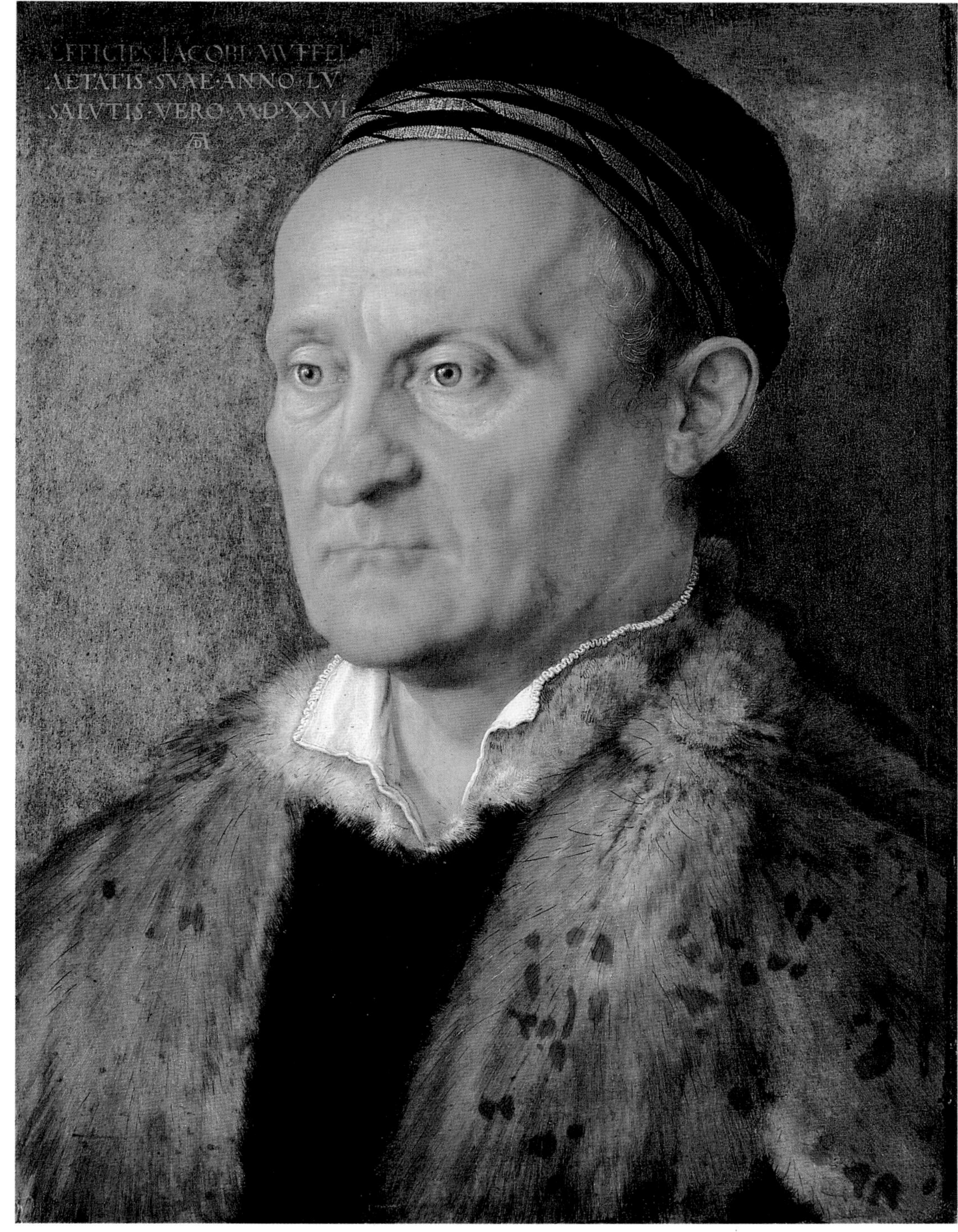

Portrait of Hieronymus Holzschuher
Berlin, Staatliche Museen, Gemäldegalerie
[pl. 73]

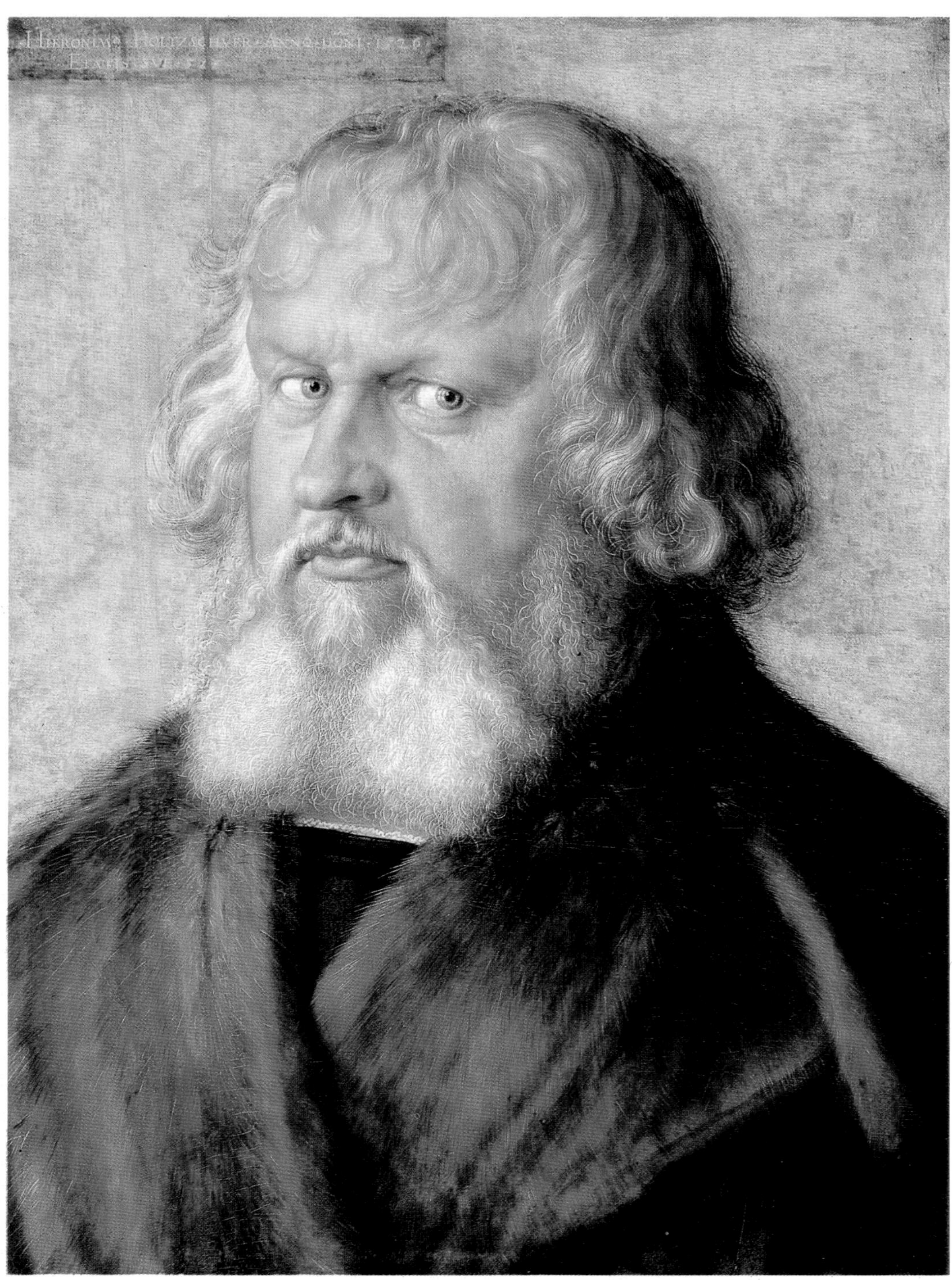

Portrait of Johannes Kleberger
Vienna, Kunsthistorisches Museum
[pl. 74]

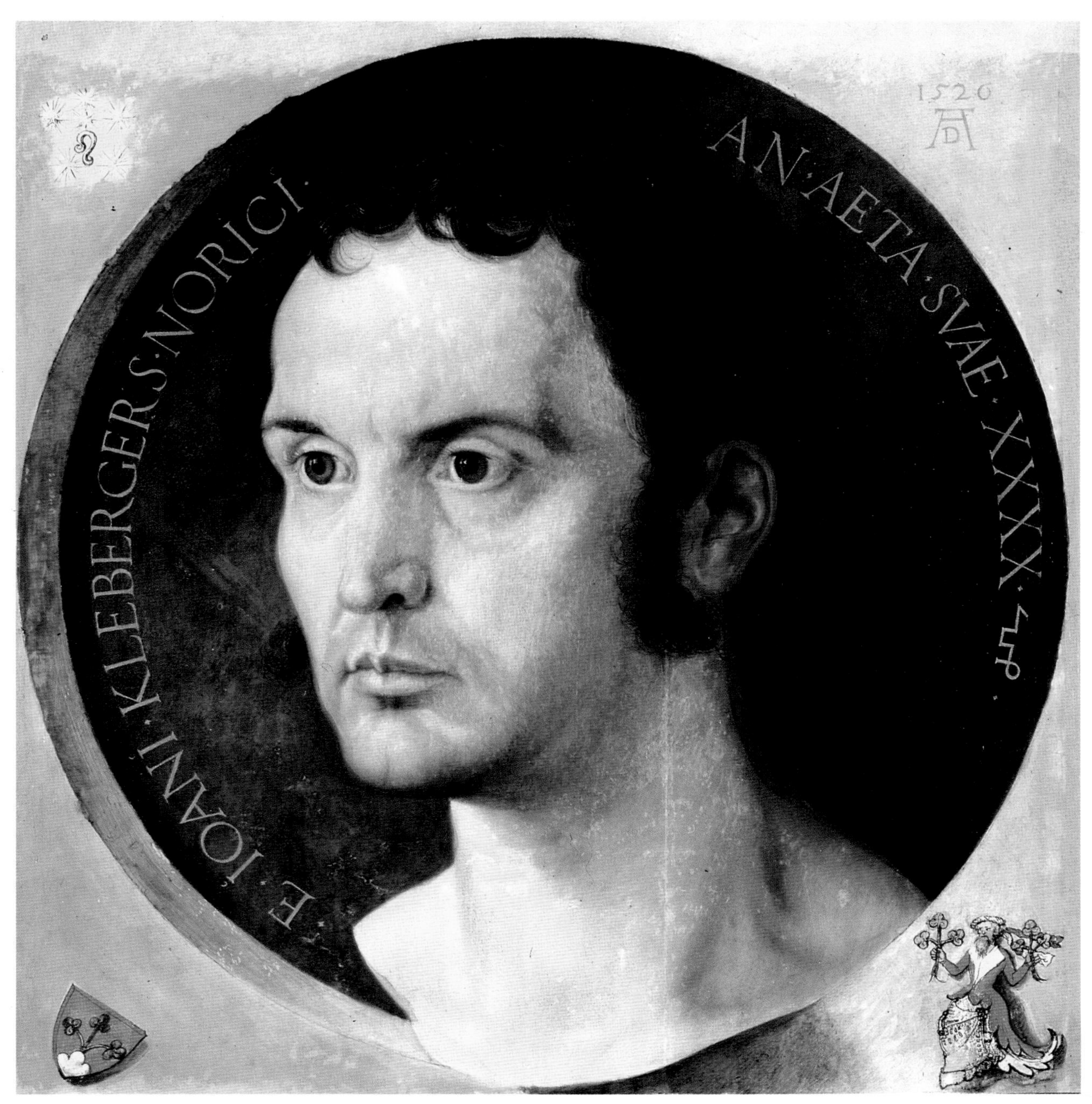

The Four Apostles
Munich, Alte Pinakothek
[pl. 75]

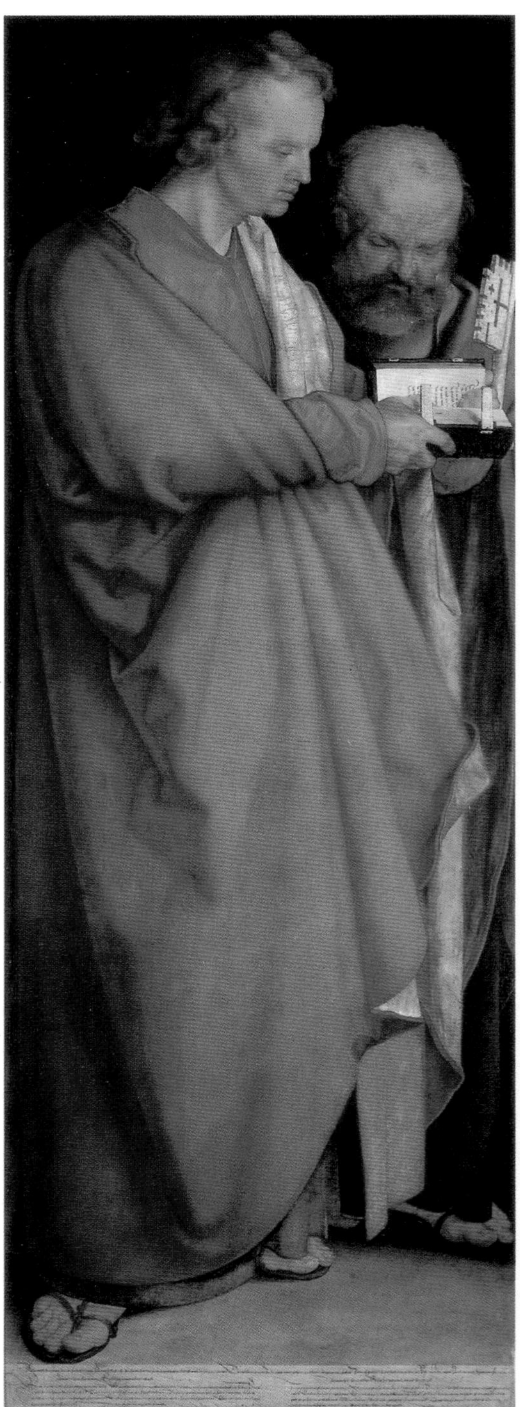

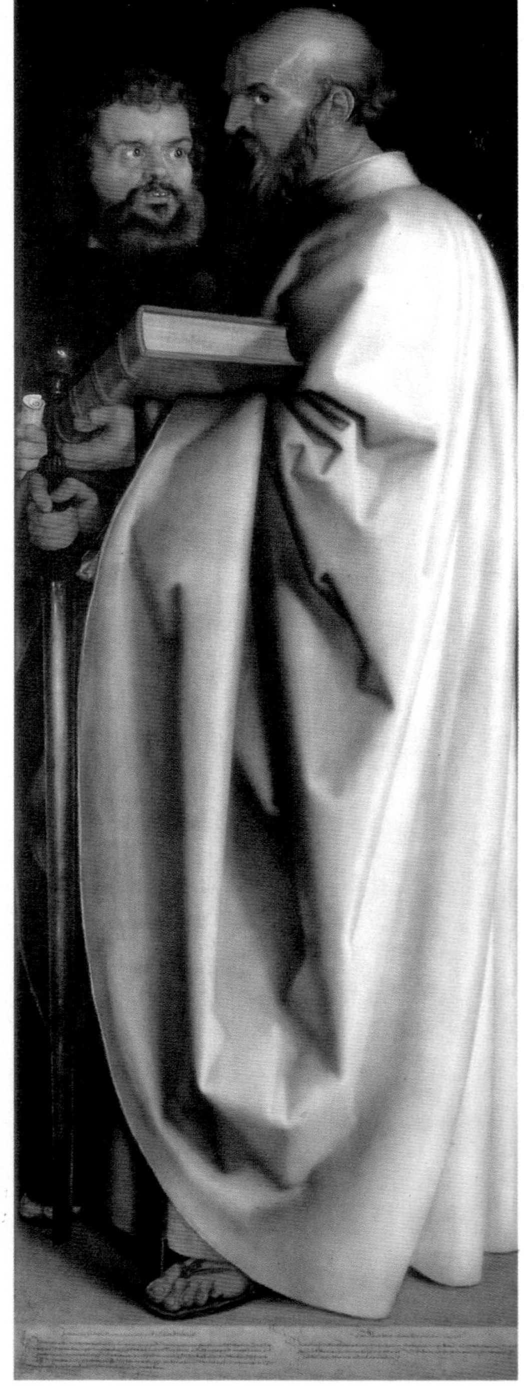

Complete Catalog of Works

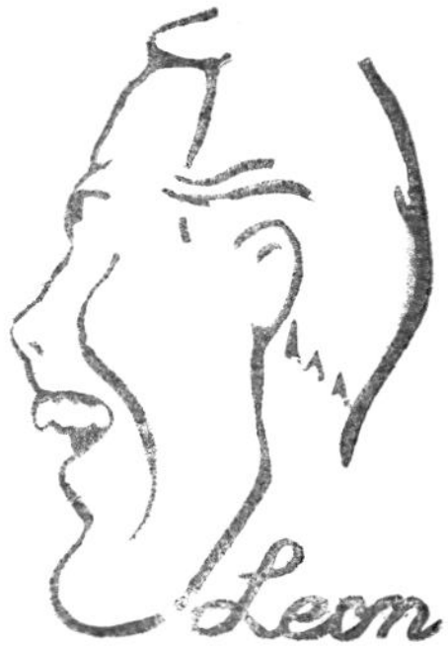

The catalog numbers in the gray squares correspond to the works reproduced in the table of color plates.

1

Portrait of Barbara Holper (Dürer's Mother)

Part of a diptych; see cat. 2.
Oil on wood, 47 x 39 cm
(on the left shortened by ca. 1 cm)
Nuremberg, Germanisches Nationalmuseum
1490

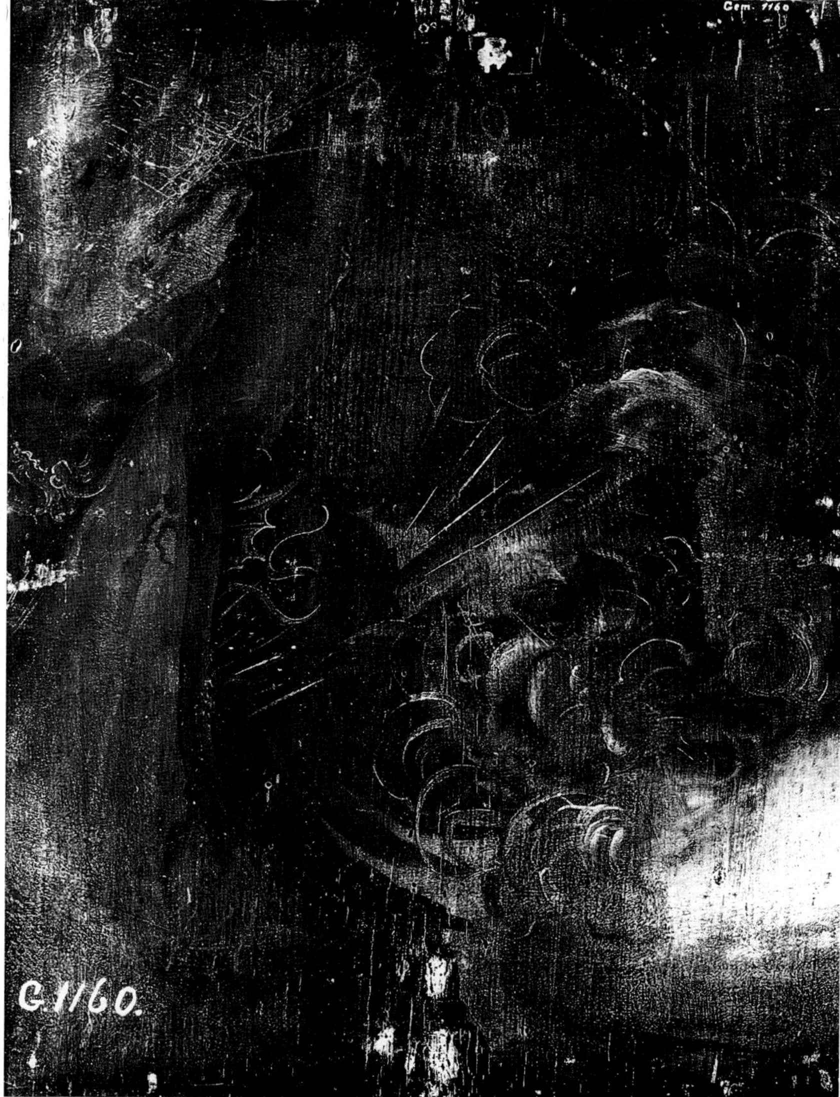

Cat 1 Verso

The portrait of Dürer's mother (1452–1514), together with the portrait of his father (pl. 2), also called Albrecht, was part of a diptych that appears as number 19 in the 1573–74 inventory owned by Willibald Imhoff, a Nuremberg patrician. This inventory also brings to light that the two portraits were acquired by Ursula Dürer, the widow of the painter's brother Endres. The portrait was seen again in Nuremberg by Carel van Mander, as is recorded in his 1604 Schilderboek. It disappeared in the middle of the seventeenth century, to be rediscovered as the portrait of Barbara Dürer only in the mid-1960s at the Germanisches Nationalmuseum (Brand Philips, 1978/79).

The museum acquired the painting from Munich's antique market in 1925. It came from the collector of Dürer's drawings, the Frenchman His de la Salle. There are several indications that it is the painting of Imhoff's inventory.

The number 19 (that is, the one corresponding to the place in the inventory), is painted on the reverse side. It is found on top of an image of a devil who takes shelter in the crack of a rock, between clouds. Furthermore, these clouds are identical with those appearing behind the coat of arms in the portrait of Barbara's husband.

The presence of the devil can only be interpreted as an image to contrast with Barbara Dürer. Since Piero della Francesca represented the triumph of virtue on the reverse side of the portraits of Federico da Montefeltro and of Battista Sforza, it is plausible that Dürer, painting on the reverse side, had wanted to represent the devil, driven out by the virtue and faith of his mother (note the rosary that she holds in her hands).

It could be a slightly different formulation of the theme of the triumph of virtue over vice, which will be treated on subsequent occasions. If there are any lingering doubts that this is the portrait of a thirty-nine-year-old woman, mother of sixteen, as was Barbara Dürer, one should remember that the portraits of women were generally much more idealized than those of men. In addition, the idealization could act as a final homage to her virtue.

Dürer shows that he does not yet have a perfect mastery of perspective in the painting (note the left arm of the mother). Even the folds of clothing are represented somewhat schematically; on the other hand, his extraordinary realism is already demonstrated by the clear, flesh-pink of the face and the white bonnet with the fallen tip.

The sleeves and the hands are only partly seen, according to the portraiture conventions of the day.

The color of the background is neutral. The pictorial tradition of his teacher is still present.

Note, in this painting, the resemblance of the mother's head to that of the Magdalene under the Cross in the Lamentation of Michael Wolgemut of 1484–85

(Strieder, Tafelmalerei in Nürnberg 1350–1550, Königstein im Taunus, 1993, ill. on p. 202).

2

Portrait of Albrecht Dürer the Elder with the Rosary

Part of a diptych; see cat. 1.
Inscription on the back, monogrammed and dated
Oil on panel, 47 x 39 cm
Florence, Galleria of the Uffizi, 1490

The portrait of Dürer's father (1427–1502) is found, in Willibald Imhoff's inventory, at the same number as the one of his mother (pl. 1). Separated from the latter, it was sold to Emperor Rudolph II between 1588 and 1628. Prior to 1675, it was part of Cardinal Leopoldo de' Medici's collection; in the eighteenth century, it was at Poggio Imperiale and, since 1773, it has been at the Uffizi. The coats of arms of the Dürer and Holper families are depicted on the reverse side of the painting, with the date 1490 and the number 19 of the Imhoff inventory. The two panels were furnished with hinges so that they could be closed, one on the other: on one side, the coats of arms in front of the smoky clouds could be seen, and on the other, the devil who is taking shelter in the crack of a rock.
The nineteen-year-old Dürer painted the portraits of his parents as soon as he finished his three-year apprenticeship under the woodcutter and painter Michael Wolgemut of Nuremberg (1490), and before undertaking his journey to Colmar, for Easter (April 11) of the same year. These are the first two documented panels of the young artist, and the oldest example of a diptych of portraits known in German art (see also pl. 20, 21).
The relief of the wrinkles of the hands, the length of the fingernails, the expressiveness of the moist gaze of the eyes—which reflects the window bars—the precise depiction of the eyebrows, and of the first hint of the beard: all these details indicate the immense talent of the still-young artist. The dimension of the head and the position, in the visual field, of the upper part of the body are also fruits of a wise, thought-out decision, which brings focus to the head, whether for the effect of light or for its relationship with respect to the dimensions

Cat 3 Votive panel for a drowned child

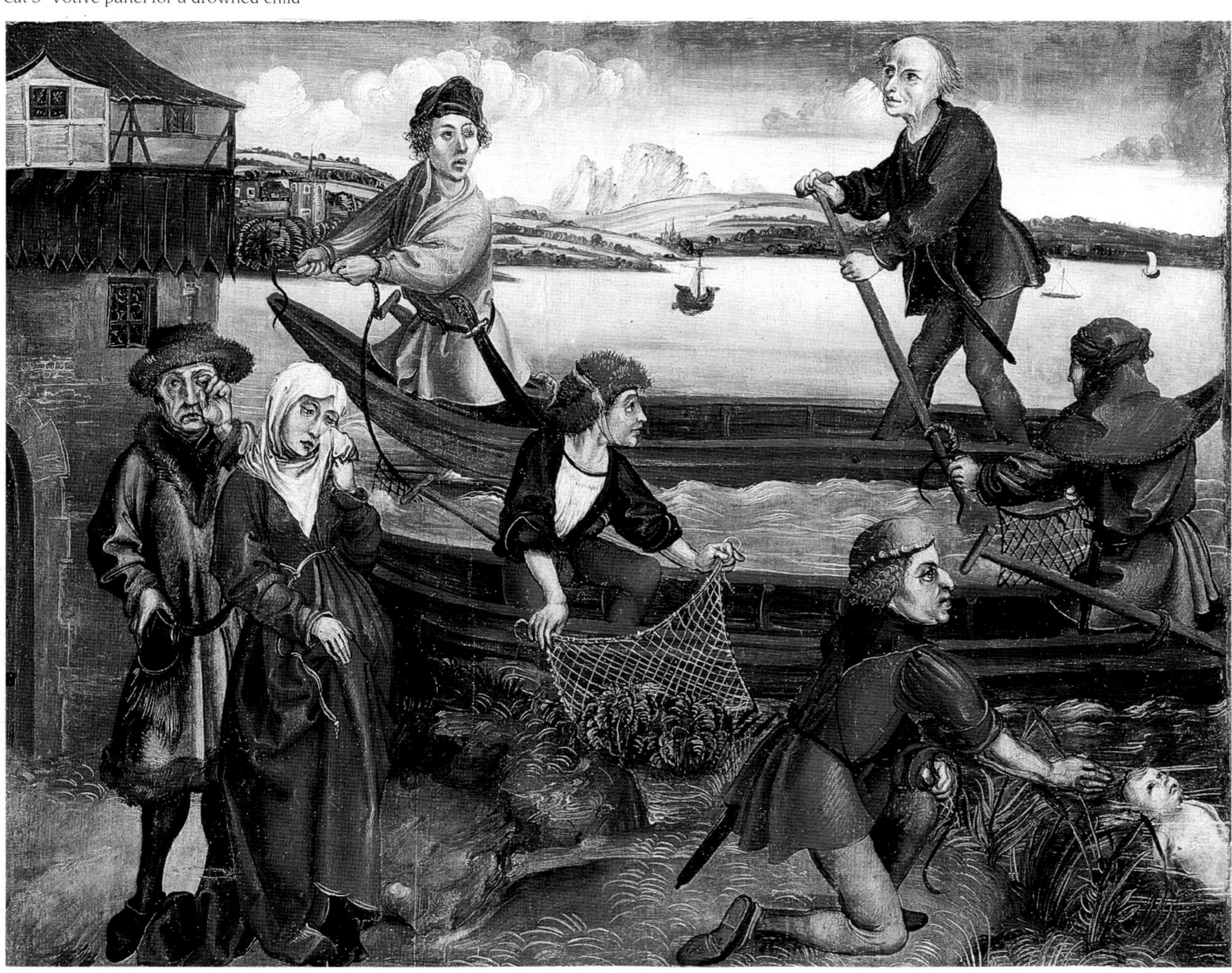

of the painting. Together they create a delicate counterpoise with the joined hands. Before such pictorial sensitivity, the slight difficulty that the artist encounters in representing the shortened right forearm appears almost negligible.
In comparison with the portrait of his mother, the one of his father is more characterized, and not only for the exterior aspect. According to Dürer's description in the "Family Chronicle" of 1524, he was "a man, gentle and peaceful with whomever," and his sensitive nature also transpires from this image.
In general, the portrait of the woman should not be to the left—for the spectator—of the man's, as it is in this case (compare the portraits of the Tuchers, *cat. 21, 22*); however, other examples like this exist.

3

Votive Panel for a Drowned Child
Spruce fir,
42 x 52 cm
Kreuzlingen, Switzerland,
Kisters collection
ca. 1493

This panel was acquired by Heinz Kisters in 1952. Previously, it was in the outskirts of Vienna, in the Gemäldekammer in the castle of Kreuzenstein, property of the Count Wilczek.
The painting had been attributed to an artist from Dürer's circle during his apprenticeship trip to Basel (late 1492-1493). Strieder (1963, 1981) and Anzelewsky (1991) attribute it to Dürer. In the panel, one cannot make out any saints who could have saved the child. After he had fallen into the Lake of Constance, fishermen searched for him and eventually found him by the shore of the lake. In front of the house, the mother and father are crying for their little boy. The panel was certainly part of a larger painting, in which the saint who saves the child would also have been represented. I submit that, as a Geselle (that is, a still-dependent artisan) and in foreign surroundings, Dürer was not able to obtain an official commission.
The principal part of the work was probably executed by a local artist, whose workshop Dürer relied on during his trip. Although all the proportions are broken, and despite the faulty perspective, one notes in the casual and modest work a glimpse of the southern shore of Lake Constance, seen from Lindau.

4

The Adoration of the Magi
Tempera on fir,
75.5 x 169.5 cm.
Basel, Kunstmuseum
ca. 1493

In 1823, this panel, which previously appeared in the Faesch collection, became the property of the city of Basel.
Some damage to the painting is apparent in cuts a few centimeters long in the upper part and a missing portion off the right edge.
As with the votive panel (*cat. 3*), here the proportions are not always respected. It is another modest work from the period of Dürer's journeys.
Besides the "Rhineland" type of Madonna, which echoes Martin Schongauer, who had inspired Dürer, the third black king—according to Nordic tradition—has a long stride and wears a flapping cloak and pointed shoes, and shows a great resemblance to a figure from the illustration in the works of Terence, which Dürer executed during the period in Basel (Anzelewsky, 1991, p. 121, *fig. 11*).

5

Christ as the Man of Sorrows
Fir, 30 x 18.8 cm
Karlsruhe,
Staatliche Kunsthalle
ca. 1493

The museum in Karlsruhe acquired this panel in 1941 from the heirs of the painter Philip Roth (1841–1921) of Munich. The head leaning on the hand and the gaze

Cat 4 The Adoration of the Magi

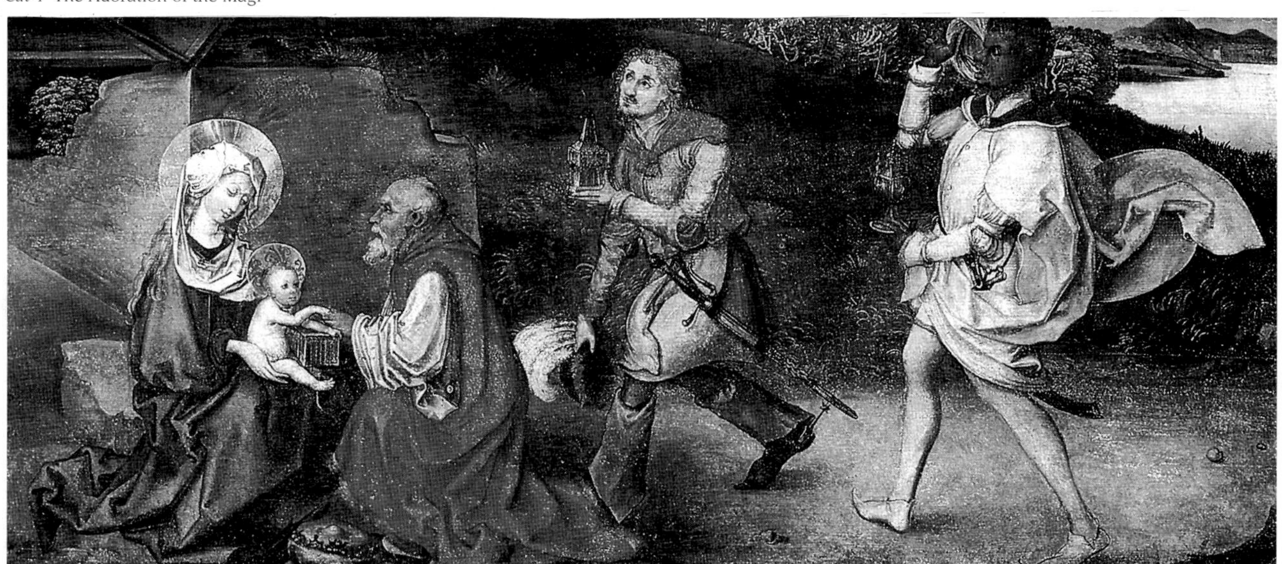

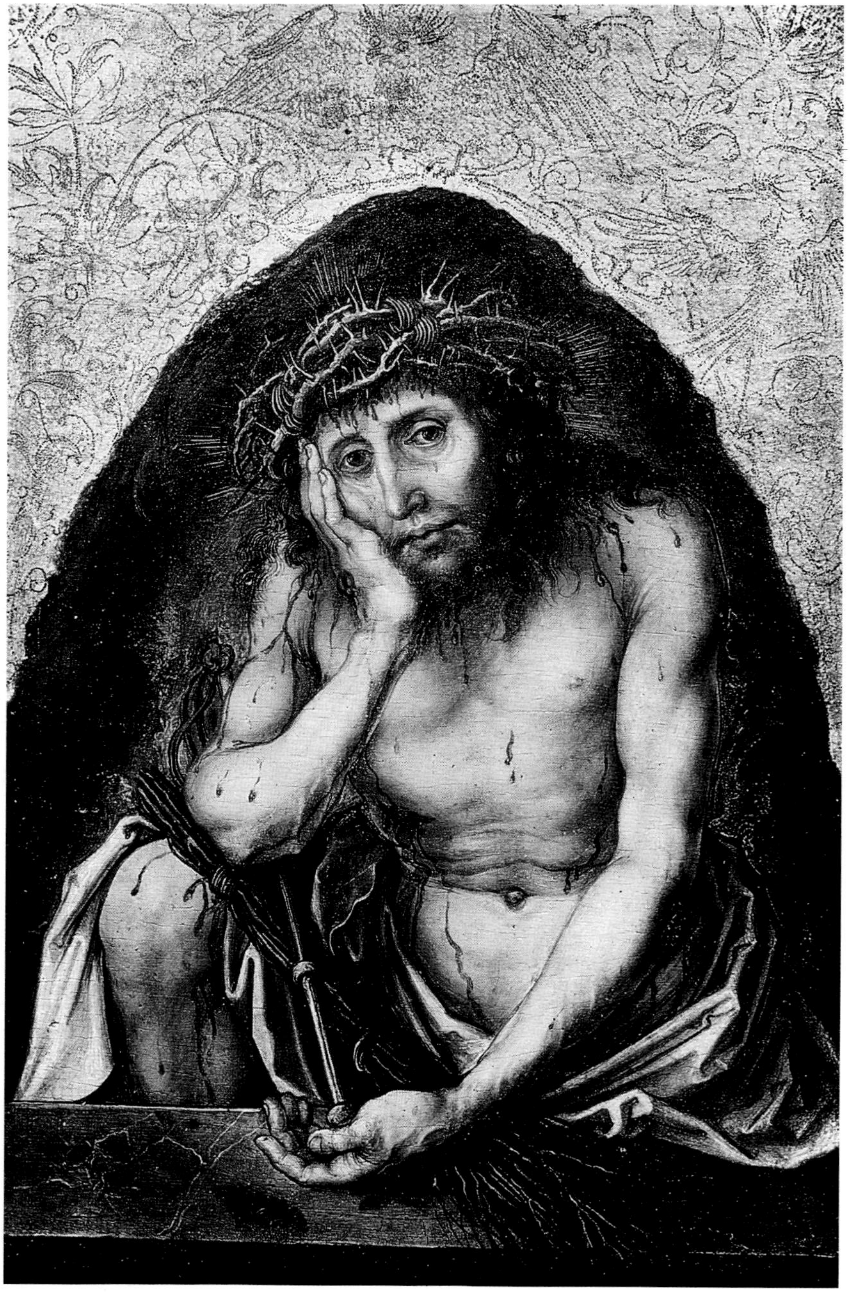

Cat 5 Christ as the Man of Sorrows

of Christ express melancholy and recall the self-portrait of Dürer in a melancholic and tormented state of mind, drawn in about 1491 in Erlangen (*fig. 11*). Nevertheless, the small panel must have been created as a private devotional panel at the end of his journeys, about 1493 or 1494 (Anzelewsky, 1991). The twigs of thistle and the little owl, who is attacked by other birds, engraved on the golden background, have prompted different interpretations, the most probable of which is the Redemption of man the sinner through the suffering and death of Christ. As in the portraits, the head of Christ is of a distinguished workmanship, both for the formal and psychological profile; the painting easily lends itself to be used as a devotional panel.

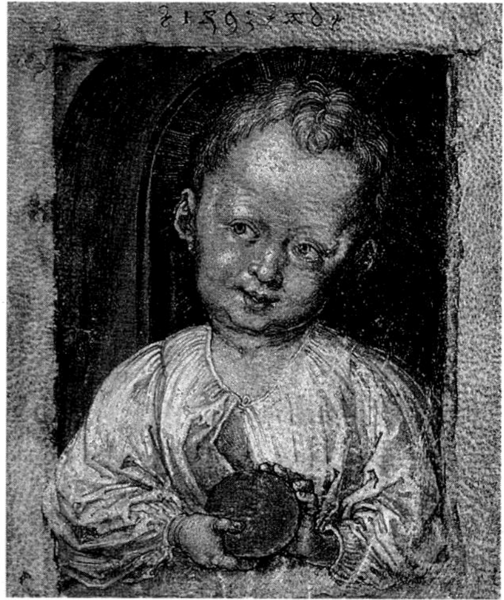

Cat 6 Infant Jesus with the Globe of the Earth

6

Infant Jesus with the Globe of the Earth
Inscription above:
the initials A.D. *and the date* 1493
Parchment, 11.8 x 9.3 cm
Vienna, Albertina, Graphische Sammlung
1493

A radiant infant Jesus, represented with the upper body in front of a niche and clad only in a shirt, holds the globe of the earth in his small hands. It is most likely a New Year message of good wishes, painted in Strasbourg toward the end of 1493.

7

Self-Portrait
Inscription above the head:
My sach die gat/ Als oben schtat;
dated 1493
Oil on canvas—transferred from vellum, 5.5 x 4.5 cm
Paris,
Musée du Louvre
1493

This painting was probably part of the Imhoff collection in Nuremberg and subsequently—though it is not for certain—part of the collection of Emperor Rudolph II.

After passing through various private hands, the last being L. Goldschmidt of Paris, it became part of the Louvre collections in 1922.

The very eloquent inscription, "my affairs are ordained from Him above," is expressed in an idiom that resembles the Alemannic-Alsatian dialect (Rupprich, 1956, I, p. 211 n. 6).

This is not surprising, since at that time (1493), during his early Wanderjahre, Dürer would have been in Strasbourg. This would also be supported by the fact that it is a painting on parchment, an easily transportable material.

Goethe, who had seen a copy of the painting, had already recognized in the drawing that the youth holds a sprig of sea holly (Eryngium) in his hands, whose current German name is Mannestreu, or Männertreu, that is, "fidelity of man." This name consequently provoked diverse interpretations as to its presence in the painting.

Thausing (1876/84) insists on seeing a request for marriage in the gesture of offering the plant.

From the times of Pliny (Willnau-Giessler, Zeitschrift für bildende Kunst, 1930), sea holly had been a sign of conjugal fidelity.

Dürer would have painted the portrait for Agnes Frey, who was betrothed to him, as arranged by their parents.

Ludwig Grote finds a link between the plant and the inscription and proposes a religious interpretation, tied to the Passion of Our Lord. Edgar Wind (Giorgione, La Tempesta, 1969) sees in the plant an allusion to the fortuna amoris or even to the constantia amoris, recalling that the plant was present in the engraving Nemisis (or Fortune) as well.

However it may be, the presence of the sea holly, given the prominence Dürer assigns it, has an important significance.

Before painting this excellent self-portrait, Dürer, from the age of thirteen on, had already executed four others.

Two of these, from his Wanderjahre period, are drawings in half-length. He is portrayed in all of them with his head covered, but in the Paris portrait, for the first time he chooses a showy, fashionable headgear: a red beret with a cluster of red ribbons, worn on a slant, as if from force of habit.

The long blond hair falling to his shoulders is similarly studied.

On the shoulders, we find a garment with a red and gold hem draping over a shimmering white blouse whose pleats are gathered by many decorative ribbons.

We also see the sleeve puffing at the right elbow. So much refinement in attire does not reveal Dürer as he was at that moment, a wandering painter and a novice without his own workshop; he represents himself in the portrait much better dressed than he would have been. He is represented here not how he actually was, but rather, how he visualized himself in the society where he wanted to be.

Only the fixed gazed reveals the artist who is portraying himself, because only in this way would he see his eyes in the mirror. The beauty of the mouth hints of Dürer's still-present vanity.

In contrast, the pronounced nose and the not-so-beautiful hands (the left one has been painted over; Winkler, 1957; Strieder, 1989 suggests that it is a later supplementation) already reveal his realism and precision as an observer.

The heavy varnish unfortunately compromises the original brilliance of the color scheme.

This painting, a self-portrait at twenty-two, represents, with the exception perhaps of Jan van Eyck and Leon Battista Alberti, the first and most significant "autonomous" self-portrait—that is, an image unto itself and removed from the context of European art.

8

Madonna and Child
Panel,
47 x 36 cm.
with cuts on the left and right
Parma,
Fondazione Magnani-Rocca
1494–95(?)

As published by Longi in 1961, this painting was located in Bagnacavallo, in the monastery of Capuchins nuns founded in 1474; evidently, it has not left Italy since Dürer's time.

The cloth that wrapped around the child's hips was considered a posterior addition and has been removed. Longhi and Musper dated the work to Dürer's second trip to Italy (1505–6). The catalog of 1971, as well as Anzelewsky, comparing it with various drawings of the artist, date it to his first sojourn in Italy (1494–95), and, more precisely, before the Haller Madonna (pl. 14), a date that seems much more probable.

Strieder has it painted in Germany, in the period after the painter's first sojourn in Venice. The small image of the Madonna, like that of a private devotional panel, is painted, as Anzelewsky rightly observes, in the Florentine style, in a three-quarter figure. The Madonna is seen through a window, with one side of the frame and the window sill projecting out. The marble wall that stands behind the Madonna is interrupted by an arched doorway, which, standing open, gives way to another brick wall, illuminated from above.

Between the Madonna and the back wall is a shallow space, typical of all Dürer's early works. The Madonna, young and graceful, with long curls, wears a red gown and a blue cloak. She delicately holds the infant in her lap, like a most precious treasure. She looks downward and smiles gently, her eyes still lowered, enraptured.

The infant, delicately shaped by the effects of the light, is anatomically perfect; his rapt gaze is facing upward, toward his father. In his right hand, he holds a small strawberry stem, which may symbolize the incarnation of Christ (Levi d'Ancona, The Garden of the Renaissance, Florence, 1957).

The small feet, one placed over the other, foreshadow the Crucifixion; the dangling right arm recalls the deposition and the lamentation; the white cloth, the sudarium.

Through the symbolic attributes and the expressiveness of the gestures, the image suggests to the faithful to contemplate the theme of the incarnation with that of the Passion.

These eventualities are foreseen and accepted by the humble pose of the Virgin Mary.

9

Saint Jerome in the Wilderness

Birch, 23.1 x 17.4 cm
Lt. Col. Sir Edmund Bacon Collection, Revening Hall, Norwich, Norfolk
Presently on loan to Cambridge, Fitzwilliam Museum
ca. 1495

This small panel, which only since 1957 has been recognized as an original, was previously attributed to the Veronese painter Giovanni Francesco Caroto (1488–1555). It was probably painted during the first Venetian sojourn of the master. This hypothesis is corroborated not only by the fact that the painting, in all likelihood, remained in Italy, but also by the presence of a lion, which is modeled on a study on parchment which Dürer did in Venice, initialed and dated 1494 (W 65) (Note: Dürer's drawings are cited with Winkler's numeration (W), 1936-1939.). Even the rocks to the right recall the studies of the master during his trip to Venice. On the other hand, the goldfinch and the bullfinch by the creek, the butterfly and the plants in the foreground appear simply as many small individual studies. The morning sky behind the rapt gaze of the penitent creates a dramatic atmosphere that we do not find even in Bellini's works. This reflects the interior struggles of the saint: an exceptional demonstration of the artist's talent at twenty-four years of age. Judging from the numerous copies that were made, the work had a strong resonance during this time, especially in the circle of Altdorfer, Cranach, and Baldung.
On the posterior side of the panel is a comet or a meteor; it is perhaps the record of a celestial event that took place on 7 November 1492, which Dürer could have observed from Basel.

10

Madonna and Child in front of a Landscape

Poplar, 89 x 74 cm
Schweinfurt, Germany, collection W. Schäfer
ca. 1495

This representation of the Madonna in front of a landscape is relatively rare among Dürer's paintings. The Madonna's face, the motif of the pomegranate she holds in her hand, and the pictorial realization in general imitate Venetian painting. On the other hand, not Venetian but absolutely typical of Dürer, are the landscape and the motif of the Madonna seated on a stone bench, holding the child.
A previous drawing by Dürer portrays the plasticity of a child's body, copied in 1495 by Lorenzo di Credi (W 84).
Another, which largely resembles the child in this painting, is portrayed in a drawing now at the Uffizi (W 86). The date that Longhi proposed (see *cat. 8*) on the occasion of the first publication of the painting, i.e., the period of the second trip to Italy, 1505–6, should be dismissed.
The melancholic gaze of the Virgin, openly directed to the viewer of the painting, contrasts with that of the infant Jesus, contrite, absorbed, and turned to endless space. His little finger, which seemingly indicates his own genitalia, could lead one to think of an intentional reference to his own human nature. Certainly, the gesture of his other hand, clutching his mother's cloak, here meaningfully red, seeking help and protection, expresses his awareness of his own future martyrdom.
The pomegranate the Virgin holds in her hand symbolizes all her good works, sublimated by her faith in the Passion of Christ (Alain de l'Isle). The dimensions

Cat. 10 Madonna and Child in front of a Landscape

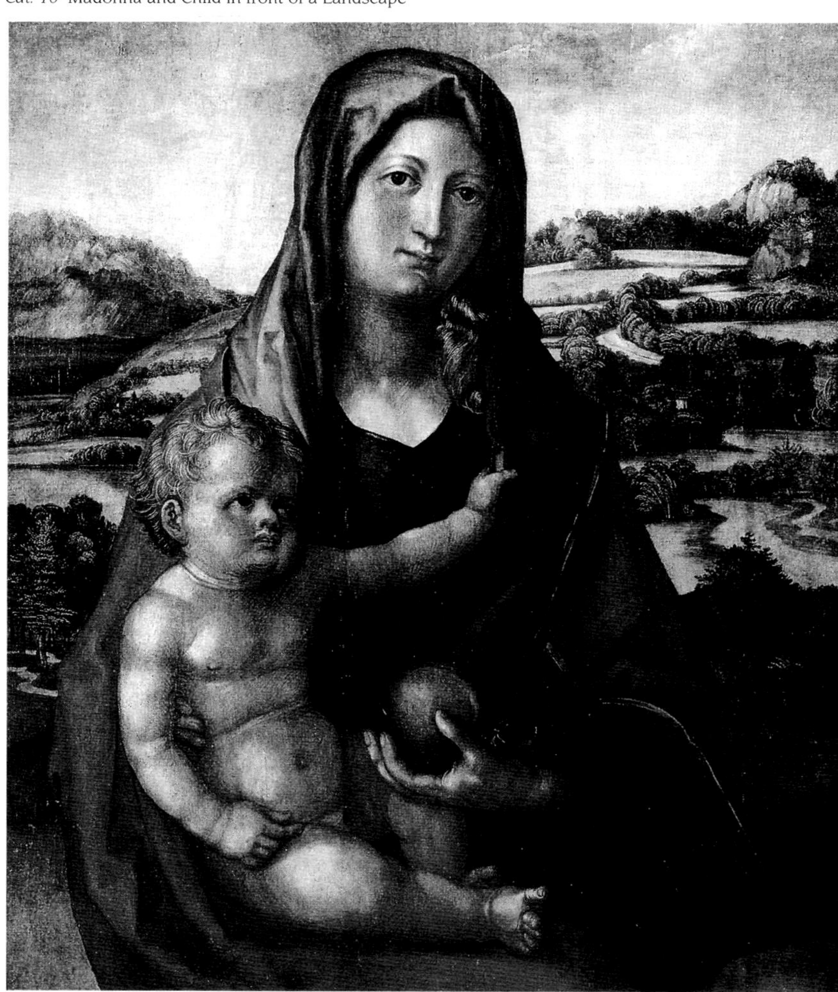

of the panel are considerably larger than all the other private devotional panels. The state of preservation is good, noticeably so for the landscape portion. Dürer's typical preparatory drawing comes through particularly around the child.

11

Frederick the Wise of Saxony
Inscription in the bottom left, monogrammed (later addition?)
Tempera on canvas,
76 x 57 cm
Berlin, Gemäldegalerie
ca. 1496

In 1700, this portrait was in the possession of an English painter, collector, and art merchant in Florence, Ignazio Hugford. It was from his heirs that the grand duke Pietro Leopoldo acquired it in 1779. From the Uffizi, it was passed on to Antonio Armano, and from him it was acquired by William von Bode, in 1882, for the gallery of Berlin.
In all probability, it was executed by Dürer in April 1496, during the prince elector of Saxony's (1463–1525) sojourn in Nuremberg.
The painting appears quite dark because the painting was not only applicated on a new canvas, but received in addition, varnish on top of the tempera painting which is not a common procedure. The position of the arm leaning on a window sill and the hands, placed one on the other, recalls the Self-Portrait of Dürer of 1498 at the Prado (*cat. 19*).
It is the first portrait done of the elector, who was twenty-four at the time. The penetrating gaze and the creased forehead are the most striking features. These characteristics were not as evident in the following portraits Dürer executes, and not even in the numerous portraits that Lucas Cranach, the court painter, made of Frederick the Wise.
The prince did have large eyes, but Dürer portrays them in this painting—and only in this one—with such an obstinate expression ("heroic-shadowy," according to Panofsky, 1955) that it makes one think that the artist's chief intention was to bring out the qualities of a learned man and a responsible and farsighted sovereign. There is also a scroll of parchment that emphasizes this intention. The aquiline nose, which does not appear as pronounced in other portraits, denotes magnanimity, according to ancient treatises on physiognomy.
At the same time, the artist wanted to provide a conciliating and relaxing counterbalance to the severe expression of the face (which was also emphasized by the heavy black garment edged with a gold brocade and by the black cloak thrown over his left shoulder) by painting the beautiful hands resting on the window sill with great finesse.
Perhaps the unusual portrayal of the prince can be explained more simply as Dürer's attempt to express in painting ancient theories of physiognomy.

12

The Holy Family
Parchment,
16 x 11.2 cm
Rotterdam,
Museum Boymans-van Beuningen
ca. 1496

The small painting has a fictive frame of intertwined branches, which constitute a kind a window through which one observes the image (compare the Adoration of the Holy Trinity, *cat. 50*) that is contained in a fairly limited space: a Madonna and child, who is approached from Saint Joseph, who has a darker complexion, from the left. Behind him is a glimpse of a landscape with a rather overcast sky.
The Madonna, her head bowed and her face absorbed, supports the child with both her hands, with her whole hand holding his while her other hand is placed under the pit of his arm.
With this same hand, she wraps the white cloth around his shoulders. It also covers her knees where he sits. From her right hand hangs a long rosary made of coral beads, while her left wrist dons a pearl bracelet.
These small details, the richness of her attire and the damask drape in the background give the image an unusual touch of preciosity.
The details concerning the infant Jesus—the dangling legs, the big toe of his right foot sticking out, his right hand clinging to the cloth wrapped around him, the other hand playing with a small bird, calling him with his arm spread to his mother's face—bring a smile to the viewer.

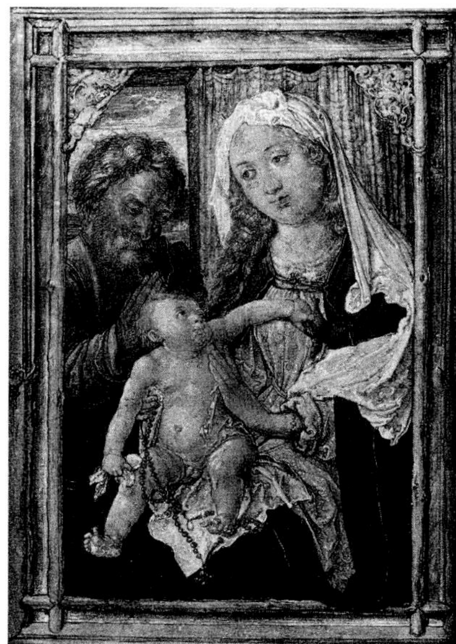

Cat. 12 The Holy Family

Yet it is an image dense with dramatic symbolism, which recalls the Passion: the sad gaze of the Virgin; the abovementioned bird; the white cloth alluding to the sudarium; and the worried gaze of the child who turns to his father.
The image has a twofold function: it offers a moment of aesthetic pleasure; and it induces a meditation of the sufferings of the Madonna and child.

13

Saint Anthony and Saint Sebastian
Side panels of the Dresden altar.
Canvas, 114 x 45 cm
Dresden, Gemäldegalerie;
from Schlosskirche of Wittenberg
ca. 1496

Dürer executed these side panels, commissioned by Frederick the Wise upon his return from his first trip to Italy; they came to the Gemäldegalerie in the eighteenth century. The recto is not painted, since these panels were firmly fixed to the cen-

tral panel.
The central one, displayed with the side panels in the Gemäldegalerie, has also been attributed to Dürer in the past (Tietze, 1937). In 1991, Anzelewsky rejected this notion on solid grounds and attributed it to a Dutch painter of the name Jan, who worked in Frederick's court.

14

Madonna and Child (Haller Madonna)

Tempera and oil on lindenwood,
53 x 41 cm
Washington,
National Gallery of Art
between 1496 and 1498

Documented in 1778 in the Praun collection, this painting passed through many hands. In 1932, it showed up in some English collections, from where it went to the Thyssen collection, to the Knoedler collection in New York, and then to the Samuel H. Kress collection. Kress donated it to the National Gallery in 1950.
It is called the "Haller Madonna" for the presence in the bottom left of the coat of arms of the Nuremberg family of this name. Another coat of arms, to the right, does not have clear heraldic characteristics and has not been identified.
The Madonna's face and the strong color scheme—azure, red, and green, obviously inspired by Giovanni Bellini—bear witness to how deeply the work of this great Venetian painter had made an impression on Dürer during his first sojourn in Venice. Nevertheless, the portrayal of the half-length Madonna reveals the Nordic character of the painter; as does the child, who stretches on his toes on the cushion, leaning on the mother with a trusting abandon and a serene knowledge (Tietze, 1928: see Schongauer). Similarly, the narrow internal space is typically Nordic, even if the imitation marble decorating the walls betrays a careful study of Italian models.
The same consideration holds for the view enjoyed from the framed window: an enclosed, flowerless garden, a wide road that bends around a rocky spur that is covered in trees and crowned by a castle, and a man and a horse that are crossing through. These landscape motifs are typical not only in Dürer's backgrounds but in Nordic painting in general.
The distant, dreamy gaze of the child, who, supported by his mother's right hand, rests against her with all his vitality, is opposed to the absorbed, sad expression on Mary, which is emphasized by the azure veil that almost completely covers her forehead. It prompts the impression of an intentional contrast between the extreme feeling of calm, further communicated by the soft fall of Mary's ample clothing, and the feeling of movement and vivacity that emanates from the brilliance of the child's body, silhouetted against the deep azure of the mother's cloak. Everything is balanced out by the intense red of the curtains in the background, which take the entire scene and confer it a grand solemnity.
Dürer has perhaps never managed to represent the majesty of the Madonna in such a clear and vivid manner, suspended between reality and symbolism, anywhere else.
It is certainly a sign of the inspiration he derived from his study of Venetian painting. Furthermore, in representing the child with an apple in hand, turned toward the background—as he did in the famous engraving of Adam and Eve—the painter might have also wanted to express the memory of Christ's death as the Redemption of mankind from the consequences of Original Sin.
Since both sides are painted, it is assumed

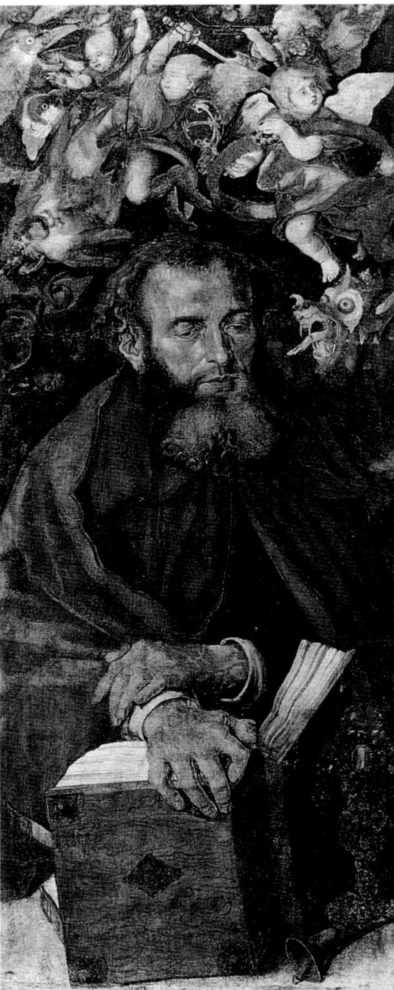

Cat. 13 Saint Anthony

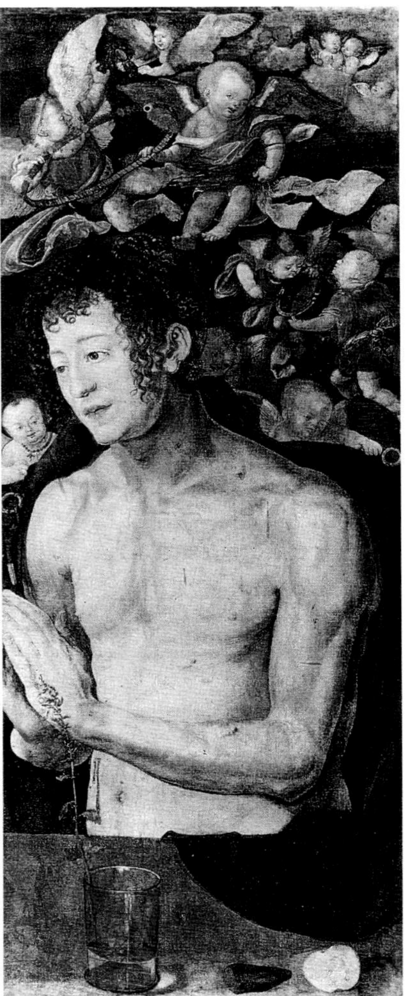

Cat. 13 Saint Sebastain

that the panel was part of a diptych, or maybe even a triptych, with portraits of the donors on either side.
Private devotional panels of this kind were quite wide-spread in the Netherlands and in Italy, whereas they were unknown in Nuremberg.

Verso:
The Flight of Lot and His Daughters from Sodom and Gomorrah

In the far background, one can make out the cities of Sodom and Gomorrah, on which Yahweh rained sulfur and fire. Just slightly in front of this is Lot's wife, who has already been transformed into a pillar of salt. Lot and his daughters are shown fleeing in the foreground, while vapors rise from the ground "like the smoke of a furnace" (Gen. 19:23–29). Painted with a light touch, the painting has always been admired for the powerful representation of the fire.
The connection between the Madonna and Child on the anterior side of the table and the scene on the recto has not yet been definitively clarified. One possible interpretation could be of the speculum humanae salvationis as the prefiguration of Christ's descent into Purgatory. Christ became man and freely accepted human sufferings to liberate the good souls from Purgatory's tortures; likewise Lot, the good soul, was saved form the destruction of Sodom (Anzelewsky, 1991). This interpretation would also lead back to the presence of the apple in the child's hand, on the anterior side of the panel. It is monogrammed (original?) in the hollow in the field behind the daughters.

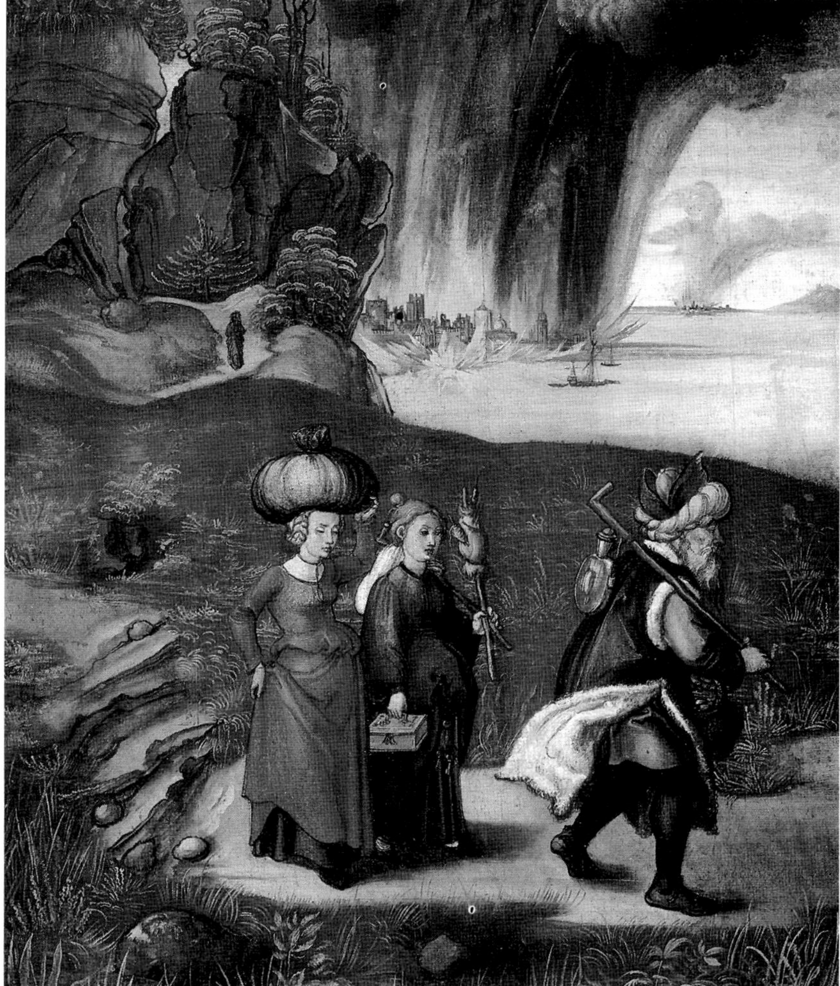

Cat. 14 verso The Flight of Lot and His Daughters from Sodom and Gomorrah

15

Dürer's Father
Part of a diptych; see cat. 19.
Inscription at the top, by someone else:
1497 ALBRECHT THURER DER ELTER UND ALT 70 JOR
Oil on lindenwood,
51 x 40 cm
London, National Gallery
1497

The city of Nuremberg consigned the portrait to Howard Earl of Arundel in 1636, along with the Self-Portrait of 1498 (today in the Prado in Madrid, *cat. 19*), as a diptych, to be given to King Charles I of England.
On the verso of the panel, visible traces of handwriting bear witness to the date of donation: 18 March 1637 (Oliver Millar, Walpole Society 37, 1958–60). The National Gallery acquired it in 1904 from the Marquise of Northampton.
After his first trip to Italy, Dürer painted his father a second time (for the first portrait, see *cat. 2*). Seven years separate the painting of the first and the second portraits, and despite the fact that his father had aged and his wrinkles had deepened, in the later image he looks more vivid and more spontaneous than in the first, dated 1490. The difference shows how much Dürer's art had matured in these seven years, and how his sensibilities and his abilities to penetrate the human character and to show it in painting had grown sharper. The weak color of the background reveals that that part of the portrait was probably not finished, but the posture of the head demonstrates that the master intended to create a portrait of his father that was characteristic and representative.
The light does not fall directly on his face; rather, one almost has the impression that it radiates from the head, the high forehead, the delicate cheeks, the thin lips, the pronounced chin, and the neck. The master shows a shadow on only one side

of the face, with a darker tone on the cheek. The clear expression of the face, with the small and attentive eyes directed to the painter and to the observer, is highlighted by the brown beret, which, with the two side flaps lifted, shows a wide forehead.
Dürer's talent for observation makes this painting, which was executed with a very fine brush, a masterpiece of intuition, psychological penetration, and great personal affection. The serious gaze of this man, revealing the great peace of mind attained through the trials of life, directs itself, with a certain pride, at the son who stands before him.
Such immediacy of expression would not have been possible for the painter to achieve for a commissioned portrait; it results from the close relationship Dürer had with the person before him, his father. It would be difficult for him to achieve such a sense of immediacy and spontaneity in any future portraits.
Various documents prove that this work was included with the self-portrait of Dürer of 1498 within a single frame, that is, when they were both still property of the city council of Nuremberg, and when they were part of the collection of Charles I of England. It is a unique example among typical diptychs, which were always composed of separate portraits of a married couple.
Even if the scale of these portraits more or less corresponds, their backdrops do not harmonize formally or chromatically. In addition, they were painted a year apart from each other.
We do not know if it was Dürer himself who framed them together to demonstrate his affection for his father, or whether it was the council of Nuremberg that wanted this framing (described in an inventory of 1625) to give homage to the city's most famous son and to his father, a well-known and respected goldsmith.

16

Portrait of a Young Fürleger with Loose Hair
Inscription in the top left, monogrammed by another hand and dated 1497
Canvas, 56 x 43 cm
Frankfurt, Städelsches Kunstinstitut
1497

This portrait, together with the following one, forms part of a rather uncommon diptych. The coats of arms, added shortly after and placed on the external side beside the portraits, were those of the same family, even though the coats of arms are different: one has a cross between two fish, the other an upside-down lily.
The emperor Sigismund had authorized the families of ecclesiastic members to add a cross to their own coats of arms. For this reason, it was deduced that the young woman portrayed with loose hair, the coral bracelet, the hands joined in prayer, and her head bowed down had devoted herself to the cloistered life. The Latin inscription added to the engraving Wenzel Hollar modeled on this painting, also recommended following in the path of Christ.
The very fine brushstrokes of this exquisite painting and the sharp distinction between the areas in light and those in shadow give the face a sense of plasticity, endowing it with a particularly vivid expression. Fritz Grossmann demonstrated, in an essay from 1944 in Burlington Magazine, that this and the following portrait truly formed a pair of portraits and that they were acquired together in 1636 in Nuremberg by the count of Arundel, whose engraver, Wenzel Hollar, made two engravings modeled from them. It should be noted that the young woman with the loose hair also rests her arms on a window sill.
In 1673, the portraits were acquired, together as always, by the bishop of Olmütz, from whom they later went on to Carl von Waagen, of Munich. Afterward, the two portraits were separated.

17

Portrait of a Young Fürleger with Her Hair Done Up
Inscription on the card, no longer legible; in Wenzel Hollar's engraving and in an existing copy in Leipzig, it reads:
Also pin ich gestalt / In achzehe Jor altt/ 1497
Canvas, 56.5 x 42.5 cm
Berlin, Gemäldegalerie
1497

When the portraits were still together, they passed on from Carl von Waagen (see *cat. 16*) to other owners, until it alone was finally acquired by the museums of Berlin in 1977. The various restorations have partially or entirely destroyed areas of the landscape and the inscription on the card at the top; the same holds true for the small statue of the prophet, inserted in the window post, which, from the side, looked toward the other portrait and in whose book Dürer had written his monogram, as Wenzel Hollar's engraving shows. At one time, the two portraits (*cat. 16 and 17*) were considered to be two representations of the same person, namely, Katharina Fürleger. The series of letters on the trim of the blouse also seemed to point to this; however, they are probably the initials of a motto. Today, it is generally believed that they are portraits of two younger sisters of the Fürleger family. The portrait, along with the following one (*cat. 17*), acts as part of a fairly uncommon diptych; it is the representation of the two Fürleger sisters of Nuremberg.
In contrast to the other young woman, depicted with loose hair, this one—an eighteen-year-old, according to the inscription—wears her hair in large braids wrapped around her head, a sign that she opted for marriage. Her defiant gaze is also proof of this. Similarly allude the sprigs of sea holly (Eryngium campestre) and Southernwood (Artemisia abrotanum), symbols of conjugal fidelity and eroticism, which she holds in her hand. Note that one of the portraits has a neutral background, while the other has a window with a landscape scene. One interpretation could be that one of the young women renounces the world, while the other welcomes it openly. In both figures, Dürer reveals pathologic symptoms: the young woman with the loose hair has goiter, and the two of them show signs of arthritis in their hands.

18

Portrait of a Man
Parchment on panel,
24.2 x 20 cm
Kreuzlingen, Switzerland,
Kisters collection
1497–98(?)

Heinz Kisters acquired this painting in 1952 from the antique market in London. The state of preservation, following the removal of one layer of a painting that had

been painted over it, appears relatively good. The painting has been included among the Dürer's original works by Fedja Anzelewsky (1991), who compares it with the portrait of Dürer's father of 1497 (*cat. 15*).
The contrast between the internal strength that emanates from his face, and the wisdom and foresight in his eyes, on the one hand—and the messy and wild hair, on the other, effectively demonstrates the breadth of Dürer's skills as a painter, even if the completely distorted perspective of the left shoulder remains inexplicable.

19

Self-Portrait with Gloves

Inscription:
Das malt ich nach meiner gestalt / Ich was sex und zwanzig Jor alt / Albrecht Dürer;
monogram follows; dated 1498,
below, on the window sill
Panel, 52 x 41 cm
Madrid, Museo del Prado
1498

For indications on the provenance of this work, which at one time was framed with the portrait of his father of 1497 to form a diptych, see *cat. 15*. It is 1498, and three years have gone by since Dürer's first journey to Italy.
The artist owns his own workshop and manages his own work. The series of woodcuts about the Apocalypse comes out. This portrait is from the same year: Dürer appears more confident than in the earlier self-portrait (*cat. 7*). This one was probably painted in Strasbourg, and shows just the beginnings of a beard around the chin, and an even more refined attire.
The neutral background used in the first portrait is abandoned; the artist depicts himself, like the Haller Madonna (*cat. 14*), beside a window that looks out onto a Pre-Alpine landscape. While there is only an enclosed garden beyond the window in the Madonna painting, here one enjoys a view of a wide valley, a lake with rippling waves surrounded by leafy trees, and some houses nestled just behind. In addition, a cluster of gentle, pleasant hills leads one's gaze to the background, where high snow-capped

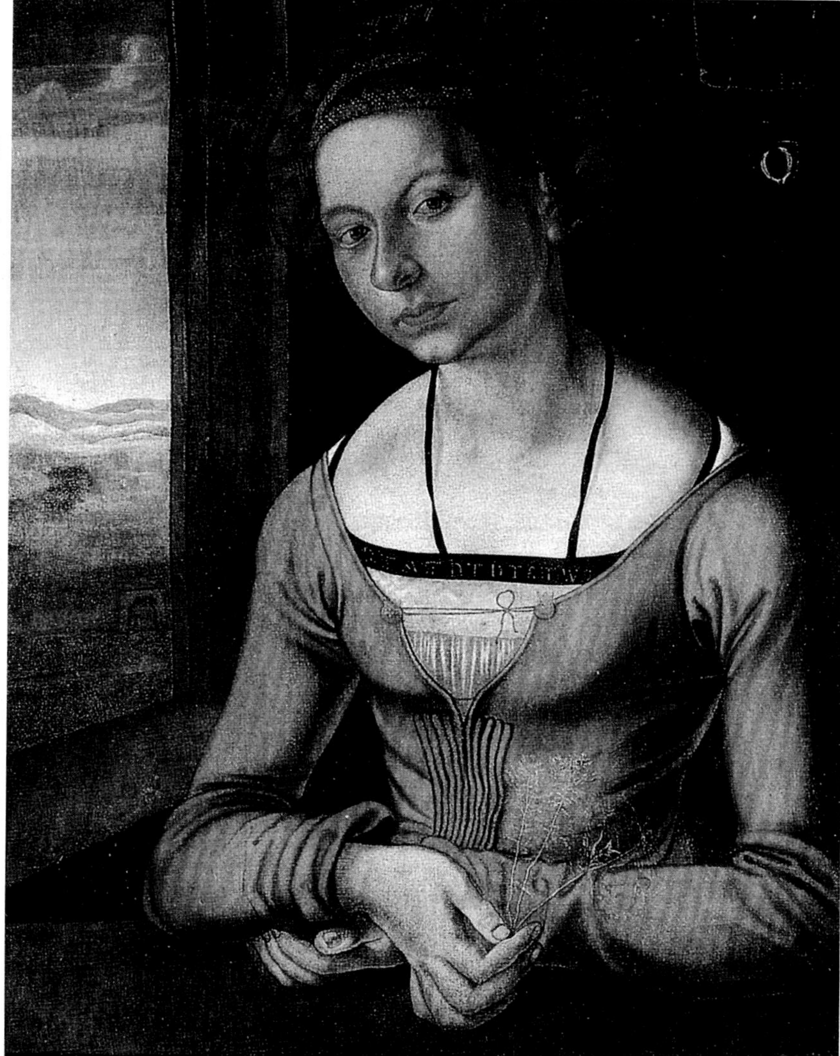

Cat. 17 Portrait of a Young Fürleger with Her Hair Done Up

mountains rise, crowned by a luminous but faintly clouded sky.
The care that Dürer dedicated to the realization of this panoramic view leads one to think that he wanted to draw attention to his abilities as a landscape artist, which he had already demonstrated by his numerous watercolors. Naturally, in the middle of this landscape, the usual wayfarer is not absent.
The architecture that he creates in the background painting does not have a logical justification within the painting. It is necessary because with just the beginning of the archway sketched, it gives the head more prominence. It is here, in the head of curly hair, and in the blouse gathered in extremely fine, tiny pleats, that we have an example of the sort of precise painting at which Dürer excels. He intended to distinguish himself from the rich merchant class, who are always clad in fur coats in their portraits. Afterward, in the self-portraits that accompany the altarpieces, he, too, will wear fur coats. Here, however, Dürer chooses clothing characterized by an elegant color scheme: it begins with the beret, alternating in white and black, grows richer in the various shades of gray in the

clothing, and finally establishes a delicate contrast with the fresh color of the skin. The white-black-gray scheme blends with the brown and purple color of the cloak, worn on the left shoulder, the white and olive green of the braided cord that holds it, and the gray of the gloves. Such refinement in the elegant harmony of the attire is not only a demonstration of a chromatic aesthetic unto itself, but is meant to introduce his new personality: that of an independent man who can choose his own social class.

Perhaps the presence of the gloves indicates this as well. Besides the portraits of his mother and father (*fig. 1, 2*), and the Christ as Man of Sorrows, these being so psychologically intense, no other work, out of all his paintings from this time until his second trip to Italy, of such a high pictorial quality has survived.

20

Hans Tucher

Left side of a diptych that includes the portrait of his wife Felicitas (cat. 21)
Inscription in the top left
in another's hand: HANS TUCHER, 42 IERIG 1499
Oil on panel, 28 x 24 cm
Weimar Schlossmuseum
1499

21

Felicitas Tucher, née Rieter

Inscription in the top right, by someone else (?): FELITZ. HANS. TUCHERIN, 33 JOR. ALT. SALUS. 1499
Oil on panel,
28x24 cm
Weimar, Schlossmuseum
1499

In 1824, the two portraits were included in the inventory of the museum in the Jägerhaus of Weimar. After 1918, they were passed from the grand dukes to the museum.

It was commissioned in the same year as the diptych of Nicolas and Elsbeth Tucher (*cat. 22*). They had approximately the same composition because Wolgemut, Dürer's master, had already done portraits of the members of the Tucher family years before. Even the setting of the portraits is very similar. The presence of an embroidered curtain in the background, the almost identical landscape passage seen through the windows, and lastly, the windowsill set equal spatial limits to the portraits. The foreshortenings of the landscape passage are imaginative and mannered, showing roads, lakes, and mountains. On the road, in the landscape behind the man's portrait, one discerns a wayfarer; on the path, in the woman's portrait, a man on horseback. The same clouds are seen in the clear sky behind the man, as in the wife's portrait, and in Elsbeth Tucher's (*cat. 22*).

Hans Tucher, a descendant of an old Nuremberg family and an important member of the city council, is depicted in lavish clothes, with a fur collar, a symbol of his high-ranking position. The head, portrayed in a more elevated position than that of his consort, is framed by soft and wavy hair. The eyes, which have slightly different size, have an open gaze, the eyelids are somewhat lowered, the nose is long and sharp, the lips thin: the result is a proud but winning look, which is also emphasized by the points of the beret folded to the back and front. Besides the ring he wears on his thumb, he holds—like Elsbeth Tucher in her portrait—another ring, gold, in his hand as evidence of his marriage, contracted in 1482 with Felicitas. She, in turn, holds a carnation, with a bud and a flower. Her plump face is turned to the left, but her gaze, with slightly melancholic eyes, looks to the right. Like her sister-in-law, she wears a gold chain around her neck, and the waistcoat , according to custom, is held by a buckle (*cat. 22*), which is engraved with the initials of her consort, H. T.

The combined coat of arms of Tucher-Rieter is depicted on the verso of the Hans Tucher portrait, which became the anterior side of the closed diptych.

22

Elsbeth Tucher, née Pusch

Part of a diptych, including the portrait of her consort Nicolas, that is, Nikolaus (lost).
Inscription in the top right, by someone else (?):
ELSPET.NICLAS.TUCHERIN.26 ALT. 1499;
monogrammed above the hand
Oil on lindenwood,
29 x 23 cm
Kassel, Staatliche Kunstsammlungen
1499

In 1499, the brothers Nicolas and Hans Tucher (the latter a member of the city council of Nuremberg) have Dürer execute their portraits and the portraits of their wives. In all likelihood, they had even determined the unusually small dimensions of the portraits and their characteristics with the artist: in a half-bust, holding a ring or flower. The background probably also corresponds to their wishes: a damask curtain, beside which a window opens sideways onto a landscape passage. The missing panel, with the portrait of Nicolas, probably had the coat of arms of the families of both spouses on the retro, as did the example of the panel of the Portrait of Hans Tucher (*cat. 20*). The dimensions of the panels and the fact that they could be kept closed leads one to consider that they were not representative portraits, but rather, objects destined for the family archive.

The twenty-six-year-old woman hides her braided hair under a bonnet with a net design, a sign of her status as a married woman.

The head is portrayed in a three-quarter profile, in the act of casting an affectionate glance to her consort. The depiction of the face is delicate: the eyes—each different—have an absent expression; the cheekbones protrude slightly; the chin is firm; the mouth is well modeled; the skin color, suffused in a soft light, is rosy. The overall impression is of a portrait of someone with whom the artist had some kind of relationship, without, however, betraying any particular emotion. It is realistic, but not particularly meaningful. The bodice is held, according to the fashion (see the Madonna who supports Christ's hand in the Lamentation of Christ, *cat. 25*), by a gold clasp with her consort's initials, N. T., and has a heavy gold necklace running beneath it. Both the clasp and the necklace are gifts from her husband.

The letters embroidered on the bonnet and the two Ws on the folds of the blouse, perhaps the initials of some motto, remain unexplained.

23

Portrait of Oswolt Krel

Inscription in the top left, by someone else (?): OSWOLT KREL 1499
Oil on lindenwood,
49.6 x 39—the side wings,
49.3 x 15.9 and 49.7 x 15.7 cm
Munich, Alte Pinakothek
1499

This portrait comes from the collection of the Princes Oettingen-Wallerstein, who had acquired it in 1812; it has been in its present location since 1928. It is presumed that Oswolt Krell, a merchant for the Ravensburg House in Nuremberg from 1495 to 1503, had asked the artist for a true portrait of representation. Its notable size, similar to that adopted by Dürer for the portrait of his father two years earlier, and its setting, a half-length, suggests this. In this way, it differs from the Tucher portraits, which were intended for private use.
The background, as in the Tucher portraits (*cat. 21, 22*), is divided between the curtain and landscape passage, unlike those, however, it is divided rather unevenly. The bright red curtain is wide and occupies most of the space on the right; the landscape, on the left, is reduced to a foreshortening that shows a small part of a river that meanders toward the back, behind a group of tall trees. The windowsill that separated the subject from the landscape in the Tucher paintings is absent. The figure represented, set with obvious grandiosity, is found in front of the curtain, highlighted by intense color.
The large fur-lined cloak is casually placed on the right shoulder only, to show, on the left side, the rich black garment with the puffed sleeve. To the disorderly folds of the cloak correspond the parallel horizontal folds of the sleeve and the vertical ones of the garment. The three-quarter position allows the painter to bring out the quality of the attire: the fur, silk shirt, and gold chain. The careful, fastidious representation of these meaningful details creates a powerful foundation for the setting of the head: vigorous, strong features, the pronounced nose and the strong-willed mouth, the furrowed eyebrows, as if from a sudden start or fright that makes him direct his gaze off to the side behind him. Everything works to make his face threateningly severe, which even the soft, light brown hair framing him does not attenuate. To the energetic expression of the face corresponds the nervous look of his left hand clutching his cloak and that of the contraction of the knotted fingers of the right hand that leans on an invisible window sill.
Color, form, and proportion heighten the expression of supreme resolution, an expression that is the result of a serious psychological study that Dürer conducted on the merchant, who was the same age as the artist and who was later to become the mayor of Lindau, his native city.
The two side panels that represent two "sylvan men" are wings to the portrait. They bear the heraldic shields of the subject and his wife, Agathe von Esendorf. They originally let the portrait be closed from the retro; one could imagine, then, that despite the large dimensions, the painting was to be conserved closed.
The present frame has been made recently.

24

Portrait of Saint Sebastian with an Arrow

Panel, 52 x 40 cm
Bergamo, Accademia Carrara
ca. 1499

This primitive portrait has been partially repainted and transformed into a Saint Sebastian with a large halo. Originally, the man wore a beret and held a broken arrow in his left hand, which rests on the window sill, as you can still see today. In the whole painting, only the landscape passage with the lake and the castle in front of the mountains have remained in its original state. The arrow is a fairly rare attribute for a portrait, although, in this case, it could become credible if Sebastian Imhoff were the person portrayed, as Thode had previously proposed when the painting was first published in 1893 (Jahrbuch der Preussischen Kunstsammlungen, 14). Sebastian Imhoff was elected to the position of consul of the Fondaco dei Tedeschi in Venice in 1493.
The painting shows many Dürerian portrait characteristics of this era, such as the landscape beyond the window and the resting of the hands in the window sill; the minimum of space between the window sill and the back wall; and the curtain that partially covers it.

25

Lamentation over the Dead Christ

Commissioned by Albrecht Glimm, goldsmith, for the Predigerkirche in Nuremberg
Oil on conifer,
151 x 121 cm
Munich, Alte Pinakothek
ca. 1500

This panel was dedicated by Albrecht Glimm, the goldsmith, to his first wife, Margareth Holzhausen, deceased 22 October 1500. During 1573–74, it was part of the Imhoff collection and, with the collection, was offered to Rudolph II in 1588. Between 1608 and 1613, it was acquired by Maximilian I of Bavaria. During a restoration that took place in 1924, the portraits of Glimm's second wife and of his seven children were destroyed. Dürer had added these following her death, in 1518. The Dürerian monogram and the date 1500 had once been on the lower edge of the sudarium.
The lamentation scene, composed of nine figures under the cross, occupies almost the entire painting. This scene is framed above by a beautiful landscape in which Jerusalem can be seen off the lakeshore, atop a hill, in the foreground. Behind the city is a mountain peak and a mountain range that disappear into the background. The city, mountains, and lake are flooded with light. A thick blanket of heavy black clouds that thins out just above the lake in the back looms over the mountains. While the presence of the black clouds is justified by the narration of the crucifixion ("and darkness came over the whole land...while the sun's light failed," Luke 23:45), and the light is explained by

the words of the apocryphal gospel of Saint Peter when he describes the position ("and the sun began to shine again," 6:21), the Jerusalem that appears in the painting—a city near water, with house, towers, and fortification walls, lying against rocky mountains—is decidedly an invented, Nordic city, which does not at all reflect the actual appearance, well known at that time, of this blessed city.
In the center, one sees the door that opens into the garden of Gethsemane. A little more ahead, on the right, is the entrance to the tomb in the rock, through which one can spot the uncovered sarcophagus. The first thing that strikes the spectator is the chorale composition of the sufferers around the figure of Christ.
One subsequently perceives the landscape, almost as if it were a second component of the painting. At this point, the two components together make the visual field explode.
The image of the lamentation is from a Dutch, not a German, tradition (Anzelewsky, 1991). Dürer interprets it in Italian terms, associating, in the composition of the scene, the figures three by three: Nicodemus, Magdalene, and Saint John the Evangelist align themselves in an ascending order under the cross. In the center, the head of the Madonna, while she wrings her hands, is joined by the heads of the other two Marys, who cry with her, the three representing three ages of life.
Last is Joseph of Arimathea, who supports the body of Christ with the sudarium. The image of the body is particularly impressive for the deathly pale color and for the complete abandon of the lifeless parts. Another Mary stands out for her clothing, fashioned from Dürer's period (note the bonnet and the gold clasp, similar to those of the Tucher women, *cat. 21, 22*). She is weeping while holding Christ's hand.
Thus, a triad is formed, be it with the head of Christ and the Madonna, or of Christ and Joseph of Arimathea.The impression of these different triads contrasts with the great chromatic variety of the clothing. However, the rhythm that characterizes the harmonious composition of the figures is not to be found in the colors, since the exaggerated dimensions of the ointment vases breaks the regularity of the proportions, which is otherwise fairly consistent.
The beauty of the work lies chiefly in the depiction of the individual physiognomies and in the gradation of pain: from Magdalene's tear-stained eyes, to the expression of muted and composed suffering of almost all the rest of the figures, to the absolute desperation, shown by the gesture and wailing of the woman next to the Madonna.
The scene with the body of the dead Christ opens up toward the spectator, so that he can directly participate in the lamentation, following the Mary, clad in Renaissance attire, who lovingly clutches the hand of Christ. Since the entire scene is illuminated by a limpid "new light," the suffering of the lamentation is accompanied by a feeling of comfort, a feeling that Dürer makes delicately transpire from the John and Magdalene, whose hopeful gazes are turned toward this light. This, apparently, is the Christian message of the panel.
According to an enduring medieval tradition, the figures of the donors are painted, kneeling at the bottom of the scene: on the right, the position of honor, the goldsmith Albrecht Glimm with his coat of arms and two sons; to the left, the late consort with her own coat of arms and daughter. A crown of thorns lies in the middle, between the two groups.
There is another painting in the Germanisches Museum of Nuremberg that is dedicated to the memory of Karl Holzschuher dated the year 1500. It comes from the same church and vaguely recalls the one described above, but it is the product of workshop.

26

Self-Portrait with Fur Coat

Inscription to the left:
ALBERTUS DURERUS NORICUS / IPSUM ME PROPRIJS SIC EFFIN. / GEBAM COLORIBUS AETATIS / ANNO XXVIII
Lindenwood, 67 x 49 cm
Munich, Alte Pinakothek
1500

Carel von Mander (1617) saw this painting in Nuremberg, and it stayed in the city hall there until 1805, the year it was sold to the gallery (Pinakothek) of Munich. Except for the background, which has been repainted, the painting has been well preserved.
Many aspects of this most famous portrait, which has prompted a number of interpretations, are, to say the least, unusual. The first observation concerns the depiction of the front profile: its symmetry, evident not only in his facial features but also in the placement of the curly hair to the sides of the head, recalls the "true icon," the true image of Christ, the model for every image of the blessed face, even in his depiction of the Holy Shroud.
The fact that the portrait is almost lifesize is as exceptional, for it is a dimension that artists commonly avoided. The third observation: the vanity and the self-satisfaction that the artist had persisted with in his previous portraits acquires a completely new appearance. He renounces any example of his exploits and cleverness and adopts a classical form, unusual for him.
This form presupposes a serious study of proportions.
According to Winzinger's calculations (Zeitschrift für Kunstwissenschaft 8, 1954), the portrait is constructed according to the dictates of the gold section, or, at the very least, according to precise rules, beginning with the proportions of the dimension of the portrait. The same had already occurred in the representation of the head of Christ. Undoubtedly, the source of this correspondence in Dürer's thought could be the biblical affirmation that God created man in His own image.
However, this does not necessarily mean that the artist intended to paint an imitatio Christi (Barinton, Art Bulletin 29, 1947, pp. 269 ff.), even if the year 1500 was also a holy year and that this sort of idea is not to be totally dismissed. We can find a plausible motivation of this autoidentification of Dürer and the image of Christ in Saint Bonaventure, who believed that the human being's creative abilities bring him closer to God. This line of thought was subsequently drawn upon by the Neoplatonic school in Florence (which Dürer had come into contact with through his friend Pirckheimer). Anzelewsky's thesis is just as convincing (1991). He sustains that the window that is reflected in Dürer's eyes—a detail that

is frequently found in his portraits and depictions of the Madonna—does not only represent reality, but mirrors Leonardo's thought: oculi fenestrae animae. Camerarius's interpretation runs similarly, holding that in Dürer's biography (Rupprich, 1956, p. 307), the artist transfers the figures seen internally "with the eye of the soul," in the visible reality of things.

To the reference to christoformitas is added also the allusion to the creative force of the artist.

It must be emphasized that Dürer apparently follows another topos in this self-portrait, what Vasari adopts in his Vite to praise the best portraits: to seem truly alive. In fact, the artist's eyes are still moist, the flesh is so bodily it seems palpable, and the fur and the material seem real. At the same time, he was concerned about rendering a spirituality in the facial expression, lengthening the features and making the forehead higher.

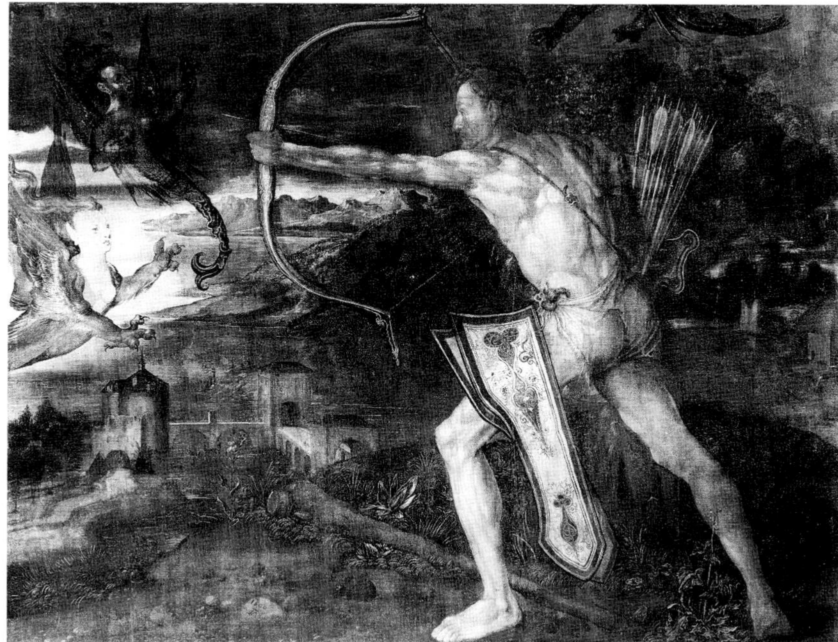

Cat 27 Hercules Killing the Stymphalian Birds

27

Hercules Killing the Stymphalian Birds

Monogrammed and dated 1500 on the rock in the lower left, by someone else (?)
Canvas, 87 x 110 cm
Nuremberg, Germanisches Nationalmuseum
1500

This canvas appears in the Castle of Schleissheim in 1761; since that time, it has belonged to the State of Bavaria. Around 1500, Dürer had repeatedly treated mythological subjects, though almost exclusively in his graphic art. His models were taken from Italian painting and drawing. The fact that only two of his paintings are about a mythological subject—this one and Lucrezia (*cat. 59*)—is a result of his patrons' meager interest in these themes. Frederick the Wise was an exception. He decorated a room of the Wittenberg Castle with a series of images of the labors of Hercules. In a description of the castle made by Andreas Meinhard in 1507, he speaks of a surrounding (aestuarium) with four representations of the labors of Hercules. On of these corresponds to the theme of the present painting. Panofsky supposes that it actually is this one, and that it was executed for the design of that room. According to Anzelewsky (1991, p. 67), the painting's poor state of preservation could then be explained in terms of the heat and humidity from its location. It must not be forgotten, however, that we are speaking about a watercolor, which is inherently delicate, and which, it had also been repainted several times and then treated with a varnish. In addition, the painting has visibly undergone various mutilations to its upper half, so much as to make one suppose that the original had a different form, with an ogival arch, which would explain why we can only see the paws from the Harpy above.

Another Harpy, to the left, is armless, which again suggests that the painting was originally larger. A copy of 1600, present in a Viennese collection, already had the form and dimensions of the current canvas. The painting shows Hercules, the pure hero, in whose face the artist's can be recognized. He is completing one of his twelve labors: fighting the rapacious and voracious monsters, the Harpies.

They are represented according to Dante's description in the Divina Commedia (Inferno, Canto XIII, 10–15; from Strieder, 1989). The scene unravels near the lake of Stymphal, in Arcadia, in a landscape whose beauty is now unfortunately only intuitable.

According to Weisbach (Der junge Dürer, 1906), the model for Hercules must be found in Antonio del Pollaiuollo: in Hercules and Dejanira of the Fogg Art Museum at Harvard. The hero has almost the same bearing and almost the identical bow. Hercules' right leg has always generated criticism, but nevertheless, the power of the figure is striking. A drawing that represents the same theme, found in Darmstadt, is no longer attributed to Dürer.

28

Paumgartner Altar

Inscription on the pillar below the porch roof, monogrammed
Oil on lindenwood, center panel, 155 x 126 cm; side panels, 151 x 61 cm
In 1619, the saints of the side panels were repainted, as were the patrons of the central piece; restored in 1902–3
Munich, Alte Pinakothek
ca. 1500–1504

Emperor Rudolph II did not manage to acquire the painting, which in 1613–14 was removed from the church of Saint Catherine in Nuremberg, to be given to Maximilian of Bavaria.

Center panel

On the left side, Dürer invented, with an almost perpendicular perspective with respect to the observer, a complex of ruins made up of huge, partly broken blocks of stone.

A large round arch made of square stones is erected upon these stones and shifted toward the left. The arch, in turn, is surmounted by a large slab in an apparently precarious balance, and by a huge angular rock. From here, rising on a step along the wall beside the arch, you reach another rounded arch. This one is much higher than, and perpendicular to, the first.

It leads to another structure to the right, where two smaller arches, resting on columns with Romanic cubic capitals, delimit the stable of the ox and donkey.

The two facades, on the left and on the right, establish a perspective series toward the landscape passage in the background. This passage is contrasted with the three planks resting on the right wall and on the transversal arch, and, lower down, with the wooden roof that stretches from the right-hand wall toward the center, protecting the Madonna and the infant Jesus.

This whole arrangement can be considered proof of the level Dürer's abilities had reached in perspectival representation—though as yet imperfect, as far as the rules of central perspective are concerned. It is the setting of the Nativity. The characters are distributed in the open space between the two houses under the shelter of a roof, as the "golden legend" says. The Virgin is in front of the small archways on the right. She stands ahead of Joseph, who remains outside the roof cover; two shepherds appear beyond and behind the Madonna.

In the distance, above a hill, is the scene of the angel appearing "in the splendor of the glory of the Lord" to the shepherds grazing their sheep, announcing the "good news." The two shepherds who enter the scene are speaking animatedly, and one of them, in a sign of devotion, has also removed his hat. However, they do not yet realize, emotional as they are, that they are so close to their destination.

The Virgin Mary is depicted on bended knee and in adoration of her son, as her gaze and her folded arms reveal. He is a little baby, held and caressed by a group of playful little angels. Jesus crosses his legs and looks tenderly at his mother, stretching his arms out toward her, a gesture and a gaze that perhaps signifies the acceptance of the task that awaits him.

The shepherds are moving toward the crèche, although the panel does not represent the "adoration of the shepherds." They are too immersed in their own conversation. The central theme of the panel is surely the "adoration of Mary." An unusually large Joseph approaches the foreground and emerges from a gap in the stones. Leaning with his right hand on the socle of the roof, he looks to the Madonna. He has a saddlebag hanging from his side, and in his left hand he holds a lamp firmly, which does not, however, emit any light.

The blessed night appears illuminated by a great, mysterious round light in the top left. It is, however, a fictive light, since the whole scene of the nativity is illuminated by an invisible source in the bottom left corner. According to Panofsky, Joseph's lantern would have an emblematic value (1955): it would represent the splendor materialis, which, according to Saint Brigid of Sweden, is obscured by the splendor divinus of the newborn Savior.

Joseph, in his role of putative father, is usually represented in Nordic art as a ridiculous figure. Here he enjoys an important position, without taking on a dominant role in the story. After all, it is true that the pole supporting the roof excludes him from the principal scene. The presence of the two male figures leaning out from the left, from the shadow of the wooden beams inserted below the arch, is curious. The meaning of the plants that sprout from the ruins is obvious: they allude to the coming of the new era that has begun with the birth of Christ. Dürer, unlike the other workshops of his day, produced very few altarpieces. In this panel, he apparently demonstrates much less interest for the christological content of the represented theme than for the formal problems: the architecture, light, and perspective. The latter remains his primary concern, even if, objectively, he did not succeed in resolving these problems in a totally satisfying way. But it is still possible that he did want to confront them, through the formal artistic solutions of Hugo von der Goes, who in 1483 was in Florence and whom he likely knew through his drawings (Panofsky). His patron was not a clergy man; neither do we find any reference to a pilgrimage to Jerusalem, for which occasion he would have commissioned the work.

The small figures of the patrons remain outside the technical and artistic problems of the painting. They were inserted a bit haphazardly wherever there was any space left over. On the left is Martin Paumgartner (died in 1478), his sons Lukas and Stephan, and perhaps Hans Schönbach, the second husband of his widow, Barbara Volkhammer (died in 1494). She is depicted on the right together with her daughters Maria and Barbara. Everyone is depicted with their coat of arms.

Side Panels

The figures of the saints are a completely different artistic matter. They are painted in almost actual size on the side panels representing the portraits of the patrons: Saint George could be Stephan Paumgartner, and Saint Eustace, Lukas. They are, according to Anzelewsky (1991), the first full-length portraits known to us, except for those of 1504 of the Stalberg spouses in the Städelsches Kunstinstitut in Frankfurt, by the "Master of the Stalburg portraits." As for the rest, from observing the bearing of the two figures, studied carefully, and their marked plasticity and expressiveness of the physiognomies, one could argue that the side panels were painted after the central one. When the side panels would be turned slightly forward, the figures of the patrons found themselves observing the scene represented on the central panel. The panels were painted even on

the back, but of these, only the left one has been preserved.
It represents the Madonna of the Annunciation (Strieder, 1933, fig. 463) and comes from a workshop. A copy of the Paumgartner altar is located in the Germanisches Nationalmuseum in Nuremberg.

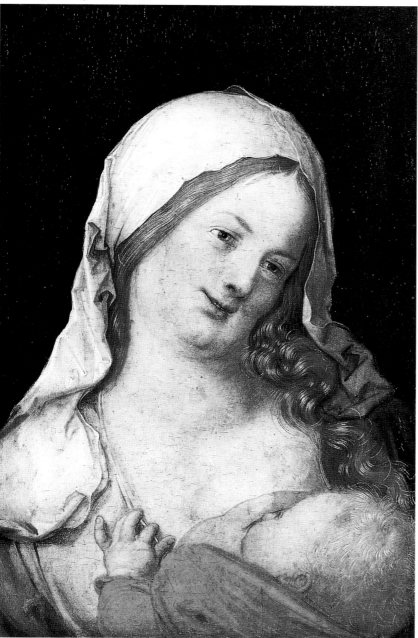

29

Virgin Nursing
Inscription at the top, monogrammed and dated 1503
Lindenwood, 14.5 x 18 cm
Vienna, Kunsthistorisches Museum, 1503

Cat 29 Virgin Nursing

In 1600, Rudolph II acquired this small panel, together with other works from the collection of Nicolas Perrenot, Cardinal Granvella, from the count of Cantecroy, Francesco Perrenot. By the end of the nineteenth century, the important influence of Jacopo de' Barbari, court painter in Wittenberg from 1503 to 1505, on Dürer had been hypothesized—and the thesis is accepted even by Anzelewsky (1991), based on the later appearance of documents. The priority of the artists, that is, which of the two had influenced the other, has also been debated. Recently, these relationships were again discussed (catalog of Vienna, 1994). The beatific, smiling gaze of the Virgin is unusual. She faces to the side in the small panel, painted with suffused and delicate colors. Besides the graceful hand of the Infant, you can only see his head of very fine blond hair.

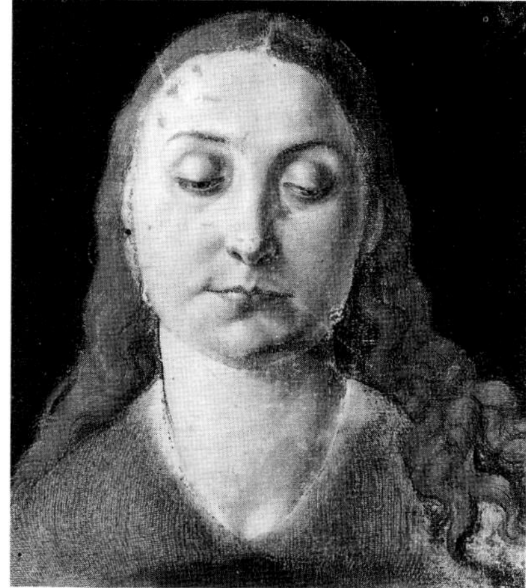

Cat 30 Head of the Virgin Mary

30

Head of the Virgin Mary
Inscription, monogrammed and dated 1503 or 1505
Watercolor on canvas, 25.5 x 21.5 cm
Paris, Bibliothèque Nationale
1503 or 1505

The colors of this canvas are quite faded, so much so as to show the preparatory drawing.
Both Dürer's studies on symmetry (see the Self-Portrait of Munich, *cat. 26*) and his deviations from it are shown by the depiction of the head.

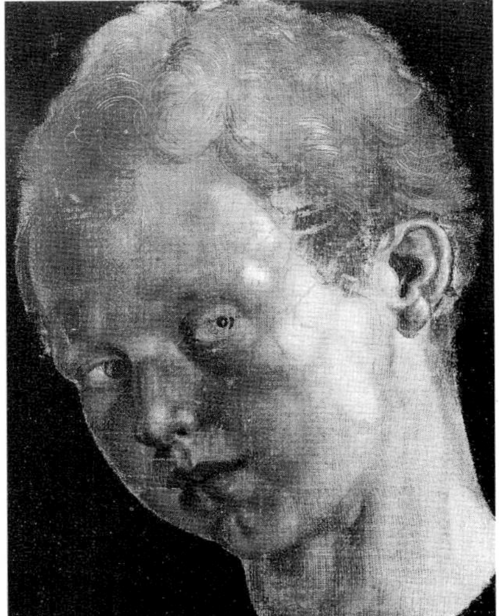

Cat 31

31

Girl's Head Leaning Left
Canvas,
23.1 x 17.9 cm
Paris, Bibliothèque Nationale
ca. 1503–5

As in the previous painting, the colors are quite faded, showing the preparatory design. But it is still possible to appreciate the studies on volume and light.

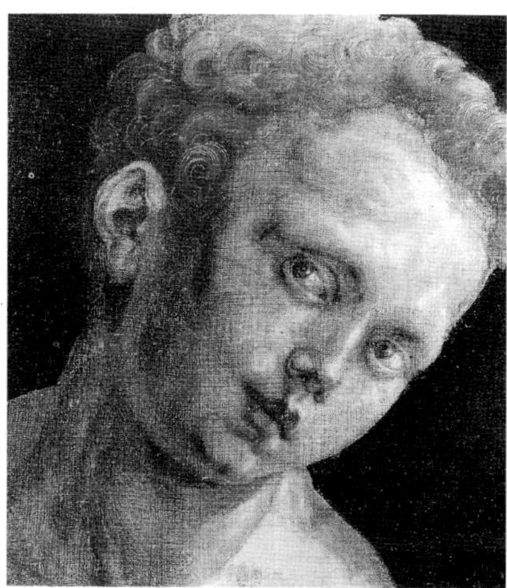

Cat 32

32

Boy's Head Leaning Right
Inscription in the top left,
traces of a monogram
Canvas, 22.5 x 19.2 cm
Paris, Bibliothèque Nationale
ca. 1503–5

Even in this painting, the state of preservation is rather poor. Cuts above and on the right edge have been noted. The preparatory drawing shows through in several places.
Both the heads captured in the foreground are fairly suggestive.

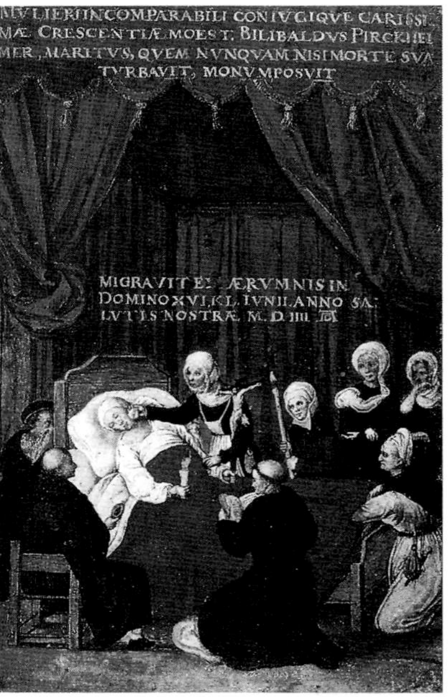

Cat 33

33

The Death of Crescentia Pirckheimer
Inscription, monogrammed
and dated 1504
Parchment, 15.4 x 9.9 cm
Bremen, Kunsthalle
1504

In 1628, Hans Imhoff the Younger offered this small painting, with other works of Dürer, to the duke of Bavaria, Maximilian. He describes it as "a little panel mounted on silver and ebony." The frame that he mentions must be the same that frames a copy of the painting in the Lehmann collection in the Metropolitan Museum in New York. It would be one of the rare original frames that still exists (see Adoration of the Holy Trinity, *cat. 49*; and Portrait of Holzschuher, *cat. 7*).

This fairly unusual scene, following the style of a "Death of the Madonna," shows Crescentia Pirckheimer on her deathbed, under a sky-blue canopy. In one hand, she holds a crucifix; in the other, a lit candle. A servant wipes the perspiration from her cheek; another servant, at the foot of the bed, has put her hands beneath the covers, probably to warm up the dying woman's feet. Still another woman kneels beside the bed holding a candle, while a friar is reading the Last Rites. Her husband, the humanist Willibald Pirckheimer, a close friend of Dürer's, hides himself halfway behind the head of the bed as he covers his face with a cloth. The scene is described in a lengthy inscription. It is likely that Dürer was not present at this final moment.

34

The Jabach Altarpiece

Two wings (inner side)

The Saints Joseph and Joachim
Inscription on the knob atop the stick
Joseph holds, monogrammed
Lindenwood,
96 x 54 cm

The Saint Simeon and Lazarus
(dressed in the garb of the bishop of Marseilles)
Lindenwood panel,
97 x 55 cm
Munich, Alte Pinakothek
ca. 1504

No documents exist that show what the original composition of the so-called Jabach Altar was.
Neither do we know who the patron was nor where he was originally placed. Naturally, hypotheses about this are not in short supply.
The name "Jabach Altar" goes back to an indication made by De Noël, a local scholar of the history of Cologne, that the altar was located in the family chapel in the house of the Jabach family of Cologne. Maybe the famous Parisian banker and collector Everhard IV Jabach (1618–95) had it sent to his father's house, especially since he collected Dürer's drawings. Even at that time, the side wings existed without the

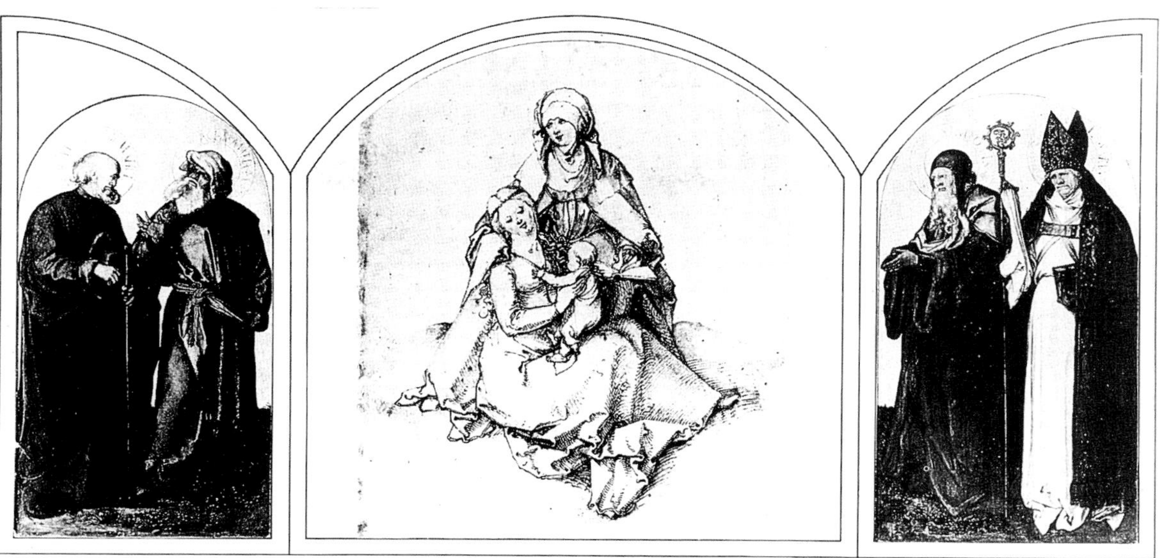

Cat 34 The Jabach Altarpiece. Reconstruction of the internal section

Cat 34 The Jabach Altarpiece. Saint Joseph and Saint Joachim

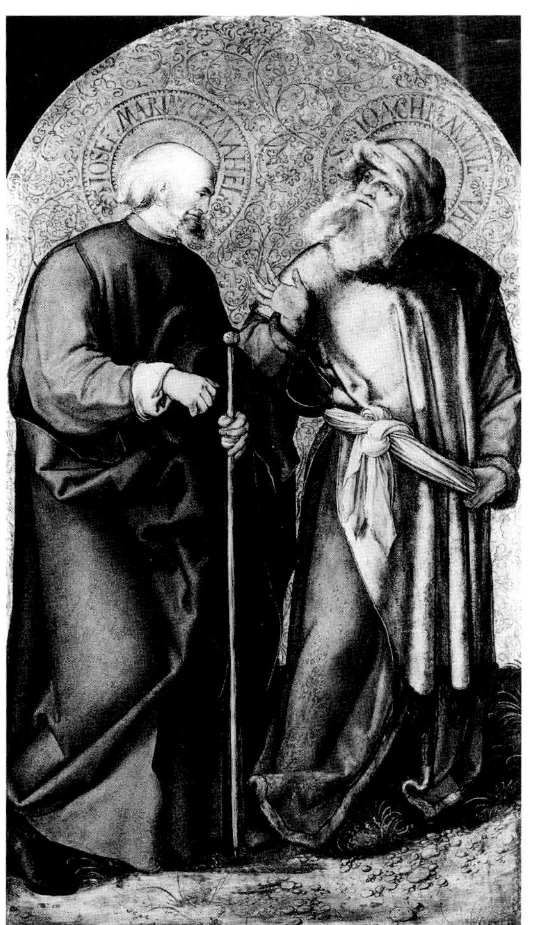

Cat 34 The Jabach Altarpiece. Saint Simeon and Saint Lazarus

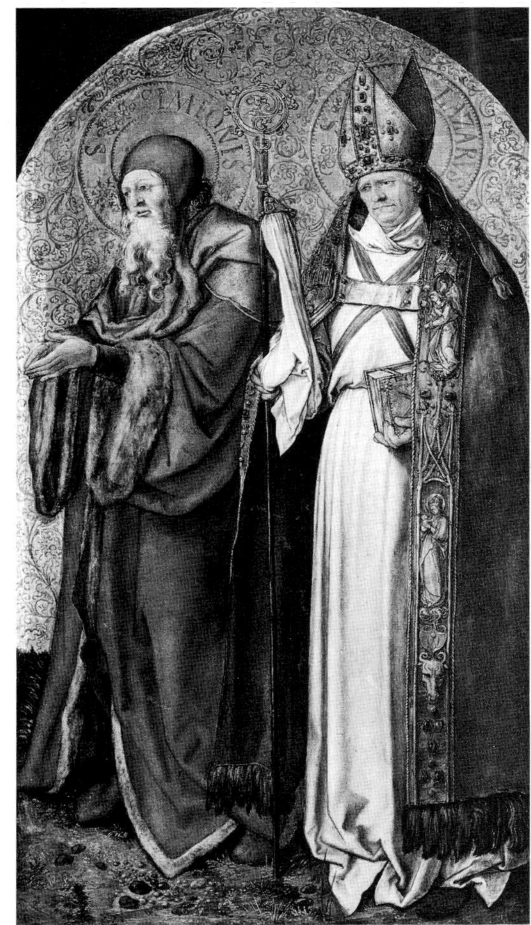

central panel.
While the hypothesis that the patron was Frederick the Wise hangs in the air, many clues indicate that the first seat of the altar was in a locality in Saxony, perhaps in the church of the Wittenberg castle.
A drawing exists (ill. in Anzelewsky, 1991, n. 67) by Cranach's school, which was active in Saxony. This drawing shows a copied and recomposed version of the story of Job and his wife, which is the subject of the exposed wings at the Wallraf-Richartz-Museum. These, in turn, would become, from technical operations executed on the wood of all four of the panels, the posterior face of those on which the four saints are represented. Once the wings are closed, the story of Job is recomposed, as mentioned for the drawing above.
The panels have undergone, over time, modifications to the upper edges.
As far as the central panel is concerned, of which no trace remains, Flechsig (1928) has hypothesized that it was a representation of a "Anna Selbdritt" e.g. *Saint Anne, The Madonna and the Christ Child*.
The proposal seems acceptable, since it is almost unthinkable that Saint Joseph and Saint Joachim were portrayed together without the Virgin Mary and Saint Anne.
For this, Anzelewsky (1991) proposed the drawing W 222 (see the reconstruction of the altar in the catalog).
The inscriptions on the saints' halos would support Flechsig's proposal: "Joseph Maria Gemahel" (Joseph, Mary's husband) and "Joachim Marie Vat[er]" (Joachim, Mary's father). In addition, Joachim is represented in the midst of a vision, and Simeon, who, upon his introduction to Christ in the temple, took him in his arms and prophesied great sufferings to Maria, holds his hands in an adoring gesture.
The four panels, unfortunately, are not very well preserved.
Despite the Dürer's monogram present in all four, and despite the preparatory drawing of Saint Lazarus, it is held that at least the doors with the four saints were painted with the assistance of the workshop. The gold background is probably an unusual return to the medieval manner.

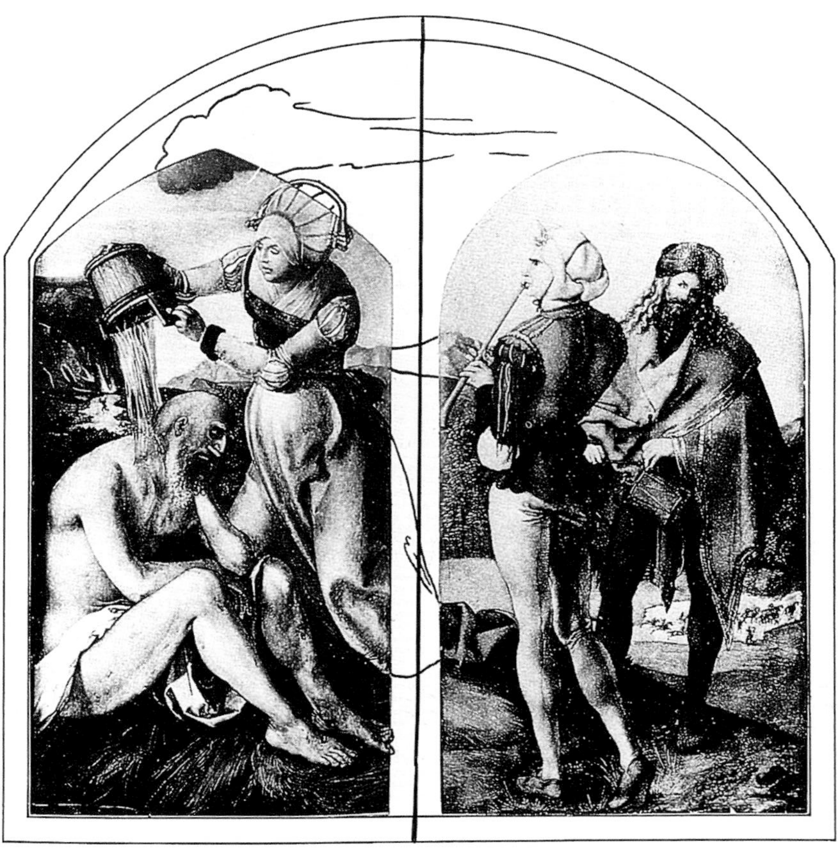

Cat 34 The Jabach Altarpiece. Reconstruction of the external section

Two wings (external part)

Job and His Wife
Lindenwood,
96 x 51 cm
Frankfurt,
Städelsches Kunstinstitut

Two Musicians
Lindenwood,
94 x 51 cm
Cologne,
Wallraf-Richartz-Museum

The episode of the mocking of Job does not exist in the Book of Job in the Old Testament. It probably came from the influence of the Biblia pauperum, which speaks of the mocking as a prefiguration to the torments of Christ. It is a rare subject in painting. Dürer interprets it with a scene in which Job is mocked by his wife: she pours a bucket of water on the poor man's naked body, which is covered with sores, and he, seated on a pile of dung, resignedly endures it; meanwhile, two minstrels join the scene by playing their instruments. In the background, at the top left, a rain of fire (Job 1, 18, 19 speak of a "great wind') (*cat.* 14) destroys the house of Job's eldest son.
A servant, however, manages to escape. We see him, a tiny figure running away from the burning house. To match this miniature scene, there is an illustration of another disgrace suffered by Job, in the background on the bottom right, behind the musicians: the assault of "three groups of Babylonian plunderers having mounted your camels and having killed all your men."
One link between the story of Job and the four saints represented in the other panels is that both Job and Lazarus are invoked as protectors from the plague. The Pre-Alpine landscape of the background and the wife's train pass from

one panel to the next without breaking the continuity, thus demonstrating what has been said regarding the probable original composition of the altarpiece.
The study of the bodies is impressive: the old nude and motionless Job, and his wife clad in typical Nuremberg dress pouring the water; and the minstrels, the one with the flute and the one with the little drum, the latter bearing a certain resemblance to Dürer. In the depiction of the two musicians that Dürer seems to have tried to represent the balance between motion and stasis of the Polycletus canon, the contrapposto, yet again (see *cat. 44*). This occurs in both figures individually and in their reciprocal interaction: between the frontal position of the drummer, and the flutist, viewed from behind, moving toward him.

35

The Adoration of the Magi

Inscription on the rock in the foreground, monogrammed and dated 1504
Panel,
99 x 113.52 cm
Florence,
Galleria degli Uffizi
1504

The elector Frederick the Wise of Saxony ordered this painting for the Schlosskirche (the church in the castle) in Wittenberg. It was once believed to be the central part of a polyptych, with, on the side wings, the story of Job, in Frankfurt and Cologne (*pl. 34*). However, this hypothesis has already been called into question by Panofsky (1948) (Anzelewsky 1991). The elector of Saxony then donated the painting to Emperor Rudolph II in 1603. An exchange with the Presentation at the Temple by Fra Bartolomeo brought it in 1793 from the gallery in Vienna to the Uffizi.
This altarpiece was probably conceived without the lateral panels, in contrast with the actual practice in Nordic countries, and at variance with the situation of the Paumgartner altarpiece (*cat. 28*). Dürer framed and delimited a large space by an architecture composed of arches of a very refined perspective. The three kings arrived at this slightly elevated space from the back and after having climbed two steps. A single figure, sharply foreshortened, followed in their footsteps from the distant background. Only the upper half of his body is shown where he now stands at the bottom of the two steps. He is Oriental and wearing a turban. The heavy traveling bag he holds probably contains precious gifts for the infant Jesus.
The Madonna is clad in azure clothes and cape, a white veil covering her head. She is holding out the infant, who is wrapped in her white veil, to the eldest king. He is offering the infant a gold casket with the image of Saint George, which the infant has already taken with his right hand. This is the only action that unfolds in the principal scene, except for the Oriental servant's gesture of putting his hand in his bag. All the other characters are motionless; immersed in thought, they look straight ahead or sideways, creating the effect of a staged spectacle set with immobile characters.
The architecture of the fictive ruins behind the Madonna is beautiful and imaginative. Dürer had previously experimented with this design in drawings and engravings. The background is stupendous: the limpid sky, in which the cumulus clouds chase one another; the light Nordic city, climbing up the cone-like mountain; the road bending into the archway where people stop, following behind the three kings. These are represented with much imagination and variety, as far as the fashion and color of their clothes and the differences in their expressions. In the far right are a lake and a boat.
This imagination and variety continue in the extraordinary depiction of the kings, in lavish clothing, with their precious jewels, and with the beautiful goblets and caskets that they bear as gifts. It is telling here that Dürer was also an expert goldsmith. According to the Nordic tradition, also adopted previously by Mantegna in Italy, one of the kings is a Moor. The physiognomy of the young king with long blond curly hair, standing in the middle of the painting, bears, according to recent interpretation, a resemblance to a self-portrait of Dürer. Panofsky attributes a Leonardesque character to him.
Dürer was passionately devoted to the study of animals and plants, which he reproduced faithfully from life. See the numerous colored drawings and watercolors: the Leveret and the Bouquet of Violets, from 1502, or the Great Piece of Turf (*fig. 6*) from 1503, just to mention a few.
He often distributed these images in his landscape passages (*cat. 9*), and particularly in his drawings and engravings of the Madonna. We find some here as well: in the foreground, to the right, a flying deer, already known from various watercolors (Koreny, 1985), which here symbolizes Christ; the plantain (plantago major) seen directly behind, whose healing properties were once much appreciated, recalls the spilled blood of Christ; in the foreground, now to the left, on the millstone beside the carnation, a small coleopterum surrounded by a few butterflies, the ancient symbol of the soul, which here may be a symbol of the resurrection.
The panel of the Uffizi represents the richest and most mature actualization of all Dürer's altarpieces, before his second trip to Italy, and therefore before the Feast of the Rose Garlands, painted in Venice (*cat. 39*).

36

Bremen Triptych

Center panel: **Salvator Mundi**
Lindenwood,
58 x 47 cm
New York, Metropolitan Museum,
Friedsam collection

Side wing: **Saint Onofrius**
Panel,
58 x 20 cm
Bremen, Kunsthalle

Side wing: **Saint John the Baptist**
Panel,
58 x 20 cm
Bremen, Kunsthalle
(lost since the end of the World War II)
ca. 1505

The center panel, already mentioned in the Imhoff inventories of 1573–74, passed in 1650 to the Hallers, a noble family of

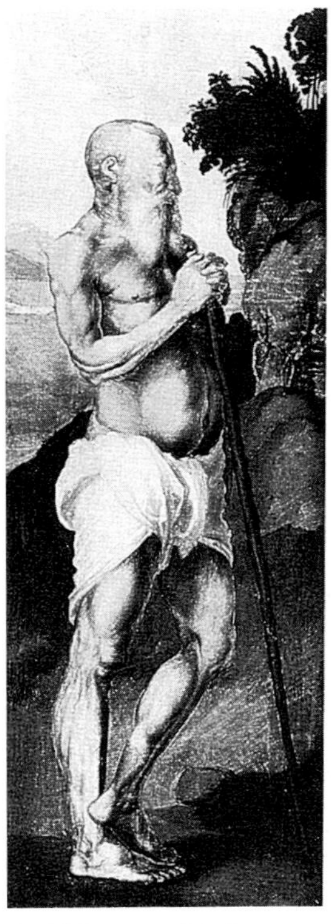
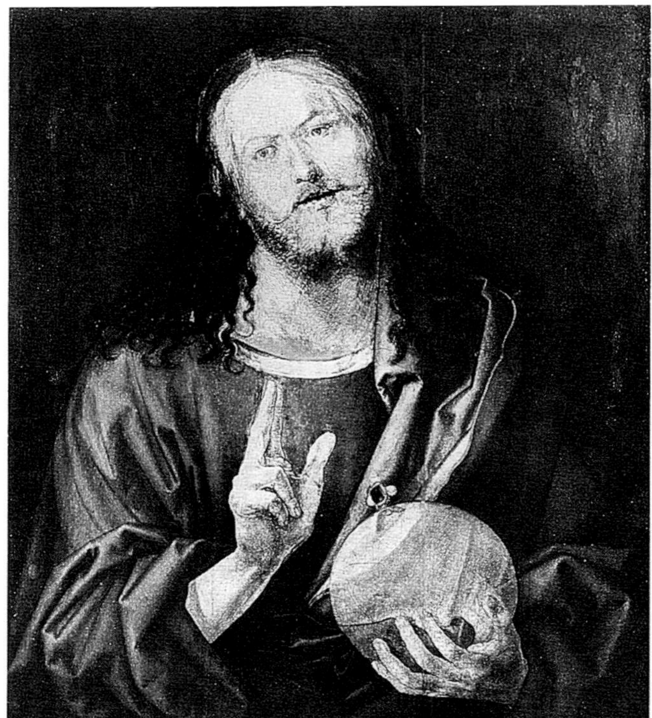
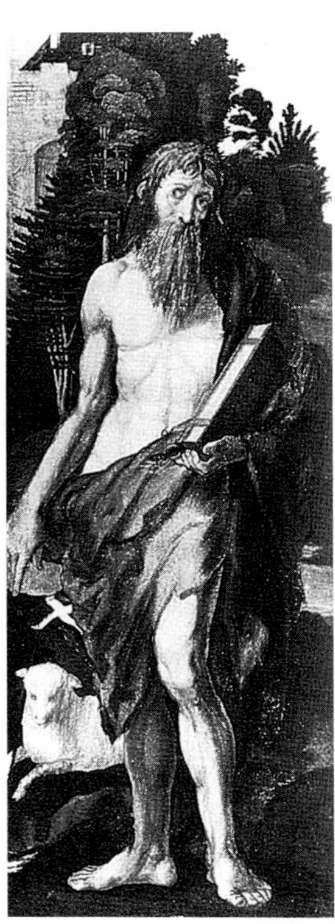

Cat 36 Bremen Triptych

Nuremberg. After traveling through many hands in the antique market and in the private collections, it landed at the Friedsam collection in 1921 and from there, it went on to the Metropolitan Museum, in 1931. The two side wings are in the Paul von Praun gallery in Nuremberg. In 1822, they were still to be found in the Heinlein collection in Nuremberg; in 1851, as a result of Senator H. Klugkist's bequest, they became part of the Bremen Gallery.
The first to suggest that the three unfinished panels probably were part of the same triptych was Flechsig (1928–31), who dated them 1505. It is probable that Dürer had begun to paint them in the period immediately preceding his departure for his second trip to Italy. The trip was possibly provoked by the reappearance of the plague in Nuremberg. This sudden departure impeded the completion of the work.
Many believe that Dürer was inspired by models of Jacobo de' Barbari for the Salvator Mundi. For Saint Onofrius, on the other hand, he was inspired by Giovanni Bellini's figure of Saint Job in the Altar of Saint Job of 1490.

37

Portrait of a Young Venetian Woman

Inscription in the top center, monogrammed and dated 1505
Oil on fir,
32.5 x 24.5 cm
Vienna, Kunsthistorisches Museum
1505

In the late eighteenth century, this panel was part of the collection of the mayor Danzica Schwartz, but in 1790 it was auctioned off by the wife of Schwartz's brother; in the early twentieth century, we find it in the Wancowicz collection in Lithuania. The portrait was then acquired from a private collection by the Kunsthistorisches Museum of Vienna, where it can still be found today. According to Schütz (1994), it represents one of the more important acquisitions made by the museum in the last hundred years.
The portrait is one of the first works of the artist during his second sojourn in Venice. It was painted in the autumn or in the winter of 1505. It was Fedja Anzelewsky (1971) who recognized the hairstyle of the young woman and the hairnet that covers it as typically Venetian, whereas the fashion of the clothing has been defined as typically Milanese by Weixelgärtner (1927), Tietze (1937) and Panofsky (1948). From the portraits, an extraordinary charm emanates, which cannot be merely attributable to the shades of brown and gold of the hairdo and clothing, which are set apart from the uniform black background. It is really the beauty of the portrait that fascinates in its entirety and in its variety of details. It is the slight wave of the hair on the clear, high forehead that imperceivably becomes curls caressing the girl's cheeks. It is the dreamy gaze that shows, under the slightly lowered eyelids, the radiant, black eyes. It highlights the play of light on the forehead and on the cheeks. It is the candor of this face, of the neck and chest, emphasized by a neckline of a contrasting color, that evoke the image of the ideal purity of a girl. With great ability, the artist includes in this image a long and pronounced

nose and large, sensual lips, immersing the whole figure in a light that reveals the important influence of the Venetian school, and, in particular, that of Giovanni Bellini.
With reference to some of the details, it has been repeatedly made known that the portrait is unfinished. It is probable that Dürer deliberately did not give the same intensity to the left ribbon as to the right: on the one hand, so as to not overwhelm the charm of the dark eyes; on the other, so as to support the subtle chromatic effect of the bodice that, from the design of the gold ribbons, contributes to the overall charm of the painting.
This charm is also shown in the movement in the double rows of pearls, interrupted by the darker shapes of doubled cones, making the pendant curve slightly from the neck.
Among Dürer's works, there is not a more beautiful portrait of a woman. Indeed, it has led one to think that there was a rather intimate relationship between the artist and the model. Some see the woman as a courtesan (Glück, 1933); others define her as an "instinctive, languorous, and melting beauty" (Winkler, 1957).

38

Portrait of a Venetian Woman

Inscription in the top left, monogrammed
Poplar, 28.5 x 21.5 cm
Berlin, Gemäldegalerie
1506

The Berlin museums acquired this panel on the antique market in London in 1893. Beforehand, it was in the Reginald Cholmondely collection.
The painting is poorly conserved. Almost all the final layers of color are missing. The eyes have been restored (Anzelewsky, 1991).
Because of the absence of the topmost layer of color, the painting has acquired a soft chromatic shading. Even if we know that Dürer executed it during his second sojourn in Italy, probably in the autumn of 1506 after the Feast of the Rose Garlands (*cat. 39*), workmanship seems particularly "Venetian." The refinement of the artist is clearly absent in the sketching of the hair (compare Portrait of a Young Venetian Woman, *cat. 37*). Some object is discernible in the curl hanging to the left.
Only a few traces of the hairnet have been preserved, and the sky blue of the background, which is inexplicably divided into two sections, is probably no longer its original shade. In its original state, however, this half-bust must have been in the Venetian style, because of her full, soft shapes, delicately modeled with a measured use of light. We must count this painting among the most beautiful works Dürer produced during his second sojourn in Venice.
The various attempts to identify the model—for example, as Agnes Dürer, because of the letters AD on the trimming of the clothes or the woman with her head turned in the middle right of the Feast of the Rose Garlands (pl. 39)—have not held up to criticism. The letters are probably the initials of a motto.

39

The Feast of the Rose Garlands

Inscription on the sheet,
in the artist's hand, monogrammed
and autograph writing:
EXEGIT QUINQUE MESTRI SPATIO
ALBERTUS DURER GERMANUS MDVI
Poplar,
162 x 194.5 cm
Prague, Národni Galerie
1506

This panel was painted for an altar for the German community in Venice, in the church of S. Bartolomeo near the Fondaco dei Tedeschi, the social and commercial center of the German colony, where it remained until 1606. It was then acquired, after many negotiations, for 900 ducats by Emperor Rudolph II. According to Sandrart (1675), four men were hired to bring the packaged painting to the emperor's residence in Prague.
Stationed elsewhere during the invasion of the Swedish troops, the painting, already very damaged, returned to its place in 1635. It underwent a first restoration in 1662. In 1782, it was sold in an auction for one florin. After having passed through the hands of various collectors, it was acquired by the Czechoslovakian state in 1930.
The painting, severely damaged chiefly in the center portion, from the head of the Madonna and continuing downward to the bottom, was clumsily restored in the nineteenth century; in this restoration, the upper side portion, left of the canopy and to Saint Dominic's head, was also included (see ill.) Three copies of the work are known: one—considered the most important and which now belongs to a private collection—is attributed to Hans Rottenhamer, who sojourned in Venice from 1596 to 1606, where he took care of many acquisitions on behalf of Rudolph II; another is in Vienna; and the third, a rather modified version of the original, is in Lyon (Anzelewsky, 1991, with reproductions of these last two).
The preparatory work of the panel occupied the artist for a long time, from 7 February until the last half of April in 1506. It consists of twenty-one preparatory drawings, executed chiefly in pen and ink on azure paper, according to the Venetian tradition; others are drawings of various characters, in the dimensions then adopted for the painting (W 380–401). In a letter dated 25 September, addressed to Willibald Pirckheimer, the artist communicates the completion of the work. (Rupprich, 1956–69, I).
It seems that the Confraternity of the Blessed Rosary was officially recognized by the Venetian authorities in 1506, that is, in the year Dürer carried out the painting. In comparing his panel with the woodcut to the writing of Jakob Sprenger about the foundation of the same Confraternity, having appeared in Augsburg in 1476 (see ill.; Wölfflin, 1905), suggests that it was well known to him. All this implies—even if no document exists to prove it, and none of the names of the members are known—that the painting was ordered by the same Confraternity.
On the whole, the majority of the figures in the painting have not been identified. The exceptions to this include the self-portrait of the artist; the portrait of Emperor Maximilian I; the one of the architect Hieronymus of Augsburg, engineer of the new Fondaco dei Tedeschi (1505–8) after it was completely destroyed in a fire, and who is recogniz-

Cat 39 Festa del Rosario, stato di conservazione

able in the far right by the square he holds; and Burckhard from the city Speyer, identified as the fourth figure form the left (see *cat. 40*).
Saint Dominic is clearly the saint whom we see to the left of the Madonna, since the institution of the rosary is attributed to him. For all the others, many names have been proposed. For example, the more recent attribution of Strieder (1989) and Anzelewsky (1991), maintain that the highly characterized figure that appears just behind the emperor bears a resemblance to a representative of the Fugger house (*cat. 62*), a powerful family of the sixteenth century, who obviously shared in the financing of the work. In fact, when Rudolph II acquired it, he sought their consent. However, the identification, especially of a specific person, is still uncertain. The Madonna is enthroned in a field, beneath a green canopy that cherubs hold up with ribbons. Other cherubs on little clouds hold a crown of precious stones suspended above her head. At her feet kneel the pope and the emperor, on the left and right, having placed before themselves a tiara and a crown, respectively. And while the Madonna places a garland of roses on the head of the emperor, the Blessed Child places an identical one over the head of the pontifice. Saint Dominic, in turn, crowns a bishop. Behind the pope and the emperor, the patrons are arranged symmetrically, some of whom, in both parts of the background, divert their gaze from the Madonna. Other Bellinian cherubs descend upon them with rose garlands. In the center of the painting, seated in front of the throne, an angel playing a lute recalls the angels playing at the feet of the enthroned Madonna in Giovanni Bellini's paintings. These details aside, the setting of the work is typically Venetian, (Panofsky 1977). The rigidly pyramidal composition of the painting is not Venetian. This painting has indicated that Dürer was one to have been of the first who created such composition (Erika and Hans Tietze, 1937–38).
The Feast of the Rose Garlands is undoubtedly the most important work that Dürer created during his sojourn in Venice and was the work that ushered in the Renaissance. Dürer was obviously aware of this, as his letters and the painting itself demonstrate. The painting shows this in the distinction he gives his self-portrait: in the top right, in front of the typically German landscape passage at the foot of the mountains, with his face framed by long blond hair, donning luxurious clothes—even a precious fur cloak, in spite of the warm season—so as to be noticed among the other characters. He alone has ostentatiously turned his gaze to the spectator. Even the writing on the paper he holds is unusual for Italy. It indicates not only the time of production (five months), but next to his own name is the indication germanus. This detail was to distinguish himself from his Venetian colleagues, who evidently held him in very high regard, since even the doge and the patriarch came to his workshop to admire his work.

40

Burkhard von Speyer
Inscription, monogrammed and dated 1506
Oil on panel,
32 x 27 cm
Windsor Castle,
coll. of H. M. the Queen
1506

This painting was present in the collection of Charles I of England. A comparison of the subject of this painting with that of a miniature dated 1506, located in the Schlossmuseum of Weimar and with its subject identified as Burkhard von Speyer, confirms that the portrayal is of the same person. This same person is recognizable, within a reasonable margin of probability, in the figure who, in the Feast of the Rose Garlands (*cat. 39*), is seen on the left, directly behind the young cardinal. This suggests that Burkhard, a relatively unknown figure, was part of the Venetian German community. Like the Portrait of a Youth (*cat. 41*), this portrait was executed during Dürer's second sojourn in Venice, between 23 September and 23 October 1506. The face in this portrait, as in the other, painted in clear pink shades, occupies almost the entire space of the painting. Even the dimensions of the two paintings are identical. It is Bellinian; even the beret is probably from Venetian fashion.
Dürer has captured the head from a po-

sition lower than the subject. The perspective from such an angle causes the very pronounced chin, mouth, and nose to occupy most of the face, leaving a fairly narrow and sunken space for the relatively small, slightly different from each other, light-colored eyes in the upper portion of the face. The resulting contrast, between physiognomy and gaze, confers a deeply pensive look to the portrait. The fine, light red hair, depicted very carefully, as usual, is somewhat darker than the face it frames. The light that originates from the left highlights the contrast in the colors of the head and the attire: the white of the shirt, the red of the garment over the shoulders, the light shade of the trim of the fur, the black of the two ribbons crossing in front. Despite the limits of the space, the result is a suggestive and serene image, typical of his second sojourn in Venice.
The height of this portrait, as of the one of Vienna (*cat. 37*), is quite small (32 cm), so it gets numbered, with the portraits of the Tucher family (*cat. 20, 22*), among the "portable" family portraits. The reduced dimensions were perhaps chosen because they would facilitate transportation, an important consideration to the subject, who was painted during his temporary sojourn in Venice.

41

Portrait of a Young Man

Inscription at the top,
monogrammed and writing:
ALBERTUS DÜRER GERMANUS FACIEBAT POST VIRGINIS PARTUM 1506
Panel, 50 x 40 cm
Genoa, Palazzo Rosso
1506

The restoration carried out of after the Second World War involved the removal of the opaque varnish that protected this painting and revealed it to be much better preserved than was previously thought. Nevertheless, the face is not finished (Anzelewsky, 1991), and it appears slightly flat, despite the vivaciousness of the eyes. The contrast of the colors of the clothing and beret (charcoal and black, respectively) against the green background elicits a remarkable effect. So does the gentle depiction of the face framed by soft, chestnut hair. The portrait, which can be considered typical of the era, according to Anzelewsky, can be dated accurately: a letter that Dürer sent at that time from Venice to Willibald Pirckheimer (Rupprich, 1956–59) makes clear that it must have been carried out between 23 September 1506, and 23 October 1506, that is, after the Feast of the Rose Garlands (*pl. 39*) and before the Madonna with the Siskin (*pl. 42*).

42

The Madonna with the Siskin

Inscription, monogrammed,
on a scroll on the small table to the left,
autograph: ALBERTUS DÜRER GERMANUS FACIEBAT POST VIRGINIS PARTUM 1506.
Poplar, 91 x 76 cm
Berlin, Gemäldegalerie
1506

In the second half of the sixteenth century, this painting was in Nuremberg; in 1600, it was part of the collection of Rudolph II, as Carel von Mander notes (1617).
In the 1860s, it reappeared and became the property of the marquis of Lothian of Edinburgh, from whom the Berlin museum acquired it in 1893.
In a letter of 23 September 1506 from Venice addressed to Willibald Pirckheimer, in which Dürer writes that he has completed the Feast of the Rose Garlands (*cat. 39*), he also speaks of having just finished another painting. It would most likely be the Madonna with the Siskin (Arnolds, 1959), which the artist brought back to Nuremberg with him.
It is astonishing that Dürer does not mention any patrons for this large painting, full of iconographical references. He created it simply by drawing on his own culture and experience.
The work is conceived following the dictates of Venetian painting: a monumental Madonna, with the red gown covered by an azure cloak, who sits enthroned before a curtain that is also red, in a landscape pervaded by an especially clear light.
A Florentine trademark is represented in the presence of Saint John, even if this detail was also rather common in the Venetian painting by this time (Panofsky, 1955). The Madonna's rapt gaze is directed slightly off to the side, while her right hand rests on the Old Testament, in which is prophesied the birth of the new king. She almost unconsciously accepts a lily of the valley (convallaris majalis) from Saint John with her other hand. It is the flower symbolic of the Immaculate Conception and the Incarnation of Christ (Levi d'Ancona, The Garden of the Renaissance, 1977).
The small saint, however, does not look at her; his gaze is directed to Jesus, whose divine nature Saint John is the first to recognize.
The infant Jesus is seated in his mother's lap on a rich red cushion. With his right hand, he elegantly lifts a sort of soother—a tiny pouch, apparently filled with poppy seeds, on which babies would suck and be calmed.
His left hand, which holds the edge of his little shirt, probably just unfastened (see the open clasp), comes toward his face. In the preparatory drawing (W 408), Dürer had represented him with a more solemn expression, while he raised the cross staff; but perhaps in changing the staff, the symbol of the Passion, with the poppy-seed soother—poppy seeds symbolic of sleep and death, if this is actually what it contains—the artist wanted to preserve the childlike manner of the infant Jesus, without altering the symbolism.
The siskin—in the place of the goldfinch—perched on his arm points his beak toward his head, where one day the crown of thorns will be; the child smiles affectionately at Saint John below him, to whom a little angel, with a meaningful gaze, is holding the cross staff out to him, though the saint and child do not take notice.
To the ruins represented in perspective on the left corresponds a tree in bloom growing from a fallen trunk on the right.
The former is a symbol of the fall of the Old Covenant, or perhaps an image of the ruins of David's palace, where, according to the legend, the nativity stable stood. The latter is a sign of life and of the New Covenant.
Two cherubs crown the Madonna with a garland of vine shoots of roses, in

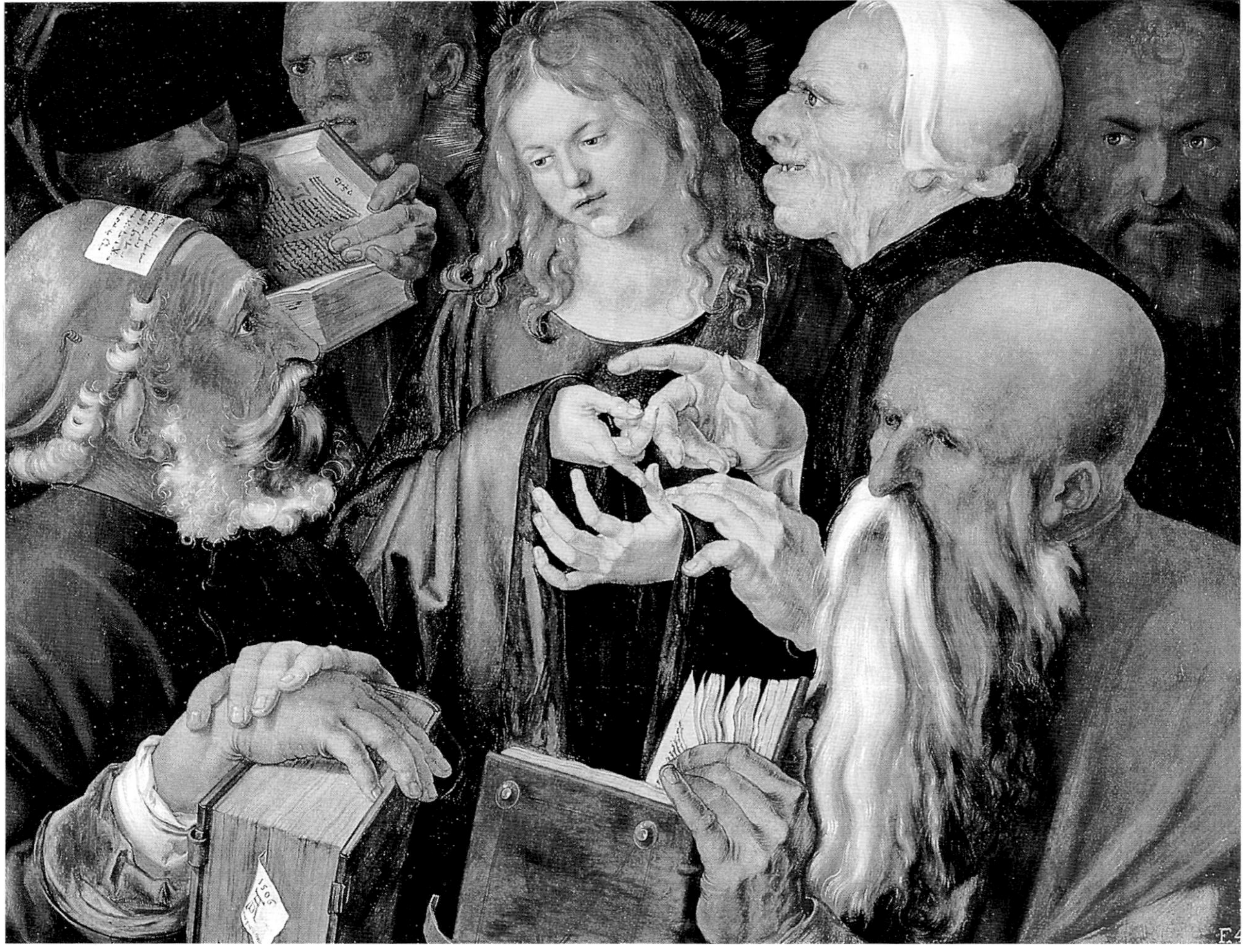

Cat 43 Christ among the Doctors

which are woven a white rose, symbol of her joy, and two red roses, symbol of her sufferings.
Dürer's main accomplishment in this painting is in the perfect combination of form and content. Each of the characters expresses his or her own emotion, yet everyone together is composed in a convincing, unified story, the symbols included.
Unfortunately, the poor state of preservation greatly disturbs the impression of overall harmony that characterizes the panel.
This can be appreciated thoroughly in another painting found in the same museum, the tondo Terranuova Madonna, the brilliant and nearly contemporary work of Raphael.

About ten years later, Titian captures the Saint John of this painting in his Madonna with the Cherries, at the Kunsthistorisches Museum in Vienna.
He takes up again the soft depiction of the hair and veil that covers his shoulders, and changes only slightly the position of the arm (Tietze, 1937; Panofsky, 1959).
This suggests that he had seen and appreciated Dürer's work during its painting in his Venetian workshop.

43

Christ among the Doctors

Inscription on the bookmark sticking out from the book on the left, monogrammed and dated 1506 (it once read: F. ROMAE / OPUS QUINQUE DIER[UM]*)*
Panel,
65 x 80 cm
Madrid,
Museo Reina Sofia
1506

Because the painting was first attributed to Dürer in 1837 by Nagler, when it was part of the Palazzo Barberini collection in Rome, it is possible that the work, painted in Rome, remained there. In 1934, it was acquired for the Thyssen collection in Lugano, and recently, it was sold together along with the entire collection to the museum in Madrid.
It was not until Günter Arnolds, in 1939, succeeded in deciphering the entire inscription from a copy in a drawing, that

Dürer's stay in Rome from the end of 1506 to the beginning of 1507 could be sufficiently established. It was apparently a brief sojourn, given that not many other traces of it remain and that, in the beginning of 1507, he was on his way back to Venice.
This painting is an uncommon work, a talented display of skill and destined to remain a collection painting. The overabundance of figures in such a narrow space has been criticized, given the fact that Dürer, on his way to Rome, had stopped off in Bologna to study perspective. The matrix matrices of this painting are mixed: Venice for its composition, Leonardo for the faces, and eloquent language of the gestures. No one has ever thought about analyzing the "story" of the painting to find out its proper content.
A young, beautiful, and tender Jesus shows with his right index finger that he is talking about a first argument, while the eldest of the doctors, beside him, ugly, pale, and indignant, has already exhausted all his arguments, as you can infer from the just lifted position of his right index finger and his folded left little finger. In turn, the doctor to the left has already closed his book and rests his folded hands passively on top of it, looking attentively though appallingly at the elder one, who has exhausted all his arguments. His younger colleague, right above him, looking rather like a simpleton, is searching frantically and uselessly through his papers for some new pretext. The old bald doctor alone, absorbed in thought, seems to distance himself from the book.
All these figures are so near to one another and pushed into the foreground that it causes an extreme sense of distress in the observer. Only the calm twelve-year-old Jesus demonstrates absolute superiority to all the very learned men.
In the top right, another old man casts a look onto the group: one understands that he has listened to everything very carefully, but that he lacks faith. On the opposite side, beside Jesus, a youth with a tense expression faces forward, telling whoever looks at him the distressing tension of the discussion.
After long preparatory studies (W 404–7), Dürer painted the panel in just five days.

44

Adam and Eve

Adam
Pine,
209 x 81 cm

Eve
Inscription on the small table:
ALBERTUS DÜRER ALEMANUS / FACIEBAT POST VIRGINIS / PARTUM 1507;
monogrammed
Pine, 209 x 83 cm
Madrid, Museo del Prado
1507

In 1587, both the works were in the collection of Rudolph II, in Prague. From there, they were purloined by Swedish troops and brought to Stockholm. In 1654, Queen Christina donated them to Philip IV of Spain.
There are several preparatory studies Dürer made of human proportions, which he had already begun during his second sojourn in Venice: a drawing in which he sketches the Apollo Belvedere; a second drawing, in pen and ink; the engraving in 1504; and finally, the important paintings that we are presently treating.
Adam's complexion is slightly darker and less bright than Eve's. His wavy hair, slender legs, the right heel just lifted off the ground, are in perfect balance, according to the classical canon of Polycletus, the contrapposto, rediscovered in the early Renaissance. The whole figure is outstretched in an amorous movement, with slightly parted lips; only the gesture of the right hand hints of Adam's instinctive initial hesitation.
Eve, on the contrary, is more active, more concrete: she shows signs of a step and while casting an inviting look to Adam, she gently smiles. Both figures are twisting slightly toward the other. Dürer determined to sing the praises of the beauty of the Creation in his presentation of the first human couple. He gave his figures life with a very skilled depiction of movement, thus actualizing one of the finest examples of representation of the human form.
One of the copies of the work, probably by his student Hans Baldung Grien, is found in Florence at the Uffizi Gallery.

45

Portrait of a Young Man

Inscription in the top right, monogrammed; in the top: dated 1507
Oil on Lindenwood,
35 x 29 cm
Vienna, Kunsthistorisches Museum
1507

This painting probably came from the collection of Rudolph II. Dürer returned to Nuremberg in the spring of 1507, after his second sojourn in Venice. Opinions differ as to the whereabouts of the painting of this portrait, which demonstrates, on the one hand, all the pictorial characteristics of the Venetian tradition (following in the steps of Giovanni Bellini, according to Winkler, 1929; or Vicenzo Catena, according to Panofsky, 1943), and shows the depiction of a youth wearing a typically Venetian beret, which would mean it was Venice; on the other hand, the type of wood used for the panel, lindenwood, would have its execution in Nuremberg, upon his return. It should be recalled that Dürer only used panels of poplar while in Venice, or, rarely, elm. The alternative, regarding the setting and brightness of the portrait being typically Venetian, in fact, is purely speculative.
The portrait almost aggressively approaches the spectator. It is dominated by a light, slightly reddish face, an intense, far-off gaze, a short and robust nose, a wide mouth, and turgid lips surmounted by a hint of downy hair. Even the beard under the chin is delicate and contrasts with the almost frizzy hair, painted with an extremely thin brush. Despite the fact that the painting is not completely preserved in this area, one can still appreciate the extraordinary skill of execution. One appreciates above all the difference between the stroke used for the hair and the one, just as skillful though different, adopted for the hairs of the fur collar, giving a showy trim to the coat. His talent drew praise from the Venetians and particular admiration from Giovanni Bellini (see introduction). The snow-white of the shirt represents the third note of color of the painting, next to the delicate pink of the

flesh and to the black, found in the elegantly worn beret and in the clothing, silhouetted against the similarly black background.
He employs what he learned from Venetian painting and his special talent for painting, with very fine strokes for hair and fur—a talent that markedly distinguishes him from his Venetian colleagues.
Dürer thus manages to vivify even a face like this one, that except for the mouth, has rigid and immobile features, and for that, on the whole, is not very expressive.

Verso

On the reverse side, without a preparatory drawing and with light brush strokes, an ugly old woman is painted, who winks rather obscenely. She reveals her nude breast and holds a bag of coins. A closer view recalls, as the Tietzes have already noted in 1937, the Old Woman by Giorgione with the writing col tempo at the Academy of Venice, which represents the allegory of human transience.
In this case, the patron of the portrait could have asked Dürer to paint a figure that represented voluptas, luxuria, and perhaps vanitas (Anzelewsky, 1991), which was to be so revolting so as to serve as a warning about the temptations of these vices. Anzelewsky (1991, p. 39) suggests that Dürer had referred to a model by Leonardo.
With the original frame lost, it is unfortunately impossible to know if this small painting was to be part of a diptych, as some have put forward.

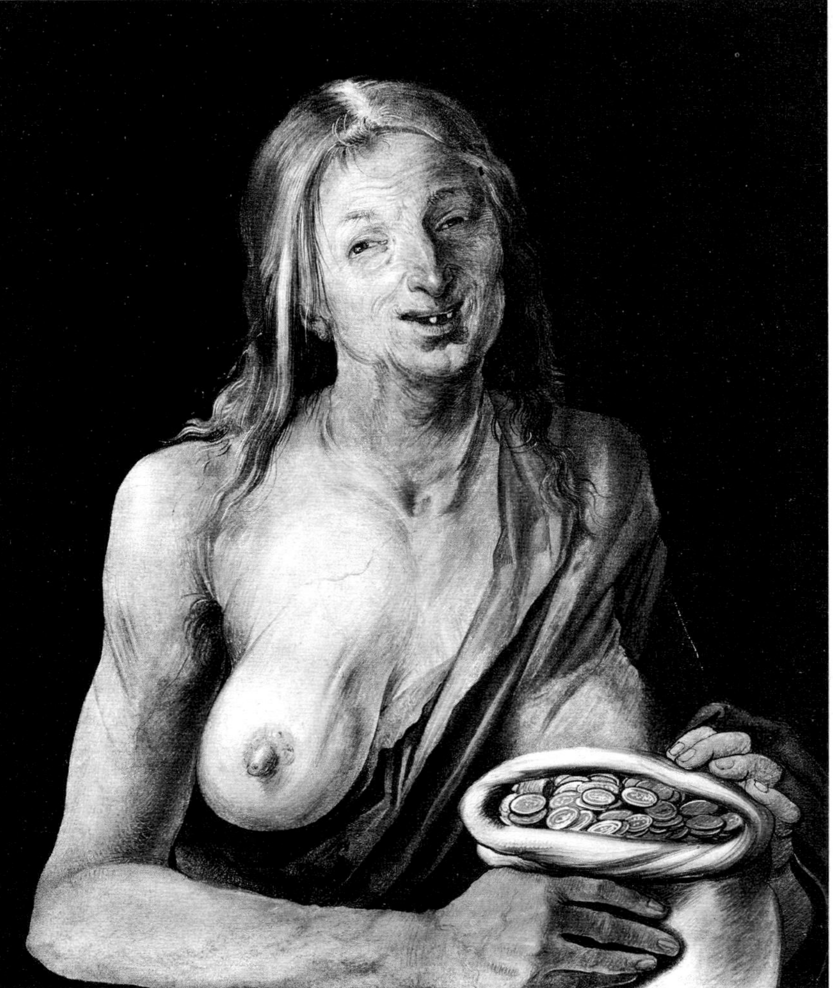

Cat 45 verso

46

Portrait of a Young Girl

Inscription in the top right, monogrammed and dated 1507
Panel, transferred from parchment, 30.4 x 30 cm
Berlin, Gemäldegalerie
1507

This small painting was in the collection of the Imhoff family of Nuremberg, and cited in their inventory from 1573–74 until 1628. In 1633, it was handed over, with the title Portrait of a Young Girl, with other works by Dürer, to Abraham Bloemart, an artist and merchant from Amsterdam.
An identical portrait, judging from the description, and cited as a "copy of Dürer," was found in the register of the collection of Archduke Leopoldo Gugliemo in 1659.
In 1899, the portrait reappears in London, and the firm P. and D. Colnaghi donated it to the Berlin art gallery (Anzelewsky, 1991).
The delicate girl is portrayed with soft, curly blond hair, slightly dreamy her eyes, one somewhat lower than the other, a gentle, melancholic gaze; and well-defined, slightly parted lips. The red beret, worn sideways, with a little slit to the side, with a long red ruby and black pearl pendant, gives her a slightly cheeky air.
The square green border of the red bodice sets off the upper part of her body. All these details put together have led to various interpretations. In addition to the fact that the "girl," when sold by the Imhoffs, was transformed into a "boy," Panofsky (1955) attributes an androgynous nature to her that could reveal the possible homosexual tendencies of the artist.
A teasing letter of 1507 from the canonical Lorenz Behaim of Bamberg and the fact that the portrait does not seem to have been ordered would support this

hypothesis.
It has also been debated whether the painting was executed in Venice or after Dürer's return to Nuremberg.
According to Anzelewsky, who considers the clothing to be typically German, there is no doubt as to its provenance. Justi (1902) speaks of a "reconstructed" imaginary portrait; but even if frontal portraits are quite rare for Dürer, the many discussions provoked by this would tend to exclude such a possibility.

47

The Martyrdom of the Ten Thousand

Inscription on the paper attached to the stick that Dürer holds, signed and dated in the inscription:
ISTE FACIEBAT AÑO DOMINI 1508
ALBERT[US] DÜRER ALEMAN[US]
Canvas, transferred from panel, 99 x 87 cm
From the Schlosskirche of Wittenberg. Vienna, Kunsthistorisches Museum
1508

Dürer executed the painting in 1508 for Frederick the Wise (*cat.*11), directly following his return from Italy. He was compensated 280 Rhineland florins. In 1549, on orders from Emperor Charles V, it was sent to Antwerp and given to Nicolas Perrenot, his chancellor. It then passed from his son, Cardinal Granvella, to his grandson, the count of Cantecroy, who sold it to Emperor Rudolph II for 13,000 talers in 1600. In 1617, the painting was still in Prague, where Carel van Mander saw and described it. Since 1619, it has been in Vienna, where Joachim van Sandrart described it in 1675.
Frederick the Wise had gathered an enormous quantity of relics in the Stiftskirche of Wittenberg, among which many were of the legendary martyrdom of the ten thousand of Bitinia, particularly those of the Saints Achatius and Hermolaus (Anzelewsky, 1991). This fact explains why he chose, for the painting commissioned to Dürer, an episode so removed from the common iconographical theme. The legend that it refers to probably arrived in Europe during the Crusades; however, it did not appear earlier than the twelfth century (Schütz, 1994). It narrates the story of Emperor Adrian, who recruited for a military campaign in Asia the pagan Prince Achatius, with nine thousand soldiers. During the advances against the enemy, who outnumbered them, an angel appeared to Achatius and promised him a victory despite the menacing superiority of the adversaries. After the victorious battle, the angel reappeared, directing him toward Mount Ararat; here, the prince and his soldiers converted to Christianity. The emperor, enraged, decided to slaughter them all and employed the Persian king Sapor II, along with other Eastern princes, for the massacre. Meanwhile, in addition to Achatius's nine thousand soldiers, the thousand Eastern soldiers were baptized; and after having been tortured and having suffered atrocious torments, they were all killed (Anzelewsky, 1991). The same legend, in a different contest, had already been illustrated by Dürer ten years earlier in a woodcut.
The character lavishly attired, seated on horseback, with an enormous turban and a scepter, who looks at the observer, represents in all likelihood King Sapor of Persia. In front of him, in the foreground, in white clothes, a white turban, and an azure cloak, another high-ranking Easterner is imparting the orders for the tortures and killings, which are readily carried out before his very eyes with clubs and axes. The representation of the violence of the torturers and the various positions of their victims, on their knees and lying on the ground, demonstrates the wide knowledge Dürer had acquired about the human form and laws of perspective. Notice, in particular, the figure whose head is about to be smashed: the artist had apparently studied classical sculpture and Italian painting modeled on classical art. An incredible display of knowledge of human physiognomy is evident in the head cut off from the man beside the first. A refined psychological sensibility and pictorial mastery characterize almost all the figures of this tragic scene: for example, the almost cinematographic sequence of the people who are made to fall from the cliff in the top left (Panofsky, 1955), or the highly dramatic representation in perspective of the crucifixions and the various fragments of crosses on the ground. The Bellinian precepts are revealed in the color scheme of the sunset; even the child who plays with the dog, in the corner on the bottom right, has Italian echoes.
The bishop of Nicomedia, Hermolaus (Anzelewsky, 1991, with a bibliography) has been identified in the figure in the center of the painting. He is being accused by a man with pointed gestures in front of an Eastern figure, who, then indicates the pathway of martyrdom. Achatius, on the other hand, is probably represented in the figure with the crown of thorns who moves in front of the crucifixions in the foreground.
In the visual center of the painting, it is clear that Dürer, as usual, looks toward the spectator. This time, he is not wearing rich and gaudy costumes; his black attire expresses his mourning for the recent death of his friend Konrad Celtis, poeta laureatus, professor of poetics at the University of Vienna and well known to Frederick the Wise as well (Panofsky, 1955). In the painting, Celtis stands beside him and with his right hand, looking out to the observer, he indicates sadly the scene of the martyrdom.
The painting, impressive also chromatically, is not an altarpiece but a devotional image; the particular care that Dürer devoted to it makes it a piece of exquisite quality, a classic collector's piece. A copy of a preparatory drawing for the painting exists in Vienna as well, in which is sketched a horizontal development of the martyrdom scene; even from the point of view of content, the definitive version presents various modifications.

48

Heller Altar

Central element
Assumption and Coronation of the Virgin
Copy by Jobst Harrich, ca. 1614
Cuts at the upper and lower parts and at the sides
Inscription on the table before the self-portrait: ALBERTVS DVRER ALEMANVS FACIEBAT POST VIRGINIS PARTVM 1509; *monogrammed*
Tempera and oil, 189 x 138 cm
From the Church of the Dominicans in Frankfurt am Main, Frankfurt am Main Historisches Museum, 1508–9

This altarpiece was commissioned by Jakob Heller (1460–1522), a wealthy merchant, member of the town council, and mayor of Frankfurt, either before or after Dürer's second trip to Italy. On 28 August 1507, Dürer informed Heller that he could not finish the work, which was intended for the elector of Saxony, Frederick the Wise (*cat. 47*), because of an illness that included a high fever. The panel was probably begun in April 1508. The preparatory works for the panel and frame—background preparation, gilding—had already been carried out by other artisans. In mid-March 1508, the external sides of the wings had been prepared for painting, and the drawing of the central panel was ready. In a letter dated 21 March, Dürer told Heller that the coloration of the background of the panel had also been completed. In a letter of 26 August 1509, Dürer assures him that he can deliver the finished work to Hans Imhoff so that it arrives in Frankfurt. Jakob Heller paid 130 florins; however, Dürer obtained seventy more, after prolonged negotiation. Nine letters bear witness to the progress of the work; copies have been published by Rupprich 1956-1969).

The center panel of the altar, with the monochromatic gray on gray wings—these made by the workshop—to which were later added two more wings painted by Grünewald (these, too, monochromatic) was dedicated to Saint Thomas Aquinas. It was placed in front of the first pillar to the right of the entrance of the Dominican church in Frankfurt, dedicated to the Beatissima Maria Virgo ad coelus assumpta. Heller had a grill stationed in front of the polyptych with two huge, tall candles perpetually burning. One hundred and five years later, in 1614, the brothers sold the central panel alone to Duke Maximilian of Bavaria for 8,000 florins. The amount was the changed into an annuity of 400 florins, which was paid until 1781. In 1729, the painting was destroyed by a fire in his residence in Munich. Fortunately, a copy of the work remained in the Dominican church. It had been executed by Jobst Harrich of Nuremberg (ca. 1580–1617) when the original had been sold. But even this one was not to remain there long. The wings of the polyptych were already detached in 1742. The remaining parts were sawed apart and the various pieces housed in different places throughout the Dominican convent. After its secularization, the Museumsgesellschaft saw to the reunification of the pieces, and in 1877, the entire Heller Altar went to the Historisches Museum. The restorations performed on the panel in 1791 and again in 1956 stripped the uppermost layer completely. Hardly anything at all remains of the work by the Dürerian copyist Harrich or from the master. The evaluation of the center panel of the largest altarpiece painted by the artist can only be based on a compositional, perhaps a formal and, limited chromatic study (Pfaff, 1971).

The theme and composition were previously discussed and established by Heller for Dürer, so that not another word was mentioned in the ensuing correspondence. There is still mention, on the other hand, of the preciosity of the colors, chiefly the sea blue. A drawing from 1503 (W 337) could perhaps represent the first outline of the work.

The theme of the assumption and of the coronation of the Madonna was familiar in Nuremberg painting of the fifteenth century (Panofsky, 1977). But Dürer gives it a particular Renaissance interpretation. The doubting Saint Thomas (or Saint John, perhaps? as the favorite apostle is absent from the group) bows over to the inside of the emptied sarcophagus in the foreground and clings to the linens that wrapped the body of the Madonna. He demonstrates the difficulty he has in convincing himself that the assumption is truly happening. His lowered head is painted by Dürer in a sharp foreshortening.

The other apostles are standing or kneeling around the sarcophagus. Saint Peter and Saint Paul, in the foreground, turn their backs to the observer opening the view onto Saint Thomas and the landscape behind the group. In the center-ground of the landscape, Dürer stands as usual with the explicative tablet and his gaze fixed straight ahead. The background presses into the far distance, toward a lake enclosed by hills, peppered with buildings. A broad and tranquil landscape contrasts with the monumental, concentrated and restless group of apostles. While the doubting Saint Thomas is still looking for proof of the Assumption, the other apostles, arranged in an ascending semicircle to the left and right, have already recognized it. In the sky, in a semicircle of clouds, accompanied and held by a flock of cherubs, the Madonna rises toward the Eternal Father and Jesus Christ, as they wait to crown her. The faces and gestures of the men express an endless bewilderment at the sight of the miracle that is unfolding before their eyes. The variety and vigor that distinguishes the apostles, who disagree among themselves, is opposed to the monumentality of the isolated group in the foreground, consisting of the princes of the apostles, Saint Peter and Saint Paul. Each detail of the panel—for example, the bare feet of Saint Peter, precluding a Caravaggio—has been carefully studied. Eighteen preparatory drawings that still exist demonstrate this (W 448–65). They are in pencil on paper, with an azure, green background. The famous Hands in Prayer also is part of these drawings.

The entire episode was conceived with an unusual grandiosity and an intimate participation. Dürer expresses this in the vigor of the colors and, most of all, in the spaciousness and wealth of the clothes. It is modeled on a Raphael citation—twelve years his younger—and his Coronation of the Madonna, painted in 1502–3 and ordered by Alessandra degli Oddi for the chapel of the Oddi in the church of Saint Francis in Perugia. In Dürer's panel, everything is more complex and splendid, but the comparison of the two paintings is nonetheless interesting. Dürer had an opportunity to see the Raphaelesque painting while in Italy. If the commission for the painting was assigned him by Jakob Heller before his first trip to Italy, one cannot consider the Raphaelesque echo to be accidental.

Differing from the frontal arrangement of the apostles and horizontal composition that Raphael gives to his Coronation, Dürer opposes to the compact group of apostles, arranged in a semicircle opening skyward, the convex semicircular arrangement of the choir of cherubs (Panofsky, 1977). They descend gently from the clouds that encircle the scene of the coronation, plucking the lute and harp, and ringing a little bell, holding the tip of Maria's heavy azure clothing, holding up the Madonna herself. She, on her knees, dominates the upper part of the painting. Christ is a little higher up, to her left. Crowned with the papal tiara, and wearing a red cloak off his shoulders that, gaping at the side, shows the wounds of his Passion, he solemnly crowns Mary. To the right, on the same level as His son, is the Eternal Father. He is personified as a venerable old man, cloaked in a rich cape and wearing the imperial crown. He touches the crown suspended above the Madonna in blessing with His right hand, while His left holds the globe of the earth, another symbol of His power. Behind and beyond this celestial hierarchy shines a great halo, resplendent with the colors of the rainbow. From it descends the dove of the Holy Spirit, completing the glorious image of the Trinity that rises over the Madonna, who humbly bows her head in prayer.

Wings, inner sides

Martyrdom of Saint James, the Apostle
Tempera and oil on fir,
148 x 61 cm

Martyrdom of Saint Catherine
Tempera and oil on fir,
161 x 61 cm
Frankfurt,
Historisches Museum

According to Anzelewsky (1991), the wings were painted by Dürer with the assistance of his workshop, though his opinion is not universally shared. On the background of the scene of the martyrdom of Saint James is depicted the transportation of his remains to the palace of the queen of Spain, Lupa. According to the "Golden Legend," the disciples of Saint James the Elder, following his decapitation and under the guidance of an angel, secretly removed his remains during nightfall to save them from the Jews. They then brought them by sea to Spain. Here, they were gathered by Queen Lupa, who, with "wolfish wickedness," offered them a pair of wild bulls to transport the coffin. But the disciples tamed the ferocious animal, which took the corpse to the palace alone. Before the obvious miracle, the queen converted to the Christian faith and wanted the saint to consecrate the palace, transforming it into a chapel, the famous sanctuary of Santiago of Compostela.

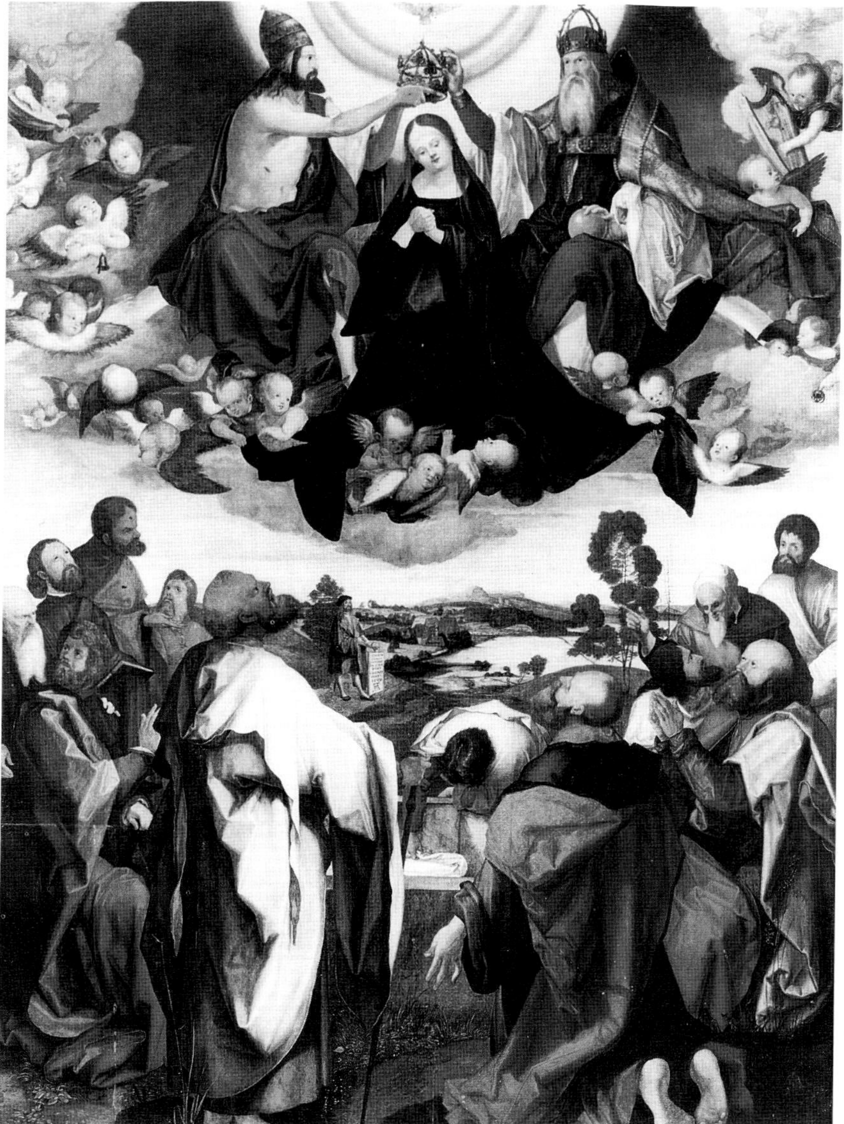

Cat 48 Assumption of the Coronation of the Virgin

In a discussion on the truth of Christianity, the beautiful and cultured eighteen-year-old Saint Catherine of Alessandria stands up to at least fifty learned pagan philosophers. Maximinus, then the Roman emperor, condemned her to the torture on the wheel; but an angel—who is not represented in the painting—breaks the wheel to pieces, which explodes in the painting, its fragments hitting the people in the foreground and the emperor in the background. He, as the target of a violent rain of boiling pitch falling from a grim and threatening sky, falls with his soldiers to the ground. In the distance, two

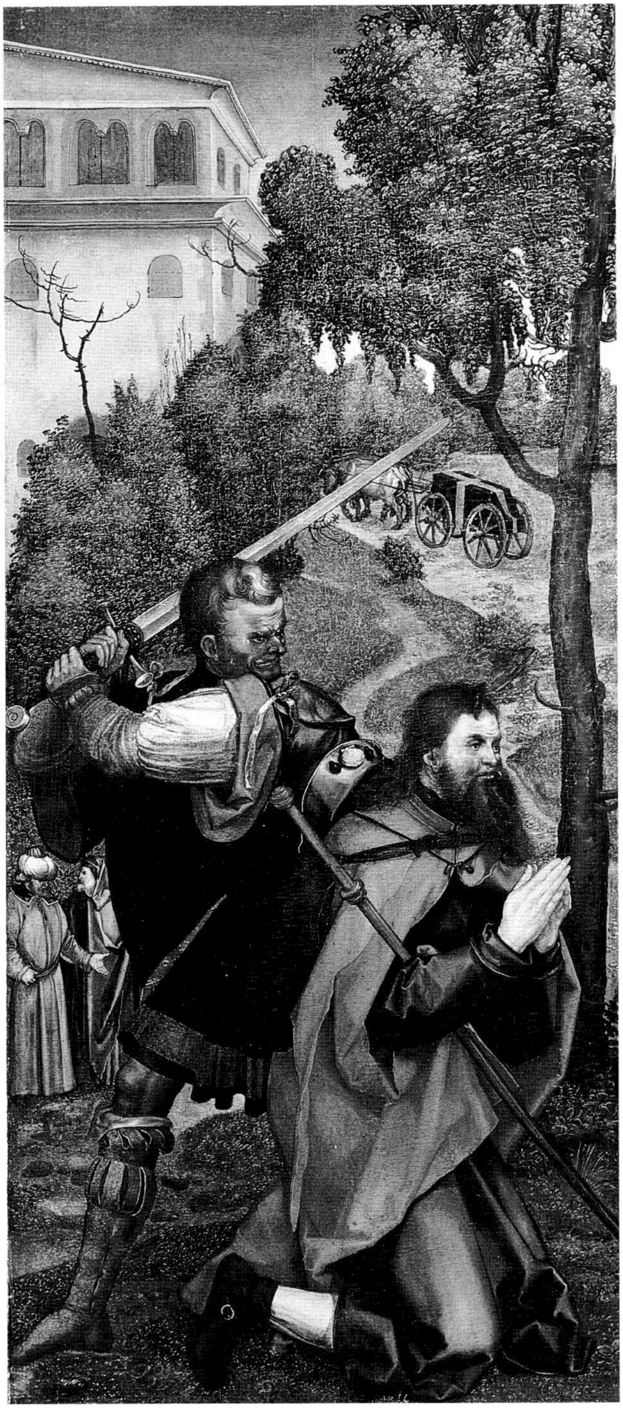

Cat 48 Martyrdom of Saint James, the Apostle

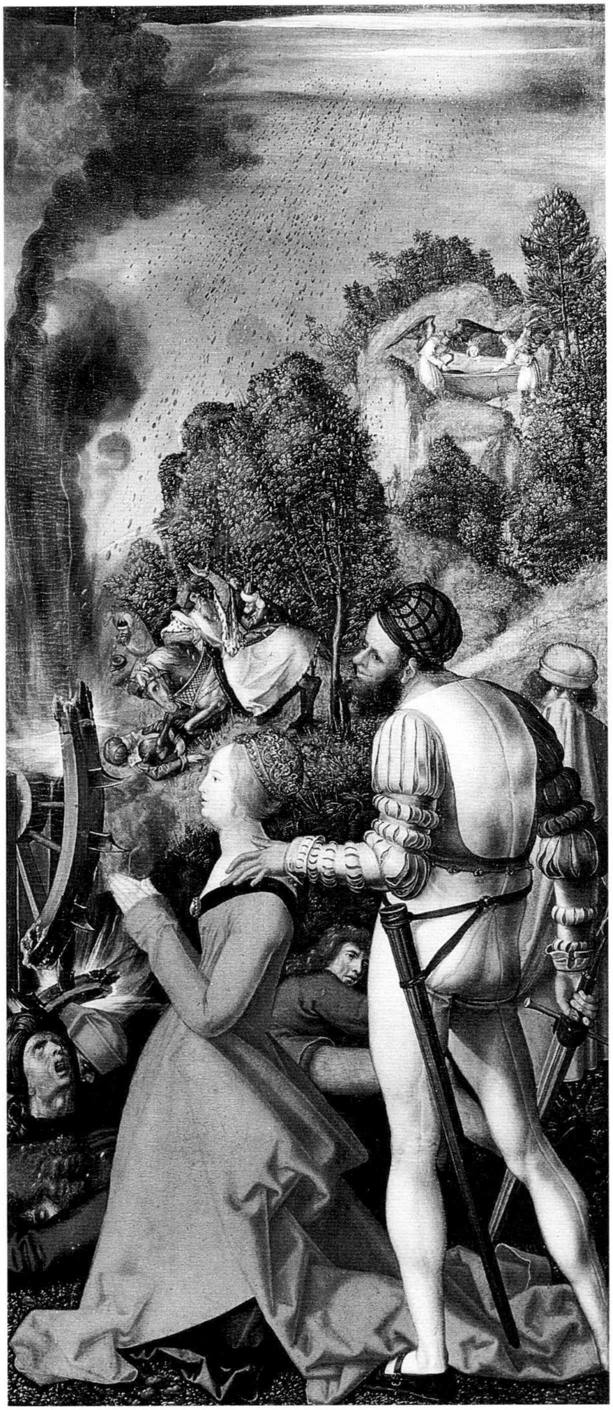

Cat 48 Martyrdom of Saint Catherine

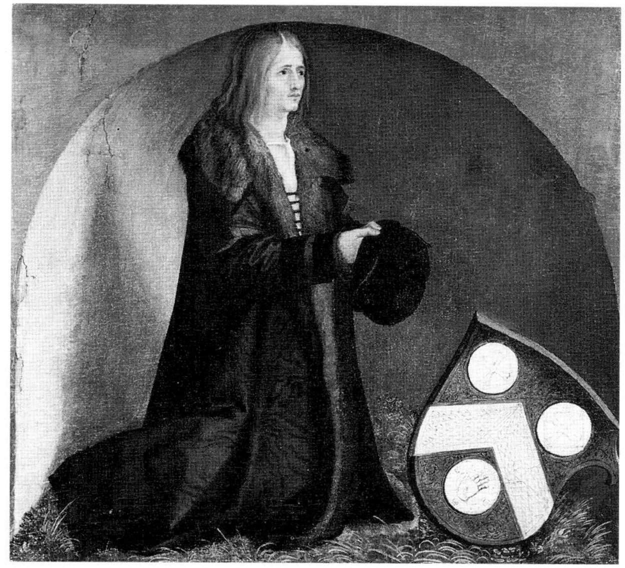

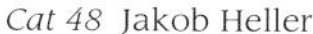
Cat 48 Jakob Heller

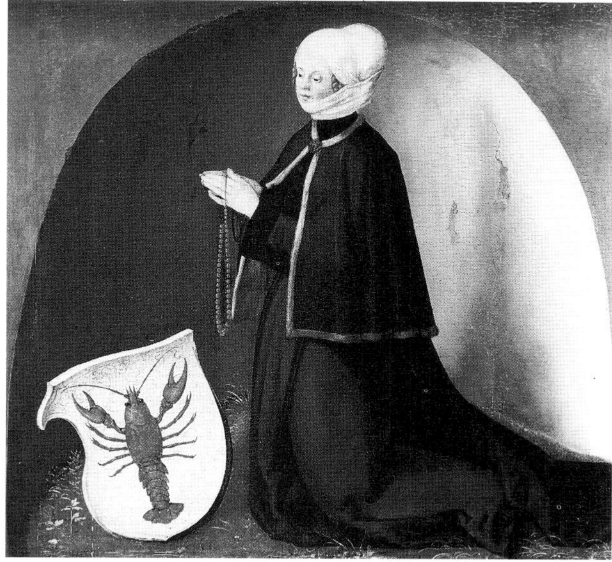

Cat 48 Katharina von Melem

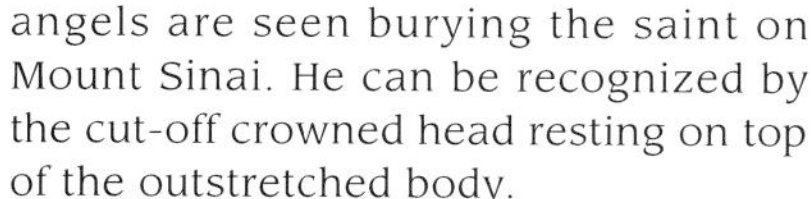
angels are seen burying the saint on Mount Sinai. He can be recognized by the cut-off crowned head resting on top of the outstretched body.

Dürer's involvement in the painting's execution is revealed not only in the depiction of the explosion of the wheel, but in the complicated expressions of the figures beneath the wheel and—a detail that has until now gone unnoticed—in the agonized scream of the man in the foreground, surely taken from Leonardo's Battle of Anghiari, which Dürer must have seen during his Florentine sojourn at the master's workshop, in Leonardo's absence. Dürer had already represented the same theme in a woodcut of 1496–97 (W120).

Portraits of the Patrons, Jakob Heller and Katharina von Melem
Tempera on fir,
53 x 56 cm
Frankfurt am Main, Historisches Museum

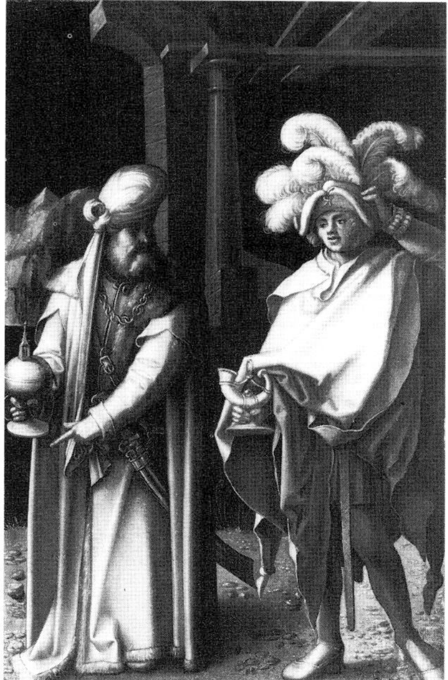

Cat 48 Two Kings from the Adoration of the Magi

An integrated polyptych, the two portraits were found under the figures of their respective guardian saints. They were represented in an adoring pose, kneeling on a field in front of a stone niche. In front of each of them lie their respective coats of arms. I tend to think that the paintings are mainly by Dürer (the catalog of the paintings of the museum). The pictorial quality of the images, or, more precisely, of the details that concern them, like the mohair cloak of the man or the gracious manner of the woman, support this notion. Anzelewsky (1991) has revealed, based on the fashion of the period, that in the portrait of Katharina von Melem, the dark portion between her neck and the fur trim of her cape was probably added later.

Wings, external facade

Two Kings from the Adoration of the Magi
(the wing with the Madonna and third king is missing)

Saint Peter and Saint Paul; Saint Thomas Aquinas and Saint Christopher
Monochrome (gray on gray), workshop works
Tempera on fir, 96 x 60 cm

Painted in "stone color," as Dürer writes, the external facades of the wings, visible when the altarpiece was closed, were carried out by the master's workshop, possibly with the assistance of his nineteen-year-old brother, Hans. For Heller, he writes, the Magi were three particular guardian saints. He professed to be devoted to Saint Peter and to Saint Paul: in 1500, he made a pilgrimage to Rome, and in a codicil to his will of 1519, he made the arrangements for a pilgrimage one month prior to his death that he should go to that city to see, in addition to the basilicas of Saint Peter and Saint Paul, the Lateran basilica, where the two heads of the saints were preserved. The altar is

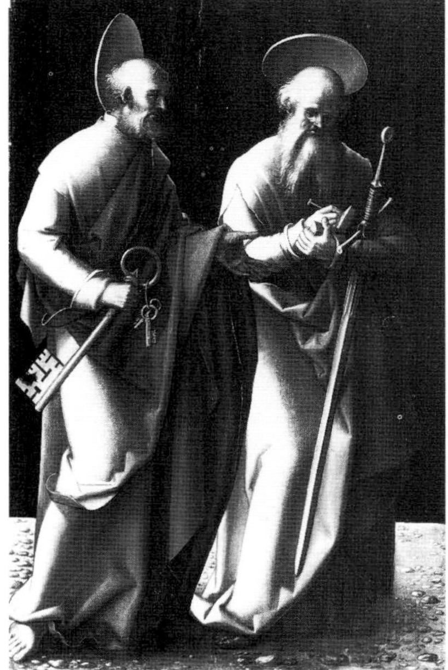

Cat 48 Saint Peter and Saint Paul

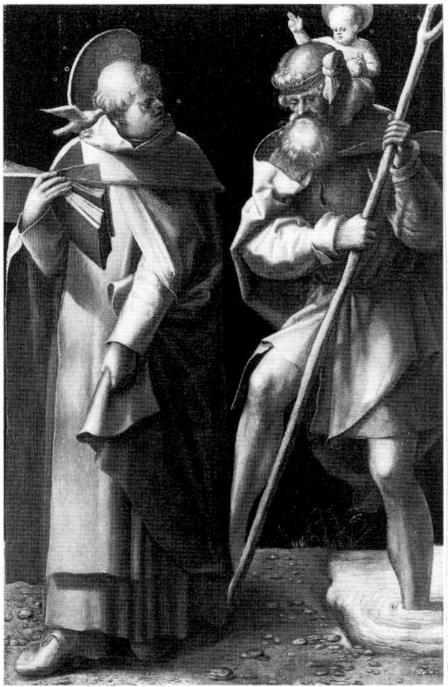

Cat 48 Saint Thomas Aquinas and Saint Christopher

consecrated to Saint Thomas Aquinas; prayers were offered to Saint Christopher for assistance in dangerous undertakings. Jakob Heller, after having ordered the work from Dürer, turned to Grünewald, who painted four other monochromatic wings for him, all of which are still preserved. No trace remains, however, of a Transfiguration of Christ, which, according to Joachim van Sandrart (1675), Grünewald would have painted; it was probably located above the altar.

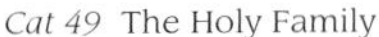

Cat 49 The Holy Family

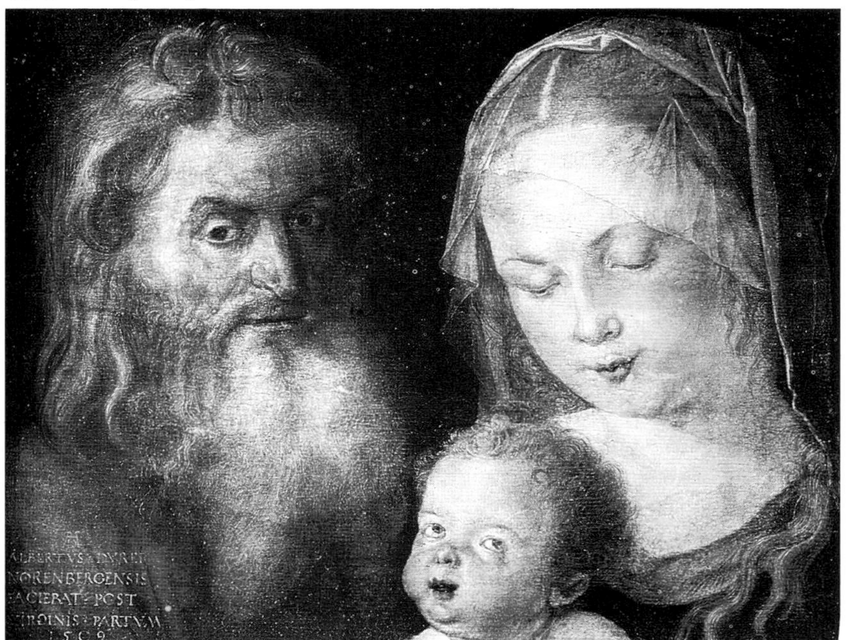

49

The Holy Family

Inscription in the bottom left, monogrammed and dated: ALBERTVS DVRER NORERNBERGENSIS / FACIEBAT POST / VIRGINIS PARTVM 1509

Panel, 30.5 x 38.7 cm

Rotterdam, Museum Boymans-van Beuningen,

1509

This small painting has been poorly preserved, and it is difficult to intuit its purpose. So much more surprising, then, is the meticulousness of the inscription. The head of the child resembles that of some preparatory studies (W 393 and W 394) for The Feast of the Rose Garlands (*cat 39*); the head of the Madonna, on the other hand, recalls that of Vienna of 1512 (*cat. 53*).

50

The Adoration of the Trinity

(Landauer Altar)

Inscription on the panel supported by the self-portrait of Dürer: ALBERTVS DVRER NORICVS FACIEBAT ANNO A VIRGINIS PARTV[M] 1511*; monogrammed*

Lindenwood,

135 x 123.4 cm

Dedicated to All Saints for the chapel of the Zwölfbruderhaus (House of the Twelve Brothers) of Nuremberg. Vienna, Kunsthistorisches Museum

1511

This panel is one of the few works by Dürer whose frame, designed by the artist himself and carved by Ludwig Krug (?) of Nuremberg, has been preserved. The actual frame of the painting is a copy made in 1880–81, and the original is preserved in the Germanisches Nationalmuseum of Nuremberg. The inscription of the frame reads: "Mathes Landauer hat entlich vollbracht das gotteshaus der szwelf bruder samt der Stiftung und dieser thafell nach christi geburd 1511 jor." (Matthäus Landauer has brought to conclusion the Chapel of the Twelve Brothers and the Rest Home and this panel in the year 1511 after the birth of Christ).

In 1585, the panel, without the frame, was acquired by Rudolph II for 700 florins. It was mentioned as being present in the Kunstkammer of Prague in 1617 by Carel van Mander and in 1675, by Joachim van Sandrart. It passed to the Geistliche Schatzkammer of Vienna in 1758, and finally, in 1780 it was set up in the Gemäldegalerie.

Matthäus Landauer, a wealthy merchant and a proprietor of foundries (Schütz, 1994), had the rest home built with a chapel attached for the twelve artisans, indigent Nuremberg citizens. He spent the last years of his life in this house that he founded and managed. The chapel is dedicated to the Holy Trinity and to all saints; in the center of the works dedicated to them was placed Dürer's altarpiece (see ill.).

Already in 1508, when the House of the Twelve was still under construction—probably at the moment of the conclusion of the contract with Landauer—Dürer presented the patron with a pen drawing in watercolor that showed the very detailed program of the entire work, including the frame. As soon as he had finished the Heller Altar (*cat. 48*), in 1511, he began to paint, while the carver worked on the frame. Once finished, the painting presented some differences with respect to the original program, in form and content. The most important of these concerns not only the portraits of the patrons but the outline of the altarpiece, which in the definitive version appears cambered in the upper portion. The corners, with a black background today, were covered in the decorative designs of the frame in his time. The ornately carved frame has two lateral columns covered, for the most part, in vine shoots. The "deeis" is represented in the tympanum, that is, Christ as judge of the universe, seated on a rainbow with his feet resting of the globe of the earth. To either side, the Madonna and Saint John the Baptist have intercessory roles. At the top, to the left and right of the tympanum, two angels trumpeting announce the Last Judgment. The angel with the cross, foreseen in the preparatory drawing and still present in a relatively recent photograph (Zampa, 1968), is missing today.

The blessed souls, who are brought to heaven, radiant with sun, are represented on one side of the architrave. On the other, the souls of the damned are pushed toward the obscurity of hell. The general disposition follows a typically Italian outline that was widely diffused at this time. In fact, according to Leon Battista Alberti's book Della Pittura, it gives the illusion of seeing the painting as if through a window—in this case, through a portal.

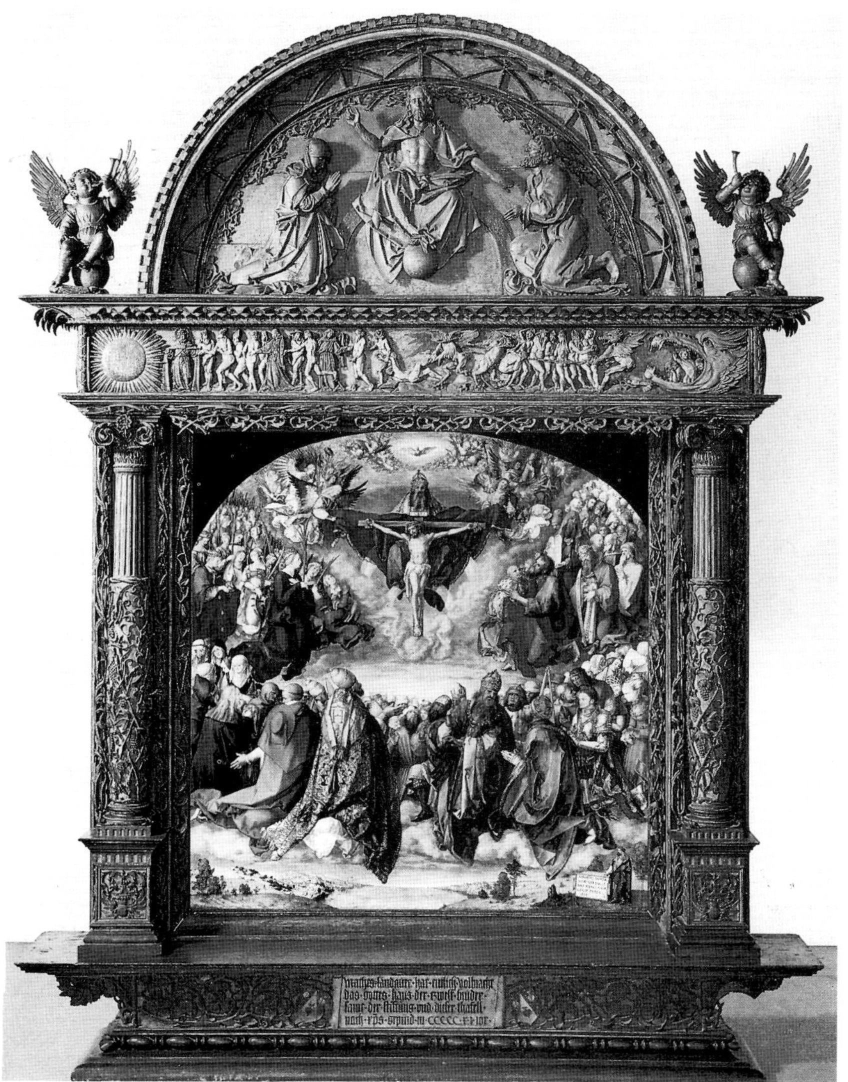

Cat 50 The Adoration of the Trinity. Reconstruction

At the top of the painting, above the clouds, the three symbols of the Trinity are found: the Eternal Father with the imperial crown, the crucified Christ—a pièce of an anatomical study par excellence—and the dove of the Holy Spirit. Angels surround them, carrying the symbols of the martyrdom and holding the cloak of the Eternal Father from behind the crucifix. Above everyone, a flock of cherubs extends into the endless sky.

Following the description of the Civitas Dei formulated by Saint Augustine (Panofsky, 1955, treated in detail), Dürer represents the glory of the Trinity, encircled in the upper zone by a score of blessed souls: to the left, the female saints, led by the Virgin Mary; to the right, the male saints, prophets, and sibyls, led by Saint John the Baptist. The Christian community hovers beneath these, in the sky between the clouds: the ecclesiastics

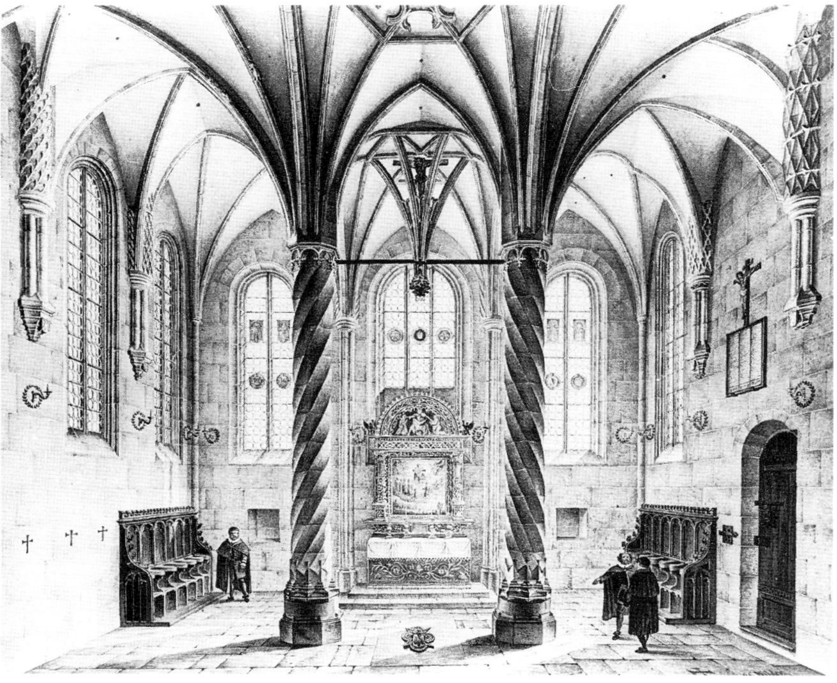

Cat 50 The Adoration of the Trinity. As seen from the original location of the Twelve Brothers' Chapel

to the left, led by two popes, viewed from behind; to the right, laymen of all ranks—the king, two emperors, and the peasant with his flail.

Among the ecclesiastics, in an impressively realistic portrait, kneels Matthäus Landauer, portrayed in prayer. He is sponsored and accompanied by a cardinal. To the right is another figure, easily identifiable from his armor, as Landauer's son-in-law, Wilhelm Haller, a mercenary captain. In the lower part of the painting, almost to contrast the suspended scores of saints and men and women, Dürer offers us, from a slightly raised perspective, the vision of a landscape passage. This one, even more than the one in the Heller Altar, disappears into an infinite background, illuminated by a most gentle evening light that also shimmers against the clouds. In this deserted terrestrial kingdom, Dürer painted himself, the only human being. He is set apart toward the right margin, dressed as usual in a rich fur cloak, and indicative of an ancient styled tablet with the inscription.

In the painting, populated by a great quantity and a variety of personages and figures, some details stand out for their true pictorial excellence: the flock of cherubs that encircle the dove of the Holy Spirit; the stupendous cloak of gold brocade of the Pope nearest the spectator; different portraits, the fashion of various clothing; the refined, veiled woman, or the one that alluringly looks out from behind someone else's back; the trimming of the clothes that hang over the clouds in the sky; or in the center, the boot with the spur in front of the clouds that rise above the landscape. Beside this preciosity, however, great uncertainty of proportion is also evident. See, for example, Saint John the Baptist or the legs of Dürer himself. The Adoration of the Trinity is the last great altarpiece painted by Dürer.

51

The Idealized Portrait of the Emperor of Charlemagne

Lindenwood, 188 x 87.6 cm,
with the frame 215 x 115.3 cm
Nuremberg, Germanisches Nationalmuseum
ca. 1511–13

This painting, and the one following, were commissioned to Dürer by the council of the city of Nuremberg around 1510, to substitute for the old portraits of the emperors of the Heiltumskammer (the room of the insignia) in which the imperial insignia (crown jewels) were preserved. Three drawings are preserved from the studies Dürer did of the insignia (W 505–7). In all likelihood, after having executed a detailed drawing in the form of a diptych (W 503), the master entrusted much of the execution of the portraits to his workshop. Even on the retro, various coats of arms are found and an inscription that refers to the preservation of the insignia.

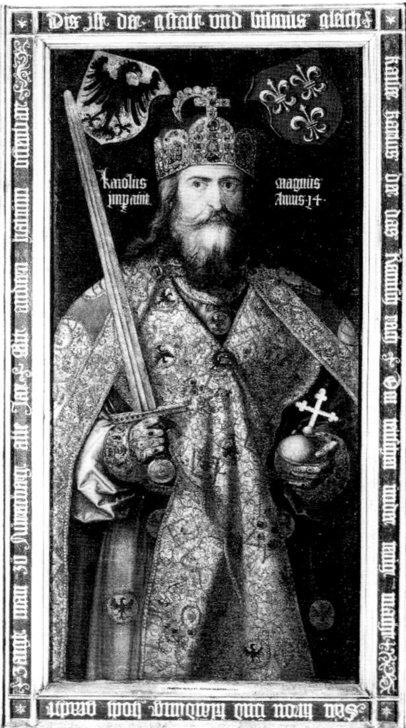

52

The Emperor Sigismund

Lindenwood,
187.7 x 87.5 cm,
with the frame 214.6 x 115 cm
Nuremberg, Germanisches Nationalmuseum
ca. 1511–13

It is said that it was Emperor Sigismund to grant the imperial insignia to the city of Nuremberg. His image in the present portrait is smaller than that of Charle-

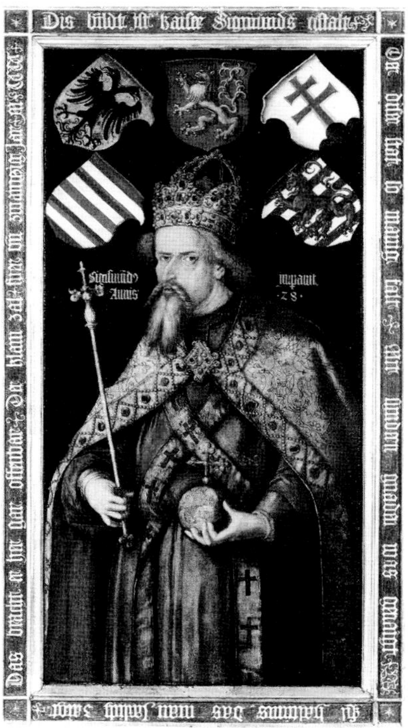

Cat 52 Emperor Sigismondo

magne (*cat. 51*), possibly because of the greater encumbrance of coats of arms, more numerous here. The posterior sides of the two portraits, with coats of arms and inscriptions, appear equal from a formal point of view.
In 1526, on orders of the town council, the two portraits were brought to the town hall from the Heiltumskammer, which was in the market square in the adjacent house, Schopperhaus, where the imperial insignia were kept each year for some time.

53

Madonna of the Pear

Inscription in the top right, monogrammed and dated 1512
Lindenwood, 49 x 37 cm
Vienna, Kunsthistorisches Museum
1512

Its provenance is probably the same as that for the Madonna Nursing (*cat. 29*), preserved in the same museum. A refined variety of details encircle the delicate face of the Virgin: the curls, the veil, and the ribbon across the forehead. The drawing of the eyes and eyebrows is sharp, and the red lips are well defined. Bowing her head tenderly toward her child and bestowing on him an extremely sweet smile, she presents him to the spectator. He lies on a sky-blue cloth, under which she hides her hands so as not to touch him, as one would not touch a precious jewel.
There has always been much discussion about the difference between the delicateness of Maria's face and the robust plasticity of the Herculean body of the child, likewise, about the differences in the pictorial technique adopted for each one: a much more physical depiction of the child than the mother. Much has been said about the marked torsion in the body of the little boy, which is splendid both in terms of formal and chromatic considerations. Other similar examples exist in Dürer's paintings and drawings (*cat. 71*). But no one, until now, has tried to resolve the meaning of the painting, or the presence of the cut pear ostentatiously presented by the child. His limpid and open gaze knowingly peers into the far distance. The pear as an attribute of Christ and Maria is not rare in Venetian painting of the Renaissance, and it appears in all Italian painting; following an interpretation of Bernardo di Chiaravalle of the Cantico dei Cantici, the sweetness of the taste symbolizes the sweetness of mouth and heart, which are, according to Saint Bonaventure, the gifts of the wise (Levi d'Ancona, The Garden of the Renaissance, 1977). Even Dürer depicted it (1509) in the middle of other fruits in a basket at Maria's feet, in the drawing of the Holy Family under the Loggia (W 466). The unusual fact in this painting is that the pear in the child's hand is cut and bitten into. However, wisdom and sweetness are certainly the principal themes of this delightful small devotional image.

54

The Madonna of the Carnation

Inscription in the top right, monogrammed and dated 1516
Parchment on pine, 36 x 25 cm
Munich, Alte Pinakothek
1516

In 1630, this panel was mentioned in the inventory of the possessions of the elector of Bavaria; it subsequently went to the episcopal palace of Freising, but it returned definitively to Munich in 1802. The main part of the space of the painting is occupied by the Virgin's head, encircled by a luminous halo against a dark green background.
The perfect regularity of her face as seen from the front leads one to think that, like the Self-Portrait with Fur Coat of 1500 of Munich (*cat. 26*), this has been "reconstructed" according to precise laws of proportion. The Madonna's gaze—her eyes reflecting, like her child's, the window beside them—is not turned toward the spectator, but is directed into the distance. Even the child has a fixed gaze and is busy with a pear in his little hands (compare *cat. 53*), while the Madonna gracefully holds a stem of a carnation, with fruit and flower, between her fingers.
Similar to the Madonna, who, for the rigid, formal composition of the head seems distant, almost rapt in an ideal world, so the child, with his wide-open eyes, who seems detached from his mother and the spectator. The small panel assumes the look of an icon, in which the carnation alludes to the Passion, and the pear that the child closes in his hands recalls—according to Saint Bonaventure—the sweetness of the wise of mouth and heart.

Cat 54 The Madonna of the Carnation

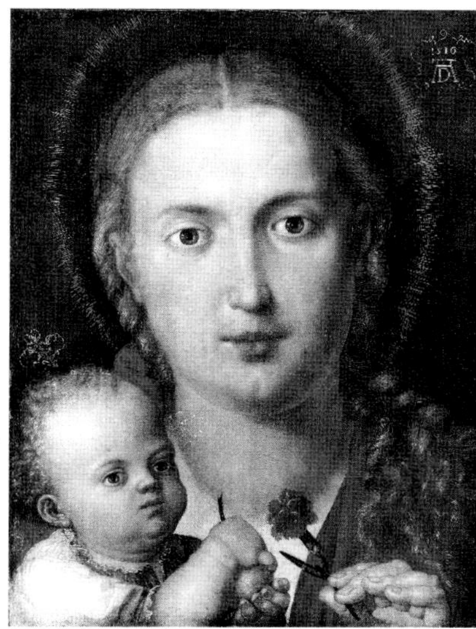

55

Portrait of Michael Wolgemut

Inscription in the top right;
in the bottom right, monogrammed and dated 1516
Tempera and oil on lindenwood, 29 x 27 cm
Nuremberg, Germanisches Nationalmuseum
1516

This painting was originally part of the Praun collection in Nuremberg. In 1809, the antique collector Frauenholz sold it for 300 ducats to the heir-apparent prince of Bavaria. It came to the Germanisches Nationalmuseum between 1909 and 1928 (Anzelewsky, 1991). Dürer was not painting on commission, but independently chose to depict his master Michael Wolgemut (1434–November 30, 1519, whose workshop he had apprenticed in from 1486. This fact can explain the unusual, impressive adherence to realism that he kept in reproducing, without embellishment, his features, against an intense green background. It is a realism that Dürer had previously experimented with two years earlier, in a charcoal-drawing portrait of his mother, which is in Berlin (fig. 2). In Gothic letters, the inscription reads: Daz hat albrecht dürer abconterfet noch siene Lermeister Michell Wolgemut jn jor 1516. Dürer later added (Rupprich, 1956–69): vnd er was 82 vnd hat gelet pis das man felet 1519 Jor: do ist er ferschiden an sant Endres dag frv, ee dy sun awff gyng. ("This is the portrait that Albrecht Dürer made of his master Michell Wolgemut." The addition: "He was 82 years old and lived until the year 1519; he passed away the day of Saint Andrew, in the morning, before the sun came out.") Another portrait on parchment, monogrammed and dated 1516—which until 1992 (sold at Sotheby's auction, in London, 9 December) was found in the Georg Schäfer collection in Schweinfurt—Winkler judges as the first version of the small work (Anzelewsky, 1991).

56

Saint Philip, the Apostle

Inscription: SANCTE PHILIPP ORATE / PRO NOBIS; *monogrammed and dated 1516*
Canvas, 46 x 38 cm
Florence, Galleria degli Uffizi
1516

It is said that Emperor Ferdinand II (1637–57) gave this painting, along with the following one (*cat. 57*), to the grand duke of Tuscany, Ferdinand II (1610–70), on the occasion of the latter's visit to Vienna. On both works, an excellent, fine painting of the very delicate canvas bears witness to Dürer's mastery, whether of the detailed depiction of the faces or, above all, of the imposing beards of the two figures.

57

Saint James the Great, the Apostle

Inscription: SANCTE JACOBE ORA / PRO NOBIS 1516; *monogrammed and dated 1516*
Canvas, 46 x 38 cm
Florence, Galleria degli Uffizi, 1516

See: Saint Philip, the Apostle (*cat. 56*). The notion that Dürer had intended to paint a

Cat 56 Saint Philip, the Apostle

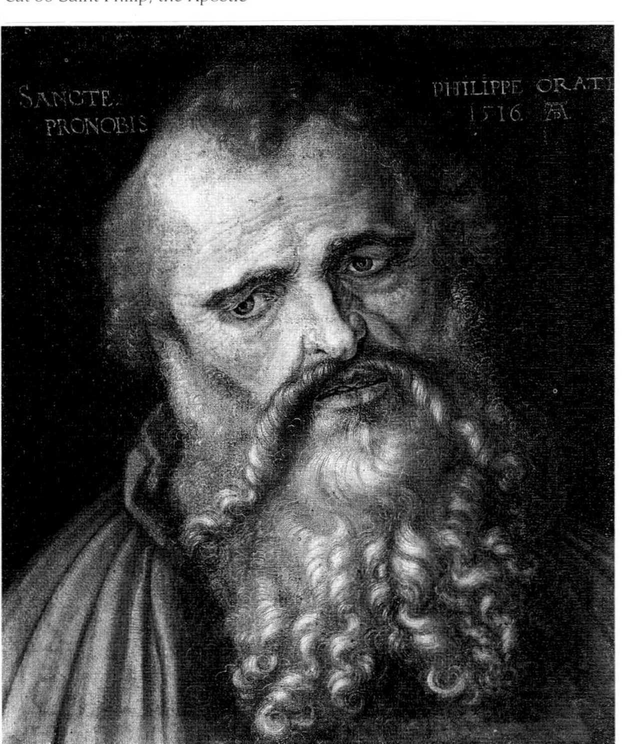

Cat 57 Saint James the Great, the Apostle

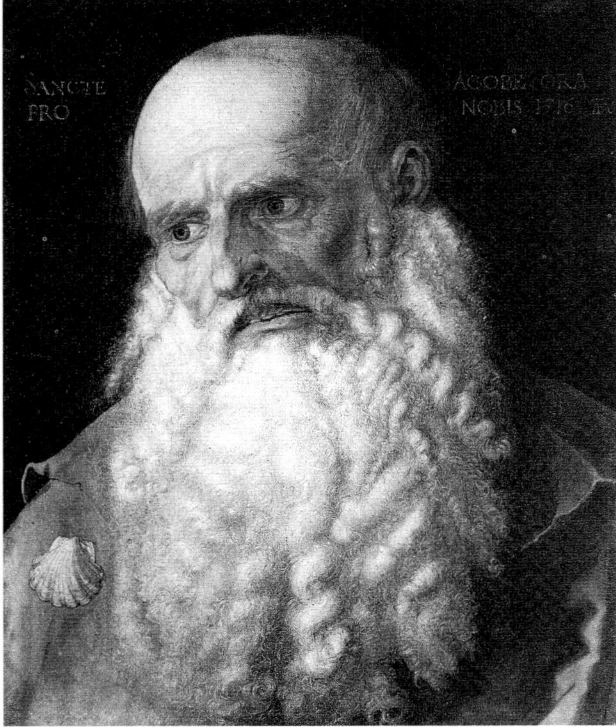

complete series of all the apostles is well supported.

58

Portrait of a Cleric

Inscription in the top right, monogrammed and dated 1516
Parchment on canvas,
42.9 x 32 cm
Washington, National Gallery, Kress collection
1516

In 1778, this painting was, along with the Wolgemut portrait (*cat. 55*), the Saint Onofrius (*cat. 36*), and the Death of Crescentia Pirckheimer (*cat. 33*), in the Paul von Praun collection. He must have acquired it from the goldsmith Wenzil Jamnitzer of Nuremberg, who, in turn, would have received it from Endres, Albrecht Dürer's brother. In 1801, the painting went to Count Rudolf Czernin, from whom Samuel H. Kress acquired it, and he subsequently donated it to the National Gallery (Anzelewsky, 1991).
The painting was considered in Nuremberg (1778) to be of Johann Dorsch, an Augustinian friar who had converted quite early on to Lutheranism. This identification, however, was challenged by various critics, since Dorsch became the parish priest of Saint John's in Nuremberg in 1528. Some have hypothesized that it was a portrait by Huldrych Zwingli, the great Swiss reformer; but only side profile portraits of him exist, which, according to Anzelewsky, do not give rise to a fair comparison or to a reliable attribution.
Anzelewsky would opt for the former identification, also because, according to more recent studies, the meeting between Zwingli and Dürer could not have occurred before 1519, on the occasion of a mission in Zurich in which he participated with his friend Pirckheimer and Martin Tucher (Rupprich, 1956-69).
As in the portrait of Wolgemut (*cat. 55*), Dürer succeeds in effectively expressing the vigorous personality of the subject, modeling the head with a slight rotation leftward, toward the light, and framing it with a severe black attire against a green background. The fine brush strokes, especially for the hair and eyelashes, are well preserved.

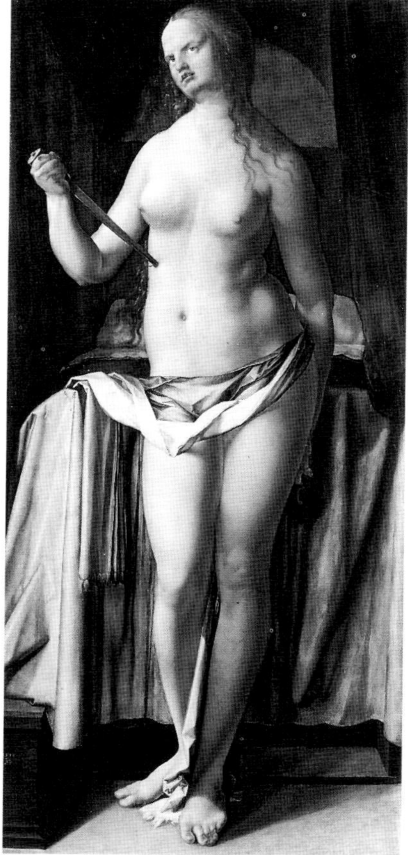

Cat 59

59

Lucrezia

Inscription on the chest in the bottom left, monogrammed and dated 1518
Lindenwood, 168 x 74.8 cm
Munich, Alte Pinakothek
1518

This panel is mentioned in the inventory, dated 1598, of the Kunstkammer of Munich. The cloth around the hips was presumably expanded upward around 1600. Fedja Anzelewsky's opinion (1991) that the Lucrezia, all things considered, was "Dürer's most unpopular work," is undoubtedly widely shared.
Because of many discrepancies and discordances in the proportions and in the expression of the figure, Anzelewsky defines it as "a parody rather than an exaltation of the classical feminine figure." The theme takes its origin from a Roman story that narrates how Lucrezia, the virtuous wife of Lucius Tarquinius Collatinus, is dishonored by Sextus, son of Tarquinius the Superb. She then takes her own life out of shame.
The Lucrezia of Dürer's painting does not pierce her heart. The artist thus follows one tradition, spread by Italian painters like Francesco Francia and adopted before him by Lucas Cranach as well. But all these represented the woman in a three-quarter profile, and they never set her in her own bedroom. The blood spouting from the wound is rather slight and does not stain the bridal bed, which remains neat and clean and undisturbed. This certainly indicates that the insult suffered is only exterior and has not contaminated the intimate purity of the chaste matron. There is one markedly commonplace and bourgeois detail in the scene, which must create the sense of a heroic-pathetic atmosphere: the presence of a night vase under the bed. The brush strokes are extraordinarily fine; the colors used for the drapes and the fabrics are predominantly various shades of red, blue, and green. Dürer made use of drawings that go back to 1508 for this painting (W 435–36).

60

The Virgin Mary in Prayer

Inscription in the top left, monogrammed and dated 1518
Lindenwood, 53 x 43 cm
Berlin, Staatliche Museen, Gemäldegalerie, 1518

Wilhem von Bode acquired the panel in Venice in 1894 in an auction of the Morosini-Gatterburg collection, and then donated it to the Berlin art gallery. The Virgin Mary in Prayer was part of a diptych (Winkler, 1928) whose matching pair was probably a representation of an "Ecce Homo" (Anzelewsky, 1991).

61

Man's Head

Parchment,
24.5 x 19 cm
on panel 26.1 x 20.5 cm
Munich, private collection
ca. 1518–20

This painting has been known since 1921,

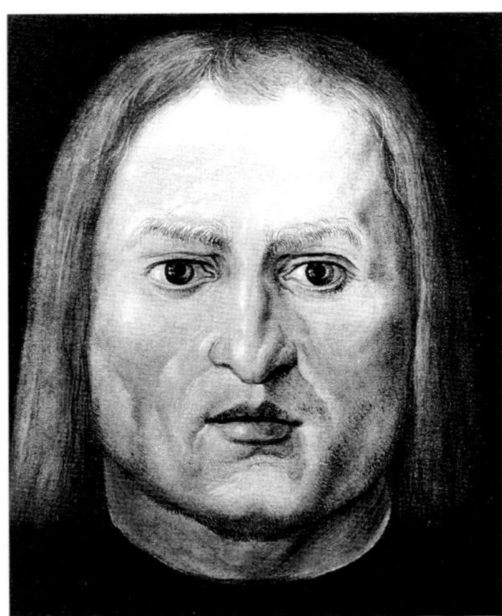

Cat 61 Man's head

when it was discovered in a London collection.
It has passed through many private collections, and was acquired by its present owner in an auction at Sotheby's in New York.
It would be difficult to assert that this painting is an actual portrait for three reasons: first, because only a head, held up by a much shortened neck, is depicted filling the entire space; second, because the head is shown in the foreground and there isn't any background; and third, because of the staring, or dazed, expression of the face. As it has always been hypothesized, we are probably observing a study of proportions, like the one, similarly probable, for the Madonna of the Carnation (*cat. 54*), which, like this head, is painted on parchment.
A copy of the head, transformed into Simone Zelota, dated 1518, exists in a private collection. A certain nearness to the Man with a Beard and a Red Beret, 1520 (*cat. 66*), leads to dating the work in the period between the two dates mentioned above.

62

Jakob Fugger the Wealthy

Tempera on canvas,
69.4 x 53 cm
Augsburg, Germany, Staatsgalerie
Between 1518 to 1520

The presence of this portrait is documented, in the eighteenth century, in the gallery of the elector of Bavaria. Because of successive restorations, the top layer of color is missing.
During the Diet of Augsburg, in 1518, Dürer portrayed Jakob Fugger in a charcoal drawing (W 571). The final painting, on canvas, differs from the drawing in the wealthier clothing of the subject, and, above all, in the framing: a half-bust in the drawing, a half-length in the painting.
Jakob Fugger of Augsburg (1459–1525), the wealthiest merchant of his day, learned the art of commerce in Venice. He possessed a network of business agencies throughout Europe. His was the most important banking institution in Europe, and he had the monopoly of silver and copper mines. He obtained the right to mint the coins of the Vatican from Julius II, Leo X, and Adrian VI, and he had an important role in the system of tax collection and payment of indulgences from the Vatican coffers. He heavily financed the political and military undertakings of Maximilian I and Charles V: just for the election of the latter, he contributed 300,000 florins. In 1508, Maximilian I conferred him a noble title, and Leo X nominated him Count Palatine of the Lateran. In 1519, he established in Augsburg the "Fuggerei," a small city within the city, consisting of 106 small houses intended for the most needy citizens.
The outer edges of his garments and fur coat, crossing and overlapping, create an ascendant pyramid effect, which solidly sets off the portrait.
At the same time, his garments sharply contrast with his face, hard and severe, atop a bull neck. Only the clear complexion of the flesh, painted with extremely fine brush strokes, which is detached from a delicate blue background, attenuates his dynamism and severity. The position of the head denotes firmness and self-assurance, and the eyes look away, possibly to indicate a far-sightedness. The wide forehead, lined with a simply-fashioned gold beret, and the thin, pressed lips, give him the look of a man who—at least according to Dürer's interpretation—has a strong personality and no need of decoration to assert himself.
This impressive characterization, if somewhat idealized, along with the one of Dürer's father of 1497 (*cat. 15*), is in my opinion one of the most significant of portraiture in that era in Europe.

63

Saint Anne, Virgin and Christ Child (Anna Seldbritt)

Inscription to the right, near the Virgin's head, monogrammed and dated 1519
Canvas, transferred from panel,
60 x 49.9 cm
New York, Metropolitan Museum of Art, Altmann collection
1519

This is a devotional image that Leonhard Tucher commissioned from Dürer. In 1628, it was offered by Gabriel III Tucher to Maximilian of Bavaria, who did not consider it to be an original. After having passed from collection to collection, it was acquired in 1910 by Benjamin Altmann, who donated it in 1913 to the museum in New York.
After having formerly been considered at times a copy, today the panel is generally held to be an original work of Dürer. The theme treated is often found in the altarpieces in Nuremberg, which are obviously of different scales and are solemn and monumental. Here the close and more familiar rapport the patron had with the requested painting led Dürer to prefer a more intimate interpretation.
The outline of Saint Anne's head is even based on a portrait drawing of his wife, Agnes, carried out the same year (W 574). The Virgin's head seems an actual portrait of a girl, so little does she resemble the contemporary iconography of the Madonna. Saint Anne, who, as in all the depictions of this sort, rests her hand on the shoulder of her daughter, has an almost reassuring, consoling character here. Very little space is left for the child because of the small dimensions of the painting.
Saint Anne's knowing gaze looks into the distance; the young Virgin's is lowered and smiling in the act of adoration of her child: both imbue the small work with a melancholic tone. This melancholy is explained by the presence of the white cloth placed under the sleeping child's lovely

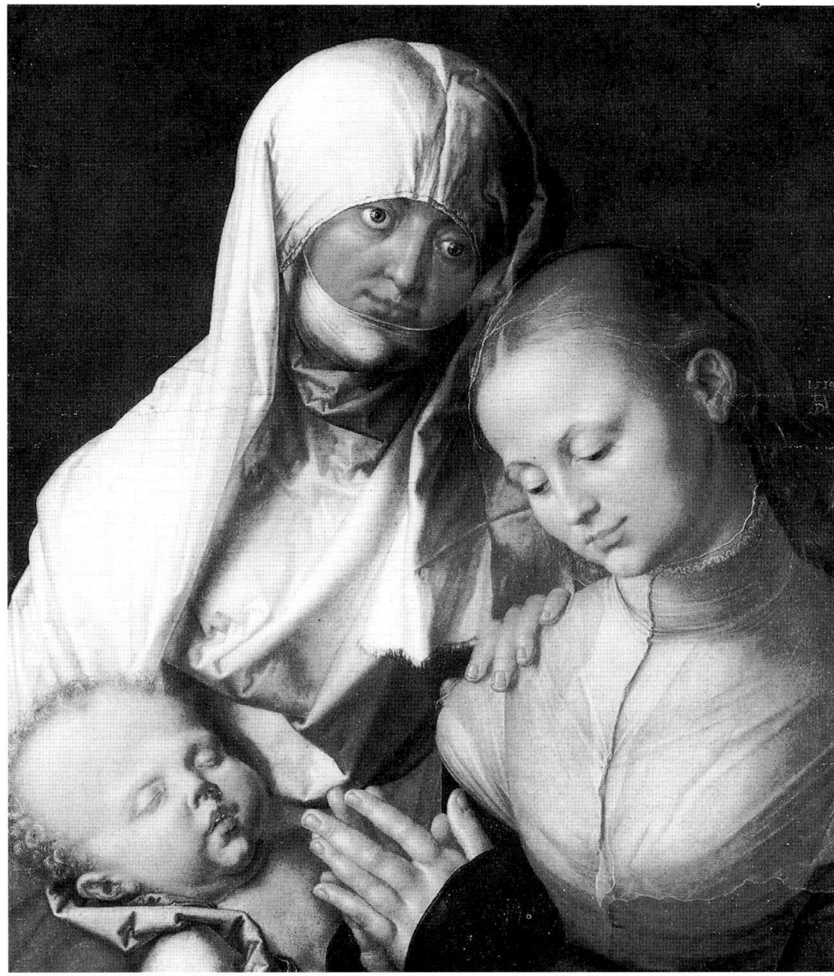

Cat 63 'Saint Anne Metterza'

head. It is a sad allusion to the Passion and death that await him.
This is obviously a work intended for meditation.

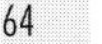

64 65

Portrait of Maximilian I
Inscription, monogrammed and dated 1519 in the top right; imperial coat of arms, surmounted by the crown and encircled by the Gold Toson chain;
in the top: encomiastical inscription
Lindenwood, 74 x 61.5 cm
Vienna, Kunsthistorisches Museum
1519

For some time, this painting has belonged to the emperors of Austria; from the end of the 1800s, it has been in the museum in Vienna. In 1518, Dürer went to the Diet of Augsburg following a delegation of dignitaries from Nuremberg. On that occasion, he did the portrait of Jakob Fugger (*cat. 62*) and also one in a half-bust of the emperor, then fifty-nine. It is a pencil drawing (W 567) carried out on 28 June (as indicated by the inscription on the same paper).
Shortly thereafter, probably still during his sojourn in Augsburg (Anzelewsky, 1991), he did a second portrait, still in a half-bust, but this time painted on canvas: Dürer probably preferred canvas to panel because it simplified the execution, for the painting as well as for the transportation.
This painting, now in the Germanisches Nationalmuseum in Nuremberg (*cat. 65*), did not have the inscription on parchment, which was added only after the emperor's death on 12 January 1519. The inscription is in German. It was transcribed, translated in Latin, in capital letters on the third panel portrait, now in Vienna.
It is this last painting that is the "true" portrait of the emperor, with even the Halsburg coat of arms. Maximilian is depicted clad in silk and cloaked by a precious, rich fur.
The pomegranate, which in the preceding portrait he held in both hands, now is held by one hand alone. It is probably a symbol of abundance, or perhaps of the conquest of Granada. The Gold Toson does not hang from his chest, but is now hanging around the imperial coat of arms.
Selecting and refining the details from one portrait to another, Dürer came to create a truly imposing and clearly humanist regal portrait—posthumous, as his blank stare surely alludes to his recent death. In both portraits, the head is traced from the first drawing (see Schütz, 1994, for the most recent bibliography).

66

Portrait of a Man with a Beard and a Red Beret
Inscription to the left, near the head, monogrammed and dated 1520
Canvas,
40 x 30 cm
Paris, Musée du Louvre
1520

It seems that this painting was part of the Crozat collection. In 1772, Katerina II of Russia acquired it. In 1852, it became the property of the Louvre.
Dürer began his journey to the Netherlands 12 July 1520, during which he carried out a great number of portraits, including, perhaps, this one. A particular fascination, emphasized also by the intense red of the beret, emanates from the penetrating eyes of this face, so spiritualized and close to the spectator. The detail of the red beret leads to the supposition that it is a portrait of a high-ranking prelate or even a judge.

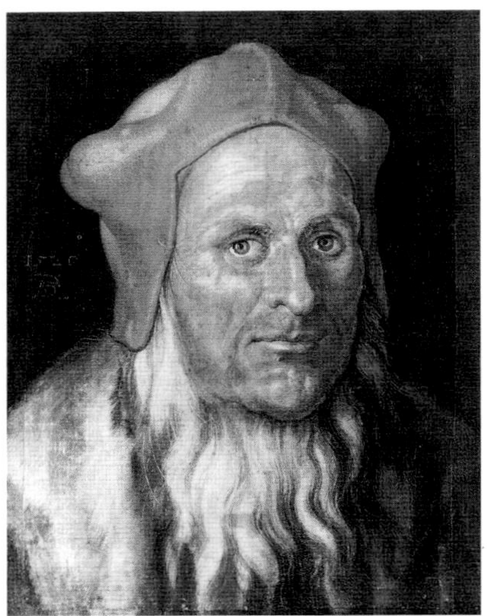

Cat 66 Portrait of a Man with a Beard and a Red Beret

Everything about it suggests that it is a work that Dürer executed all at once and that it was not commissioned, as tells the lack of concern about rules and patterns, composition and everything else, all of which are evident in his other panel portraits of that period (*cat. 67, 69, and ff.*). Maybe it is for this reason that it is one of his most fascinating works.
The original canvas has been trimmed at the sides and top; these pieces were later replaced.

67

Portrait of Rodrigo de Almada
Inscription above the head, monogrammed and dated 1521
Panel, 50 x 32 cm
Boston, Isabella Stewart Gardner Museum
1521

This portrait is preserved poorly, and the arm and hand have surely been repainted. It has been known only since 1902. Bernard Berenson passed it on to Isabella Stewart Gardner through the antiquarian Colnaghi. Even the monogram and the date have been rewritten.
The identification of the subject is possible by means of a comparison of a pen drawing (W 813): it is of Rodrigo de Almada, of a Portuguese business agency in Antwerp. Dürer had probably met him previously in Nuremberg in 1519. In fact, he speaks of him often as an old friend in the diary of his trip to the Netherlands. He also gave him his Saint Jerome (*cat. 68*).
The work, in its origin surely a display of excellent craftsmanship, is representative of Dürer's sojourn in the Netherlands.

Cat 67 Portrait of Rodrigo de Almada

68

Saint Jerome
Inscription on the slip of paper sticking out of the book, monogrammed and dated 1521
Oak, 59.5 x 48.5 cm
Lisbon, Museo Nacional de Arte Antiga, 1521

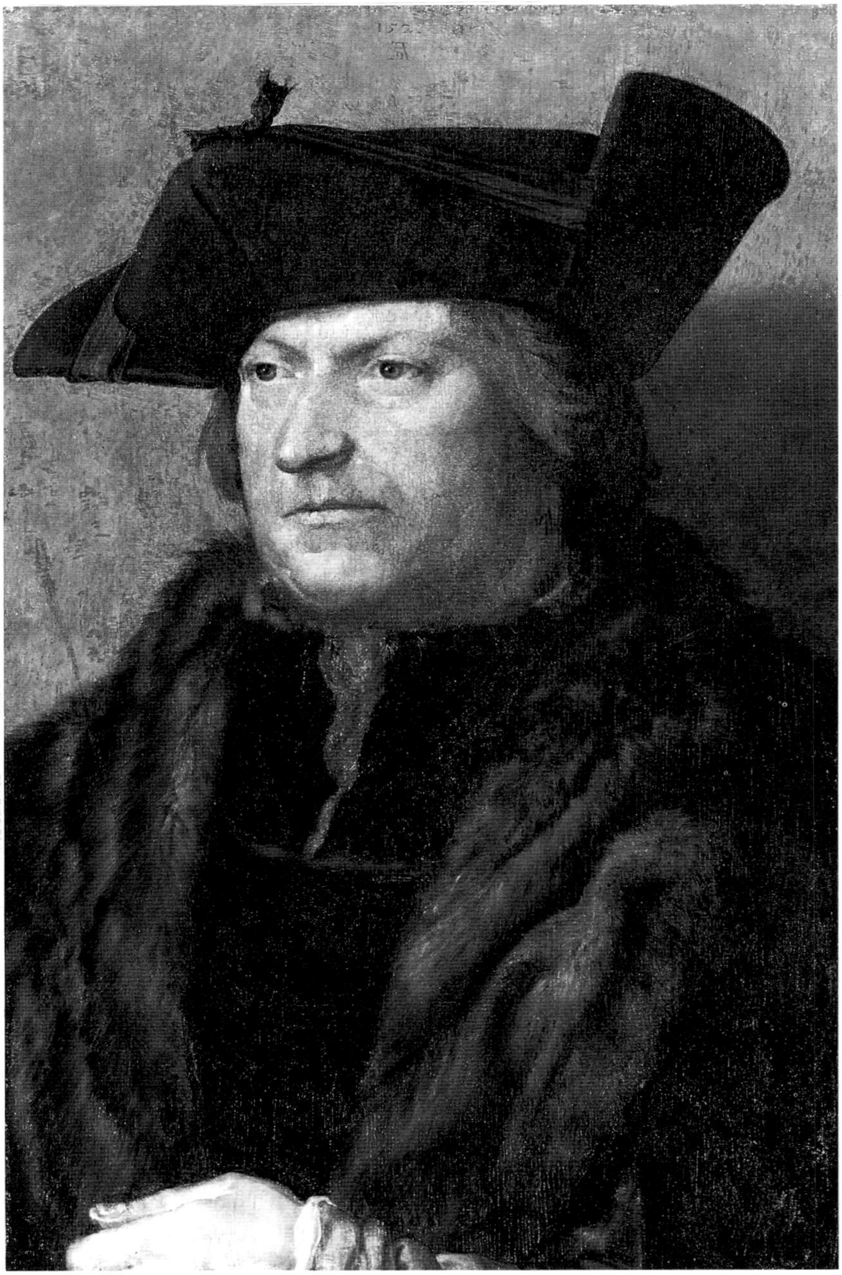

In 1521, during his sojourn in the Netherlands, Dürer depicted in pen and ink on violet paper an old man of ninety-three from Antwerp, noch gesunt und vermuglich (still bright and healthy), as his annotation reads (W 788). In that study, the expression and the position of the subject were very similar to those of the Saint Jerome of the painting, while the gaze is closer to that of the old man of a later drawing (W 789), in which only the head is shown.
The two drawings and the painting demonstrate an extraordinary capacity of observation and a mastery of execution. Other drawings also exist, executed with great care concerning the details of the painting.
Saint Jerome, one of the four fathers of the Church, translated the Bible: Dürer expresses this with the presence of a pen and ink-pot and an open book on a book rest. The old man has a melancholic air, his posture as in his gaze. His index finger, which indicates a skull, admonishes the spectator: "remember the ephemeral nature of all earthly things." Already in a famous engraving, Saint Jerome in His Study (Hieronymus im Gehäus) of 1514, judged as one of the three all time masterpieces of copper engravings, Dürer had added a skull, placed on the window sill, to the figure of the cardinal saint. But only in the Lisbon painting is there a clear declaration: memento mori. At the same time, the presence of the sacred texts seems intended to recall invariability and continuity. The still life of the books and the skull, typical of painting in the Netherlands, reveals the influence of the time and place in which the painting was made.
Another characteristic distinguishes this one from other paintings: Dürer represents the saint in a half-length, thus creating a new type of image. In the Netherlands, the painting and the new manner would have many imitators (Panofsky, 1955).
In a note in his travel diary, written after the date 16 March 1521 (Lugli, 1995, p. 112), Dürer sais that he gave the painting to "Rodrigo of Portugal." It would be Rodrigo Fernandez de Almada, of a Portuguese business agency in Antwerp, with whom Dürer had struck up a friendship (*cat. 67*). The painting remained property of the de Almada family until the nineteenth century; the Portuguese state acquired it between 1880 and 1882.

69

Portrait of a Man with Baret and Scroll

Inscription near his head, monogrammed and dated 1521
Oil on Oak, 50 x 36 cm
Madrid, Museo del Prado
1521

The last digit of the date is not clearly legible (1 or 4?), but the fact that the panel is oak indicates that the painting must have been carried out during Dürer's trip to the Netherlands. The hypotheses regarding the name of the subject are various. The most frequent are: the one of Lorenz Sterck, an administrator and financial curator of the Brabant and of Antwerp, and that of Jobst Plankfelt, Dürer's innkeeper in Antwerp. These names are frequently suggested since Dürer writes in his diary that he had done oil portraits of them (Luigi, 1995, p. 119).
I find it difficult to imagine an innkeeper who made himself depicted with a scroll in his hand. Whereas it seems much more plausible that the imposing subject characterized by a severe and scrutinizing gaze—clad in a silk shirt, a cloak with a fur collar, and a large beret—corresponds to a tax collector. But whoever the subject is, the portrait is regardless one of the most beautiful and incisive that Dürer ever created. He manages, with an image constrained by such a limited space, to communicate the impression of being in front of a personality of a supremely concentrated energy—and all that by using simple and pale colors, whose effect is unfortunately partly obfuscated by the heavy varnish covering the painting.

70

Portrait of Bernhard von Reesen

Inscription above the head, monogrammed and dated 1521
Oil on Oak,.
45.4 x 31.5 cm
Dresden, Staatliche Kunstsammlungen
1521

This painting has been in its present location since the eighteenth century. An annotation Dürer made in Antwerp in his travel diary of the Netherlands in March 1521 reveals: "Item I did Bernhart Resten's oil portrait. He gave 8 florins to me, a crown to my wife and a florin worth 24 stüber to Susanna" (the maidservant who accompanied Dürer and his wife) (Lugli, 1995, p. 115).
The name of the subject, written on the folded letter that he is holding, is still quite decipherable.
Rodrigo de Almada, portrayed in the same year 1521 (*cat. 67*), poses in front of a neutral, pale sky-blue background; Dürer chose a warm shade of red for Bernhard von Reesen.
The well-preserved state allows for a full appreciation, from a formal point of view and a pictorial one, the mastery of the painter.
He gives the thirty-year-old subject an intense physical and spiritual charm. This work further demonstrates the extraordinary span of Dürer's portraiture up until his final years.

71

Madonna and Child
(Madonna with the Pear)

Inscription to the right, monogrammed and dated 1526
Oil on Panel, 43 x 32 cm
Florence, Galleria degli Uffizi
1526

In the beginning of the eighteenth century, this painting was in the guardaroba (cloakroom) of the Pitti Palace. From there, it moved to the Villa di Poggio a Caiano. It has been at the Uffizi since 1773.
Dürer made the pear smaller as the painting process progressed. Despite its small scale, the Madonna is depicted in a half-bust; the child is seated, though it is unclear on what—maybe the mother's arm. The artist leaves that up to the spectator.
According to Anzelewsky (1991), it is the last and most stylistically mature version of the Madonna's image painted by

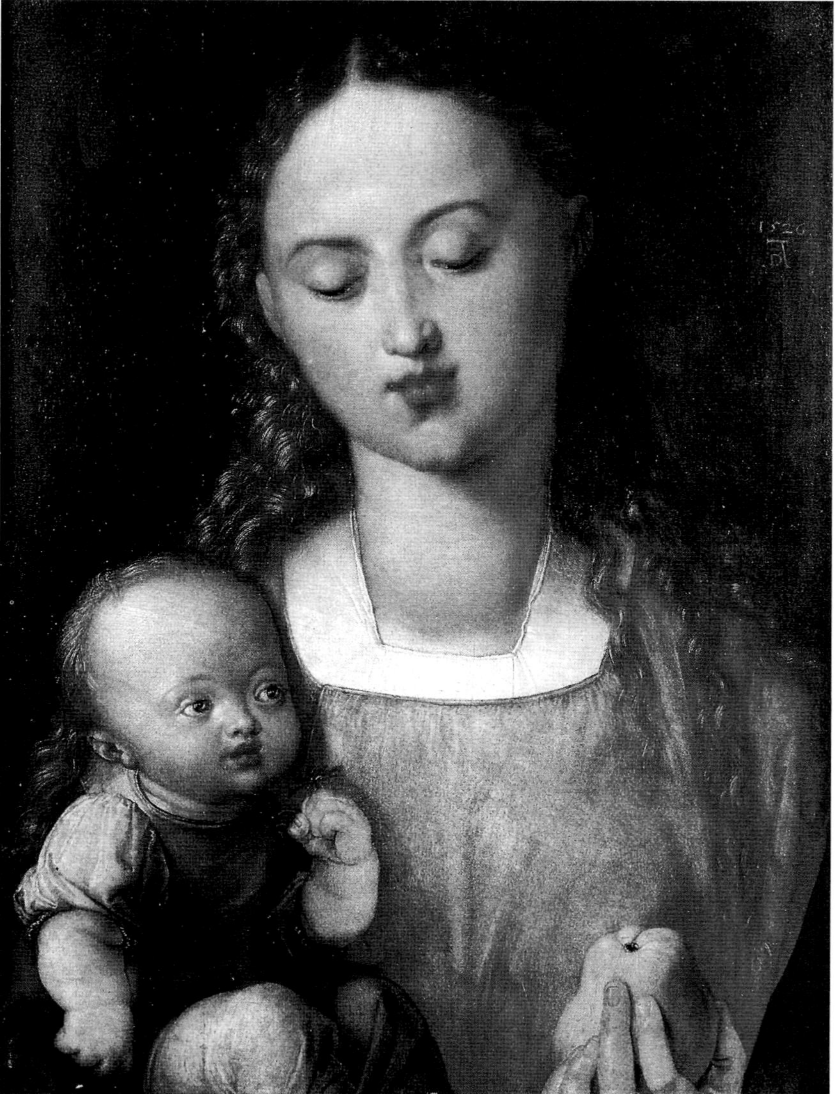

Cat 71 Madonna and Child

Dürer. The image of Munich (*cat. 54*) from 1516, though not revealing any emotional rapport between the mother and child, like this one, is nevertheless fascinating for its iconic aspect; but the Florentine image lacks intimate and formal tension.

Here, too, the Madonna is frontally depicted, holding a pear in her left hand—of which we see only the fingers. And here again, the long blond hair falls on her shoulders almost symmetrically to the right and left. The necklines of the white blouse and red dress are also nearly symmetrical, contrasting with her softly curved facial features. Her downward gaze shows meditation and pensiveness. Even the gaze of the clothed child is absorbed and immobile. The right hand holds on to the edge of the mother's cloak, and the left hand's fingers close around a nondescript flower. Evidently, this devotional image also was intended for meditation on the mother of God and on the Passion and Redemption of Christ, even if until now it has not been possible to discern any connection between the pear and the flower.

72

Portrait of Jakob Muffel

Inscription in the top left:
EFFIGIES JAKOBI MVFFEL AETATIS SVAE ANNO LV SALVTIS VERO MDXXVI*; monogrammed*
Canvas, transferred from panel, 48 x 36 cm
Berlin, Gemäldegalerie
1526

This painting was passed into a private Russian collection from the Schönborn collection in Pommersfelden, where it was in 1867. In 1870, in Saint Petersburg, it was transferred on canvas. In 1883, it was acquired in an auction from the Narischkin collection, in Paris, for the Berlin art gallery.

Jakob Muffel, first a town councilor, then a mayor for the city of Nuremberg (1514), was a friend of Dürer's. He died 26 April 1526; the portrait, dated 1526, must have been from the first months of that year. Even if its dimensions correspond roughly to those of the portraits Dürer executed in the Netherlands, it stands out from these for some particulars.

As in the Portrait of Hieronymus Holzschuher (*cat. 73*), of the same year, Dürer brings the head close to the spectator, moving it upward at the same time. There is no sign whatsoever of any decoration or of representativeness. On the contrary, the artist dwells affectionately on the details of the physiognomy of the subjects. He retouches the pronounced nose of Jakob in the shape of a duck's beak and brings out the calm expression of the open face, with the high forehead edged by a simple black beret decorated with three golden ribbons: a personal and incisive way to expose the incorruptible virtue of his friend.

73

Portrait of Hieronymus Holzschuher

Inscription in the top left: HIERONIMVS HOLTZSHVER ANNO DO[MI]NI 1526 AETATIS SVE 57*; to the right, near the head, monogrammed*
Lindenwood, 48 x 36 cm
Berlin, Gemäldegalerie,
1526

This painting belonged to the family until it was acquired by the Gemäldegalerie in 1884.
As in the case of Jakob Muffel, portrayed the same year (*cat. 72*), Dürer portrayed Holzschuher (1469–1529)—another friend who was a mayor many times in Nuremberg—without arms or hands, from the shoulders up.
The head almost touches the upper edge of the painting.
The person, clad in an overcoat trimmed with a fur collar, is drawn slightly from the side, and the animated eyes are looking with severe gaze at the spectator in the opposite direction. This technique was adopted by Dürer in only one other instance, for the Portrait of Oswolt Krell (*cat. 23*).
The face, from the well-defined lips is framed by flowing, wavy hair, and thus takes on a particularly alive expression, chiefly due to the brightness of the eyes.
This is the penultimate portrait that Dürer has left us. One more time, the master unfolds his exquisite ability in finely sketching out with a brush the details of the fur, the beard, and the hair, distinguishing one from the other. It is an ability that was highly appreciated and praised by his colleagues during his Venetian sojourns.
This portrait, besides being a masterful interpretation of the subject's character, has another characteristic: along with the very simple frame, the sliding lid that was used to protect the painting was preserved (see ill.).
It is not a portrait meant to be hung, but rather, to be put away, perhaps in a wardrobe.
The date is reproduced on the lid, as are the coats of arms of the Holzschuher family and the Müntzer family, the latter the wife Dorotea's.

74

Portrait of Johannes Kleberger

Inscription: E[FFIGIES] IOAN[N]I KLEBERGERS NORICI AN[N]O AETA[TIS] SVAE XXXX, *followed by the cabbalistic symbol (conjunction of the sun with the ascendant star Regulus of the constellation of Leo); in the top right, monogrammed and dated 1526*
Oil on Lindenwood, 37 x 36.6 cm; shortened on all sides
Vienna, Kunsthistorisches Museum
1526

In 1564, Willibald Imhoff, the child from the first marriage of Johannes Kleberger's second wife, Felicita Pirckheimer (who had first married Hans Imhoff), acquired the painting in Lyon from Johannes's son, David Kleberger. In 1588, it was sold by Willibald's heirs to Emperor Rudolph II. From Prague, it went to the Schatzkammer in Vienna and, in 1748, to the gallery.
Among the three portraits Dürer painted in 1526—Hieronymus Holzschuher, Jakob Muffel, and Johannes Kleberger (1486–1546)—the last was distinct for the format of the frame and for the depiction: the man, in fact, is sketched in a bas relief, in a half-bust, and inserted, classically, in a clypeus. It is an unusual depiction among Dürer's works, which has largely puzzled art historians. But since portraits in bas-relief on medallions were often found on the facades of Renaissance buildings in France, where Kleberger lived for a long time, it is quite likely that the patron himself had requested the artist to portray him in this way. Dürer's innovation was that of vivifying the portrait in bas relief on a medallion of fake stone, giving him the colors of a live, if pale, complexion. Dürer, as has already been noted (by, among others, Rabel, 1991), takes up again the age-old theme of the comparison of the figurative arts, or, more specifically, the discussion of the predominance of one on the other. He interprets this discussion by presenting an image in sculpture, with its light and shadow, giving at the same time the signs of a painted portrait. Thus, even while maintaining, in the steadiness of the gaze, the immobile plasticity of a sculpted image, characteristic of the portraits of emperors during classical times, the result is a particularly vivid portrait, since it expresses the power of the subject and his extremely ambitious character.
Johannes Kleberger, on the whole, had good reason to be proud of himself: working for the Imhoff merchants in Bern and especially in Lyon—a city that, because of its geographical position, had become a huge trading center with branches of very important German merchants—he had accumulated a sizable wealth that allowed him, in 1522, to provide a loan for Francis I of France. During his sojourn in Nuremberg, in 1525–26, he had Dürer paint his portrait and, after having married the daughter of Willibald Pirckheimer, Felicita, the widow of Hans Imhoff, he returned to Lyon, where he acquired various properties. In 1543, Francis I appointed him his valet de chambre.
Johannes Kleberger thus became one of the ten wealthiest and most influential inhabitants of Lyon. He gave enormous financial donations to the city, as in 1531 when, during the plague epidemic, he gave 500 livres to benefit the orphans of the plague victims. He was called le bon Allemand (Kellenberg, 1977; Rabel, 1990), and a monument was erected in his honor, of which a replica still exists today.
Upon his death, along with the bequests to the hospitals in Bern and Geneva, he left the French city huge sums to assign to charities. Yet the portrait Dürer delivers shows a very hard-looking man: a hardness underscored from the classical type of pose and from the indication of the coldness of the stone.
Behind the inscription lies the cabbalistic sign of the sol in corde leonis, which is the conjunction of the brightest star of Leo, with the sun that was taken from the De occulta philosophia of Agrippa von Nettesheim (1510). He, too, was a German whom Kleberger likely met in Lyon, and according to whom the men born under this sign were destined for greatness. The symbol also represents an amulet against melancholy. Even the symbol of Leo surrounded by stars, depicted in the upper-left corner of the painting, would have a divinatory significance and again, according to Agrippa von Nettesheim (Rebel, 1990), it would represent the particularly fortunate position of the person portrayed. In the lower corners, to the left and right, are the *redende Wappen* (figurative coats of arms) of the Kleberger family.

75

The Four Apostles

The Apostles John and Peter

Inscription in the top left, monogrammed and dated 1526

Lindenwood,
215.5 x 76 cm

The Apostle Paul and Mark the Evangelist
Inscription, monogrammed and dated 1526
Lindenwood,
214.5 x 76 cm
Munich,
Alte Pinakothek
1526

Dürer did not paint these four paintings on commission. It was he who wanted to donate them to Nuremberg, his native city. The city accepted and reciprocated by giving the sum of 100 florins (see the correspondence regarding this in Rupprich I, 1956). The four monumental figures remained in the municipality of Nuremberg until 1627, when, following threats of repression, they had to be sold to the elector of Bavaria, Maximilian I, a great enthusiast of Dürer's work.

On that occasion, however, the prince had the inscriptions, at the bottom of the paintings, sawed off and sent back to Nuremberg, as they were considered heretical and injurious to his position as the sovereign Catholic. The city handed them over to the museum in Munich in 1922, where they were rejoined with their respective panels.

As it was common in many cities in Italy to bestow the town hall with a work of art that would serve as an example of buon governo, so did Dürer want to provide his native city with a work of his that had been purposefully made to this end.

The Four Apostles, witnesses to the faith, were to simultaneously function as a warning. For this, their figures had inscriptions affixed that the calligrapher Johann Neudörfer had added to the bottom of the panels, which reproduced biblical passages from the recent translation of Martin Luther (1522).

The first line of both are references to the Apocalypse of Saint John (22:18 ff.), but the essential content has another origin: it is a reproach to the secular powers not to conceal the divine word in seductive human interpretation. Besides, it reads that everyone should take the warning of the "four excellent men" to heart: almost a formulation of the symbolic program represented in the choice of the four figures, of three apostles and an evangelist, Mark, an unusual choice that Dürer does not explain or illustrate.

The Four Apostles undoubtedly represents his personal religious credo through the inscriptions. His position is to be on guard against the "false prophets." This becomes understandable if one considers the political-religious background of that time and the violence and passion of the religious upheavals, which favored the onset of false doctrines.

Dürer knew that his support of the Lutheran movement, which surely came out from the words of the inscriptions, would have been shared by important and influential citizens; in fact, different from the majority of Nuremberg sovereignties, firmly embraced Protestantism in toto.

In his Bulletin on the Artists and Artisans in Nuremberg of 1546, the aforementioned Neudörfer writes that Dürer wanted to represent a sanguine, a choleric, a phlegmatic, and a melancholic. Panofsky (1943) believed that it was possible to subdivide them according to the following attributions: John would be the sanguine, Peter the phlegmatic, Paul the melancholic, and Marco the choleric. In addition, each temperament would correspond to one of the four ages of life. Preparatory drawings exist for the heads in Berlin and Bayonne (W 870–72).

76

Head of a Child with a Long Beard
Inscription to the right of the head, monogrammed and dated 1527
Canvas, 52.5 x 27.8 cm
Paris, Louvre,
Cabinet des Dessins
1527

It is generally held that this is a depiction of a monstrous creature. According to the Tietzes (1928), "it is a hieroglyphic traceable to Dürer's interest in the works of Horapollo (Egyptian scholar of the fourth century a.d.), representing the pedogeron, whose two components—the child and the old man—express the ancient and the new, that is, the past and the future. A source for the image is the description of the temple of Minerva in Sais, made by Plutarch in De Isi et Osiri, which was similarly known in the humanist circles of Nuremberg through the translation of Caelius Calcagnini, published between 1509 and 1517.

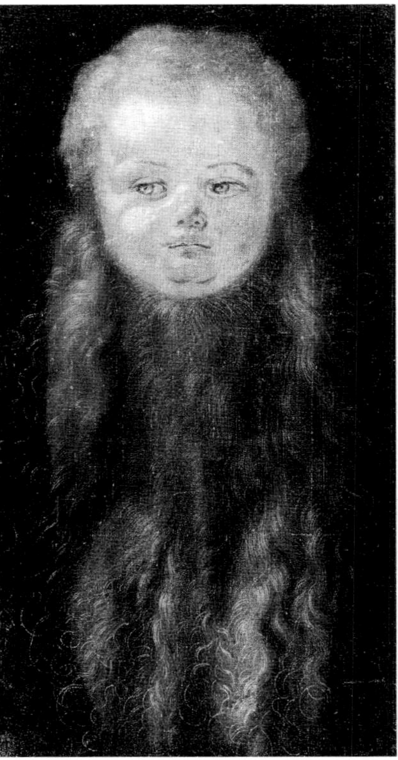

Cat 76 Head of a Child with a Long Beard

Epilogue

Dürer did not have children. Not having made a will, the inheritance went to his wife, Agnes, who, with a regular contract, divided it in 1530 with those of Dürer's brothers who were still alive. Thus, Endres and Hans each received a quarter of it.

The latter, having moved to Poland, was represented by a deputy during the division; Endres took a conspicuous share of the artistic works.

Subsequently—though it is unclear how—the main part of the inheritance went to Willibald Pirckheimer, and upon his death, in 1530, to his heirs, that is, the Imhoff family. It is through him that nearly all Dürer's works have been preserved. Among the great collectors who acquired his works, Rudolph II figures first.

His collection went in large part to the Kunsthistorisches Museum in Vienna. Maximilian I of Bavaria follows, whose collection became part of the Alte Pinakothek in Munich.

Several copies exist of many of the paintings.

Topographical Index

Chronological Table

1471
Albrecht Dürer was born 23 May, the third of eighteen children, to the goldsmith Albrecht Dürer and his wife, Barbara Holper. The Dürer family—horse and cattle breeders—was originally from Ajtòsfalva in Hungary. The German name and family coat of arms confirm this: Ajtòs, in Hungarian, means "door," and a door lies open in the center of the Dürerian coat of arms (fig. 1). "Door," in German is Tür, and, in the old spelling, Thür; and Thürer was the first German name of the family, which was then changed to Dürer. His father, also named Albrecht, left Gyula at a young age, where the family had moved (the grandfather was a goldsmith), and had gone through Germany and the Netherlands, finally settling down, at twenty-eight, in Nuremberg in 1455. Here, he entered the workshop of the goldsmith Hieronymus Holper, whose fifteen-year-old daughter, Barbara, he married 6 August 1467.

1475
The master goldsmith Albrecht acquired, after his father-in-law's death, a house-workshop near Michael Wolgemut's workshop, and other important workshops which belonged to the cultural and artistic elite of Nuremberg.

1483
The younger Albrecht entered his father's workshop to complete a three-year apprenticeship as a goldsmith.

1486
Instead of continuing to work at his father's, he entered as an apprentice the workshop of the famous painter and woodcutter Michael Wolgemut, where he remained for another three-year apprenticeship.

1490
As the family chronicle read, having finished this period and in accordance with the custom of apprentice-artisans, the younger Albrecht set out on 11 April auf Wanderschaft, and went to Colmar, Basel, and, toward the end of 1493, to Strasbourg.

1494
In May, he returned to Nuremberg, where he took Agnes Frey as his wife, 12 July. The plague broke out; in October, Dürer left, and, going through Augsburg and Innsbruck, arrived in Venice.

1495
In the spring, Dürer returned to Nuremberg and started his own workshop.

1500
The Venetian artist Jacobo de' Barbari settled in Nuremberg, the "counterfeiter" and "illuminist" of Maximilian I. Dürer hoped to learn more about on proportion and perspective under him.

1505
In February, Dürer left again for Venice, which he then left for Rome in the late autumn of 1506, stopping on the way in Bologna and Florence. He returned to Venice at the beginning of 1507. It is known that during his sojourn in Italy, the artist kept a sort of diary, a Schreibpüchle, which unfortunately has been lost.

1506
During his absence from Nuremberg, his wife, Agnes, and his mother, Barbara, were to sell his woodcuts and engravings, one at the Frankfurt fair, the other in Nuremberg.

1507
In the spring, Dürer returned to Nuremberg, passing through Augsburg. He hired first Hans Suess from Kulmbach, then Hans Baldung from Strasbourg, and last, Hans Schäufelein from Nördlingen as assistants in his workshop. Lorenz Behaim read his horoscope (Rupprich, 1956, I, p. 254).

1509
Dürer bought a house in Tiergärtnertor, since then known as "Dürer's House." The artist was elected Genannter by the council of the city.

1512
Emperor Maximilian arrived in Nuremberg 4 February. With the assistance of other artists, Dürer began to plan the Triumphal Arch of Maximilian—a monumental woodcut consisting of 192 panels—almost three and a half meters high and about three meters wide. He executed other works for the emperor as well, which assured him a lifelong annuity of 100 florins.

1518
During the summer, Dürer went, along with a delegation of ambassadors from his city, to Augsburg to participate in the Diet.

1519
Maximilian I died 12 January. At the end of April, Dürer went to Zurich with Willibald Pirckheimer and Martin Tucher on a diplomatic mission.

1520
Angling to have his 100-florin annuity confirmed by the successor of Maximilian I, Charles V, Dürer started off with his wife and maidservant to the Netherlands 12 July. During the journey, he stayed in Antwerp, Bruges, Brussels, Mechlin, and Aachen. He participated in the coronation of the new emperor, and went to Zeeland, where he probably caught malaria.

1521
In August, after going through Louvain, Aachen, and Cologne—where his diary breaks off—Dürer returned to Nuremberg.

1525
Dürer's first theoretical work is published, Die Underweisung der Messung, a treatise on geometry that he dedicates to his friend Willibald Pirckheimer.

1527
The publication of his treatise on the fortifications of the city, castles, and small cities, Etliche underricht zu befestigung der Stett, Schlosz und flecken.

1528
Dürer dies 6 April, shortly after turning fifty-seven years old. He is buried in the Frey family tomb, in Saint John's cemetery; the following day, the corpse is exhumed to execute a death mask. A lock of hair is cut off, of which the painter Hans Baldung Grien took possession, and that is now kept in the Fine Arts Academy in Vienna. The Vier Bücher von menschlicher Proportion (Four books on the proportions of the human body) are published, which in the following years are published in Latin, French, and Italian.

Bibliography

1568

Giorgio Vasari, *Lives of the Painters, Sculptors and Architects*, New York.

1584

Raffaello Borghini, *Il Riposo*, Florence.

Giovanni Paolo Lomazzo, *Trattato dell'arte de la pittura*, Milan, ristampa 1968.

1617

Carel van Mander, *Het Leven der doorluchtige Nederlandtsche en Hooghduytsche schilders*, Amsterdam, first edition Alkmaar 1604.

1660

Marco Boschini, *La Carta del navegar pitoresco*, Venice, ed. Critica a cura di Anna Pallucchini, Venice/Rome, 1969.

1675

Joachim von Sandrart, *L'Academia todesca della architectura, scultura & pittura: oder Teutsche Academie der edlen Bau- Bild- und Mahlerey-Künste*, Frankfurt.

1678

Carlo Cesare Malvasia, *Felsina Pittrice*, Bologna.

1728

Filippo Baldinucci, *Notize de' professori del disegno da Cimabue in qua...*Secolo 3.e 4. Dal 1400 al 1540, Florence.

1791

Johann Ferdinand Roth, *Leben Albrecht Dürers des Vaters der deutschen Künstler*, Leipzig.

1819

Adam Weise, *Albrecht Dürer und sein Zeitalter*, Leipzig.

1827

Joseph Heller, *Das Leben und die Werke Albrecht Dürers. Dürers Bildnisse Kupferstiche, Holzschnitte und die nach ihm gefertigen Blätter*, Bamberg.

1837

Georg Kaspar Nagler, *Albrecht Dürer und seine Kunst*, Munich.

1876

Moritz Thausing, *Dürer. Geschichte seines Lebens und seiner Kunst*, Leipzig trans. Francese 1878.

1892

Anton Springer, *Albrecht Dürer*, Berlin.

1860

August von Eye, *Leben und Wirken Albrecht Dürers*, Nördlingen.

1886

Marcus Zucker, *Dürers Stellung zur Reformation*, Erlangen.

1900

Marcus Zucker, *Albrecht Dürer*, Halle/Saale.

1902

Ludwig Justi, *Konstruirte Figuren und Köpfe unter den Werken Albrecht Dürers. Untersuchungen und Rekostruktionen*, Leipzig.

1904

Ludwig Justi, *Dürers Dresdener* Altar, Leipzig.

Ludwig Lorenz, *Die Mariendarstellungen Albrecht Dürers*, Strausborg.

Valentin Scherer, *Dürer. Des Meisters Gemälde, Kupferstiche und Holzschnitte*, Stuttgart/Leipzig.

1905

Heinrich Wölfflin, *Die Kunst Albrecht Dürers*, Munich, 6. ed. K. Gerstenberg, 1943.

1906

Ernst Heidrich, *Geschichte des Dürerschen Marienbildes*. Leipzig.

1909

Ernst Heidrich, *Dürer und die Reformation*, Leipzig.

1910

Sebastian Killermann, *Albrecht Dürers Pflanzen- und Tierzeichnungen und ihre Bedeutung für die Naturgeschichte*. Strausborg.

1915

Erwin Panofsky, *Dürers Kunsttheorie, vornehmlich in ihrem Verhältnis zur Kunsttheorie der Italiener*, Berlin.

1916

Emil Waldmann, *Albrecht Dürer*, Leipzig.

1919

Hans Schuritz, *Die Perspektive in der Kunst Albrecht Dürers, ein Beitrag zur Geschichte der Perspektive*, Frankfurt.

1919-1920

Emil Waldmann, *Albrecht Dürers Leben und Kunst*, Leipzig.

1921

Max J. Friedländer, *Albrecht Dürer*, Leipzig.

1923

Gustav Glück, *Dürers Bildnis einer Venezianerin von 1505, in "Jahrbuch der Kunsthistorischen Sammlungen in Wein,"* 36 pp. 97-121.

Kurt Pfister, *Albrecht Dürer. Werk und Gestalt*, Vienna.

1927

Arpad Weixlgärtner, Alberto Duro, in *"Festschrift für Julius Schlosser zum 60. Geburstage,"* a cura A. Weixlgärtner e Leo Planiscig, Zürich/Leipzig/Vienna, pp. 162-186, Infussi dell'arte du Dürer sull'arte italiana.

1928

Albrecht Dürer. Ausstellung im Germanischen Nationalmuseum, 2 and 3. ed., Nuremberg.

Han Tietze and Erika Tietze-Conrat, *Kritisches Verzeichnis der Werke Albrecht Dürers, vol. 1: Der junge Dürer, Verzeichnis der Werke bis zur venezianischen Reise im Jahre 1505*, Augsburg 1928, vol. 2: Der reife Dürer, Basel/Leipzig, 1937-1938.

Friedrich Winkler, *Dürer. Des Meisters Gemälde, Kupferstiche und Holzschnitte*, 4 ed. Berlin/Leipzig.

1928,1931

Eduar Flechsig, *Albrecht Dürer. Sein Leben und seine künstlerische Entwicklung*, 2 vols., Berlin.

1930

Alfred Neumeyer, *Dürer*, Paris.

Hans Rupprich, *Willibald Pirckheimer und die erste Reise Dürers nach Italien*, Vienna.

1934

Hugo Kehrer, *Dürers Selbstbildnisse und die Dürer-Bildnisse*, Berlin.

1935

Gustav Pauli, *Der knieende Schmerzensmann. Ein neues Gemälde aus Dürers Frühwerk*, in "Pantheon" 15-16, p. 347 and foll.

Wilhelm Waetzold, *Dürer und seine Zeit*, Vienna and other editions.

1936

Antonio Rusconi, *Per l'identificazione degli acquerelli tridentini di Alberto Durero*, in *"Die graphischen Künste,"* N. F. 1, pp. 121-137.

1936-1939

Friedrich Winkler, *Die Zeichnungen Albrecht Dürers*, 4 vols., Berlin.

1937

Hans Tietze and Erika Tietze-Conrat, *Kritisches Verzeichnis der Werke Albrecht Dürers; vol 1: Der junge Dürer, Verzeichnis der Werke bis zur venezianischen Reise im Jahre 1505*, Augsburg 1928; vol. 2: Der reife Dürer, Basel/Leipzig, 1937-1938.

1943

Erwin Panofsky, *The Life and Art of Albrecht Dürer*, 2 vols., 1. ed. 1943, 2 ed. 1945, 3 ed 1948, 4 ed. 1955, Princeton.

Heinrich Wölfflin, *Die Kunst Albrecht Dürers*, 6 ed. K. Gerstenberg, Munich.

1952

Hans Jantzen, *Dürer der Maler*, Bern.

Heinrich Theodor Musper, *Albrecht Dürer. Der Gegenwär-*

tige Stand der Forschung, Stuttgart.

1953

Ernst Buchner, *Das deutsche Bildnis der Spätgotik und der frühen Dürer-Zeit*, Berlin.

1955

Erwin Panofsky, *The Life and Art of Albrecht Dürer*, 4 ed., Princeton.

1956

Ludwig Grote, *"Hier bin ich ein Herr,"* Dürer in Venedig, Munich.

1956-1959

Hans Rupprich, *Dürer, Schriftlicher Nachlass*, 3 vols., Berlin.

1957

Friedrich Winkler, *Albrecht Dürer, Leben und Werk*, Berlin.

1958

Alfred Stange, *Ein Gemälde aus Dürers Wanderzeit*, in "Studien zur Kunst der Oberrheins. Festschrift für Werner Noack," Konstanz/Freiburg i. Br. pp. 113-117.

1959

Günter Arnolds. *Opus quinque diedrum*, in "Festschrift Friedrich Winkler," Berlin.

Jan Bialostocki, "Opus Qunique Dierum:" *Dürer's Christ among the Doctor's and its Sources*, in "Journal of the Warburg and Courtauld Institutes," XXII, pp. 17-34.

1960

Kurt Martin, *Der vier Apostel*, Stuttgart.

1961

Meister um Albrecht Dürer, exhibit catalog at al Germanisches Nationalmuseum, Nuremberg.

1964

Michael Levey, *Dürer*, London.

1965

Heinrich Theodor Musper, *Albrecht Dürer*, Köln.

1966

Otto Benesch, *Die deutsche Malerei. Von Dürer bis Holbein*. Genève.

1968

Roberto Salvini, *Noterella su Romanino e Dürer*, in "Festschrift fur Ulrich Middledorf," ed. a Kosegarten e P. Tigler, Berlin.

Giorgio Zampa and Angela Ottino Della Chiesa, *L'opera completa di Dürer* (Classici dell'arte 23), Milan.

1970

Mattias Mende e U. von Dewitz, *Albrecht Dürer*, Königstein im Taunus.

G.M. Wagner, *Albrecht Dürer. Vier Bücher von der menschlichen Proportion*, London.

1971

Albrecht Dürer 1471-1971, exhibit catalog at manisches Nationalmuseum, Nuremberg.

Deutsche Kunst der Dürezeit, exhibit catalog at Albertinum, Dresden.

Albrecht Dürers Umwelt, in "Festschrift zum 500. Geburtstag Dürers," Nuremberg.

Fedja Anzelewesky, *Albrecht Dürer*. Das malerische Werk, Berlin.

Walter Jürgen Hofmann, *Über Dürers Farbe*, Nuremberg.

Walter Koschatzky, *Albrecht Dürer. Die Landschafts-Aquarelle. Örtlichkeit, Datierung, Stilkritik*, Vienna/Munich.

M. Mende, *Dürer-Bilbiographie*, Wiesbaden.

Heinrich Theodor Musper, *Albrecht Dürer*, Köln.

Annette Pfaff, *Studien zu Albrecht Dürers Heller-Altar*, tesi, Nuremberg.

Roberto Salvini, *Dürer, mezzo millennio: La mostra di Norimberga e il catalogo*, in "Commentari" 22, pp. 289-304.

Peter Strieder, *Die Bedeutung des Porträts bei Albrecht Dürer*, in "Kunst einer Zeitenwende," ed. H. Schade, pp. 84-100.

Franz Winzinger, *Albrecht Dürer in Selbstzeugnissen und Bilddokumenten*, Reinbeck (Hamburg).

Franz Winzinger, *Dürer und Leonardo*, in "Pantheon" 29 pp. 3-13.

1972

André Chastel, *Zu vier Selbstbildnissen Albrecht Dürers aus den Jahren 1506-1511*, in "Albrecht Dürer, Kunst im Aufbruch," pp.37-45.

Kristina Herrmann-Fiore, *Dürer Landschftsaquarelle*, Bern/Frankfurt.

1973

Lisa Oehler, *Das Dürer-Monogramm auf den Werken der Dürer-Schule* in "Städel-Jahrbuch," N.F. 4, pp. 37-80.

1974

Jörg Rasmussen, *Die Nürnberger Altarbaukunst der Dürerzeit*, thesis, Munich.

Walter L. Strauss, *The Complete Drawings of Albrecht Dürer*, 6 vols., New York.

1975

Walter L. Strauss, *The Intaglio Prints of Albrecht Dürer: Engravings, Etchings and Drypoints*, New York.

1976

Kristina Hermann-Fiore, *Sui rapporti fra l'opera artistica del Vasari e del Dürer*, in "Il Vasari storiografo e artista," Atti del Congresso internazionale nel IV Centenario della morte, Arezzo/Florence.

Peter Strieder, *Dürer*, Milan.

1977

Erwin Panofsky, *The Life and Art of Albrecht Dürer*, Princeton.

1978-79

Lotte Brand Philip, *The Portrait Diptych of Dürer's Parents*, in "Simiolus," 10, p. 5 and foll.

1979

Peter Strieder, *Albrecht Dürer. Das Gesamtwerk*. Frankfurt/Berlin/Vienna.

1981

Terisio Pignatto. *Dürer e Lotto*, in "Lorenzo Lotto," Atti del Convegno internazionale di studi per il V centenario della nascita, pp. 93-97.

Peter Strieder. *Albrecht Dürer*, 3. ed., New York 1989.

1983

Fedja Anzelewsky, *Dürer-Studien, Untersuchungen zu den ikonographischen und geistesgeschichtlichen Grundlagen seiner Werke zwischen den beiden Italienreisen*, Berlin.

Làszló Mészàros, *Italien sieht Dürer, Zur Wirkung der deutschen Druckgraphik auf die italienische Kunst des 16. Jahrhunderts*. Erlangen.

1985

Bernhard Decker, *Notizien zum Heller-Altar*, in "Städel Jahrbuch" 10. pp. 179-192.

Fritz Koreny. *Albrecht Dürer and the Animal and Plant Studies of the Renaissance.* Munich.

1986

Günter J. Janowitz, *Leonardo da Vinci*. Brunelleschi. *Dürer. Ihre Auseinanderzetzung mit der Problematik der Zentralperspektive*. Einhausen.

1987

Alexander Perrig, *Albrecht Dürer oder die Heimlichkeit der deutschen Ketzerei*, Weinheim.

Roberto Salvini, *Raffaello e Dürer*, in "Studi su Raffaelleo," Atti del Congresso internazionale di studi, Urbino, Florence, pp. 145-150.

1988

Fedja Anzelewsky, *Dürer, Werk und Wirkung*, Erlangen.

1989

Peter Strieder, *Albrecht Dürer, Paintings, Prints and Drawings*, 3 ed.

1990

Jane Campbell Hutchinson, *Albrecht Dürer: A Biography*, Princeton.

1991

Fedja Anzelewsky, *Albrecht Dürer: das malerische Werk*, 2 vols., Berlin, also see 1971 Anzelewsky.

Colin Eisler, *Dürer's Animals*, Washington/London.

1994

Karl Schütz, *Albrecht Dürer im Kunsthistorischen Museum*, exhibit catalog, Milan.

Lukas Mandersbacher, *Albrecht Dürers Allerheiligenbild* in: "Sinnbild und Abbild. Kunstgeschichtliche Studien," Innsbuck 199, p. foll.

1995

Albrecht Dürer, Viaggio nei Paesi Bassi, ed, Adalgisa Lugli, Torino.

Doris Kutschbach, *Albrecht Dürer.Die Altäre*, thesis, Stuttgart, Zürich.

Pierre Vaisse, *Albrecht Dürer*, Mesnil-sur-l'Estrée.

Recent publications of Dürer's writings:

1956

Rupprich, Hans, *Dürer, Schriftlicher Nachlass*, Berlin. Vol. 1: Personal chronicles. Maxims, letters, poetry, travel diary of the Netherlands. Books Dürer owned. Dürer in documents and writings.

1966

Vol 2. The beginning of his theoretical studies, until his return from Italy in 1507. *Das Lehrbuch der Malerei, Die Lehre von der menschlichen Proportion, Vom Mass der Pferde, Vom Mass der Gebäude, Von der Perspektive, von Licht und Schatten. Die Umkonstruktionsmöglichkeiten für den menschlichen Körper.*

1969

Vol. 3: *Die Lehre von der menschlichen Proportion. Die Unterweisung der Messung. Unterricht zur Befestigung der Städte, Schlösser und Flecken*. Various topics.

Note:
Dürer's drawings are cited with Winkler's numeration (W), 1936-1939.

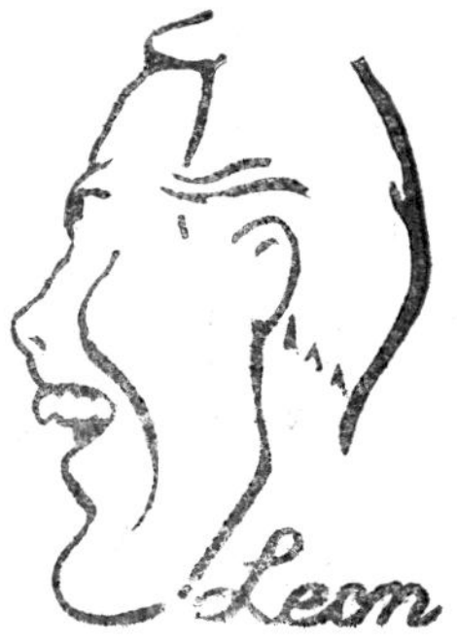

Leon

P9-ECX-149

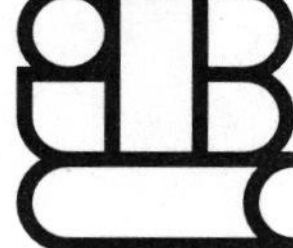

Thought Leaders

THOUGHT

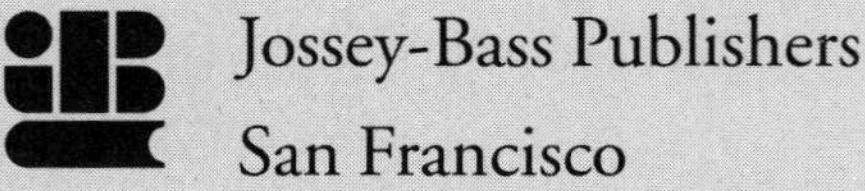

Jossey-Bass Publishers
San Francisco

A *Strategy & Business* Book
Booz·Allen & Hamilton

LEADERS

Insights on the Future of Business

Joel Kurtzman, Editor

Foreword by Brian N. Dickie

A *Strategy & Business* Book

Substantial discounts on bulk quantities of Jossey-Bass books are available to corporations, professional associations, and other organizations. For details and discount information, contact the special sales department at Jossey-Bass Inc., Publishers (415) 433-1740; Fax (800) 605-2665.

For sales outside the United States, please contact your local Simon & Schuster International Office.

Jossey-Bass Web address: http://www.josseybass.com

Manufactured in the United States of America on 100% recycled paper with 20% postconsumer fiber.

Library of Congress Cataloging-in-Publication Data
Kurtzman, Joel.
Thought leaders : insights on the future of business / Joel Kurtzman.
p. cm. — (The Jossey-Bass business & management series)
Includes index.
ISBN 0-7879-3903-X
1. Management. 2. Businesspeople—Interviews. I. Title. II. Series.
HD30.19.K87 1998
97-37425
658—dc21

Text Design by Ralph Fowler

FIRST EDITION
HB Printing 10 9 8 7 6 5 4 3 2 1

The Jossey-Bass
Business & Management Series

Contents

Foreword

Since early in this century, Booz·Allen & Hamilton has been working with the world's largest companies and the teams that lead them. Although this period of history has been as furious as it has been fruitful, the topics that now occupy the busy calendars of CEOs and their leadership groups have not changed much from two or more decades ago. As this volume will show, many of these "perennial" topics not only continue to occupy the minds of today's high-level leaders but also remain at the forefront of academic research in business and economics.

Indeed, the big concerns—over defining values and vision, managing people and risk, adapting to changed markets and new technology, and assessing performance and portfolio mix—have only become more important as competition intensifies, the speed of computers multiplies, and the economy becomes increasingly global.

At the same time, because of external pressures and changing management approaches, new ways of thinking about those concerns have swept through boardrooms and across factory floors with remarkable synchronicity, as shown by this collection of interviews with top executives, authors, and academicians between 1995 and 1997. We call this cutting-edge group "Thought Leaders." Some of these shifts reflect radically different orientations, such as management theorist Charles Handy's musings on corporate federalism or author-professor Gary Hamel's views on bottom-up strategy. Others are wholly pragmatic in nature, such as the views on teams and teamwork expressed by Jean-René Fourtou, chairman of Rhône-Poulenc S.A. of France.

Our own client work and research activities confirm the importance of the topics that this book addresses, although our ideas **do not** always agree with the interviewees' provocative conclusions.

In our own work, we have recently seen the focus of the CEO agenda shift toward growing the top line rather than cutting costs and toward managing the new corporation instead of restructuring the old one. As we see it, three variations on these themes reflect the new agenda for CEOs and their top teams:

- Managing for growth
- Business process redesign, the next generation
- The new organization

It seems clear what has caused CEOs to shift their focus. Many major companies, though not all, have completed the first wave of business process reengineering (BPR) and have thus achieved the first 80 percent or so of cost restructuring. They must now look to revenue growth for the next quantum leap in performance improvement. This situation puts managers in an expansive frame of mind that the rebound in corporate profits over the past three years undoubtedly reinforces.

At the same time, the wave of delayering, restructuring, and reengineering has left many companies in a twilight world between the old and the new. Traditional management processes have been discarded and dismantled; new ones are not always comfortably in place. Learning to manage in the post-restructured world has become a life-and-death priority, according to one Thought Leader, Keshub Mahindra of Mahindra & Mahindra, India's biggest maker of utility vehicles.

Broadly speaking, our clients seek growth from four sources, each of which has implications for the CEO's role in shaping a company's core capabilities and critical priorities.

- *Emerging markets.* Most CEOs look to the emerging markets of Asia and Latin America (and to a much lesser and potentially myopic extent, eastern Europe) as the keys to future growth. On the one hand, there is the infrastructure boom ($1 trillion by 2000, according to some estimates); on the other, there is an almost infinite potential consumer market as more and more segments of these huge populations enter the market economy. Already, there are about 300 million "consumers" who can purchase power parity in the world's emerging markets. And that number represents only 10 percent or so of the total population of those areas.
- *New products and services.* The ability to sustain innovation in products and services is becoming a principal source of competitive advantage across a broad range of industries.
- *Acquisitions.* As balance sheets have improved, the number of corporate acquisitions has started to rebound. In fact, there is even evidence that part of the value liberated by recent acquisitions is being captured by the acquirer's shareholders and not just by those of the acquiree,

which has overwhelmingly been the outcome historically. This trend is consistent with our observation that today's acquisitions appear to have a greater fit with the acquirers' core strategies and capabilities than was true in the past. This pattern also dovetails with the comments of another of our Thought Leaders, John T. Chambers, the president and chief executive of fast-growing Cisco Systems, Inc., who has made growth by acquisition his company's performance engine.

- *Strengthened "block and tackle."* Our clients are placing increased emphasis on the basics in their businesses: enhanced customer care; better marketing and sales force management; and improved, tactical pricing. Much of this change is overdue. Despite the claims of many analysts of BPR, recent rounds of reengineering and restructuring have left many of these basic processes weaker than before.

Relative emphasis among these growth channels necessarily varies. Our own analysis of one hundred companies with an above average increase in shareholder wealth over the past two decades suggests that expansion in emerging markets is the greatest source of growth; breakout strategies that redefine the basis of competition in mature industries come second; and continuous product innovation and brand building come third. Acquisitions worked less well, with a few notable exceptions.

To capture differentiated growth, CEOs need to foster new and enhanced competencies and attitudes within their organizations. Innovation, for example, has long been viewed as being as much the product of lucky breaks as of a business capability that one can design, upgrade, and manage. As a result, many organizations avoid managing their innovation capability for fear of tampering with creative forces that they do not wholly understand. In fact, as companies such as the Chrysler Corporation and the Sony Corporation have shown—and as another Thought Leader, Harvard's John Kao, has argued—companies can design and manage innovation capability in a number of ways. These include strengthening the business processes associated with understanding markets, planning product lines, managing technology, and developing products or processes; improving measurement systems that track innovation; and developing systematic processes to capture and deploy organizational learning and best practices.

Similarly, to capture the full long-term potential of emerging markets, CEOs will have to move the center of gravity of their organizations, their managerial brain trusts, and their own mind-sets toward these markets—and there is a long way to go.

Winning in emerging markets also requires a different type of decision-making process. The pace of change is so fast that traditional planning processes simply do not work. For example, markets that took a decade to develop in the United States and six years in Japan are evolving in less than two years in some parts of China.

What is needed is strategic entrepreneurship, a relatively clear view of long-term objectives, and a strong set of strategic boundaries that can be used to screen opportunities. CEOs also require a highly entrepreneurial approach to creating and exploiting opportunities and shifting between scenarios as they unfold.

Growth also brings uncertainty, however, which has implications for how companies must think about risk management. Among the "perennials" on the CEO agenda, we have found that risk management is the issue demanding the most attention.

As CEOs think about growth, their time frames are lengthening. I love to ask clients to estimate their time horizon. Answers vary, depending on the near-term health of their businesses, but strategic focus has moved out to about seven years. On earlier occasions, eighteen months was not unusual. During the past year, our firm has experienced a surge of engagements focused on modeling the relatively distant future and on leading management teams through strategic simulations or sophisticated war games for their industries.

Changing demographics, technology advances, and global shifts have far-reaching implications for competitive boundaries and patterns of demand in virtually every industry. CEOs increasingly view one of their core roles as stimulating their companies' perspectives on what the future will bring. The boldest among them will select a scenario and remold their businesses accordingly.

CEOs have long understood their role in building the corporate vision. Today, this focus is being complemented by a drive to establish and entrench clear *corporate values.* These are not simply a means to edify the spirit but are vehicles to communicate strategic focus and operating boundaries to all employees. When Warren Bennis, the noted leadership expert at the University of Southern California and another of our Thought Leaders, assesses corporate strategy, he does so more in terms of values than of growth or share matrix dynamics. This represents a shift from the focus of most strategists ten years ago.

The breakthrough implies a focus on both vision and communication. As explained by Minoru Makihara, the Mitsubishi Corporation's president and a Thought Leader, the entire organization must understand the company's strategic direction and feel empowered to reach that goal.

A related trend in organizations is renewed interest in the role of the corporate center or core. At a recent symposium at which Booz·Allen partners discussed the most important business issues on the agendas of the firm's clients, we discovered that thirteen of the twenty-five participating partners were working with major companies to retune and redefine the role of the corporate center.

To some degree, that reassessment relates to the need to change management processes to fit the post-restructured corporation. It is also driven by external, competitive pressures, however; the same market pressures that compelled companies to lower costs are forcing them to rethink the integrative logic of their business portfolios.

Much of the thinking in this field comes back to address which businesses belong in the corporate portfolio and how the parent can add value rather than subtract it, as is too frequently the case. In addition to the traditional debate over the most appropriate forms of strategic and financial performance systems, this wave of reexamination is focused on building truly global organizations (in many cases, with traditional "center" functions being distributed geographically), on conceiving and managing strategic alliances and other extended enterprise relationships, and on some of the "softer" forms of added value.

The latter include the inculcation of shared corporate values and identity and the capture and deployment of organizational learning and best practices. Increasingly, corporate added value is more a matter of applying intellectual capital than of sponsoring scale economies in unit costs. Stanford economist Paul M. Romer, a Thought Leader, is articulate on these points.

We are also seeing greater top-level attention focused on *managing through processes.* The wave of restructuring, reengineering, and delayering demands different management approaches than those used in the past. Yet the new approaches have been slow to develop. In a recent analysis that we conducted of twenty-eight "post-reengineered" companies, we found that in most cases, the CEOs and their top management teams were continuing to manage essentially as before. They used the same decision, planning, and control processes and the same management information and reporting systems. Most recognized the disconnection but were uncertain about how to resolve it. The answer lies in taking the following actions:

- Reorienting top executives to manage and enable "processes" rather than organization units

- Explicit reengineering of the decision-making processes involving top management itself, with related changes in authority delegation and style
- Creating new performance management systems that complement the reengineered world and incorporate an ability to learn

In beginning to address these issues, CEOs are also beginning to take more seriously some of the concepts that they nominally embraced over the past several years. The horizontal organization, team-based management, the learning organization, empowerment, and similar concepts have had their place in the executive lexicon for several years. The body language of most CEOs continued to reinforce older, more hierarchical traditions, however. This is now beginning to change as CEOs gain a greater understanding of these ideas and become more sincere in their desire to practice them.

The final element of the new organization relates to the players themselves. Building the management team is always a CEO agenda item. Today, virtually all CEOs with whom we talk say that creating greater *entrepreneurship* and *teamwork* among their top one hundred managers is their Number 1 challenge.

There are several drivers behind this renewed focus on the top team. Above all, the pace and volume of change that most corporations face demand that the load be shared; the CEO cannot typically expect to shoulder it alone. Then, too, there is a need to rebuild the social contract between managers and the company. One consequence of restructuring and downsizing has been a unilateral revocation of implied loyalties, as Charles Handy has suggested.

CEOs are exploring various approaches to reengineering their teams, including explicit team-building exercises, adjustments to measurement and rewards systems, and experimentation with such devices as internal "venture funds" designed to stimulate entrepreneurship. We are also seeing a renewed focus on selection, including a willingness to reach outside the home team to enlist the best athletes.

As CEO agendas evolve, the natural question is whether the current focus is correct. In our view, the new agenda is properly directed. Nevertheless, it is almost certain that the next decade will see a sorting of winners from losers at least as significant as the one that occurred during the last two decades. Fewer than half of the Fortune 500 listed twenty years ago are still on the list today, and a fair number of the survivors owe their position to their leviathan scale rather than to stellar performance.

Companies that lost their position failed because they had insufficient insight into their customers' needs and the implications of technology and other trends. In addition, they allowed service bottlenecks and excess costs to accumulate in their delivery systems. As a result, overseas and greenfield competitors were able to outdeliver and undercut them.

In theory, the new CEO agenda will help business leaders avoid similar missteps in the future. It will do this in a number of ways: the concentration on growth and innovation implies improved customer understanding and strengthened value propositions; the second wave of BPR will improve value while keeping costs lean; and the new organization will focus on shared learning, continual improvement, and greater entrepreneurship. Overall, we observe a more concerted attempt by CEOs to understand and position their companies for the future.

In practice, of course, some companies and some CEOs will do better than others. That is the nature of competition. From our vantage point, though, it is clear that the winners will be those CEOs who can integrate the new agenda with their own clear vision while simplifying the execution challenge and inspiring their organizations to perform beyond all expectations.

New York
October 1997

Brian N. Dickie
President and COO,
Booz·Allen & Hamilton

About the Editor

Joel **Kurtzman** is the editor-in-chief of *Strategy & Business,* a quarterly business publication. He is the former executive editor of the *Harvard Business Review* and former business columnist at the *New York Times.* An economist and international business consultant, Mr. Kurtzman has written fifteen books and numerous articles that have appeared in newspapers and magazines around the world. He has testified before the U.S. House of Representatives and the General Assembly of the United Nations on economic matters. Mr. Kurtzman has lectured at Columbia, Georgetown, Harvard, and Oxford Universities; the Keidanren, Tokyo; and at many companies.

He was the host of the PBS television special *Four Weeks in the Life of the Global Economy.* In Japan, he hosted an NHK television special *The Death of Money!* He has also hosted *Hodotokushyu,* the Japanese equivalent of *Sixty Minutes.* Mr. Kurtzman appears regularly on CNN.

For Eli Kurtzman

Introduction

More than ever, business is a game of ideas in which companies and individuals compete on the strength of what they know.

This fact is reflected in the rise of business schools, the increased number of MBAs, and the latest professional perk—the executive bookshelf.

I have observed this change myself as I have wandered through the hallways and offices of some of the world's greatest companies. When I began my career, it was rare to see books in the offices of corporate leaders. Shelves were stuffed with reports, coffee tables were piled with printouts, and desks were covered with papers.

Although papers still make their home on desktops (even with the advent of computers), the shelves are now filled with books and the coffee tables sport copies of the *Harvard Business Review, Strategy & Business,* and the *Sloan Management Review.* Executives are buying books, attending conferences, reading specialized periodicals, and surfing the Internet to discover new insights before the competition does.

But which insights and from which thinkers? And which books?

Over the last dozen or so years, I have conducted hundreds of interviews with some of the most renowned thinkers. These interviews have appeared in publications all over the world. If I wanted sympathy, I suppose I could complain about the travel, moan about how difficult it is to prepare for such encounters, and talk about the laboriousness of reading and rereading each subject's publications—not to mention deciphering my own handwriting and trying to make sense of the hisses and pops on the tape.

But the truth is that the experience of interviewing and then publishing the insights of today's most interesting Thought Leaders is very rich. There is also the thrill of the hunt, because few things are as enjoyable as being the first to discover and bring to people's attention someone whose insights are valid and important.

This volume contains a mixture of "sung" and unsung heroes. Some of the interview subjects are quite well known, although I have tried to have them talk about their newest work. Other subjects are only now developing followings.

I conducted all of the interviews in this book except for those with Stan Shih, founder of the Acer Group, and John T. Chambers, president and chief executive of Cisco Systems, Inc., both of whom were interviewed by Glenn Rifkin.

My reasons for selecting the people who appear here were straightforward. In each instance, I was looking for an individual who was addressing the big questions with which today's most senior executives are wrestling.

These questions relate to issues of business strategy, growth, and human resources, as well as the new social contract that is taking shape among companies, employees, and shareholders and the ways in which society itself is changing.

In every instance, the individuals in this book have global perspectives. These Thought Leaders come from the United States, Britain, France, Germany, Japan, Taiwan, and India. In almost every case, they have lived, worked, or studied outside their own countries.

It is a diverse group. For example, John Kao, who discusses creativity in the workplace, was trained as a psychiatrist. Charles Handy, the British management philosopher, worked in Asia for Royal Dutch Shell and once lived in Buckingham Palace, where he put on seminars. Warren Bennis, an economist by training and an expert on leadership and groups, was a soldier, professor, and university president.

All of these interviews first appeared in *Strategy & Business,* which in a short span of time has become one of the leading business journals. *Strategy & Business* is sponsored by Booz·Allen & Hamilton, the global strategy and technology consulting firm.

This volume inaugurates a publishing alliance between Booz·Allen and Jossey-Bass Publishers. Each year, two or three new books will be published in the *Strategy & Business*/Booz·Allen series. These books will address core topics for business managers and executives and will focus on the challenges that managers will face in the next century. The series will draw on the "intellectual capital" of top Booz·Allen consultants and of leaders in business and academia.

No book series or magazine could be produced without a group effort. These publications required the support of Charles E. Lucier, Booz·Allen's first chief knowledge officer; Sam I. Hill, the firm's former chief marketing officer; and, of course, Brian N. Dickie, its president and chief operating officer.

The publications are also the result of the creative efforts and exertions of the entire *Strategy & Business* team: Barry Adler, Lawrence M. Fisher, Glenn Rifkin, Barbara Presley Noble, and David Berreby on the editorial side, and Max Henderson-Begg, Rebecca M. Church, Mary Workman, Jamie MacLachlan, and Jackie Collette in management and production.

Together, this group produces wonderful material in an amazingly efficient and thoughtful manner.

Boston
October 1997

Joel Kurtzman

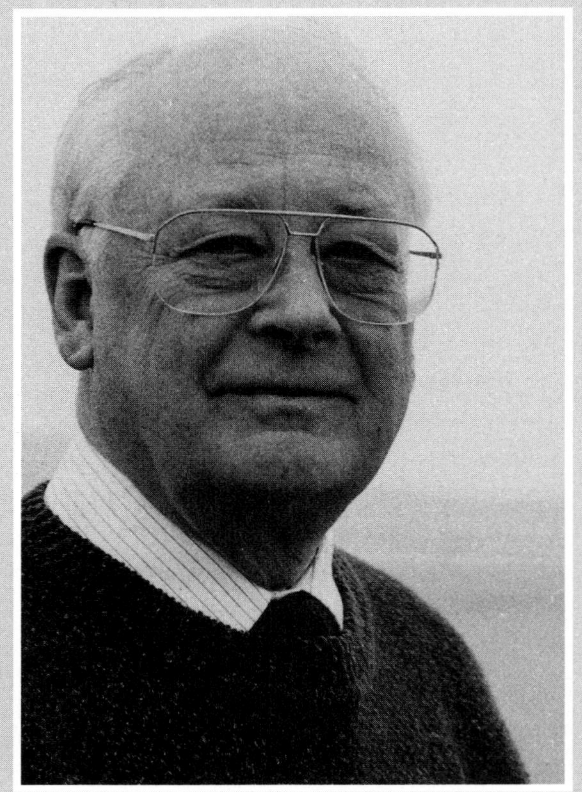

An
Interview
with

CHARLES HANDY

Professor, London Business School, and Author of *The Age of Unreason* and *The Age of Paradox*

Charles Handy is Europe's best-known and most influential management thinker. Walk into any bookstore and you will probably see stacks of his latest work, *The Empty Raincoat* (*The Age of Paradox,* Harvard Business School Press in the United States) in large displays with life-size portraits of the author. Switch on the BBC and you are likely to hear his voice.

Mr. Handy, who was born in 1932 in Kildare, Ireland, has had a long and distinguished career in business and academia. He started out at Oriel College in Oxford and Royal Dutch Shell in Asia, went on to the Sloan School at M.I.T., where he received his MBA, and was later a founder of the London Business School. His early books were about organizational dynamics and behavior.

Mr. Handy does not see business as being removed from society. He views it as an integral element in the life of humanity. As a consequence, he thinks of himself as more of a social philosopher than a management theorist. He sees business as an important element within the overall social fabric of any nation. But business must change to keep pace with the new realities. It must change structurally to be more competitive and to fit with society's transformation, and it must change strategically. In Mr. Handy's view, businesses must no longer simply be places to work and to produce a profit for the shareholders; they must become "membership communities." What follows are excerpts from a conversation with Mr. Handy in March 1995 at his home outside London.

Suddenly, growth for its own sake seemed to be a very funny notion.

S&B *You have written that the corporation is in the midst of a profound and historic transformation. Other management thinkers have offered similar observations. But you also offer a new model. How would you describe that model?*

CHARLES HANDY The old corporate models grew out of the Machine Age, and that age is passing rapidly. Recently, I was talking to some German executives in Frankfurt. They were engineers who had built their organization as engineers build organizations. Their company was a work of great precision, rather like an automobile engine. Its functions could all be accurately designed and accurately measured. This model had served them well. But they began wondering about their organization in the future. They began to wonder if the model would work when the commodity that was being passed around was information, not metal. "We understand what we have to do to our organization with our brains," they said, "but in our hearts we don't know how to design an organization that is not a machine."

S&B *What did you tell them?*

CHARLES HANDY Well, I told them that not many people really do know how to design an organization that is not a machine. I also told them there are a few places to start. For example, we no longer need to have all the people in the same place at the same time to get work done. There is now the core-periphery model with people working in the core while others work outside of the core. There is also the federal model, where power is distributed. But I also told them about what I have been trying to do most recently, that is, design the corporate model around the concept of what I call the "membership community." I believe that corporations should be membership communities, because I believe corporations are not things; they are the people who run them.

S&B *How is a membership community structured?*

CHARLES HANDY It is something quite different from what we now have. Let me give you some background. The old model of the corporation was a piece of property, a piece of real estate. It was, quite simply, the property of its owners. The owners were in the first instance the people who created the corporation. Then, increasingly, the owners were the financiers. That's just rubbish now. It's rather like saying that the people who provide you with a mortgage actually own your house when in my view they only do as a matter of last resort. It is also like saying, as people used to do, I'm afraid, that a man owns his wife, which now sounds quite absurd. So the property model of the corporation is outdated. Why should financiers have such power and talk the language of ownership just because they provided the money? People don't own people and corporations are people. It's all part of the Machine Age model.

S&B *So tell me, what is a membership community?*

CHARLES HANDY Here, then, is the premise. In order to hold people inside the corporation, we can't really talk about their being employees anymore. To hold people to the corporation, there has to be some kind of continuity and some sense of belonging. We also have to talk about commitment, but we have to talk about it both ways—corporation to member, member to corporation. With the way corporations are evolving—with all this virtual business and all these alliances—my worry is that unless we develop a more sophisticated model of the organization, the corporation will become just a box of contracts with no commitment on anyone's part at all. That would be a tragedy. If that were to happen, it would mean that people would be put together on project teams from all over with no real sense of responsibility. What I want companies to develop is a concept of membership, which says that people with a large stake in the organization, those who are the great contributors—and yes, they include the financial contributors sometimes, the major shareholders—should be given membership rights. At the moment, we're asking for responsibilities from people and giving them very few rights.

S&B *What would these rights entail?*

CHARLES HANDY The right to have a say in the strategy of the company. The right to have a veto on the sale of the company and even in the merger of a company. You would have mergers, but they would be by the members' agreement. And, of course, the right to a share in the value-added of the company, which I would express not so much by stock options (which I think are a rather dubious invention) but by having a share of revenue.

S&B *Don't you think it would be more difficult to raise capital if investors had less of a say in how the company was managed?*

CHARLES HANDY You know, when *Fortune* magazine reviewed my latest book, *The Age of Paradox,* they wrote that "Handy's solution is to abolish the stock market." That is not my intention at all. My aim is to reduce the powers of the shareholders—yes. But I believe in a strong, vigorous market. I don't think shareholders should have the power to sell the company over the heads of its people. Nor do I believe that the shareholders have the right to sack the board. But I do believe that those members of the stock market who have a serious commitment to the company—that is, a big stake in it, 1 percent or more—should have membership rights, that is, voting rights. They should have rights as should the senior employees and perhaps even the junior employees through the form of a trust fund. These trusts would have some block votes. So at least in one sense, performance would continue to be measured by return on shares and the market would serve its function. The markets would also ensure transparency. These are not antimarket propositions.

S&B *Would everyone who works for a corporation, in your model, be a member with the same rights and responsibilities you describe?*

CHARLES HANDY In a word, no. Not everyone in the core, for example, has to be a member. There can be some people with whom you enter into ordinary contractual relationships and who simply work there. But the people upon whom your long-term future depends must be members.

S&B *Are you proposing a two-tier system with the members employed for the long haul and with others working on an as-needed basis?*

CHARLES HANDY My model is not quite so simple. The members are the people on whom the corporation is dependent for its long-term future. But as far as titles go, I prefer to use the word *professional* rather than *member* because the thing about professionals is that they are competent in their own right and acknowledged as such. They are not just tools of the organization. This goes back to my basic concept of *subsidiarity,* which says you must leave as much power as possible as low as possible in the organization because that's where the knowledge and experience are. Subsidiarity is also at the heart of federalism.

Now it seems to me that the principle of subsidiarity is at the heart of professionalism. Think for a moment about the doctor in the emergency room of a hospital. The doctor is in charge even though she may be straight out of medical school and her specialty training. The doctor is in total charge in that place at that time because she has the knowledge and skill. As a consequence, all the decisions are hers to make because she is a *professional* and because you are dependent upon her knowledge. The same is true for the lawyer in the courtroom and the teacher in the classroom. They are professionals. When a student asks a question, the teacher in the classroom doesn't say, "I'll have to go and ask my boss before I let you know the answer." The teacher has power by virtue of the fact that he is a professional.

In order to hold people inside the corporation, we can't really talk about them being employees anymore.

This is how I conceive of the members of the corporation. The long-term future of a corporation depends upon its professionals just as surely as your survival depends upon the professional in the emergency room. Decisions have to be made where the knowledge is. So I believe professionals should have rights within the organization. Indeed, I believe they require rights to do their jobs. So you see, I am only talking about membership as a requirement for those upon whom the corporation's future depends. Those people—by virtue of their professionalism—are at the heart of the high-commitment organization. Other workers need not be members. I am not talking about Machine Age organizations. I am talking about something new.

S&B *You mention a high level of commitment. Does that mean lifetime employment in your model?*

CHARLES HANDY No. I believe in membership and a high level of commitment, but not necessarily forever. The British army offers an example I like. It is an organization with terrific commitment, both ways. But it's not forever. The army says to a young person, "We want you, but only for fifteen years." The army needs a few wise old owls with lots of experience. But it doesn't need that many. What it needs are highly trained, bright young people. And it needs to keep its overall age down. I mean, you couldn't have a bunch of old men storming the beach, could you? You would have nothing but heart attacks.

So the army says it will start out offering a new recruit a seven-year contract. It also says, "We'll train you so you'll be more valuable when you leave." After seven years, the army can offer you another contract for ten years or so. But it is the army's decision alone to offer you a subsequent contract, which you may or may not accept.

Now the army doesn't offer that contract to everyone. It assesses its needs and winnows out those people it no longer requires. It does this, offering contracts to fewer and fewer people, to keep itself young and with the right number of generals and so on. But here is the point. In that context it is perfectly permissible—and there is no social stigma—to be a former junior officer who has retired at thirty-two years old. Nor is there a stigma to have retired as a major or a colonel when only forty-four years old. In fact, it works the other way. Retired army personnel have skills that are desired in other settings.

S&B *So commitment is not necessarily a lifetime offer.*

CHARLES HANDY Precisely. The army is a high-commitment learning organization. But the expectation of most of its members is not for lifetime employment. They have predictable points of decision and no social penalties if their contracts are not renewed.

And when members of the army are not going to be offered new contracts, they know it well in advance and have plenty of time to prepare. So the British army gets what it needs for as long as it needs it and there is a nearly total commitment from the soldiers during that time.

S&B *How would this apply outside the military?*

CHARLES HANDY Is it very different in investment banking? If you run a bank, you know that you need traders of a certain sort. They have to be streetwise but not necessarily wise in other ways. They need to be young and without much need for sleep. They need to be driven by money and have quantitative minds, and so on. And they're probably best if they're under thirty years of age.

I think you would be foolish to give someone like that anything like the expectation that they would move from being a trader to being a general manager of the investment bank. So why not give the good traders ten-year contracts and make sure they have a bloody good raise, lots of money, and then let them move on to something else? Just don't tell them at twenty-nine years old they have to leave at thirty. That would be cruel. But why not design for total commitment, but with the recognition that you are not responsible for your traders for the rest of their lives? This is something especially suited to the future and to today's far-flung organizations.

S&B *Why is this important for today's global companies?*

CHARLES HANDY It's very natural. With people scattered around the world, you really have to let them be on their own. The assignments are often difficult and you need them for specific purposes. Those purposes may change. That means you have to run the organization on the basis of professionalism and trust—subsidiarity. If you run an organization like that, you really have to base it around relatively small, long-term, continuing units where each member has a high level of commitment. Now you may have all kinds of stringers too, but at the core there must be a community of trust, which is the membership community. You let the Brits run Britain, the Germans run Germany, and the Japanese run Japan—with as little meddling as possible. The young Silicon Valley companies are learning this. But at the heart, there must be the mutual bonds of commitment.

S&B *Aren't you simply advocating decentralization?*

CHARLES HANDY Yes and no. What I am really talking about is the federal model of organizations and about building high-commitment, professional organizations. You see, the really interesting thing about federalism is not its decentralization. It is actually much more complicated than that. Yes, it is decentralized when the local pressures are important. But it is also centralized whenever that works to the benefit of all.

So, for instance, Unilever used to manufacture soap powders in every European country. And it marketed them in every European country. In a sense this was total decentralization. But of course, once soap powders became a commodity, where price mattered far more than anything else, it became rather ridiculous to be so decentralized. They were sacrificing economies of scale. So they now actually manufacture soap powders in the center of Europe—in one place—which seems to me an appropriate use of centralization. The problem, of course, is deciding which goes where.

S&B *How does a manager make those decisions?*

CHARLES HANDY The process is important because the principle of federalism is that this must be a contractual negotiation or agreement between the parties. Between—as you might say—the barons who are in the countries or regions and the center. You see, if the center tries to impose its solution on the barons, they will resist it. The process is important because it is only when you get the barons to say "Yes, it is sensible for us not to do our own manufacturing" that you will get things running smoothly. So the process has to be one of negotiation and the savings from centralizing have to be distributed fairly for the benefit of the organization as a whole, and not just for the center.

S&B *With all the negotiations you talk about, isn't this a very slow way to run an organization in today's rapidly changing world?*

CHARLES HANDY People would argue that it is a very cumbersome and time-consuming decision-making process and that the world is moving incredibly fast. So how can a federation keep up with the pace of change? My answer is to look at the United States. If the pace of change becomes such that the whole federation is threatened, as in a large-scale war, the power of the center increases.

But the opposite is also true. Now that it appears that the United States is not going to be fighting any massive wars, the power of the center is waning and the power of the periphery—the states—is increasing. You simply do not need a massive central government at all times in a federal constitution.

The same is true in business. If there is an all-out war—if Motorola is going to fight for its very existence, for example—then you will see power going to the center. If it is a matter of survival, you will not see centralization resisted by the barons because they understand that their own survival is threatened too, and that they will need to mobilize resources very quickly. If, on the other hand, that kind of rapid change is not required—if the issues are those of opening new markets, developing new products, getting into China, whatever—then the federal model says, "You should decentralize power because moving into the future is going to require a set of diverse responses." If the change is one of threat, federalism collapses into an oligarchy. If the challenge is one of variety, federalism goes the other way. Typically, people don't think about this. It just sort of happens to them.

S&B *So setting up as a federal corporation gives you the ability to respond more appropriately?*

CHARLES HANDY I think so. I believe that what typically happens is that we react intuitively and then people like me come along afterward and explain it. I like to say that life is understood backward, but unfortunately it has to be lived forward.

S&B *So you put federalism at the heart of the post–Machine Age organization.*

CHARLES HANDY Well, yes, as a conceptual model. The value of the model is that it tells you what is happening. It helps to have a model that says if the problem is one of innovation, and if you centralize to respond to it, you are probably doing the wrong thing.

S&B *What is the role of the corporate center in the federalist model?*

CHARLES HANDY Ah yes, the corporate center. In my federalist model, the center does not run the corporation except in times of war or its equivalent.

S&B *So what exactly does the corporate center do to add value?*

CHARLES HANDY The corporate center is not in charge of the operation unless the organization is under direct threat. You see, in normal times, the job I give to the corporate center is to be what I call "in charge of the future." It means keeping an eye on the competition, on new markets, and on strategy.

The organization's overall architecture and design are also the center's responsibilities. That means that the center can move some key people from one operating unit to another, if need be, for the good of the whole. If China is important long-term, you can't expect China to be able to generate everything on its own, straightaway. The center would move people and resources there.

If the center is in charge of the overall future, some of the money from the operating divisions must also be used to invest in the future. The center guides those investments. And when it comes to marshaling the corporation's overall forces, including its financial resources, the center is in charge of that. Those are some of the ways it adds value.

S&B *You don't need a large staff to do that, do you?*

CHARLES HANDY Oh no. If you have a global corporation, having about a hundred people at the center sounds about right. Boots, the big British drug and chemical company, went so far as to build its corporate headquarters so it can't possibly hold more than a hundred people. Now that's a statement. The company wants its core to be restricted to very broad oversight. Its job is to make certain that the lights in the cockpit are all green and all agreeing. If they are red, the center sends somebody out to have a look. And, of course, the center keeps track of all the money, does planning, and so on. It's responsible for the future.

Boots, the big British drug and chemical company, built a corporate headquarters that can't hold more than a hundred people.

S&B *Is the center concerned with the financial markets?*

CHARLES HANDY That depends upon the kind of federation you are. If you are an American corporation, you would probably raise your capital in America because it's easier. You might also do that if you are headquartered somewhere else. There are a lot of different scenarios.

S&B *And what about monitoring performance?*

CHARLES HANDY Yes, that's part of what the corporate center should do, but only in very broad terms. At Asea Brown Boveri [ABB], the big Swiss-based power generation company, the center monitors something like eighteen or twenty numbers that are delivered from the operating units every month. These would be money numbers, sales numbers, satisfaction and quality numbers, and so on. The center has a kind of multiple scorecard, with target zones for those numbers. That's enough information to illuminate the warning lights.

There is something else the center does that is important and that adds value. The center has the task of building the commitment of the whole federation. Percy Barnevik, chairman of ABB, says that one of his major jobs is not taking decisions but meeting with key executives and putting on seminars about the future. That's an educational mission. Another chief executive of a federal corporation said to me that his job is to be a missionary and to go around and say, "You know, this is what we stand for. These are our values." He's a kind of diplomat.

S&B *How else does the core add value?*

CHARLES HANDY There's a British company called Unipower that makes spare parts for automobiles. Unipower is a federal corporation and has even introduced a new sort of language. There are the operating divisions and then there are the functions—marketing, finance, research and development, and so on. They renamed the functions the *faculties* and renamed the center—where the functions reside—the *campus*. The idea is that the faculties are the company's reservoirs of wisdom and knowledge and expertise. But they have no real power, only influence. People from the operating divisions are rotated through the faculties for two-year stints. What this does is maintain and spread the faculties' intellectual capital. What I am saying is that a federal organization is not a command-and-control organization. It is a learning organization. That is another important role for the center.

S&B *Are there size limits for federalist companies?*

CHARLES HANDY Do you mean how do you get to be big? In the federalist model, you do so by combining communities of trust for certain purposes, which have to be negotiated and agreed upon. You form constellations. Federalism is a negotiated, contractual arrangement between individual groups. The individual groups can be quite small, flexible, and independent, yet the overall organization can be quite huge. ABB is really a federation of something like five thousand business units. Royal Dutch Shell is a huge company with 120,000 employees operating in nearly every country. It is a federation.

But why would you want to be huge? I once sat up on stage with a CEO in front of the senior members of his company. The CEO said his goal was to create the world's largest organization. He wanted to grow at a truly astronomical rate. I said to him that the two largest organizations in the world today are the Red Army in China and the British National Health Service. And I asked him whether either of those two models was what he had in mind. He was rather embarrassed. Suddenly, growth for its own sake seemed to be a very funny notion.

Twenty-five years ago, I was at a large, international, high-tech company headquartered in the United States. I looked at a chart that showed the company's rate of growth versus the rate of growth of the GDP of the United States. By 1993, the CEO said—with a straight face, mind you—that the revenue of his company would cross the line of the United States. He actually said his company's revenues would be larger than the GDP of the United States! Now, that was absurd. But he showed it to me on the chart. Of course, it didn't happen. You see, it is not about size.

S&B *What is it about?*

CHARLES HANDY I think it is about commitment, flexibility, and effectiveness. I think it is about mutual responsibility and rights. I think it is about membership. It is not about size. The British army is an amazingly wonderful example of how you can maintain a high-quality organization and actually get smaller. At the end of World War II, Britain had a huge army. Everybody had to do two years of service. Then in 1955, ten years after the end of the war, we decided to turn it into a relatively small professional army. Today, the army has a fighting force of only about sixty thousand—that's smaller than Royal Dutch Shell, to make a comparison, and far smaller than just after the war. But the army does an amazing job. It is very effective, highly trained, and efficient. It employs all sorts of sophisticated high-tech equipment. It's also cheaper. It has really reengineered itself since the end of the war. The British army is a true high-commitment organization. That's what I think it's all about. It's not about size.

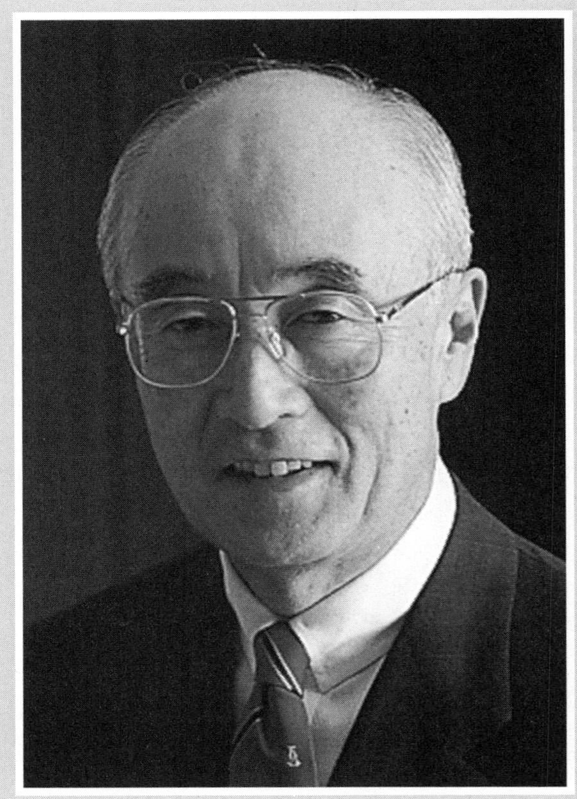

An Interview with

MINORU MAKIHARA

President, Mitsubishi Corporation

With about $176 billion in revenues, the Mitsubishi Corporation—a trading company headquartered in the Marunouchi district of Tokyo, adjacent to the Imperial Palace—is the world's largest company. It is also one of the most complex, with operations in eighty-seven countries and joint ventures and investments in businesses as diverse as energy exploration, raw materials, space imaging, foods, textiles, chemicals, metals, machinery, information systems, and multimedia.

Like the company, Mitsubishi Corporation's president is at home almost anywhere in the world. Minoru Makihara grew up in London—his father worked there for Mitsubishi—and was educated in the United States. He attended the St. Paul's School in New Hampshire and Harvard University. After graduating from Harvard, he went to work for Mitsubishi, where

Where there are changes, there are always opportunities.

he held positions around the world, including the United States.

At Harvard, Mr. Makihara's roommate was Robert A. G. Monks, the American shareholder-activist and investor who was instrumental in forcing Sears, Roebuck & Company to sell most of its financial businesses and to focus on retailing. The two men remain good friends and the sixty-five-year-old Mr. Makihara credits Mr. Monks with influencing the way he manages the Mitsubishi Corporation. That includes helping him decide to use return on equity targets to measure performance, a management method that is still unusual in Japan. Shareholder activism is also rare in Japan, but Mr. Monks recently gave a speech at the Keidanren, the most prestigious Japanese business group, at Mr. Makihara's invitation.

So how do you lead a company as vast as the Mitsubishi Corporation? One way you do it, according to Mr. Makihara, is through global "trust networks"—the myriad of value-adding business, personal, institutional, and investment relationships that Japanese trading companies have carefully nurtured, sometimes for generations. These relationships move products, but they also move information. While they link Mitsubishi to the outside world, they also serve as the glue that binds the company and its seven business units. These relationships help Mr. Makihara understand what is happening inside each business unit and enable him to know whether his messages about strategy and direction are getting through. Communicating effectively is a vital component of leadership, in Mr. Makihara's view.

Some of these relationships link the company to the Mitsubishi *keiretsu*—a group of thirty or so independent but related companies, most of which share the Mitsubishi name and three-diamond logo and have common roots. Companies in the *keiretsu*—Mitsubishi Bank, Mitsubishi Mining and Cement, Mitsubishi Heavy Industries, among others—do business with each other to varying degrees and often own shares in one another. Once a month, the presidents of the companies meet for lunch. The related companies may join forces in a crisis, but Mr. Makihara says they mostly discuss ways of preserving their common name, reputation, and heritage. What follows are excerpts from a discussion with Mr. Makihara that took place in October 1995 in his Tokyo office.

S&B *How do you measure success in a company as vast and global as yours? How do you know when you're doing well?*

MINORU MAKIHARA Up until now, it was really very simple—we measured the percentage of revenue that was profit. That was all right when our funds were limited and labor was cheap. But now the most prevalent measure we use is return on equity [ROE] or return on investments [ROI].

S&B *That is unusual in Japan, isn't it?*

MINORU MAKIHARA Well, it depends. ROE is beginning to be very popular, and people everywhere are talking about it. But you know, I think we were probably one of the first companies in Japan to introduce it as a way of managing.

S&B *By "return on equity" you mean return to your shareholders?*

MINORU MAKIHARA Yes. It comes down to that.

S&B *Do you set targets, then, as to what is an acceptable ROE for the company?*

MINORU MAKIHARA For us, it depends on the business. We are divided into seven groups. We set an expected ROE target for each group. We set it quite low for some of the groups. Our information technology group, for example, is working in the new field of multimedia. As a result, it has an ROE target that has been set quite low.

But until the bubble economy burst, we didn't have to manage by looking at ROE. Japanese shareholders were not really interested in a company's performance as long as the stock prices went up and there were stock splits and so on.

S&B *Setting a target is one thing, but how do you know that it is set high enough? How do you know that you are getting the full potential from a business?*

MINORU MAKIHARA Very simply, we don't know yet.

S&B *You don't?*

MINORU MAKIHARA No. You see, in allocating equity to each business group, we had to look at past performance and we also formed some expectations. We are aiming at an overall ROE of 8 percent by the year 2000. I'm sure that in the United States or Britain, people would say that's very low. But from a Japanese general shareholder's point of view, I think 8 percent is about right. It is an equilibrium figure where shareholders' expectations and what we see as a reasonable overall target meet. Based on this figure, we assigned targets to each of our groups.

S&B *Which groups have the highest targets?*

MINORU MAKIHARA Right now, for example, the food division has a very high target. And the newer businesses would have the lower targets.

S&B *Does ROE become a strategic investment tool for you? I mean, if the food business has a high target and it can make that target, do you aim your investment at that group in an attempt to get more of those high returns?*

MINORU MAKIHARA Not exactly. If a business can achieve high returns, then it will accumulate more equity and it will have more leeway to reinvest on its own. Right now we're still looking at the return ratios and the capital allocations that we've made in the past to determine whether they were right or wrong. That helps us so we can either increase the capital or raise the ROE bar for a particular business. Eventually, I believe that we will have to fix ROE at a certain rate. Doing that will create a greater incentive for each group to perform on its own.

S&B *Was one reason for going to an ROE-based management system the weakness of the Japanese financial system?*

MINORU MAKIHARA No, not directly. The bursting of the bubble economy was, of course, connected to the overheating of the financial system and ultimately to the situation we are in right now. But the necessity for thinking about ROE was based on the change in the expectations of the shareholders, of which in our case about 70 percent are institutional investors.

S&B *Many Japanese business leaders and commentators have criticized the United States for taking an approach to management that they say is too financially driven. Are you worried that an ROE-based approach will draw the same kind of criticism in Japan?*

> Eventually, I believe that we will have to fix ROE at a certain rate. That will create greater incentives.

MINORU MAKIHARA Theoretically, I think it is possible. But the main criticism of the United States has been that it is too financially driven and also too short-term. We are not looking at this in the short term. To a certain extent, this is a corporate governance issue, and governance in the United States is different from governance in Japan. In the United States, the shareholders are the owners. Period. They have the final say. But here it is an accepted fact that if you were to list who owns the company, it is first the employees and then the shareholders. So if you think of who owns the company more broadly—as we do—then you are obliged to think from a longer-term point of view. I think that is an advantage that will enable us to avoid making some mistakes.

S&B *Is it enough to prevent what critics in the United States and Japan call the "hollowing out" of the economy, which basically means sending jobs overseas?*

MINORU MAKIHARA Well, if we are told, for example, that it will be very advantageous to move our manufacturing from Japan to China from the point of view of costs, that is something that requires careful consideration. But the discussion must be made very carefully and with a long-term perspective.

S&B *So how are the interests of the employees taken into account? Do they have representation on the board, as in Germany?*

MINORU MAKIHARA No. Employee-oriented management is just part of our business culture, a result of having lifelong employment.

S&B *But isn't that changing? Nissan, for example, recently announced that it would lay off seven thousand workers.*

MINORU MAKIHARA It is changing to some extent, in some areas. But if you look at these actions very carefully, you will find that these people haven't been just laid off. Some Japanese steel manufacturers, for example, announced layoffs. But what they really did was relocate these people to other parts of the business. They have, in fact, been transferred, and it takes them off the payroll of the main company but guarantees them their incomes.

S&B *This is the traditional method. But a lot of people in Japan are questioning whether the old social contract can survive when so much is needed in the way of efficiency and productivity gains. Do you think Japan's social contract will remain in effect?*

MINORU MAKIHARA Yes. I think lifelong employment will remain, for the most part.

S&B *And how about outplacement?*

MINORU MAKIHARA We do some of that. We have a group of people who are exclusively concerned with this problem. They tell some of our employees that within our structure and within certain age groups, we have too many people. These people are told that it makes sense for them to think earlier than they otherwise would have done about opportunities outside the company. They are then counseled and told what they might do and given opportunities to train themselves for positions on the outside. This shows the relationship between employees and companies in Japan.

S&B *A few moments ago, you used the word "incentive" when talking about the business groups. What about incentives to increase individual performance within the company?*

MINORU MAKIHARA Right now, the bonus level is the same from group to group. At the moment, there are sufficient incentives for people to perform, based on the recognition that they achieve what we thought they ought to achieve. We have increased the proportion of employees' pay that is "at risk" over the past few years, so our salary structures have become performance-based. But you ask a very difficult question. We have had long discussions about whether, for example, bonuses should vary between the different groups, depending upon the performance of that group. The answer so far has been no. The reason is that general trading companies have to do business even in declining areas. We feel that you can't penalize someone for having been assigned to work in a declining area.

S&B *So the current egalitarian system will continue, no matter where a person works in the company?*

MINORU MAKIHARA It will continue at least for the short term.

S&B *I understand that Honda has been one of the first Japanese companies to change its* *pay structure so that it resembles a Western-style, merit-based bonus system. Will other companies do the same?*

MINORU MAKIHARA I think you can do that in a single-line business like a commodity business or a manufacturing operation. But a trading company is different. I think it would be very difficult to do that in a multiline business like ours unless you were prepared to split the company into seven separate groups.

S&B *There is a lot of discussion in business schools, within consulting firms, and in companies around the world about the role of the corporate center. The question most asked is this: "How does the center add value?" How do you view the core of Mitsubishi with respect to how it and how you add value to the enterprise?*

MINORU MAKIHARA The corporate center has the responsibility of making certain that the company's overall morale is high. It has the responsibility of seeing that people are not too internally oriented—that they are really motivated to expand the business. Working on these morale or motivation issues is a very important priority for me. On top of that, there is the very important role of setting direction and in communicating that direction. Setting the direction of the company has become one of my priorities over the past years.

S&B *Why has direction setting occupied you more over the years?*

MINORU MAKIHARA Before the bubble economy burst, the direction was automatic. You could have everybody running in any direction and it seemed to work out all right. We were also still protected within the overall Japanese business and economic framework. But we are now finding ourselves in a much more competitive world. It is also a world that is rapidly changing and that requires a lot of thought as to the company's overall direction.

S&B *You mentioned communicating as one of your roles. How do you communicate messages within the company about the Mitsubishi Corporation's changing direction?*

MINORU MAKIHARA It is a very complicated process, but we have many channels of communication. We have formal channels, like convening monthly meetings of the hundred or so top people in the company, where we can talk with them. From these meetings we can start the process of letting the message filter down to the total organization. Of course, we also use e-mail. We use internal TV. We use occasions like New Year's to convey formal messages.

Another method I use is to bring middle-level and young people into my office twice a month—about forty to sixty of them—and I just talk to them. There are many channels that we use to get out messages and to keep morale high.

S&B *How do you know if the right message is getting out?*

MINORU MAKIHARA Well, that is my job! But it is also a very difficult thing to do with precision. But when I make a significant announcement, my staff scatters around the company. Each of them comes from one of the seven groups and goes back to those groups and asks if the message was really understood. Sometimes they find that it was received and that it went straight through and everyone has gotten it. But sometimes they find that the message was stopped somewhere. So we repeat the message or try to find out why it stopped. It is very painstaking but very important.

S&B *How do you lead a broadly diversified, far-flung company like the Mitsubishi Corporation? Is it similar to the way single-line companies are led?*

MINORU MAKIHARA Leadership in a company like this—a general trading company—is probably different in at least one way from, let's say, a retail company or a manufacturing company. Our operations are really so wide-ranging and so complex. I think we have to lead people by being good listeners. That is to say, we lead in a company such as ours by drawing out ideas from people. That is something that leaders of trading companies have to do and it may be different from the way single-line companies are led. We can't simply issue commands. But apart from that, I think the qualifications are probably the same for a trading company or manufacturing company: you must be able to convey messages when required, you must keep morale high, and you must see where and when change is necessary. You must make certain that the best people are promoted and that they are in the right jobs.

S&B *You mentioned the importance of listening. Is it difficult to get the kind of information that you need in order to set the proper direction and keep morale high?*

MINORU MAKIHARA This is really the strength of Japanese organizations. It is where having lifetime employment makes a lot of sense. For instance, in the chemical group, I have a few people that I have known for many years and that I can count on for correct information. Some of them may have ideas that overlap almost completely with my own; others might not overlap entirely with my own views but would probably come very close. The point is that there are people to talk to who have an in-depth, long-term understanding of the company and who know what is really going on.

S&B *Can you keep such close communication open as you move into the future?*

MINORU MAKIHARA It is very important to do so. You know, although one of our main tasks is to transform ourselves from a Japanese trading company into a global trading company, I feel that we won't be a 50 percent Japanese company and a 50 percent non-Japanese company. Probably we will become a 90 percent Japanese company and a 10 percent non-Japanese company in terms of our top executives. Overall, 30 percent of our staff worldwide were hired overseas, but many of these are auxiliary and clerical staff, so this 90 to 10 ratio is a realizable proportion with respect to the nationality of personnel at senior management levels. I am sure that close communication can be maintained at all management levels between various nationalities. If this proportion is attained at the top, the cohesiveness required of a global general trading company will be maintained.

S&B *You mentioned that the Mitsubishi Corporation is changing and becoming more global. How else will it evolve in the future?*

MINORU MAKIHARA General trading companies are a Japanese phenomenon and are not well understood outside of Japan. They have been tried in the United States, in Korea, and in China without very much success. In Japan, these companies have been built up over long periods of time. They have established reputations. As a result, they attract very good people. They also have information and access to information—let's call these their "trust networks." These are things that can't be built up right away and that we are not intending to change.

But we are not standing still, and we have things to do. Up until now, we were Japan-centered. We imported raw materials and exported products. That was half of our business. The other half was our purely domestic business.

Now, we are becoming much more globally oriented. As we do this, we will also be moving more vigorously into making investments. Taking an equity stake in what we do will be much more common. In fact, it is already under way. About half of our income is related to our investment projects.

S&B *What would be an example of that?*

MINORU MAKIHARA In the United States, we own Aristech, Inc., a chemical company. We do a lot of business with Aristech, which we take in as dividends or show on our consolidated balance sheet. That is the kind of investment I mean.

S&B *How do you decide on the company's direction?*

MINORU MAKIHARA It is becoming more of a top-down decision-making effort, because the changes in the environment are really very unpredictable. I have an excellent core staff of people who help. This group is composed of middle-rank and upper-rank managers from our various business groups and staff. They all happen to be very highly capable and knowledgeable people with multiple perspectives. I depend upon them. So when we get together, we talk about information technology and its direction and what could happen there that would affect our businesses and so forth. That is how we think about our future direction.

> We feel that you can't penalize someone for having been assigned to work in a declining area.

We also talk about our assets, by which I mean, principally, our people. Not just our Japanese staff but also our internal and external network—our established customer base, our accumulated know-how from our staff who are hired from all over the world, and so forth.

S&B *One of the directions that is associated with Mitsubishi is multimedia. Is that something you are discussing?*

MINORU MAKIHARA No one can deny that multimedia will be very important in the future and I think there will be a lot of business opportunities there. But it is a very vague term that is used to describe anything to do with communicating back and forth through computerization. But certainly, looking at multimedia development in the United States, it is obvious that there are going to be changes in the worldwide business communication environment. Where there are changes, there are always business opportunities. My personal feeling is that the first markets for multimedia applications will be in the fields of education and business. Entertainment probably will take place, but it will be a little difficult for us to get into it. But that is my personal point of view.

S&B *So far, not very many people have figured out how to make money from multimedia. Do you have a sense of where it will come from?*

MINORU MAKIHARA I'm trying to do just that. For example, I think there is a lot of promise in home shopping. I think the concept is already there. But while it will provide some consumer opportunities, it won't be suitable for everything. Home shopping where we can probably intervene would typically be, I believe, for certain items that cannot be assembled easily in one physical place but that people want to look at. It can also be instrumental when the items are of substantial value.

S&B *You mentioned the way Japanese companies are organized. Outside of Japan, there is a great deal of misunderstanding about . . .*

MINORU MAKIHARA The *keiretsu* system?

S&B *Yes. Many people outside of Japan think of it as a closed and even insular system where member companies do business with one another almost exclusively and others are frozen out. Are they right?*

MINORU MAKIHARA Not at all. You know there is the trading company—which is our company, the Mitsubishi Corporation—and it is one of about thirty companies that make up the group. There is Mitsubishi Bank, Mitsubishi Heavy Industry, Mitsubishi Mining and Cement, and so on. In the past we did a great deal of business with each other. But that's all changed now. In our case, we really only do around 12 percent of our business within the group.

S&B *Would you say there is still a sense of being part of a bigger family of businesses? A community?*

MINORU MAKIHARA Well, the presidents of each of the companies in the group meet monthly for lunch at what we call the Friday Club. And there is a person—one of the presidents—who is nominated as a kind of caretaker and who convenes the lunches. It used to be the head of our corporation, but now it is Mitsubishi Bank. But when we meet, it is almost exclusively to talk about things like who uses the trademark, to discuss issues like philanthropy, or to talk about business trends. It is, in a way, like a seminar.

S&B *How close is this group?*

MINORU MAKIHARA It is actually very loose. As I say, most of our business is outside of this group. We—Mitsubishi Corporation—would of course like to monopolize business within the group, with regard to exports and imports, for example, but realistically it is not feasible.

S&B *Is there a sense of common purpose?*

MINORU MAKIHARA I believe there is—particularly when there is a crisis. Then the group is a very useful vehicle and that is when we come together. For example, when Mitsubishi Petroleum was about to be taken over a few years back, it would have meant that someone else would have owned the Mitsubishi name. That was a crisis because it meant we would have lost something of our identity. So very quickly, we responded to the situation. The bank and ourselves and some others bought out the outside interests to prevent the takeover. It was all done in the interest of preserving the name, which is to say, it was in all of our interests. So we acted together to manage a crisis, as it were.

You see, the *keiretsu* is really only a type of strategic alliance, and a rather weak one at that. It is not in any way exclusive or exclusionary. Even the cross-ownership of shares is declining.

S&B *Does that mean non-Japanese companies could become members?*

MINORU MAKIHARA No. Because, again, most of our discussion is about the use of the name, which is our trademark.

S&B *Due to the recession and the high yen, lots of Japanese companies are under very intense pressure. Is this the type of crisis that would bring the Mitsubishi group of companies closer together?*

MINORU MAKIHARA No. I don't think those are issues where coming together would solve the situation.

S&B *So recession and economic pressure are not enough.*

MINORU MAKIHARA That's right. What keeps us together is the idea of preserving the Mitsubishi name.

S&B *And what about the merger of Mitsubishi Bank and the Bank of Tokyo? It will form a new entity with a changed culture. Will it still be a Mitsubishi company and a member of the group?*

MINORU MAKIHARA I am confident that they will be part of our group and play a very important role. The name, of course, will change. I don't know what logo will be used.

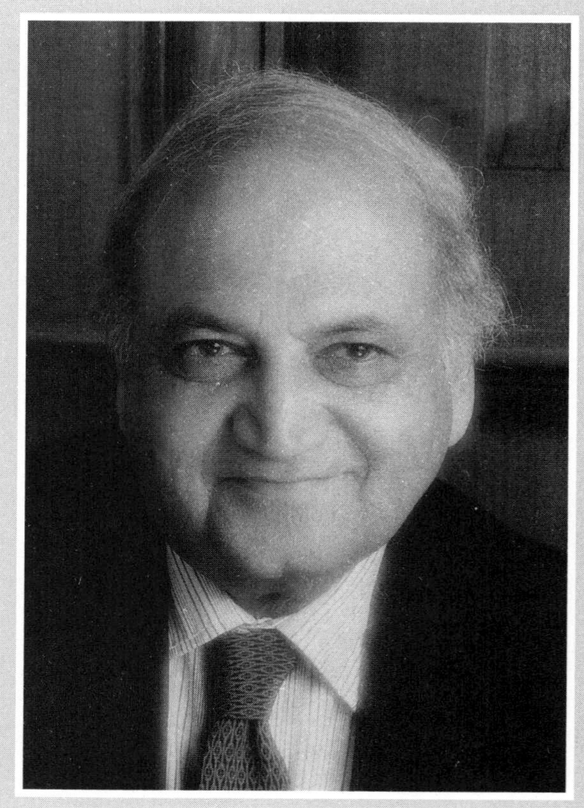

An Interview with

KESHUB MAHINDRA

Chairman, Mahindra & Mahindra

Mahindra & Mahindra, with annual sales of 14 billion rupees (about $500 million), is India's tenth largest company. It is India's largest manufacturer of utility vehicles, with 70 percent of the domestic market, and of tractors, with a 27 percent share.

During the last three years, under the direction of Keshub Mahindra, the company's Wharton-educated chairman, M&M has undergone a radical reengineering of its shop floor, a restructuring of its corporate core, and a refocusing of its strategy around a smaller group of businesses. The aim of the change was to position M&M to compete in the "new India," which—since the early 1990s—has been welcoming investment from foreign companies, many of them extremely large, well capitalized, technologically advanced, and global.

Although M&M functioned well within the protected walls of

Within a certain span of time, our products must become globally competitive.

India's post–World War II economy, it could never be called "provincial." Since Mr. Mahindra's father and uncle founded the company in 1945, it has been producing Jeeps. At first, the company had a succession of foreign partners, including the now-defunct Willy, American Motors, and then Chrysler. Then, it began to produce the vehicles wholly on its own. For engine technology, M&M has worked with

France's Peugeot and Japan's Nissan. In addition, M&M and Ford recently entered into a 50–50 joint venture to produce Ford Escorts and Fiestas in India. In other areas, such as telecommunications and software, M&M has teamed up with British Telecom and other partners from around the world.

How does a company operating in a protected, regional market—albeit a potentially huge one—ready itself for global competition? And what changes are likely to occur in the new India? What follows are excerpts from a rare interview with the seventy-two-year-old Mr. Mahindra that took place in February 1996 in his Bombay office.

S&B *There is a lot of talk about the "new India," by which people mean that the country is now open and ready for investment. Is there really a new India?*

KESHUB MAHINDRA Before answering that, let me go back to the 1950s and 1960s. That's when the story of economic development in India begins. But it begins under the influence of the Fabian socialist school of thought. This was really the British idea that economic development follows from state planning. As a result, a whole host of very strenuous rules and regulations were set up by the government. These rules covered the whole gamut of industrial activities. Everything was regulated and licensed.

Let me give you a very small example of how things worked. Under the licensing system, the government would say that we could produce ten thousand tractors a year. That figure was not based on supply or demand. If the market needed fifty thousand tractors a year, nothing doing. The government would say, "Mahindra, you can only produce ten thousand tractors a year." We could not exceed the rule.

S&B *Were you allowed to adjust your prices, or were they also set by the government?*

KESHUB MAHINDRA In the beginning, there were very rigorous price controls set by the government so that you really couldn't make any money in business. You couldn't adjust prices to costs. And when you did make adjustments, it was not based on actual costs but on historical costs.

It was all quite draconian. In addition, there were monopoly laws in India, so competition was very limited. These laws were exactly the opposite of the monopoly laws in the United States, where they were set up so no one dominant player could gain too much influence over the market. In India, the fundamental error was that these laws created a concentration of economic power. But these were not the only things that tied our hands.

S&B *What else characterized this period in India?*

KESHUB MAHINDRA There were extremely rigid labor laws. What the laws meant in practice was that if the market failed and you had to cut production, you couldn't lay off people. This was a very difficult rule under which we had to operate. All of these rules were made in the rather foolish belief that the only people who had enough wisdom to do anything right in this country were the people in the government.

S&B *Were the reasons philosophical or political?*

KESHUB MAHINDRA My own perception, and it may be wrong, was that the government was fearful of change. Perhaps this had something to do with being colonized for two-hundred-odd years. It was scared of foreign and Indian capital. So it tied our hands with all these rules and regulations. It was absolutely ridiculous. The result was that we didn't have growth at all. We were struggling, on the average, with about $3\frac{1}{2}$ percent a year growth. But India needs a great deal more growth than that, especially since the population is growing at such a rate.

S&B *So what happened?*

KESHUB MAHINDRA In 1990, we began to see some real progress. A new government came in, headed by P. V. Narasimha Rao. He had the guts, or should I say the conviction, to review the situation and say, "This is all wrong, I want this whole process changed." What helped, of course, was that the country was facing a tremendous foreign exchange crisis.

S&B *What did he do?*

KESHUB MAHINDRA Well, he set forth some principles for real economic reform. The point is this: real reform in India started only in the early 1990s. We've been at it only four or five years.

S&B *But it seems to have already paid off, in terms of growth.*

KESHUB MAHINDRA Yes, but let me tell you the problem. In terms of growth, we are doing OK. But we still have all the problems that are associated with a society where the literacy rate is only about 50 percent. As a result, people find it very difficult to relate to what might be called the "new technologies."

In addition, people want to see quick results. Unfortunately, real results don't come that quickly. They take time. Personally, I think the results have been outstanding. But that view hasn't gotten down to the people yet. My guess is that we will need some really strong growth—6 to 7 percent per annum—before we have enough funds to provide the kind of care that the country needs.

S&B *During the last two years, India has grown at about that rate.*

KESHUB MAHINDRA A little bit less than that—more in the $5\frac{1}{2}$ percent range. But we need faster growth for everyone to be on board with the reforms. You know, India is a truly democratic country, with free elections every five years. So people have to be on board. That requires good growth.

S&B *Is there a danger the reforms may be stopped?*

KESHUB MAHINDRA No. I don't see that as a danger. Both major parties are in favor of reforms. It is just a matter of speed. The Congress Party is in favor of bringing on the reforms more quickly. The major parties are headed in the same direction.

S&B *Are both parties in favor of privatization?*

KESHUB MAHINDRA That is an interesting question. There are, of course, the loss-making public companies in this country. To privatize them, you have one big handicap to overcome that makes it a very difficult problem. That problem is that in the absence of any social safety net—we have no social security system in the country—what do you do? How do you sack thousands of people and still say to yourself that there must be no social unrest? That we must have political stability? This is all very contradictory. It is still a very difficult and unresolved thing.

> These rules were made in the foolish belief that the only people who had enough wisdom in this country were the people in the government.

S&B *Are there other unresolved issues that are associated with the reforms?*

KESHUB MAHINDRA Let me give you some examples. To have real economic reform, subsidies must go. We have subsidies for food and so forth. The minute we start removing these subsidies, prices go up. People will object. Here is another example. As the process of reform moves forward, productivity will have to be improved in order for our companies to compete internationally. That means we have to bring in new technology. But that also implies that you need fewer people—at least at the outset. Trade unions are very strong here. So how do you tell a trade union leader, "Look, I will sack a thousand of you, but don't worry. In five years, there'll be two thousand more employees on the payroll." Nobody's going to believe it.

S&B *Just how difficult, then, is the business environment?*

KESHUB MAHINDRA It is very difficult. But there has been progress. Four years ago, if you talked to trade unionists about productivity, they would throw you out. Now, they are beginning to understand. Even so, last year we went through a six-month strike because of productivity issues.

S&B *Was that when you were putting in place your reengineering program?*

KESHUB MAHINDRA Yes. We had a strike at one of our operations over the question of productivity. We said to the union, "There are twelve hundred of you producing x number of parts. Now we need six hundred to produce 2x number of parts." And we showed that it could be done.
The strike lasted for six months before it was settled.

S&B *What was the outcome?*

KESHUB MAHINDRA We settled the strike and our productivity today is 100 percent more than what it was, because of the reengineering. But this is how we settled the strike. Since there is no social security system, we said to our laborers, "We will pay you, but you must stay at home. You will stay there until we can find you alternate jobs." I can't tell you how many kinds of problems that created. You see, people here don't like to take money for doing nothing. But fortunately for us, we were expanding some of our operations in some other plants in the same region. In the end, we were able to absorb some of those workers. That is how things are here.

But there are other ways of dealing with productivity issues. There is, of course, the golden handshake, which works here. But it's a very expensive business. However, in the long run, the payback is good.

S&B *Have the rules and regulations been amended so you can lay off workers?*

KESHUB MAHINDRA No. Not at this stage. But I do not believe that the answer lies simply in changing the laws. The laws may allow you to do some things differently, but the culture of the country will not allow you to do it. I would say that all of us in business in this country are facing these problems. We simply must do our best to navigate through the changes.

S&B *You recently attracted a lot of attention in India for undertaking a restructuring of your management system and corporate structure. At the same time, you reexamined your overall strategy. What have you changed?*

KESHUB MAHINDRA We used to do all kinds of things. We were in oil drilling, we were in business machines, construction, and so on. When the reforms in India started in the early 1990s and it was apparent that foreign competitors were destined to come into the market, we said to ourselves, "What is the focus of our business?" And then we made a deliberate decision. We sold our oil-drilling business, which was a very profitable business. We sold our business machines business. And we decided that our corporate mission really was in the area of vehicle production. So we refocused our business around our core competencies, which were primarily in manufacturing, joint ventures, and so on.

S&B *How did you arrive at that conclusion?*

KESHUB MAHINDRA The way we got to that was to ask ourselves a question. "Where do we have the greatest chance of becoming globally competitive?" We asked the question with a great deal of introspection. We answered by saying that our two main businesses today are automotive and tractors. So the whole focus of this company is now on that.

But that was not enough. After we arrived at that decision about two years ago, we then began to restructure the company. What we did was to split the company into six proper divisions. We then created a president for each division. The president of the automobile division, for example, has the whole lot. He is responsible for marketing, research and development, finance, and so on. And then we said, "You are now no longer able to pass the buck." Simple as that.

The structure now is that we have one division for automobiles and related businesses, a second for tractors, a third for infrastructure, a fourth for trade and financial services, a fifth for telecommunications, and finally, a division for automotive components. On top of all that, we set up a corporate body for monitoring each division's performance and the company's performance as a whole. We did this all by ourselves—the managing director, the deputy managing director, and I—and we did it quietly. Nobody in the company knew anything about the restructuring plan until we released it.

S&B *What happened then?*

KESHUB MAHINDRA After we released the plan, we came out with a thick list of instructions for each president. But what we really conveyed to the presidents of the divisions was what they can do and what they cannot do. You know, we never had presidents before, only managing directors. Now that we have presidents, the job of the managing directors is to sit on top of these businesses and monitor the work, look at long-term strategies, look after human resources and over corporate finance. Now we've only had this plan in place for about fifteen months. But the results are quite good.

S&B *What is your oversight role as chairman?*

KESHUB MAHINDRA I ask the presidents to come in with their figures for, say, the next year or the next three years—we do five-year rolling plans—and meet with the managing directors. So the president comes in with his figures. The managing director and the deputy managing director will then sit with him and say to him, "Oh, hold it, hold it, hold it. Your profits are not good enough." The managing directors will go through discussions and give the president their rationale for their questions or reservations and work out a solution together. The managing directors do that with each of the presidents and then they bring their conclusions to the board, which is where I sit. But the board rarely interferes.

S&B *What are the targets that the managing directors use with the presidents? Do they use return on equity, return on net assets? Which figures are relevant to them and to the board?*

KESHUB MAHINDRA The first target is the full cost of each president's plan. We include in that our guess for inflation. We also take a guess at what the company's economic growth will be and what the national economic growth rate is likely to be. Then we set all sorts of efficiency targets. Like return on assets, the return on investments, and so on. We have a whole gamut of efficiency targets.

S&B *How often do you look at each president's progress?*

KESHUB MAHINDRA We have a very varied system of reporting. Each president is required to report his division's overall performance every month. They are also required to report their production every day, which I get on my computer. And if we find out something is not right, we go and find out why.

S&B *What is the role of the managing director and deputy managing director?*

KESHUB MAHINDRA Although the responsibility of the operation of the whole company rests with the managing director and the deputy managing director, their role is not day-to-day operations any longer. Their role is more long-term thinking, strategy, technology, new products—what to do. For example, one area where we are concentrating is in human resource development. This is a corporate function. Corporate finance is a corporate function generally, as well. That ensures that the presidents don't overindulge the budgets given to them. So some limited degree of control over money stays with corporate headquarters.

S&B *If the president in the automotive division wanted to develop products and move into Europe, for example, could he do it?*

KESHUB MAHINDRA As long as he can afford to do it. What he has to do is put forward his plan to the managing director and the deputy managing director. He needs to get their permission. And if any capital is required, he has to be able to obtain that too. Then he does what he needs to do.

S&B *Do other Indian companies use this system? Do they have divisional presidents, for example?*

KESHUB MAHINDRA No. But I think it's coming. What is happening is that Indian companies are becoming more professional. I take great pride in the fact that our company uses professional managers, for example. My family used to own 100 percent of this company. Now it is public. We have more than a hundred thousand shareholders. But even when we owned 100 percent, we hired professional people in every sphere—and we have taken tremendous pains to do that. Right now in this company, the only family members working here are my cousin, my nephew, and me. That's it. Just three of us.

S&B *This is not typical of Indian companies.*

KESHUB MAHINDRA No. It's not typical of Indian companies at all.

S&B *India has very low-cost labor. How relevant is that to the competitiveness of your company?*

KESHUB MAHINDRA It is a myth that low-cost labor is an advantage. For instance, Indian labor, in terms of dollars per hour, is very cheap. No question about it. But if you look at overall productivity, the cost of Indian labor looks very different. Take automobiles. Today, we produce roughly sixty-thousand-odd vehicles. With truly world-class technology, our competitors could produce in excess of a hundred thousand or so vehicles with far fewer workers than we have today. So what happened to the advantage we were supposed to have from our so-called cheap labor? It is a myth.

S&B *You have a number of licensing and technical assistance agreements covering technology. How are you approaching the technology issue? What are you doing to become more competitive?*

KESHUB MAHINDRA Our philosophy on technology is very simple. In all our businesses, we have technology agreements together with investments with foreign firms. I really do not believe in just buying technology. I believe that technology should come with investment. So our partners have a long-term interest in what we do. And I must say that's good for them and it's very good for us.

S&B *You recently made a significant deal with Ford.*

KESHUB MAHINDRA It is a 50–50 joint venture with Ford. Together we set up a separate company. Now, it is very interesting. Ford said to us, "You know, our only concern is that we'd like to manage the plants because of new technology." And I think we shocked them, because it took us only one minute to say, "Go manage it." In fact, we said, "We'd love you to manage it." That is unusual.

S&B *What was your rationale?*

KESHUB MAHINDRA We don't know how to build passenger cars. We make utility vehicles. It's entirely different. True, we have an automotive business and we have local knowledge that they can use, but we are not aware of the latest technologies and so forth. So we said, "You know, it is crazy for us to do it." Our people will learn what they should do by working with Ford. Production hasn't started yet, but the whole process is working extremely well. And our people are learning. It is something of a laboratory for us.

You see, this is not a pure technology transfer issue. Ford shows us how it manages purchasing, for example. How they manage their personnel. How they manage their internal systems. From us they will get input as to how to do business in India. And it's not that simple. You just can't come in. Doing business here is complex.

> India's literacy rate is only about 50 percent. As a result, people find it very difficult to relate to the "new technologies."

S&B *You also have a joint venture with Nissan, don't you?*

KESHUB MAHINDRA It is more complicated than that. Years ago, Nissan joined a state government to make trucks. In those days, they were licensed to make only ten thousand trucks. Which is ridiculous, given our country's needs, but that's how it was. The local company went into bankruptcy. The state government said to us, "Will you please take over this plant and this company?" Which we did. So today we have a technical cooperation agreement with Nissan. We then took this company and merged it into our own company last year. So it's now a division of our company. But it is not really a joint venture, only a technical agreement with Nissan. I think Nissan has only one man here.

S&B *Events are changing very rapidly in India. Can Indian companies keep up with the pace of change?*

KESHUB MAHINDRA In my opinion, we opened up too fast. I don't think that you can suddenly jump from total government control of the economy to something that is truly open. Today, you know, India is more open than China. We have foreign companies coming here with 100 percent equity. Hyundai of Korea, for example, is coming here to make passenger cars in a 100 percent equity investment. Because their plant will be brand-new, they will come here with no excess workers to shed. Now, how do I compete with them with all my old processes?

S&B *Many of the foreign competitors are technologically very advanced.*

KESHUB MAHINDRA That is a problem. This is why I say that India opened up a little too fast. In the old days, there were so many restrictions, you couldn't come in. You couldn't have equity of more than 40 percent. India did not really invite foreign investors. The attitude toward foreign investors was totally ambivalent.

S&B *In the white-goods sector, Electrolux and Whirlpool are coming into India with 100 percent equity deals. Similar deals are being made in the automobile sector. How will Indian companies compete against these overseas firms?*

KESHUB MAHINDRA These 100 percent equity deals make it very difficult for a number of reasons. So what we are saying is this: "For God's sake, let's have level playing fields." Now, what does that mean in our context? A big company like Hyundai or Samsung can borrow money overseas at 6 percent. Our interest costs today in India are 19 percent. But I can only borrow overseas in limited ways. So all of my working capital requirements come from India and at 18 to 19 percent. How do you compete like that? It must change. Then, on top of this, these companies are bringing new technology into the country. So it is very difficult for Indian companies right now.

S&B *Are you restricted in the technology that you import?*

KESHUB MAHINDRA No, not anymore.

S&B *As a strategist, how do you take aim at your new foreign competition?*

KESHUB MAHINDRA What we are trying to do in our company is to say that within a certain span of time, maybe four, five, or six years, our products must be globally competitive. Now if that means more investment, OK, fine. If it means new technology, fine. New products, fine. But we must be globally competitive. To get there, we will develop our exports and as we do, we will begin raising our productivity to world-class levels. We will do that alone and through joint ventures.

We will also begin expanding our exports and set up a trading company, which is in its very earliest stages. But let me give you an example of where things stand. We have sent a thousand tractors to the United States—mostly in the Southern states—as a test. They were small horsepower tractors for smaller plots of land and they worked beautifully. But if I am going to sell the utility vehicles that we make, which are really diesel Jeeps, I would not have a chance at all in the United States. We tried an experiment to sell them in Europe. It was a complete disaster. Our product is not refined. It is just not as good as those on sale there. However, my Jeep does have great appeal in, say, Africa and South America.

S&B *Are there specific Indian characteristics of the company?*

KESHUB MAHINDRA Let me put it like this. If you studied the Indian social culture, you would find that it is very much a patriarchal system. Now, I think that you cannot get too far away from it, even in our company. I think that sometimes these workers of ours, they look to a father figure. And you know, I must tell you of an experience that I had that absolutely shook me.

Last year, we completed fifty years of our existence. The workers at our plants said to me, "Please come out on the day of the fiftieth year." So my wife and I went to the plant. And do you know what? Ten thousand workers standing around put my wife and me in a Jeep and they took us for a ride around the grounds. And as they did, they were cheering and throwing rose petals on us. It was an unbelievable kind of affection that they showed. It was true affection.

So if there is a characteristic of an Indian company, I would say it is rather like a large village, or family even. And you know, we try to give our workers the feeling of family. We take a lot of trouble looking after them and we care for them. I mean, we fight with them on wage agreements and so on, but we care.

I think that's the nature of an Indian company.

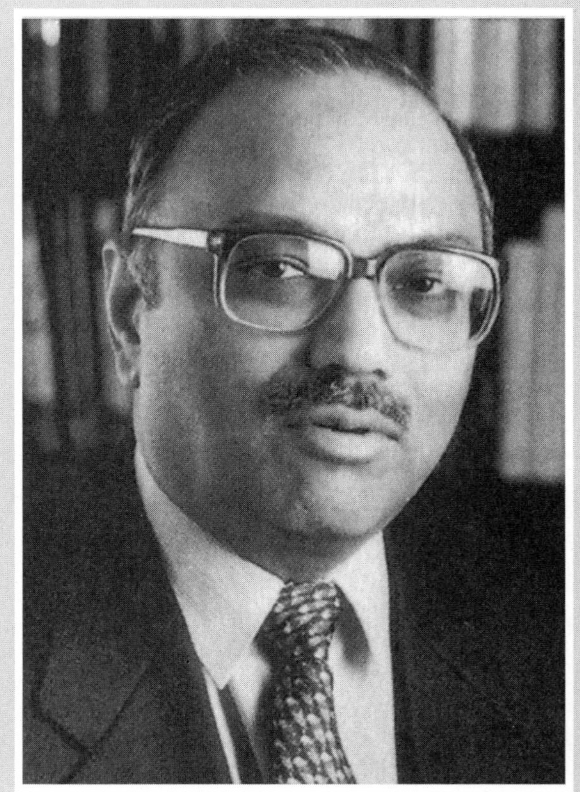

An Interview with

C. K. PRAHALAD

Professor, University of Michigan, and Coauthor of *Competing for the Future*

Over the years, C. K. Prahalad, the Harvey C. Fruehauf Professor of Business at the University of Michigan Business School, has earned a distinguished reputation from numerous contributions to academic publications that shed light on strategy, global competition, marketing, and corporate structure.

With his most recent coauthor, Gary Hamel, a professor at the London Business School, Professor Prahalad has written a number of pathbreaking articles and coined such phrases as the "core competencies of the corporation," "strategy as stretch and leverage," and "strategic intent." The articles were more than just scholarly, well-researched presentations. They also withstood what Professor Prahalad has called the "managerial test"—they were capable of being implemented. Indeed, the professor's consistent ability to articulate leading-edge, workable ideas has made him a popular speaker at gatherings around the world, as well as a sought-after adviser to chief executives.

No monarchy has ever fomented its own revolution.

Although Professor Prahalad and Professor Hamel drew attention with their articles, it was not until the 1994 publication of *Competing for the Future* that they attained the level of recognition that their new research deserved. Even though an academic publisher (Harvard Business School Press) brought out the book, it immediately attracted the interest of the major media. It also quickly gained a large following among managers and other readers, who have snapped up more than

250,000 copies in hardcover, making it one of the top-selling business books in history. *Business Week* named it the best management book of 1994, and its insights have been taught in business schools throughout the world.

Since the book was published, Professor Prahalad, who is fifty-five years old, has confined himself to teaching, doing research, speaking, and consulting. Although he is not yet ready to write another book, his thinking has progressed. One of his major concerns is whether large companies are appropriately governed and adequately managed to compete against new rivals in the future. He is also greatly concerned about the strategy-making process. At most companies, he says, that process is elitist, involving only top-level managers. But strategy is revolution, he says, and "no monarchy has ever fomented its own revolution." Instead, many people throughout the company should be involved, he argues, even those who are at low levels or are new to the enterprise. What follows are excerpts from an April 1996 conversation with Professor Prahalad that took place at his home in Michigan along a tranquil river outside Ann Arbor.

S&B *C. K., you said recently that one of management's traditional functions has been to break the company into what you call "bite-sized pieces" so that it can be correctly structured and managed. You have also said that the way this was done in the past may not be suited to the future. What do you mean by that?*

C. K. PRAHALAD These bite-sized pieces are the business unit, national organizations, and so forth. They are the basic units of analysis, accountability, and resource allocation.

There is, however, a problem with this. The problem is that the basic unit of analysis can be quite different for different tasks. For managing existing businesses and creating accountability, the business unit may be a good starting point. On the other hand, if you want to look at competence building, then you have to transcend individual business units. As a result, one of the really interesting questions is how to define the basic unit of analysis in a large firm. Is one definition appropriate for all tasks? The answer is probably not.

Take, for example, building a global brand franchise, or "share-of-mind" for a company. That is not the task of a single business unit. It transcends business units. Think, for a moment, of Sony. Sony's identity is consistent around the world. This identity is an important asset to protect. Are the Walkman and a broadcasting system both consistent with Sony's overall identity? Yes, they are. But you can't have *Sony* mean high-end, innovative products in one market, say the United States, and low-end, cheap products elsewhere. The company's identity, its skills, its reputation have to be consistent across all of its products, all of its business units, all of its markets. Is the business unit the unit of analysis in managing Sony's brand franchise? I would argue that it is not.

Now think of Canon. Canon has many, many businesses—cameras, copiers, printers, and so on. When you hear *Canon,* you have certain expectations, certain assurances, promises of what the product will be like, whichever branch of the company produces it. Is the business unit the correct unit of analysis in Canon's case? Again, I would argue that it is not.

Take also competency building. It, too, is larger than the business unit, as are management development, skill building, and relationships with partners. These issues cut across multiple business lines. If this is the case, who provides the gateway? Who shepherds those relationships?

S&B *You are not arguing that the era of the business unit is over, are you?*

C. K. PRAHALAD No. There are many aspects of managing that are still within the domain of the business unit. People have spent a lot of time thinking about how to divide companies into bite-sized pieces. They've done so for reasons that made sense in the past, not necessarily for reasons that make sense for the future. Business units were focused on accountability. They are inappropriate vehicles for corporate resource leverage–creating skills and new business opportunities. I am saying that if we imagine the future, examine management's needs and processes, we will conclude that a total dedication to the business unit approach might be very limiting.

S&B *So, just how would you change things?*

C. K. PRAHALAD Let's go back to the basics for a moment. Each layer of management has its function. One of those functions can be termed *consolidation.* This is really just collecting and adding up the data. It is purely a mechanical task that moves information about how the business is doing—particularly financial information—up the hierarchy. Then, there is the job I call management's "checking-and-cost-correction" function. As part of that function, each layer checks on the levels below to make certain they are following the trajectory that is appropriate and in line with the expectations of the company or the sector as a whole. Then, there are the wisdom-and-mentoring roles of management, which are to provide support to people who are on their way to higher levels of management. Finally, there is the function that we just spoke about of getting the company into bite-sized pieces.

This enables people to track performance and it creates administrative structure.

Now, if you think about it, the consolidation role has been made very easy due to the advances in information technology. I can get data on any operation today in any number of ways. I don't need a particular level of management assigned to do the task.

In addition, the checking-and-cost-correction function—making sure the company is on the right trajectory—was quite important when people did not have a shared view of where the company was going. This function was particularly important when communication was poor. However, if we get people to agree to a shared agenda, so everyone knows where the company is going and how they fit in that vision, then there is little need for this layer of management either.

A good example of what I mean is quality. If we have deployed a quality program in a company, and everyone understands its importance, then we don't need thousands of people checking the quality of every product. The deployment of the program eliminates the need for the checkers. So why do we still have management checkers? The only reason we need them is that we have not yet been able to deploy strategies effectively and build a shared agenda within companies. My conclusion is that the more we are able to build a shared mind-set within companies, the less we will need this administrative layer of management. This layer can become much smaller.

However, while the other layers shrink, there is going to be an increasing need for the mentoring role of management. Here, the question is whether mentoring should be done only by people who have an administrative position higher than one's own, or whether it can be done by counselors and helpers who can provide mentoring even though they are not necessarily in a higher position administratively. That is an open question.

We don't want people who are satisfied with how things are. We want people who are curious, impatient, trying to buck the received wisdom.

S&B *They say that Konosuke Matsushita, the founder of Japan's Matsushita Electric, viewed his driver as one of his mentors and never failed to ask him for advice.*

C. K. PRAHALAD Yes. Mentoring requires special skills, but it does not require hierarchical position.

S&B *Even so-called flat organizations have some hierarchical layers of management. Are these simply legacies from the past?*

C. K. PRAHALAD Partly they are legacies of the military system of command, and partly they are the legacy of Taylorism and so-called scientific management, where people were expected to specialize so much that a lot of coordinators were needed. It is also simply an element in the way we think. In the sciences, we tend to take complex problems, disaggregate them into their components—or what we think are their components—and study each component in great depth without understanding too much about the interrelationships across those components.

The goal has been to understand, in great detail, an isolated element, not the place of that element in the totality of the system. Increasingly, however, people are learning that they must understand the big picture and then the place of the elements of their specialization inside that big picture.

S&B *How do you get people to see the big picture and their place in it?*

C. K. PRAHALAD You train people to do this. You do it by getting people with different functional backgrounds to work together in common tasks under time pressure. You do it by getting them to achieve goals where they must understand what the other person can contribute and why the other person's contribution is important. This learning has to be experiential, not intellectual.

S&B *You have spoken about business units. What about the corporate center? Are you in favor, as so many people are, of shrinking it? Some companies, like Britain's Boots, a pharmaceutical and chemical company, have limited the size of the center to about a hundred people. Do you agree with decisions like that?*

C. K. PRAHALAD I am always hesitant when people come out with simple formulas for complex tasks, like saying that the corporate center should have no more than a hundred people. I don't feel comfortable making a statement like that. My answer to size, structure, and role questions with respect to the corporate center is that it all depends.

It all depends on the nature of the business, the complexity of the business, and the tasks to be performed. For example, the Hanson Trust can run a large, multibillion-dollar portfolio of companies with only twenty-five to thirty people at the top. But the reason is that Hanson is a pure conglomerate. Each business has very little in common with the other businesses and the role of the corporate center is to bring fairly strict financial discipline to the companies, most of which operate in traditional, low-tech industries.

That is very different from running IBM or very different from running Hewlett-Packard. In these instances, there are extraordinarily complex relationships that run across a wide range of businesses, with many shared technologies, shared distribution channels, and so forth. In order to at least understand the nature of those interlinkages, and to determine what to manage and what not to manage, a very different type of top management from the people running Hanson Trust is required. The question for me is not whether we need a hundred people or two hundred people, but how the nature of the internal governance process changes, given the nature of the portfolio and the way in which value is created.

S&B *Are there rules by which you can make those determinations?*

C. K. PRAHALAD Not rules, exactly. Look at Hanson. I think of it as a "disciplined owner" that has a portfolio of stand-alone businesses. When I think of Hewlett-Packard, it is as a family of businesses, not a portfolio. HP's family of businesses has common competencies, technologies, channels, and opportunities. These present different internal governance challenges for the corporate center.

Hanson's internal governance is based on financial discipline, for example. In fact, one of the vice chairmen said he had never even visited the factories of the companies that Hanson owned. He's comfortable with that and I must say I have a lot of respect for Hanson as a company. On the other hand, if someone in senior management at Hewlett-Packard said he never visited a lab or factory or division, I would be extremely worried.

For these reasons, I have great difficulty in understanding why people look at a company like General Electric, for example, and say we should be like that. GE is a unique entity. There is only one GE.

As you can see, the question of the corporate center has a different answer, depending upon who is asking it.

S&B *You mentioned internal governance. How do you see that working?*

C. K. PRAHALAD I have been giving a great deal of thought to a number of closely related ideas. These have to do with strategy and with the processes of governance within companies. I'm less worried about the external governance issue, which is a topic of debate among shareholders, boards, and CEOs. By *internal governance,* I mean the ways in which things are actually accomplished—or not accomplished—inside companies. It also has to do with who does those things and for what reasons.

The focus of my analysis is the internal governance process. By the time the CEO sees a negative result in the P&L statement, in market-share loss statistics, or in the company's inability to deliver new products quickly, it's simply too late. The cancer has already set in and large companies have an enormous amount of inertia when it comes to change. That means the real issue is how do you prevent the cancer from developing in the first place? How do you develop a methodology for assessing the quality of internal governance, especially in a multi-business company?

I think that question raises interesting issues about the nature of the relationship between headquarters and subsidiaries—which is an old problem—but it does so in a new context. It also raises interesting questions about the future and who should think about it.

S&B *What is the new context to which you are referring?*

C. K. PRAHALAD It is simply that today you cannot allow subsidiaries to be totally autonomous—nor can you expect them to be slaves of headquarters. That presents a tension.

S&B *Is the debate, therefore, about autonomy versus control? Is it, as Charles Handy maintains, about subsidiarity? Or is it about centralization and decentralization?*

C. K. PRAHALAD I am afraid it is about neither of these. My starting assumption is that the debate gets framed as centralization versus decentralization. But that is the wrong way to look at it. I think the debate ought to be framed in terms of the value that is added by each layer of management. The debate should be about how various groups—staff groups and line groups—at various levels and in various places in the organization really add value to customers and add value to the people who have to deliver a functionality to the customer. The debate should not be about power, nor should it be about egos, span of control, decentralization versus centralization, or size. The debate should be about adding value throughout the organization.

If that is the case, then the question really becomes, How do you create structures internally so that relationships are based on value creation? If you look at structure from a value-adding perspective, then there is an important issue related to internal governance that must be addressed. I frame it this way: Who has responsibility for competitiveness?

Almost all traditional views of strategy have been very elitist when it comes to this question. The assumption is that top managers develop strategy and everybody else implements it. I don't think that is the correct answer to the internal governance question.

S&B *What is the correct answer?*

C. K. PRAHALAD Let me say the following before I get to my answer. We are in an era of discontinuous change, whether we are talking about telecommunications, health care, financial services, high-volume electronics, retailing, or the Internet. As a result, we are no longer talking about fine-tuning or improving the organization's efficiency. We are talking about nothing less than reinvention—reinventing the business in fundamental ways.

Reinvention requires a new skill mix and new ways of approaching the business. It may require different business models. It may also require different people. It is not at all clear to me that the same people who are socialized in the standard way of doing business—and who understand a certain recipe for how to manage—can change very quickly and become the inventors of the new business model. As a result, companies have been looking outside their basic industries for people who can thrive in the new environment. Look at George M. C. Fisher—he came from Motorola to run Kodak. Or look at Louis V. Gerstner Jr.—he came from RJR/Nabisco to run IBM. They were hired to bring a different perspective to these companies.

Now, to your answer. I have been experimenting with ways to enable people lower down in the organization—people who are closer to new technologies, to customers, and to competitors—to create the point of view and dialogue that are needed as prerequisites for change.

S&B *How has it worked?*

C. K. PRAHALAD So far, where we have tried it, the results have been successful. We have found people deep down in the organization to be receptive to change. We have also found tremendous creativity and knowledge there—so much so that senior managers have been quite surprised.

S&B *It sounds as if you are saying that people lower down in the organization—or from outside the organization—are able to embrace change and are able to lead it, while people at the top are more set in their ways.*

C. K. PRAHALAD I would rather put it this way: not long ago, it was popular to say that there were no natural constituencies for change inside large companies. But I would now argue that it is not a matter of constituencies but of forums. There are no natural forums for focusing the energies of people who are waiting for change to happen and who understand that change needs to happen. Almost all of our current management forums, be it planning or budgeting, are status quo oriented, not change oriented.

What we need to create inside companies are forums wherein people can contribute to the changing dynamics of the industry, talk about how they can best add value, and then move on from there.

S&B *How do you create these forums? Who takes part?*

C. K. PRAHALAD Initially, we create them in an ad hoc way. We select between sixteen to twenty people who meet the following criteria: they have four to five years' experience in the industry, they've accomplished something, they're respected by their peers, they have a contrary streak.

S&B *You want people with a contrary streak?*

C. K. PRAHALAD Yes. We don't want people who do not think outside of the box or who do not have a natural predilection for creativity focusing on change. We don't want people who are satisfied with the way things are. We want people who are curious, impatient, and who are constantly trying to buck the trend of the received wisdom.

People at lower levels have less of a problem accepting their new strategic roles. The more difficult transition is for senior managers.

S&B *Once you have chosen these people, what do you do?*

C. K. PRAHALAD We give them some training on how to think of the future and then we separate them into two teams so they can compete with each other on developing a point of view about where their industry is going and how the company should position itself. Then we let them make competing presentations to top management. In this program, top management gets two views of the future, rather than one. The assumption is that some of the critical issues that probably were overlooked or underemphasized by one team will be captured by the other.

S&B *Why do you have new, relatively inexperienced managers develop competing notions about the future? Why not have a group of really experienced people leading the teams? Or why not have a mixed group?*

C. K. PRAHALAD If you think about strategy as revolution, strategy as discovery, strategy as innovation, strategy as changing industry norms and industry patterns, then you must acknowledge that no monarchy has ever fomented its own revolution. In other words, senior management does not have a great propensity for change.

S&B *Where have you tried this approach and seen it work?*

C. K. PRAHALAD I have seen it work in a wide variety of companies, in so-called mature industries (a concrete mixing company, for example), in state-of-the-art technology-oriented companies, and in service-oriented companies. Companies that come to mind are Marriott, Steelcase, Oracle, Quantum, and Eastman Chemical. There are others as well.

S&B *What you're suggesting sounds similar to the strategy-formulation process of some Japanese companies. In those companies, younger managers get together and propose new directions to older, more seasoned managers. Good ideas go all the way up the organization. If they come down again and there is consensus about the merit of the ideas, they are put into action. Conflicting views are sometimes merged, good ideas are incorporated regardless of where they originated, and bad ideas are silently discarded. Is that comparison fair?*

C. K. PRAHALAD It is fair and not so fair. It is fair in the sense that the process involves active dialogue between multiple layers in the company and multiple functions within the company. It is fair in the sense that there is a great deal of responsibility placed on people at lower levels in the organization for thinking about the overall company—not just their particular functional area. Of course, it is fair in that there is a certain humility required of top management. They must listen, after all, to people who are not on their level administratively.

It is not fair, however, in the sense that what I am talking about is not cultural at all. It is a way of managing that rests on the belief that people can think and can be creative, no matter what their nationality. It is also democratic. *Democratic* in this context means everyone has the chance to contribute to the overall direction of the company. True, ultimately a company has to focus and choose a direction. But at least everyone's voice was heard.

S&B *Because everyone is heard—including the team that lost the strategy debate—is the result more cohesion with respect to the company's direction?*

C. K. PRAHALAD Yes, but I do not believe there are winners and losers in such a forum. You start by bringing to the table a discussion about a wide variety of issues. Over a period of time, through discussion and analysis, these issues are formed into your company's point of view. When you finally decide on the company's strategic architecture and strategic intent—when you decide what it should do—the actual individuals who contributed the ideas become impossible to isolate.

S&B *What you're suggesting puts new demands on lower-level people in an organization. But it also puts new demands on the people at the top.*

C. K. PRAHALAD Yes. But my experience is that people at lower levels have less of a problem accepting their new strategic roles. True, they may be a little apprehensive at first, but they accept their new roles easily and seriously and they usually do an incredibly good job. The more difficult transition is for senior managers. Their perception is that they lost control and influence because of the process and that their power and influence have been diluted. They have to come to terms with that.

S&B *How do you implement this program?*

C. K. PRAHALAD There are stages. First, you must get broad support for the program, get perspectives from deep in the organization, and put together a synthesis of what the teams come up with, which includes the judgments of top management. You must also craft a point of view on how the company is going to compete. Then you have to deploy the ideas throughout the organization so everyone understands the direction the company is taking and where they fit in the new framework.

And once you have done that, you have embedded the company's strategy within the entire firm.

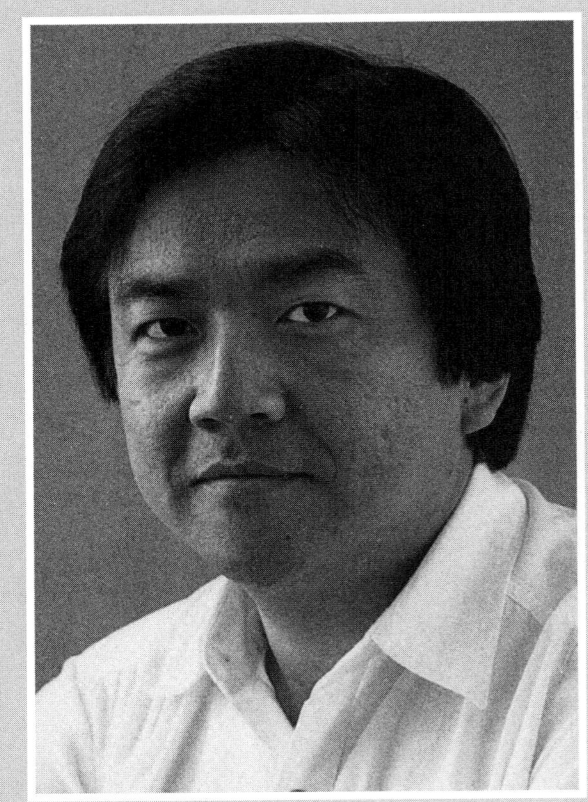

An Interview with

JOHN KAO

Professor, Harvard Business School, and Author of *Jamming*

> **Jamming is when you improvise and adapt to conditions. Jamming follows rules, not individual notes.**

When it comes to creativity, John Kao practices what he preaches. Trained as a medical doctor and a psychiatrist at Harvard and Yale, Dr. Kao, who is forty-six years old, has also had a long love affair with business and academia. For the past fourteen years, he has taught courses on creativity in the MBA and advanced management programs at the Harvard Business School, where he is a senior lecturer and program chairman and where he also did graduate business study. Not content with one university affiliation, Dr. Kao is also academic director of the Managing Innovation program at Stanford University, as well as a visiting professor at the Media Lab at M.I.T. At Harvard, Dr. Kao's research has formed the basis for books, monographs, and articles in the *Harvard Business Review.*

While at Harvard, Dr. Kao (pronounced KAY-oh) came up with the idea of the *impresario,* a term he borrowed from the music world, as the type of executive best suited to managing creative people. There, he also began to see the similarities between the creative processes in business and jazz.

Dr. Kao is not merely a student of business. He is also a practicing entrepreneur who has put his ideas about creativity into the marketplace. Over the years, he has started several businesses, including Genzyme Tissue Repair, now a publicly owned biotech company specializing in advanced tissue engineering techniques, and K.O. Technology, a next-generation cancer diagnostics and therapeutics company. In addition to his scientific and technological pursuits, Dr. Kao has produced feature films, including *sex, lies, and videotape,* which won the Palme d'Or Award at the 1989 Cannes Film Festival, and *Mr. Baseball,* which starred Tom Selleck. He is also a pianist and jazz musician.

Dr. Kao's most recent effort has been to write a book, *Jamming: The Art and Discipline of Business Creativity* (HarperCollins, 1996), and to produce a documentary film based on the same subject. The book has been favorably reviewed around the world and has made it onto a number of best-seller lists. Among other things, it resulted in a profile of Dr. Kao in *The Economist.* What follows are excerpts from a conversation with Dr. Kao that took place in July 1996 at his office in Cambridge, Massachusetts.

S&B *John, when you talk about creativity, you use the metaphor of jamming, as in jazz improvisation. Is it true that you once brought a jazz ensemble into a company to teach people about creativity?*

JOHN KAO I'm guilty of that, yes.

S&B *What were you trying to show people at that company?*

JOHN KAO Jazz musicians can be great teachers of business. Their creativity is not dependent on their mood. It does not have to be coaxed out of them. It has nothing to do with the phases of the moon or even how they feel that day. They go on stage and start playing. Being creative is their job.

Now, jamming—which is about collaborative improvisation—has to do with getting people together to be creative musically. But it is a very powerful metaphor for understanding the grammar of the creative process. It applies to business and to other pursuits as well. The capacity to creatively improvise is an important factor that differentiates successful companies—or teams—from those that are not successful.

Improvisation in the jazz sense—like the business sense—is not formless. It is built on a skill set. Jazz, for example, involves selecting a tune. Tunes have notes and tempos and rules. If the tune is "All the Things You Are," you have to adhere to its structure and to the tradition behind that structure. Jazz is not about getting up and playing whatever notes you want. It is about reworking themes in a manner that sounds good, that can be followed by the other musicians, and that the audience enjoys. You cannot do that without first acquiring skills. In the end, as Duke

Ellington said, "If it sounds good, it is good," which is to say, ultimately, jazz has to work. It has to play with the audience and with the marketplace. I think that is relevant to business.

S&B *How do you know whether a company is sufficiently creative?*

JOHN KAO There are some pretty obvious ways of benchmarking creativity. One way is to perform what I call a "creativity audit," which is to look at your capabilities and look at your performance and examine the percentage of revenue that comes from products that are less than five years old, less than three years old, and that are current with the present accounting period. You can then compare those figures to those of your competition along the same axes.

You see, my notion is that an organization is really a factory for producing new ideas and for linking those ideas with resources—human resources, financial resources, knowledge resources, infrastructure resources—in an effort to create value. These are processes that you can map with results that you can measure. Organizations are about putting ideas through one or more types of gating procedures. In this way, ideas go from being a whim to becoming a project, from being a "skunk works" effort to becoming an official, mainstream effort, from being an unfunded program to a funded process, and so on.

Now, all companies do what I just described with their ideas. But most companies do it unconsciously, unintentionally, or almost by default, which is to say not very effectively. As a result, conducting a creativity audit can be very illuminating, because it can tell you how the process is working internally and against the competition.

You can do it quite simply by gathering people together in a room and asking them about the creative process and then diagramming it. You can create a map and by doing so gain a new understanding of how it works, who the gatekeepers are, who has the power, where the ideas really come from, and so on.

You can ask yourself whether you are happy with the source of your organization's ideas. Do the ideas come only from official, specially anointed, idea-generating sources, or do they come from people who are off the radar screen? How are they rewarded? What does that say about the quality of creative collaboration? What does it say about the rigidity or appropriate flexibility of the organizational structure as a whole?

S&B *When you do an audit, are you able to show how new, creative ideas translate to the bottom line?*

JOHN KAO If you come up with a new product, you can very easily track its contribution to the bottom line. But often the challenge can be both large and subtle.

If you are at Coca-Cola, for example, the creative challenge is one of maintaining—rather than creating—a tremendous level of consumption for your products. Every day, there are 770 million Cokes consumed, which means that there are 770 million purchasing decisions made each day regarding the product. To support those decisions, the company must constantly reinvest in its marketing links to its customers. As a result, a high level of creativity must go into everything the company does, from cause-related campaigns—Coca-Cola and its sponsorship of the Olympic Village in Atlanta, for example—to new catchphrases, commercials, marketing slogans, advertising campaigns, and promotional tie-ins.

All of these creative ideas and decisions about new ways to reach the consumer can be tracked with regard to how well they are working, whether and how they are building awareness for the product, how well they motivate the consumption of the product, and so on. So there's real "right brain" creativity that goes into all of the organizational processes that a company utilizes and must continually reinvent in order to conduct its business. But there are also the "left brain" accounting functions that must continually ask how the company is doing financially and whether the creative processes are working for the bottom line.

The management of creativity is intimate. It deals with an individual's personal, psychological landscape.

S&B *Do you manage those "right brain" creative processes the same way you manage "left brain" functions?*

JOHN KAO I would argue that the management of creativity requires a skill set that's relatively different from the traditional management skill set that is appropriate to a large, complex, industrial-era organization.

S&B *Can you describe how they differ?*

JOHN KAO Let me put it this way. The management of creativity is more intimate. By that I mean that it deals with an individual's personal, psychological landscape. It deals with the way you create relationships. It deals with creating an atmosphere and environment that support the creative process. As a result, it is a management skill set that is inherently psychological and that encourages desired outcomes rather than demands those outcomes.

You see, the traditional managerial mind-set is an analytical mind-set. It is about creating accountability and defining responsibilities. But when you come into a creativity-driven environment, things are very different and there is the danger that a traditional managerial mind-set could even do damage. That is because managing creative teams and people is very different from managing the factory worker–foreman relationship. The creative process is different from the traditional production and work-flow process. It is not so linear. Instead of command and control, managing the creative process is about facilitating and permitting.

S&B *What about people skills?*

JOHN KAO Managing the creative process means selecting the best people and then letting them do their work. That means nurturing. It also means, from time to time, creating drama—even uncertainty—so that the creative environment has an edge to it, a charge, and does not run out of steam. In jazz, performances have this function. Performers may play in the studio, but they need to go out and tour every once in a while to keep their edge, or a performer who is a stranger may be asked to "sit in" on a set.

So rather than managing by clarifying events, the creative process may require raising the level of uncertainty. Sometimes this can be done by issuing a creative challenge that has resonance, in that it inspires the team to activity.

S&B *Can you give me an example of what you mean by "a creative challenge"?*

JOHN KAO Yes. Take Sony. A few years ago, a senior manager went to see a group of engineers who were working on designing tape recorders. He walked into the group, took a small wooden block out of his pocket, and threw it on the table. Then he said to the engineers, "Make it this big," and he left the room. Well, the only way that they could make a stereo tape recorder so small was to eliminate the loudspeakers, use headphones, and eliminate recording. Once the engineers decided on this, it led to a whole raft of innovations in tape transport, electronics miniaturization, and so on, all culminating in the first Walkman.

Now, the manager did not go to the engineers and say, "Market research wants a tape recorder this size but without loudspeakers." Instead, he challenged them. He didn't tell them how he wanted his problem solved, either. Perhaps he did not know. He did not provide them with too many directions or too much clarity, for that matter.

S&B *The management style you are describing sounds more like art than science. Are certain types of people more adept at it* *than others? How do you make certain it is practical?*

JOHN KAO The metaphor that I like to use for the leader of a creative process is that of the head of a record label. The CEO's job in a creativity-driven company is to be an impresario, not a manager. The impresario's job is to pick the right people who can pick the right people. He picks the people who can pick artists and relate to them. People who know what the market craves. The head of a record label sets up structures, but he also defines the sound of the label, which is to describe what is desirable, what fits, and what is quality for that label, and then to create an environment where that sound can thrive.

As a result, a large part of the impresario's job has to do with maintaining and communicating standards of performance. Knowing how to set those standards—which are often more subjective than analytical—means knowing how to communicate the difference between something that is great and something that is just OK. It means that you are able to monitor and police your standards of quality once you have defined them. It also means that you are able to create an environment so that the creative process can take place and so that you can get people to perform at their highest levels.

But ultimately the impresario must also know when to simply get out of the way. You see, to continue the musical metaphor, in the end it is the musician who actually plays the notes. The impresario—or the project leader—is only there to make sure that happens. That is a very different type of management mind-set.

S&B *What else does the impresario do?*

JOHN KAO The impresario functions as a bridge and a translator. He or she is a bridge between the creative point of view—which is often very focused on the creative task itself—and the resource-allocation process. The impresario has to make certain the funds and people required to get that task completed are available. The impresario function is also about intervening with the company's more administrative management structure. It is about trying to establish a sense of boundaries and budgets and milestones and so forth on a project that does not necessarily lend itself to milestones. It is about translating between the intimate interior environment of the creative work team and the company's need to make money. And, finally, it is about positioning the fruits of the creative process in the marketplace and selling them.

S&B *Are there companies that use the impresario management model?*

JOHN KAO Neutrogena does this. Lloyd Cotsen, the CEO, explicitly says that his job is managing the creativity of his people and that maintaining the creativity of the company is his most important responsibility.

S&B *How would you characterize the environment?*

JOHN KAO Well, it's everything from the physical attributes of the environment—which is to say the internal design, the furniture, the decor—to the culture of the organization. The culture must underscore, in no uncertain terms, the primacy of the creative talent as the way the company competes. At Neutrogena, if you're in product development, you are a hero.

S&B *Has that translated into superior results?*

JOHN KAO Neutrogena is a highly profitable company. Other profitable companies embrace the same view of creativity. Silicon Graphics has gone so far as to say it will now treat its engineers like recording-label superstars, by providing them with money and whatever they need to excel at their creative work.

Coca-Cola also takes the view that creativity is a corporate discipline. M. Douglas Ivester, Coca-Cola's president, told me his company is way beyond thinking about creativity as a momentary epiphany or as something to learn over a weekend at an executive-training course.

He said that creativity is something the company cares about and takes seriously every day. It does not think of creativity as a whim or a lightning bolt or a company fad or even as a campaign but as a discipline to be fostered. That discipline translates directly into the company's competitive capabilities. To do that, Mr. Ivester explained, people must get respect for their new ideas. It must be ingrained in the culture, which is one hundred years old—even celebrated. Coca-Cola does that. They have historical displays, museums. They are proud of their invention of the contour bottle in 1915 and of their reinvention of Santa Claus in the 1930s and 1940s.

S&B *Is there a "department of creativity"? Does Coca-Cola outsource it?*

JOHN KAO Coca-Cola has it in its own culture and it has created relationships to foster it when necessary, too. The traditional model for a company like Coca-Cola is to hire one big advertising agency and essentially outsource all of its creativity in that area. But Coca-Cola does not do it that way. It knows how to manage creative people and creative teams, and it has been quite adept at building a network that includes the Creative Artists Agency in Hollywood, which is a talent agency. And rather than relying on a single advertising agency, the company's unique global structure and independent bottling company relationships have enabled it to put together a network of four or five dozen boutique advertising, marketing, and communication agencies on a global basis.

In broad terms, what this means is that the company can benefit from what I call "knowledge and creative arbitrage." It can take the Brazilian creative team and put its work to use in a project in Japan. It can use this work in a project in eastern Europe. The output of one team can be used to stimulate another.

What that means is that Coca-Cola can get really fresh output, because it is getting people who are outside the traditional model and they are combining ideas in very novel ways. F. Scott Fitzgerald said that the mark of the developed intellect is that it can accommodate two contradictory ideas at the same time. That is a skill at which Coca-Cola excels.

S&B *Fitzgerald mentioned intellect. How is knowledge related to creativity?*

JOHN KAO It takes creativity at every stage to make the discontinuous leap from one level of knowledge to the next. These discontinuous leaps of understanding lead to insights that, in turn, lead to value creation.

So in a corporate context, companies have to try very hard to oppose the enticements of conventional wisdom. They must aim for the leaps, which means that companies have to do more than simply manage their knowledge, which is composed of the insights and understandings they already know. They also have to manage the knowledge-generation process. It's not just about, "Oh, we're going to create a data warehouse and we are going to invent a computerized filing system to get at all the stuff we know." Companies have to take risks to get new knowledge, in a manner similar to how jazz musicians take risks when they go after a new approach to a tune or a performance.

Let me give you an example of what I mean about the knowledge-generation process in a business context. The Global Business Network, a trend-forecasting firm, creates scenarios about the future for its clients. It wanted to figure out whether there is a single global teenage market, and if so, what characterizes it. How did the GBN do it? In a very creative way. It hired a teenager and sent him on a worldwide market-research tour. It then put that teenager in front of GBN's top corporate clients to talk to them about what he found out. So it employed a radical method to create knowledge, rather than simply digging through a data warehouse of existing knowledge. It was a risky, jazzlike approach.

S&B *I know of an Italian restaurant in Kyoto, Japan, that closes for two weeks each year so the owner can take the staff on a culinary tour of different regions of Italy.*

JOHN KAO That's the same intent. On a larger scale, Meiji Seika, a major Japanese confectionery firm, sends its executives on confectionery eating and purchasing expeditions to places like Belgium. At Coca-Cola, Mr. Ivester himself makes field trips.

S&B *How does a company decide which ideas to fund?*

JOHN KAO That's where it is essential for the various stakeholders in the company to get involved in the collaborative process of decision making. In a large pharmaceutical company, where it's a big bet, you're going to need finance people to be involved in the decision making, because the investment can run into the hundreds of millions of dollars. You're going to have to run scenarios. You might even need agreement from the CEO to make that type of decision. If it's an incremental, low-cost decision in a marketing-oriented company, it may be a very different set of stakeholders a lot further down in the organization.

> The traditional managerial mind-set is analytical. In a creativity-driven environment, a traditional managerial mind-set could do damage.

Let's say you are funding a motion picture, which requires an investment in the $20 million to $50 million range. You're making that bet based on certain assumptions regarding the market, its size, the appeal of what you're funding, the talent associated with the project, and so on. Those decisions are not that different from the ones regarding funding a new car model or a pharmaceutical research project. You have to take into account the size of the market, the likelihood of success, the proposed payback, and whether your talent can pull it all off. The only real differences are those of scale.

S&B *What else do you look at in deciding which projects to fund?*

JOHN KAO The larger the price tag, the more you have to adopt what I call the "postmodern management approach." What I mean by that is that you have to use everything when you make a decision. You need judgment, you need to utilize conventional resource-allocation analysis, you have to work backward from estimations of the market to the current investments, and you have to do some benchmarking of your product and its potential against your competition.

However, if that's all there is—if that's the only way you make your resource-allocation decisions—then your process is both flawed and limited. You are not taking advantage of all the tools that exist or all of the potential in your organization.

Now here is where I use my jamming metaphor. You see, the conventional asset-allocation method is like sheet music. It is prescribed, it has right answers and wrong answers, and it sounds about the same every time. But jamming is different. Jamming is when you make the music, when you improvise and adapt to conditions, when you are creative. Jamming—which follows rules but not individual notes—gives you a different result each time, depending upon the players and the conditions in which they find themselves. It is adaptable to changing conditions.

S&B *The metaphor sounds as if it applies only to companies like software producers or entertainment companies. Do companies in more mundane businesses jam?*

JOHN KAO One of my favorite companies is Oticon. It is a Danish company that is in the hearing aid business—not the sexiest of industries. It had a Number 1 share in that business. But in the words of the CEO, the company got sleepy. It failed to keep pace with the competition and it fell from Number 1 to Number 3 worldwide.

It was also suddenly facing intense competition. Siemens, the big German electronics concern, entered the market and spent more on hearing aid research and development in a year than Oticon's entire market capitalization. Oticon could not keep up with Siemens by traditional measures. Oticon decided the only way it could compete was by being more creative as well as faster than its rivals.

So what did the company do? It changed from sheet music to jazz. In one quick change of focus, it rebuilt the organization. Now, Oticon's change was very radical. It eliminated all reporting relationships, all job descriptions, its traditional accountability structures. The company also eliminated the functional organization structure. It changed the organization from being built around a traditional flow of processes to one that was structured around a bag of projects and new ideas. People at this company were essentially given full permission to pursue objectives according to the way they saw fit and understood the market.

S&B *It does sound radical.*

JOHN KAO It was, but there was still accountability. There were group structures and processes created for approving skunk works projects and for moving informal skunk works efforts into more formal efforts. This was done by representative committees of the company. Yet, while there was an approval process, there was also plenty of latitude for these projects.

They did another thing that was interesting. The company moved into new offices that had a completely open plan with modular furniture, and each worker's credenza was put on wheels. Everyone was suddenly together. The result was that an engineer and a technician would sit down together and the technician could wheel over his credenza full of tools to wherever it was needed to work on new ideas. The traditional assembly method was changed into a musical-chairs arrangement of build-it-on-the-spot.

Now, not everyone was moving around every day. But the point is they all knew that they could move if it was required to fulfill the objectives of the company. They also knew that a microchip designer, for example, could sit next to the marketing people for a few days to work on designs, listen in on conversations, and get involved in the discussions. At the same time, next to them both, people could be working on manufacturing prototypes. All of the machinery, in fact, was sprinkled throughout the corporate headquarters.

S&B *Was it at all chaotic?*

JOHN KAO When you say *chaotic,* what do you really mean? It was energetic, yes. Unorthodox, yes. But don't forget—it *is* a health care company, so there are very high standards of quality and manufacturing control that have to be met. These standards in no way declined. In fact, they actually improved. And, of course, because it is a health care company, it still must be perceived as a serious company to its customers. So, in that sense, it was not chaotic at all.

But it was suddenly open to new ideas, which were free to bubble up from people anywhere in the organization. What all the changes actually did was to improve the quality and the quantity of the conversations within the company about fulfilling the firm's objectives. What the changes also did was to create networks instead of hierarchies. People were free to take on multijob assignments, instead of thinking of themselves as narrow specialists. Some people at the company had two or three different jobs!

As a result, there was knowledge arbitrage going on inside many workers' heads. Because they could find all sorts of different people with different points of view and they were free to talk to them about anything with regard to the company and its methods, ideas flowed. At the same time, the company made some speculative money available to nurture little projects of an individual nature.

S&B *What were the objective changes that resulted?*

JOHN KAO There was an overall and very dramatic improvement in the company's performance. It regained a great deal of market share, even against its giant competitors, though it is not yet Number 1 again. Product development time was cut by more than 50 percent. The company was able to go public. And by opening up the corporate "mind," so to speak, the company was able to develop several new products by mining its old intellectual property assets.

S&B *Is this an isolated case, or are there other companies that have radically changed themselves?*

JOHN KAO One company that is very interesting is Senco Fasteners, a maker of industrial staple guns, nail guns, and fasteners for use in prefab housing. It is a privately owned company located outside Cincinnati. It has been as aggressive as any company I know in creating a corporate culture that does creative work.

Senco has invested heavily in terms of management, time, and energy in developing what they call "Senco management concepts." It is actually one of the few companies I know of that has an explicit epistemology—an attitude and approach to knowledge. Their epistemology says basically that an organization has two states. It has the state of operating to assure its own survival and then it has the state of operating to assure its advancement. Those states require different types of functions.

> The challenge is not to let people do whatever they want. The challenge is to create accountability in a nonmechanistic way.

S&B *How does that approach work in practice?*

JOHN KAO First, it works as a conceptual platform for management's two goals. There is, for example, on the advancement side, something at Senco called the Business Development Information Resource Team. The goal of this team is to look outside the company and to carry out disciplined speculations about the future—to do creative scenarios and analyses and to gather new kinds of cognitive expertise to help the management of the company navigate its way through growth. But on the other side of the company, there are procedures to disseminate basic management concepts to everyone—including people who work on the assembly line—so they can do their jobs better.

Now, both sides come together as well, and everyone knows what the advancement team is doing, as well as what the survival team is doing. Communication is open and during my visits to the company, I found that everyone pretty much understands what's going on. This includes people on the factory floor assembling nail guns, and so on. That gives them a lot of coherence about the company's purpose. If they were a jazz ensemble, they would be very "together."

S&B *How do you define "coherence," or "togetherness"?*

JOHN KAO The whole company shares a common frame of reference. Now, it has paid off at Senco in different and creative ways. For example, workers are taking the initiative for redesigning processes. Everyone also knows the importance of knowledge within the company. In the executive suite, for example, they have some really sophisticated software to represent in digital fashion the strategic knowledge of the company.

Down on the factory floor, they don't need the software, so they have white boards and clipboards everywhere to represent and capture the knowledge they need. They are labeled "OFI" (opportunity-for-improvement) boards. If you are a blue-collar worker, you just write on the board, "We need such and such a part or element." Or you write, "This is my idea to improve the process." And it is management's responsibility to provide a response. It may sound simple, but it is a method for harnessing the company's creativity.

S&B *So what is the challenge to managers?*

JOHN KAO The challenge is to manage creative people so that the output is fruitful. The challenge is not to have an open environment and simply let them do whatever they want. I mean, you would not let your kids do whatever they want. So the challenge is to create accountability in a nonmechanistic way. You cannot come in with a clipboard and check off boxes and figure out why something has not been done on schedule.

But obviously businesses do not operate like an artist commune. Business involves deploying finite resources to achieve goals in a competitive environment to make money. That is something creative people understand. The manager's job—the impresario's job—is to preside over the company's efforts to jam so the business runs really well.

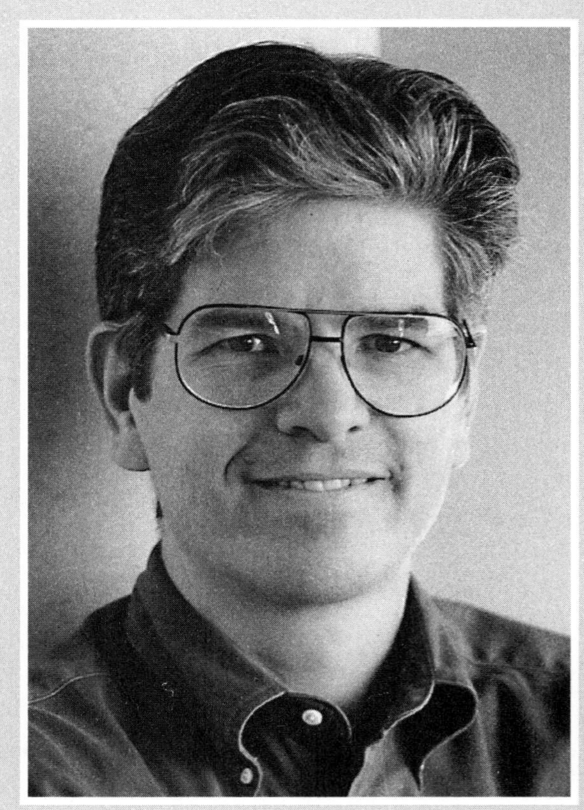

An Interview with

PAUL M. ROMER

Professor, Stanford Business School

It is hard to label an economist who just turned forty "venerable," but that is what Paul M. Romer's peers call the Stanford University economics professor. Professor Romer, who also teaches at the University of California at Berkeley while conducting research at the Hoover Institution at Stanford and the Canadian Institute for Advanced Research in Toronto, is best known for his theories about the dynamics of growth. In Professor Romer's view, knowledge is the unsung hero of the growth game. Whereas most classical economists—not to mention Marx—have focused on production, labor, and capital, Professor Romer adds knowledge and technology to the mix.

The classical approach operates well in the physical economy of resource extraction and commodity production, according to the professor. That economy is characterized

The first thing that you lose in the knowledge economy is the classical notion of the right price.

by diminishing returns, because each additional ton of copper or barrel of oil is harder to find than the previous one. Being scarcer, it is more expensive to extract from the earth.

The information economy is different, however. Writing a complicated piece of software or discovering specific gene sequences incurs large, up-front costs. But after the initial work is done, the cost of each additional "unit" is minimal or sometimes even nil. Software can be copied onto disks at very low prices or sent out over the Internet. Each gram of protein produced by genetically altered bacteria only adds to the world's supply. As a result, whereas returns diminish in the physical economy, they increase in the knowledge economy. This is a cause for hope, according to Professor Romer.

There is another important tenet in the professor's worldview: the more we discover new things, the better we become at the process of discovery itself. Knowledge builds on itself. As a result, the capacity to create wealth and value increases over time—surely another reason for optimism.

Professor Romer's work is serious and academic. Whereas most economists have their cadre of on-the-one-hand, on-the-other-hand adherents and detractors, however, Professor Romer's work has thus far attracted much more support than dissent among his peers, prompting speculation that he may someday receive the Nobel Prize for economics. Economist Paul Krugman and management theorist Peter F. Drucker are among Professor Romer's biggest and most public boosters.

Professor Romer recently spoke with *Strategy & Business* at his Stanford office in Palo Alto, California. What follows are excerpts from that conversation, which took place in March 1997.

S&B *For the most part, knowledge, like technology, has been taken for granted by economists who look at the factors that propel growth. But in your work, you assert that knowledge can raise returns on investments and that it is a factor of production, like capital, labor, and raw materials. Does the information economy work differently from the classical economy?*

PAUL ROMER Let's back up. My work on growth can be traced back to an attempt to isolate the differences between the information or knowledge-based economy and what came before it. My belief is that those differences are important for our understanding of growth. Those distinctions matter to people running firms, and they should matter to policymakers. They are issues that show up at a number of points in the economy. And since those issues are topical right now, it makes my work in this area a lot of fun.

S&B *What differences are you referring to?*

PAUL ROMER Let me articulate it this way. One feature of knowledge can be summarized by Isaac Newton's statement that he could see far because he could stand on the shoulders of giants. In other words, his notion was that knowledge builds on itself, which means that as we learn more, we get better and better at discovering new things. It also means that there's no limit to the amount of things we can discover.

This is a very important fact for understanding the broad sweep of human history, and it is very different from what we are used to thinking about in terms of physical objects, where scarcity is the overwhelming fact with which we have to deal.

S&B *You say we are getting better at finding new things. What exactly do you mean by that?*

PAUL ROMER There are only a finite quantity of things with which we can work—basically, the matter in the earth's crust. We've had essentially the identical amount of physical stuff for millions of years. Now, a lot in the language of economics—and in the popular language, as well—makes it appear as if we are wealthier today because we have more of this physical stuff. It makes it sound as if we have actually produced more physical things. But in truth, that is not right. If you think about it the way a physicist does, the law of the conservation of matter and energy states that we have essentially the same quantity of things we have always had.

S&B *So what have we done?*

PAUL ROMER We have taken the fixed quantity of matter available to us and rearranged it. We have changed things from a form that is less valuable into a form that is more valuable. Value creation and wealth creation in their most basic senses have to do with taking physical objects and rearranging them.

Now, where do ideas come in? Quite simply, ideas are the recipes we use to rearrange things to create more value and wealth. For example, we have ideas about ways to make steel by combining iron with carbon and a few other elements. We have ideas about how to take silicon—an abundant element that was almost worthless to us until recently—and make it into semiconductor chips.

So we have physical materials to work with—raw ingredients—which are finite and scarce, and we have ideas or knowledge, which tells us how to use those raw materials. When I say there are always more things to discover, what I mean is that there are always more recipes that we can find to combine raw materials in ways that make them more valuable to us.

S&B *What you are saying sounds straightforward enough. What does it mean for the economy and for growth?*

PAUL ROMER The claim I made a moment ago about standing on the shoulders of giants tells us something important. It says that we can take advantage of a form of increasing returns in the process of discovery. Now, it could have been—I suppose—that with each new discovery, it got harder and harder to make additional discoveries. In that case, we would, at some point, simply give up. Progress would be slowing down and eventually would come to a halt. Of course, this is not what we see when we look at history. From one century to the next, the rate of technological change and the rate of growth of income per capita have been speeding up.

S&B *This is contrary to discovery in the physical world, isn't it?*

PAUL ROMER Yes. The physical world is characterized by diminishing returns. Diminishing returns are a result of the scarcity of physical objects. One of the most important differences between objects and ideas—the kinds of differences that I alluded to before—is that ideas are not scarce and the process of discovery in the realm of ideas does not suffer from diminishing returns.

The law of conservation of matter and energy states that we have the same quantity of physical stuff we have always had.

S&B *"One" of the differences? Are there other differences as well?*

PAUL ROMER Yes. Let's take a particular piece of knowledge, such as a piece of software, and think about the costs of production that a supplier faces. If we do that, we see that this piece of knowledge is very unusual from a traditional economic point of view.

To make the first copy of Windows NT, for example, Microsoft invested hundreds of millions of dollars in research, development, testing, and so forth. But once Microsoft got the underlying bit string right, it could produce the second copy of Windows NT for about 50 cents—the cost of copying the program coded in this string of bits onto a floppy disk. Since then, all subsequent copies of the program have the same cost or even lower costs. For example, if Windows NT is distributed over the Internet, the cost of every additional copy is basically nil. So the first copy costs you hundreds of millions of dollars, but all other copies are free, no matter how many you produce.

This kind of falling cost per unit is a different manifestation of increasing returns. This is very different from the physical economy, where an important part of the cost of each good comes from the process of making an additional copy of that good.

S&B *Paul, is this kind of increasing return the same as or different from the standing-on-the-shoulders-of-giants effect that you mentioned before?*

PAUL ROMER These two kinds of increasing returns are logically distinct. For example, we could have falling costs of production for copies of a specific piece of software, even if the standing-on-shoulders effect were not operating.

Suppose, for a moment, that Windows NT were the last piece of useful software that could ever be written. Once it is finished, it will be impossible to develop any new pieces of software. I know this sounds crazy, but bear with me. This would be an extreme case that is the opposite of the shoulders-of-giants effect.

But even if this were true, the production costs for NT would still have the unusual character of huge costs up-front and very, very low costs for each subsequent copy. That feature is very important for understanding what we call the "industrial organization" of the economy, because it means that you are going to see a great deal of monopoly power in the new economy.

S&B *How does knowledge lead to monopolies?*

PAUL ROMER Traditionally, in economics, you would assume that there would be a couple of leaders in a field, that their success would make it attractive for other people to come in, that there would be rivalry among all the firms, and that the industry segment as a whole would grow and benefit as competition intensified.

For example, in the physical economy, suppose you've got a firm that owns a big ore deposit somewhere in the world, and there are other firms that own other ore deposits in other parts of the world. Each of these firms will operate under conditions of increasing costs and diminishing returns. One of those firms may be able to produce 100,000 tons of refined ore per year. But it can't easily scale up to 200,000 or 300,000 tons because of the nature of its physical resources. There's only one way to mine the ore and it gets more expensive as you do it faster. The physical structure of your assets means that there's a limit on how fast you can exploit it.

So you might ask: Will one company take over the whole world's supply of ore and become a monopolist in world copper? The answer is no, because the firm that wants to do that would produce up to a point where it would become more and more expensive. Other firms would be drawn into the market and might produce and sell their ore more cheaply. When firms face increasing costs and diminishing returns, no single firm can supply the whole worldwide market. If it tries, it faces increasing cost disadvantages relative to its competitors.

S&B *So there are limits to monopoly power in the physical world?*

PAUL ROMER Yes. In the physical economy, there is a natural equilibrating process. If one firm tries to take over the whole market, other firms will gain an advantage and will enter. When this whole process settles down, there will be many firms and a competitive market.

S&B *How does this differ in the knowledge economy?*

PAUL ROMER Let's think about operating systems and the world of computers for a moment. Let's say you have one firm, like Microsoft, which is going to produce Windows NT. Once it produces its first copy, it then faces no cost disadvantage. It can produce millions or billions of copies of NT at little additional cost. It truly can supply the entire worldwide market with operating systems. If anything, it probably gets even easier for Microsoft, because the larger its market size gets, the more attractive it is to adopt its software, because of what we call "bandwagon effects." If everybody else is using a particular piece of software, it usually makes it advantageous for you to use it, too.

Now, this difference between diminishing-returns industries and increasing-returns industries completely changes the dynamic of competition. Under conditions of increasing returns, competition is driven by various firms trying to capture as much market share as possible as quickly as possible and by being the first to develop a product and to flood the market with it, even—at least initially—at a loss. To see how different this is, think again about mining. If you discover a large deposit of copper ore, do you think you would want to give lots of it away for free to increase your market share? Of course not.

S&B *What does this mean in a business sense?*

PAUL ROMER First of all, it means that the kind of strategies you see in the knowledge economy are those like Netscape's. In that strategy, a new company comes into a new market and gives away its browser and tries to move very rapidly to supply a large part of the market. Netscape did this and it ended up with a large percentage of the total market for browsers. It is now trying to leverage that advantage into a larger advantage in the more lucrative market for server software. That kind of competition is driven by falling costs and increasing returns in the information economy. That is the way competition unfolds in the information economy.

So we are talking about two extremes: one is software, the other is resource extraction. A lot of traditional business fits somewhere in between.

S&B *How are monopolies sustained in the knowledge economy? Don't new companies come along with new products that replace the old ones?*

PAUL ROMER Yes, that is true, and it brings us back to the two notions of increasing returns that we were discussing a minute ago. Recall the thought experiment where we shut down the increasing returns associated with the shoulders-of-giants effect but assumed that the increasing returns associated with cheap copies were still present? This leads to a rather pessimistic implication. A firm like Microsoft would become the monopoly supplier of operating systems software. It would remain a monopolist forever, because no entrant could compete with it with a similar product and, according to our assumptions, there was nothing better that was left for someone else to discover.

Fortunately, we don't get this pessimistic result, because the two kinds of increasing returns go together. This means that even though one firm may control a large fraction of the market at any point in time, there is another way for new firms to compete. Instead of trying to enter the market by providing exactly the same product as the incumbents at a lower price, they can enter and compete by selling something that is new and better. This is precisely what Microsoft and Intel did when they displaced IBM as the dominant force in the computer market. It is what firms like Netscape, Sun, and Oracle are trying to do now by leveraging the emerging power of the Internet. Economists call this "monopolistic" competition. It's a form of competition between different firms, each of which sells a different kind of product and can behave like a monopolist, at least temporarily.

Of course, it takes various kinds of institutional infrastructure to make this system work. For example, the government has to grant property rights over intangible assets like ideas.

S&B *The property rights you are referring to are patents, copyrights, and so on?*

PAUL ROMER Yes, and these differ from the property rights we are familiar with for physical objects. You can give dispersed ownership to something like timber or ore. Many different people can own different pieces of the same kind of asset, so they can all compete to supply ore. But if you consider, for example, a pharmaceutical product, you see that once the government gives a firm a patent on a new drug, this firm becomes a monopolist with regard to that piece of knowledge, that recipe for how to make that drug. We give this company a legal right to keep everyone else from using its knowledge, and this means that the company can gain the dominant position in the market. So it is the combination of low replication costs to the producer and the protection of intellectual property rights that creates the monopoly position.

S&B *This means that competition tends to take place via the introduction of new goods, rather than by competing on price in existing goods?*

PAUL ROMER Yes, that is right. It is a very different vision of how competition works and why markets are so successful in generating high standards of living. You see, the traditional intellectual justification for laissez-faire comes from dealing with a hypothetical world filled only with scarce objects. In effect, you're just trying to figure out which mine should produce how much copper and how much total copper should be produced. In such a world, the classical notion of perfect competition is feasible and it works well. Competing firms will end up charging the right price for copper in a precise sense. The market price will determine the total amount of copper that should be produced. It will also determine how much of the total each mine will produce. Classical economists were able to show that, under competition, these production and allocation decisions are efficient.

In this kind of world, it is important for policymakers and the government to step in and break up any monopoly or cartel. If they keep the cartels at bay, the price will adjust to the efficient level and the right quantities will be produced and sold.

Now, let's go to this new world, where the key challenge is to produce and distribute knowledge or ideas. The first thing to notice is that you lose the classical notion of the right price. For example, with the concept of a vaccine, the best thing to do might be to give any firm the right to use this concept for free and let everybody in the world use it to make serums so that people in general can benefit. To do this, you want the price for using the concept of a vaccine to be zero after it has been discovered. Thus, for example, we could have granted a perpetual patent on the basic concept of a vaccine to Edward Jenner, who discovered the concept in the 1700s. In fact, he and his heirs have no intellectual property rights over this idea. They collect no income when researchers and doctors all over the world use vaccines and the concept of immunity to protect us from disease. After the fact, this is efficient.

But let's back up for a moment. If you want to get people to discover extremely valuable concepts like vaccines, you would like to offer them really high prices for their discovery. This creates an incentive to do the work necessary to make the discovery. So, in this world of knowledge and recipes, there is always an unavoidable tension between wanting to have low prices after the fact, so a knowledge good can be distributed widely, and wanting to promise strong property rights and monopoly protections in advance, as an incentive and a motivation for discovery.

S&B *How do you resolve the problem, Paul?*

PAUL ROMER What we have to do is work out a balance between tolerating some monopolies and monopoly profits—since that's how we motivate people to discover new recipes—with competition to keep prices low and distribute products widely.

We encourage this competition by granting property rights that are partial or incomplete. In practice, what this means is that while in the physical economy with diminishing returns there are perfect prices, in the knowledge economy with its increasing returns there are no perfect prices.

S&B *Are you suggesting that we must simply tolerate monopoly prices?*

PAUL ROMER Yes. I'm also suggesting that we have to establish property rights that are incomplete. In the world of objects, you don't have to make these kinds of compromises. We use government policy to limit monopoly. We also establish very strong property rights. For example, it would be very wasteful for property rights on land to expire after a certain period of time and then for everyone to be able to use it freely. But this is precisely what we do with patents. One key difference is that in the world of ideas, you cannot have both strong property rights and competition. The other is that you don't get congestion over the use of ideas. When we look back on systems where a group of people did have free access to a physical resource like land, we speak of a "tragedy of the commons." But there is no similar tragedy of the intellectual commons.

> The physical world is characterized by diminishing returns. The realm of ideas does not suffer from diminishing returns.

Now, as I suggested above, if there were not all these additional things to discover, we would be pessimistic about this new world of ideas, because of all the monopoly power we are creating with patents and copyrights. In fact, if there were nothing left to discover, we would treat all knowledge the same way we treat the knowledge behind the principle of vaccination. It would be common property and everybody would be free to use it.

But fortunately, in the knowledge economy, there are always new things to discover. We grant property rights over knowledge, and this leads to a leapfrogging process whereby the potential of future monopoly profits induces new discoveries. As a result, a new entity will emerge and come into a market at some point and leapfrog all the existing entities. When that happens, you'll get a big jump in terms of productivity and economic value, and the old monopolists will typically be displaced. Remember, this is a different dynamic from the one we described in the classical economy, where all competition was to produce existing goods at lower prices.

So over in this idea part of the economy, we worry much less about having the government actively intervene to strike down any hint of monopoly power and keep all firms small. We rely much more on the process of what Schumpeter called "creative destruction," where you have a sequence of temporary monopolies that are superseded by new monopolists selling new products and services.

S&B *What are the policy implications of the knowledge economy?*

PAUL ROMER There are big implications stemming from the recognition of the difference between the classical world of objects and the idea-based world. With objects, we have a good idea of what the right institutional arrangements are. We just establish infinite-lived property rights, make sure that there is no monopoly control, and then let the market operate. This will lead to efficient allocations of physical objects. That is the lesson of laissez-faire, and it is still a very powerful lesson, one that too many politicians still do not understand.

S&B *And the aim of laissez-faire in that respect is greater economic efficiency?*

PAUL ROMER Yes. But more important, I would say the aim in both of these worlds is to generate or create more value. The kinds of problems you've got to solve in the classical realm are relatively simple. You just have to allocate scarce commodities among alternative users and between alternative producers.

S&B *It would seem that the aim of regulation in the commodity-producer world is to foster efficient production, while the aim in the knowledge world is to bolster future discovery. These are different roles for the government, aren't they?*

PAUL ROMER Yes, they are. There is something inherently static about the classical vision—that if there were nothing changing, nothing new being discovered, the price systems would be a good way to decide which mine should produce the next unit of copper. It also works well to decide which power plant should generate the extra megawatts of electricity, and so on.

But over here, in the knowledge economy, there are these other imperatives. We have to worry not just about getting efficient usage from what we've got right now but also about figuring out ways to discover all the new things we might need or be able to use. That is not a set of static problems. It is very dynamic.

S&B *Do the right institutions exist to make those policy choices?*

PAUL ROMER What's interesting about the knowledge economy is that we haven't figured out what the optimal institutions are. That's still a wide-open question. What is the best way to structure our economic world? This is true at the level of policy formation not only for a nation but also for firms. Firms are really struggling with how they should organize themselves internally.

S&B *What are some of the policy issues within firms?*

PAUL ROMER The traditional logic within companies was like that in government. In the government, people might look at medical discovery, for example, and say, "Gee, this is a market failure. We can't make the market work perfectly here." So the government would then step in. It would collect taxes, use the revenue to pay for research taking place at universities, and use that research to develop discoveries, like the principles behind vaccines. It would then give this knowledge away for free. We invented nonmarket institutions like universities to aid us in the production and distribution of ideas.

Firms, to a certain extent, have mimicked that solution. They say, "OK, we need to generate new knowledge. We have different divisions that we can treat as profit centers. So what we will do is tax those profit centers to create something that looks like a mini–internal university—the R&D department." They then gave the funds to the R&D department and told it to do good work, just like the national government does with the universities. Over time, when the R&D department produces something, it gives that something away for free—gives this knowledge away—to any of the operating divisions that need it.

S&B *That's the classical, prebreakup AT&T-Bell Labs model.*

PAUL ROMER Yes, but you also saw it at IBM and at GM and on smaller scales in many firms. A number of firms mimicked the institutions and economic policies of government when they realized that knowledge creation and discovery were central to their growth.

S&B *What came next?*

PAUL ROMER The firms found that these institutions did not work so well, so now they are trying to come up with modified institutional arrangements. They are recognizing that the simple solution that recreates the government's command-and-control and tax-and-subsidy mechanisms is not the perfect solution. What they are finding is that while there are a billion haystacks in which there will be some very valuable needles, it is an enormously expensive proposition to go about looking underneath every one. So what they are asking themselves is, How do you allocate the resources that you devote to research most effectively? They are realizing that they cannot just give scientists lots of money and let them follow their curiosity. If they do, this form of tax-and-subsidy system runs the risk of dissipating efforts by looking in too many different directions that don't necessarily lead to the highest returns for shareholders. One way to think about the problem here is that a tax-and-subsidy system does not have the built-in checks on wasteful activities that are present in a market system.

As a result, firms are beginning to create marketlike mechanisms that impose market tests on things like R&D departments. In some instances, this goes all the way to the extreme of the profit-center model. In these instances, they have set up R&D units as profit centers, and they charge different divisions for any of the results they produce that other divisions use.

When firms face increasing costs and diminishing returns, no single firm can supply the whole market.

S&B *Does that work?*

PAUL ROMER Well, it gets back to one of the problems with knowledge, which is if you charge high prices for knowledge, you don't end up with the efficient distribution of that knowledge.

Let me provide you with an anecdote. Someone at a company I know told me that he had taken over the market-research division. The company used to be operated on the tax-and-subsidy model. The corporation used to give the marketing division lots of money and it went out and worked on anything that it wanted to. That system meant that the department was not really working on the right problems. So this manager took the market-research budget and allocated it to all the different business units and told the units that they could buy whatever they wanted from the researchers. This, of course, made the market-research folks focus more on the actual marketing problems that the different divisions were facing.

But then he ran into a problem. One division would pay the market researchers to work on problem x. Another division in the corporation would then come in and want the group to do a study on a very similar problem. It was inefficient for the market researchers to go out and redo the study, but the first division had property rights over the existing study. The market researchers could not just give it to the second division without getting permission from the first, and complicated negotiations would sometimes ensue over what the second division should pay the first. This sometimes led to restrictions on flows of information that would have helped other divisions, and this is clearly bad from the point of view of shareholders.

The lesson is that as soon as you start to price knowledge, you get into awkward situations where your knowledge is not being as widely used as it could be. This is just a fact of life.

S&B *So how do you price knowledge? What is the model?*

PAUL ROMER There is nothing so far that is perfectly neat and clean. My guess, however, is that the answer lies between the two extremes of the market system and the tax-and-subsidy system. My guess is that we're going to start to find much richer institutional arrangements to control the flow of information. For example, firms are doing things like making people in the R&D units go out and spend time with the divisions, just so that they communicate more closely with people in the divisions. Firms are even making R&D people go out on sales calls to talk to the customers to see what they are really interested in.

This is one way to get people in the R&D unit focused on their markets, their market opportunities, and their final customers. It's a weak, but apparently effective, way to impose a kind of market discipline on what the researchers do.

But it is an institutional arrangement, not an explicit price system. Firms could eventually augment an institutional arrangement like this with things like promotion and compensation systems, which reward being attentive to customers, as opposed to more traditional systems, which just give rewards for the number of scholarly publications or the number of patents, whether they are useful or not. So what I expect is that there will be a lot more experimentation with arrangements that are neither pure market systems nor pure tax-and-subsidy systems.

S&B *Another model is to view the R&D department as the center of the firm and the rest of the company as the channel for getting the discoveries of the R&D department to market.*

PAUL ROMER Embedded in your question is what people call the "linear model" of science and discovery. It was one in which the people in the research lab said, "Look, the whole game is to create knowledge. That's where value comes from. We're the center of that process. We're going to create the knowledge. Once we've created that knowledge, we'll give it to you, so you can market it and make a profit for us."

In practice, that turned out to be a very bad way to structure corporations and a very bad way to think about economic activity. The problem is that it is not well guided. There are many different kinds of knowledge that researchers can produce. Some of these will be more valuable than others, and researchers may not be in the best position to tell which ones are the most valuable ones. So what's happened is that we've kind of turned this process around.

The new perspective says, "Look, the most valuable things we could do will be things we learn about from the problems we are facing in the field." In terms of information flows, that means it goes from the customer to the operating people to the R&D people.

The point I am making is that the problem-solving agenda should not be determined by the R&D unit but by somebody else. So even though we now recognize that knowledge creation is really central to the business process, we don't think of it as being a kind of pyramid model where the R&D unit is at the top and everybody else is kind of subservient to it.

It is very important to realize that the immense potential for new discovery brings with it an even more immense potential for wasted effort. Discovery is therefore associated with really hard choices. For example, what's the set of all possible software programs that could be written? If you just do a simple mathematical calculation about how many bit strings could fit on a CD-ROM, it is an unbelievably large number, far larger than the total number of particles in the universe. It's larger than any physical quantity that we can understand. Most of these possible bit strings would be useless junk. A few of them will be the "killer apps" of the future.

What's the significance of this? At the same time that we know there are good things out there to discover—new pieces of software—it would be very easy for an organization to produce a lot of software that isn't very useful. As a result, we need marketlike mechanisms to focus the research efforts.

S&B *What is the government's role in the knowledge economy?*

PAUL ROMER What we have done very effectively in the United States is tried to encourage the process of discovery by subsidizing the inputs that go into the discovery process. What I mean is that ever since the Civil War and the creation of the land-grant universities, we have heavily subsidized higher education. We have also subsidized training scientists and engineers, who are the key input into the research process.

In addition, the United States has maintained a regulatory and financial system that makes it easy to create new companies, raise capital, and start new businesses. We also tolerate failure in the United States.

That combination seems to have worked very well. And it's very different from, say, the European perspective, where national policy—especially since World War II—has focused on what they call "national champions," which they identify as a few big firms whose monopoly positions they try to protect. That really goes in all the wrong directions. What the Europeans really should be doing is thinking about the process that brings new entrants into the market. How do you get people out there working on interesting new questions to start new enterprises?

The real success of American economic policy has been to have moderately strong property rights with lots of subsidies for inputs—like research and education—that are used in the innovation process. Then we hold the government back and let firms fight it out in the marketplace.

S&B *Should the government do anything different?*

PAUL ROMER Many people think the government should have a much more direct role over outputs by actually contracting for research in specific areas. They feel that the government should go out and decide which areas are most promising for technological development—synthetic fuels or hypersonic planes, for example. Then, these people argue, the government should play an active role in leading the direction of technology development. The evidence these people cite for this argument is that the government has been successful in the past in bringing new technologies into existence.

But this was really only the case in specialized instances when the government happened to be the lead customer. It was the lead user with regard to a number of different military technologies. So it gave the academic and the corporate R&D sectors very specific problems to solve—as a user. In effect, what the government said was that it wanted to solve a particular problem—as a customer. It did not know how to solve the problem in detail, but it did know the capability it required. This arrangement took advantage of the reverse information flow that we talked about before, the one that corporations are now trying to create, back from users to the research department.

But the problem these days is different. Most of the key technologies that need to be developed are those things for which the government is not a lead user. In these new areas, no one in the government has any special knowledge about what should be done. This means that unlike military applications, where the government was a well-informed customer, in many areas of technological development the government is likely to fail if it gets into the business of picking which technologies to develop.

S&B *So how would you make the present system better?*

PAUL ROMER I would focus much more on the input side and I would subsidize those inputs. At the moment, in the United States, we are not training as many scientists and engineers as we could and should. We're not training people in areas where they would be the most valuable.

The federal government in the United States and governments in every country in the world are going to be extremely constrained by entitlements in the next several decades—actually, for the rest of our lives. This is a result of the baby boom and the commitments made in entitlement programs and pensions. What this means is that the government won't have as much in the way of resources for R&D as it used to have.

My argument is that we should concentrate those government resources as investments in the people. At the same time, generally speaking, you'll probably have to strengthen property rights a little bit and let the market handle a little bit more of the discovery process than it has handled in the past.

S&B *What would you do differently with regard to the inputs like training?*

PAUL ROMER The problem—in my opinion—is that the university system is not producing the kinds of scientists and engineers that the private sector needs. It is still locked in the academic model and it is producing scientists and engineers who are copies of what their professors are. As a consequence, there are many areas in the private sector where there is a big demand for scientists that is not being met.

At the moment, we produce Ph.D.'s in our university system for two reasons. One is that we give research money to professors, including money for assistants, so they can use them as inputs in their research. As a result, we produce Ph.D.'s in areas where we're doing research, whether or not there's a private sector demand for people with these skills. We also produce Ph.D.'s where the universities need them as teaching assistants—as inputs in the teaching process for undergraduates.

This means that universities are responding to incentives that are dictated by research funding priorities, a good deal of which come from the federal government. They are also responding to their own teaching priorities, which come from university administrations and state governments. But they are not responding to the market's demands for particular types of scientists and engineers.

Now, in this system, students—who are arguably worried about their ultimate job prospects—do not control any of the resources, since most Ph.D. training is subsidized. In my view, what we really need to do is to redirect the system toward the market while, at the same time, giving people bigger incentives to go into scientific fields.

When it comes to how you redirect it, the approach I prefer is one where you give students more control over their own funds. Instead of giving the money for student fellowship positions to the research professor in the department, why not give it to the student? That way, a student could take the fellowship and say, "I've seen the numbers. I know I can't get a job if I get a math Ph.D. But if I go into bio-informatics, there is this huge demand for people right now." If students could control the funds, the universities would start to cater to their demands, which would be in line with the market and the private sector's needs.

We're going to start to find much richer institutional arrangements to control the flow of information.

S&B *What would happen if that kind of plan were put into place?*

PAUL ROMER If students controlled the funds, you would start to see programs that are more practical, more like high-tech apprenticeships. You would see arrangements where graduate students spend time with firms and work on problems that come up within firms and you would see more movement back and forth between the universities and the private sector.

What is interesting here is that we saw a great deal of this in the American system before World War II, before the federal government stepped in and began to play such a big role in funding decisions. When the federal government came in, it broke the links between universities and the private sector.

There is another way to go, as well. I think if you gave an industry some control over research funds that are allocated to universities, the companies would focus much more on training people along the lines I was describing. In a sense, I think the students who are looking for employment and the firms who are looking for employees have interests that are very much in common.

So if you give either piece some control over the system, we will get back to where we want to be.

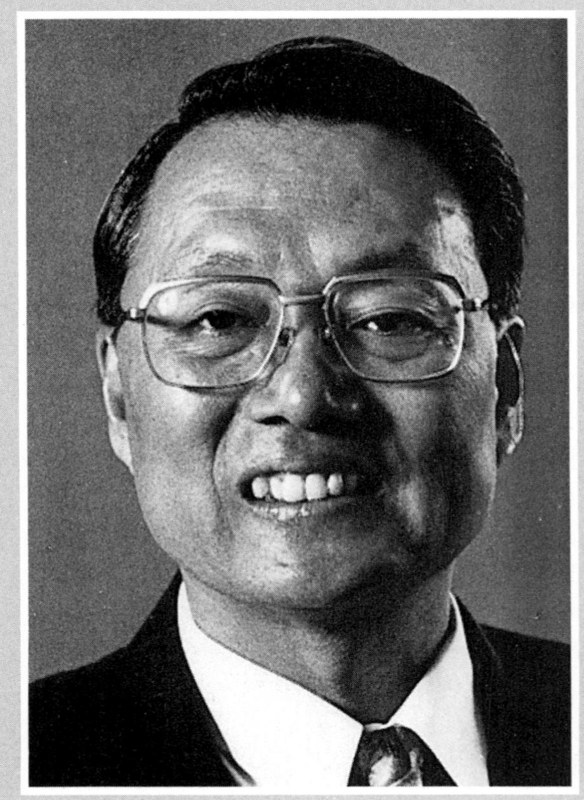

An Interview with

STAN SHIH

Founder, Chairman, and CEO, Acer Group

In Taiwan, where business anonymity is the cultural norm, Stan Shih stands out. Name recognition is anathema in Taiwan, which built its massive computer industry by manufacturing systems for technology giants from the United States, Japan, and Europe. Yet Mr. Shih, founder and chairman of the $5.8 billion Acer Group, has spent the past twenty years fighting to make Acer a global brand name, as recognizable in computers as Fujitsu, IBM, NEC, or Hewlett-Packard. Indeed, the fifty-one-year-old Mr. Shih, an urbane engineer and entrepreneur, has long railed against Taiwan's willingness to toil in obscurity. The country's most visible business leader, Mr. Shih is outspoken, aggressive, and never shy. In many ways, he is the antithesis of his Taiwanese counterparts, once telling *Business Week* that "even bankrupt companies in Silicon Valley have better images than Taiwan companies."

We are really something of a virtual corporation.

Using Taiwan's manufacturing might and his own unique management concepts, Mr. Shih (pronounced SHE) has made a name for himself and his company by building Acer from a tiny chip distributor for Taiwanese makers of arcade games into one of the world's five largest manufacturers of PCs, components, and peripherals. Although Acer also acts as an original equipment manufacturer for the likes of Hitachi and Texas Instruments, Mr. Shih is intent on having his company become a model for the rest of Taiwanese industry by shedding its copycat image and becoming an innovator.

Mr. Shih's new book—published by Acer—is aptly

titled *Me-Too Is Not My Style.* In it, Mr. Shih outlines a model for changing the bad reputation that has long been associated with his country's products. "The negative images of 'Made in Taiwan' have accumulated over a long period of time," he writes. "The reasons are twofold. First, many poor-quality products are sold under Taiwan brands while many of the fine-quality products are manufactured for foreign brands (O.E.M.). Second, although there are good Taiwan-made products, there is not enough promotion or marketing of them. With better packaging and better marketing communications, Taiwanese products still have the opportunity to break through the current image."

Although Mr. Shih is a strenuous booster of his nation, he is not waiting for the rest of Taiwan to catch on. Employing a carefully honed strategy that he calls "global brand, local touch," Mr. Shih has, during the last four years, remade Acer into a decentralized conglomerate of autonomous businesses, selling off majority stakes to local investors in more than twenty countries. Acer now has thirty-nine assembly sites in thirty-five countries and has become the Number 1 PC maker in Indonesia, Malaysia, Mexico, South Africa, and other emerging markets. Mr. Shih is pushing Acer into new markets, such as consumer electronics and inexpensive computers for developing countries.

Despite Mr. Shih's ambitious efforts, these are tough times for Acer. This year, growth has stagnated in its core PC business, and falling prices in the semiconductor business have hammered profits. But Mr. Shih is undaunted, having survived enough roller coaster business cycles to believe that his goal of becoming a $15 billion internationally renowned technology giant by the year 2000 is well within reach. The following conversation between Mr. Shih and *Strategy & Business* took place in April 1997 in his office in Taipei.

S&B *The Acer Group is known as an innovative competitor, especially for the way it has been structured to compete globally. You are the company's chief strategist, as well as its founder. How do you think about strategy?*

STAN SHIH Before you can create a strategy, you need a vision of the company. Before you set that vision for the future, you have to understand your current position in the market, as well as your limitations. To me, strategy means trying to overcome your limitations and your weak points. To do that, I try to enhance and leverage my strong points. As a result, my strategy-setting process involves simply saying, "This is my goal, these are the key success factors for reaching that goal, and in these areas I am weak." After I have done that, I find a way to overcome my weak points.

S&B *Your method sounds deceptively simple. Can you give an example of how it works in practice?*

STAN SHIH Yes. We ultimately developed two strategies that are very important to us. One is what I call our "global brand, local touch" organizational structure, and the other is what I call the "fast-food" business model.

The company needs to globalize, but Taiwan is too small a place to do it from. It doesn't have enough human resource talent to manage the globalization process. It doesn't have enough capital to invest overseas. I mean, we have capital, but Taiwanese investors get concerned if you invest too much overseas. They want to know how you can control those foreign investments.

So how can we effectively globalize from a Taiwan base? To do that, I decided on "local touch." By that, I mean that we develop local shareholder majorities around the world, as well as local management teams. Through this process, we get the talent we need. That is because I can convince my investors in Taiwan that we have local partners who are willing to take risks with us. Such a method gives us global strengths from the local areas where we actually do business. It overcomes significant weaknesses. As a result, it is our primary objective.

Another part of that objective is this: people always want to have ownership and decision making and autonomy. So I structured the company around what I call the "client-server" model.

Every unit of the company in every locality is independent, and because they are all independent, they have different shareholders. Usually the local management team is the local majority shareholder. We're in the final stages of putting this structure in place in Europe and the United States. In the rest of the world, we are already structured that way. Now all of our local businesses make their own decisions their own way. As a result, these businesses are our clients. But we provide the vision, guidelines, and strategy from Taiwan, so we are the server.

If you think about this model, you will see that we are really something of a virtual corporation, or a networked company. Our local touch concept and our local shareholder majorities give autonomy to each business. Our central strategic and technological function gives us our global identity and direction.

S&B *You also mentioned the "fast-food" business model. How would you describe that?*

STAN SHIH In the past, when we shipped our finished desktop products by sea to the marketplace, they would arrive in the stores one or two months later. As a result, our products were no longer up-to-date and fresh. So we were not competitive. In addition, by the time the products arrived, the price had already dropped. The reason we shipped these products by sea was that it was too expensive to ship finished goods by air.

To get around this problem, beginning in 1992, we developed the fast-food model, which revolves around each of our local businesses doing local assembly from components manufactured here. So today, we have thirty-nine assembly lines in thirty-five countries. We operate these assembly lines globally the way fast-food restaurants operate locally. We airship components from Taiwan—which is cost effective—to the regional business units overseas for assembly into products. This approach provides "hot and fresh" computers to our local customers. Not only does this provide fresh products, it also accelerates the speed of new-product introduction, and it accelerates the inventory turnover rate. This fits with our strategic philosophy.

S&B *The local touch, fast-food model was derived from your philosophy of identifying and addressing your problems head-on.*

STAN SHIH Yes. It is our problems that teach us. For example, we had a problem that we could not make money in the early 1990s. In our first ten years, the company developed quickly and profits were relatively strong. We doubled our revenue every year. Only our first two years weren't profitable. Then the company went public in 1988, and growth suddenly was almost flat. We could only break even or lose money. At the same time, IBM and some of the other computer companies also got into trouble. Because of the external market shifts and our internal difficulties, we had no choice but to change. We had to think about change constantly. So we developed the new strategies.

S&B *What influenced you to make the particular changes that you did? Did it come from the books you read, from sending your managers to business schools, or from somewhere else?*

STAN SHIH It didn't really come from books. I mean, I had heard about networked organizations. But for me it was simply a case of going back to basics.

Our original plan, when we started, was to be decentralized. That was an early objective, even though it was contrary to the Chinese tradition of centralized or family-owned businesses. We had that as one of our objectives for twenty years.

Let me give you an example of what I mean. In 1979, when I formed the Taichung-Kaohsiung branch of Acer in those two cities in the south of Taiwan, I was already using the local touch model. We had a local partner in those cities who owned 60 percent of the company. The Taipei part of the company only owned 40 percent of the Taichung-Kaohsiung venture. And we saw that it worked. It made money. So the local shareholder majority concept has been one of our earliest traditions.

> We call it the Dragon Dream. The dragon is the Chinese people, and we Chinese want to contribute in a big way to global society.

S&B *Did other business leaders or companies influence you early on in the way you set up Acer?*

STAN SHIH Akio Morita, Sony's cofounder, really brought a global image to Japan. We have always aspired to be like Sony—quick, creative, product-driven. We also aspire to be like Philips, which is a big global company that comes from a very small country. And Philips believes in localizing its operations, as we do. It has even done that in Taiwan.

S&B *Your "client-server" strategy requires that Taiwan become not only a strategic center but also an innovation center for your network of companies. How do you keep your "innovation engine" running?*

STAN SHIH Right now, we own more than four hundred patents all over the world. These patents are valuable and they enable us to have cross-licenses with excellent companies. We have cross-licenses, for example, with IBM, Intel, and Texas Instruments on PC technology. We are beginning to collect patent-license revenues from local and Japanese companies.

One of our advantages—and why we think our approach will work—is that the basic cost of engineering is low in Taiwan compared with the United States. The same amount of investment is two or three times more cost effective here as in the United States.

Of course, our technology base and also our understanding of marketing are different. Some of the technology innovation here is not as advanced or as creative yet as in the United States. But we are still competitive from a global standpoint, compared with the average American company. If you compare what we can do with what can be done within our region, in many areas we are ahead. I am including the Japanese companies, too. We are ahead of many of them.

S&B *Yes, but keeping up with the competition is one thing, and taking on the creativity in the United States is another. How will you derive a leadership position on that front?*

STAN SHIH There are two ways. One has to do with our culture. We call it the Dragon Dream. The dragon is the Chinese people, and we Chinese want to contribute in a big way to global society. We want to do it in a number of directions, including technology. So we have a very powerful cultural momentum behind us.

The second way is purely pragmatic. We are providing strong incentives for innovation. That includes incentives for our people to apply for patents. We even have a special profit-sharing plan set aside, for which revenues are generated from our patent licenses. We split some of the income with our engineers, who apply for the patents.

S&B *You mentioned that research and development expenditures in Taiwan are more efficient than in other countries. How much money do you devote to research as a share of revenue?*

STAN SHIH As I mentioned, Acer is made up of many different companies. Some of the companies spend 3 percent of revenue on research and development, some spend only 1 percent or 2 percent. The average, across the entire network, is about 2 percent right now. In competitive companies, like Compaq, research and development accounts for about 2 percent of revenue or less. So we are in the ballpark.

S&B *In a company as decentralized as Acer, how do you measure success? What metrics do you use?*

STAN SHIH I like to say that we measure it by a person's contribution to the company as a whole. If I make a good contribution—whatever that is—I can measure its return in a monetary form.

But I think you have to look at how a person contributes on a number of levels. For example, the number of people you are able to train is a contribution. My personal impact—and the company's impact—on the image of Taiwan is a contribution. And, of course, you have to consider the impact of a person's work on the customer.

We put it all together in what I call our "1–2–3" philosophy. The customer is

Number 1, the employee is Number 2, the shareholder is Number 3. I keep this message consistent with all my colleagues in all our companies. This is the only way to protect the shareholders and their returns. Now, I am one of the company's biggest shareholders and since I am one of them, I will protect them.

I even consider that the company's banks, suppliers, and others we do business with are our stakeholders; even society is a stakeholder. I believe that the company belongs to society. Here, we believe that way. So I do my best to run the company that way.

Why do I need a company? Because I believe companies contribute to society.

S&B *Do you use specific managerial measurements, like return on equity, growth of shareholder value, economic value-added, or return on invested capital?*

STAN SHIH We measure return on equity, return on assets, and what we call return on human assets. We employ fifteen thousand people, so we need a measurement of return based on head count. Roughly, what I measure is how much a person makes—his salary—against that person's share of revenue. It is a rough estimate of the productivity of our human resources. With regard to the other measures, on return on equity, we are usually looking for a return that is in excess of 10 percent to 15 percent. In good times during our twenty-year history, our average has been in the 20 percent to 25 percent range. In addition to these measures, I also measure productivity every year. In fact, we like to benchmark our productivity against [that of] our rivals. With regard to our measurements of return on equity, we like to average this figure, because businesses have up-and-down cycles.

Now, it is difficult, but we try to set goals for these figures every year. We circulate these goals through the company and then we compare them to how we actually did.

S&B *What were your performance numbers like in recent years?*

STAN SHIH We're quite pleased. In 1995, our revenue came in at about [U.S.] $463,000 per employee, companywide. Meanwhile, the average annual salary of our Taiwan employees is about $15,300. Overall, our costs have stayed almost flat, but our productivity has grown at about 20 percent a year in the last three or four years. The reason our salaries have stayed flat is that we have more and more people working in the Philippines and Malaysia to offset the overall average cost. Our return on equity over the last two years is in the 30 percent–plus range.

S&B *You mentioned that your employees were Number 2 on Acer's list of priorities. How do they share in your growth? Microsoft awards shares to its employees, and there are many "Microsoft millionaires" as a result. Are there Acer millionaires?*

STAN SHIH Thousands of our employees are millionaires—if you measure it in New Taiwan dollars. But at the current exchange rate, an NT dollar is worth only 27 U.S. cents!

But yes, every employee is entitled to own shares. Our system is different from the American system, however. We have a stock purchase plan instead of stock options. In good times, this results in the same thing, with Americans exercising their options and our people purchasing shares. But in bad times, the results are different. In the United States, in bad times, the options can't be exercised and there are no incentives and people just quit. But in our case, in bad times, our people work harder—to protect their own money in the stock plan.

> The customer is Number 1, the employee is Number 2, the shareholder is Number 3. I keep this message consistent with all my colleagues.

In addition, we offer profit sharing and our employees are entitled to free bonus shares. In good times, in Taiwan, engineers earn several years' worth of salary as their bonus. What that means in practice is that a Taiwanese engineer's salary may be low when compared with an American engineer's salary. But if you add the incentives—and in Taiwan in semiconductors and computers, 1994 and 1995 were very good years—then the two groups compare favorably.

S&B *How about during a downturn? Do you have layoffs, or do you abide by a lifetime employment policy?*

STAN SHIH We have had layoffs. In 1991, for example, we laid off about three hundred people in Taiwan. It was very unusual for us, but we did it.

S&B *Some people say that Taiwan's younger generation is not as interested in working as hard as your generation. If it is true, do you worry about that?*

STAN SHIH I don't worry about it. You know, I respect the younger generation for not wanting to work as hard. You see, we worked hard and our purpose in doing so was to improve conditions so that the next generation could have a better quality of life. That was our aim. So I am not complaining if the younger generation wants an easier life. They have higher education and have better ways to create productivity. So why can't they enjoy a better life? I don't think we need to be concerned. That's the point of progress.

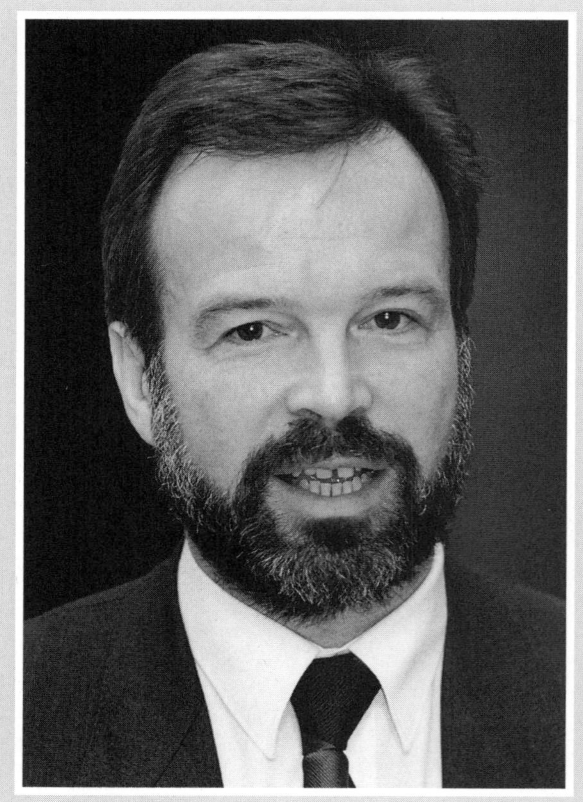

An Interview with

NORBERT WALTER

Chief Economist, Deutsche Bank

For nearly four decades, Germany was the miracle economy. Unemployment was low, inflation barely registered, and growth was steady. With one tough central banker after another and a government that eschewed red ink, Germany was the world's benchmark with respect to monetary and fiscal policy. It was also something of a maverick economy. Whereas multinationals took root in Britain, the Netherlands, Sweden, and France, Germany—with its myriad high-quality, middle-sized producers—remained primarily an exporter. This was so much the case that in dollar terms, Germany sent more of its goods abroad than any other country, including the United States and Japan. About 60 percent of Germany's exports went to other European Union (EU) countries.

But beginning in the early 1990s, something changed. The German economy, as the saying goes, fell to earth. One reason, of course, was the unification of the eastern and western portions of the country. Not only did people's savings have to be converted from East German marks to German marks—at very favorable terms—but factories had to be closed, workers had to be trained in the latest business practices, and investment had to flow. Then there was the global downturn that began around 1991.

There is the notion that if you failed once, you are basically dead. As a society, we are very risk averse.

Under the strain, the German economy sputtered. Unemployment rose to about 10 percent, budget deficits increased, and growth went negative. In 1993, the economy contracted by 1.3 percent before growing stronger again in 1994. But 1995 was a lackluster year with the GDP growing at just under 2 percent, and most forecasters expect 1996 to be slower still.

All of this would be difficult enough—even for a powerhouse economy like Germany's—without added pressure from the Maastricht Treaty. This treaty, which is to go into effect in 1999, calls for the establishment of the European Monetary Union. The EMU, as it is called, will do for the EU what the Federal Reserve did for the United States. It will create a single currency, the euro; establish a single central bank to be based in Frankfurt; and require all participating countries to coordinate their fiscal and monetary policies.

But unlike the Federal Reserve Act, which created a single currency for the United States through an act of Congress, the EMU is a membership organization with extremely high entrance requirements. No country may join, for example, unless its budget deficit is less than 3 percent of its GDP. Countries must also put their monetary houses in order. Their inflation rates can be no higher than 1.5 percentage points above the average rate of the three European countries with the lowest inflation numbers.

The clock is ticking on Maastricht. Countries will become eligible to join in 1997, and so far the only EU country that qualifies for entrance into the EMU is Luxembourg. All of the others that have expressed their intention to join, including Germany, have fallen short in some respect. In some cases, the problem is inflation. In others, it is the budget deficit. In fiscal 1995, Germany's deficit overshot the Maastricht criterion by 0.7 percent, a significant miss for a country known for its fiscal discipline.

So whither Germany? And what effect will its future have on the rest of Europe?

To find out, the editors of *Strategy & Business* asked Professor Norbert Walter, chief economist of the Deutsche Bank Group. Professor Walter, who is also managing director of Deutsche Bank Research, is one of Europe's leading economic analysts and forecasters. He has written extensively about European economic integration, Germany's economy, and the restructuring of the eastern European economies. Before joining Deutsche Bank in 1987, Professor Walter held senior positions at the Kiel Institute of World Economics in Kiel, Germany.

In 1986 and 1987, he was John J. McCloy Distinguished Research Fellow and resident scholar at the American Institute for Contemporary German Studies at Johns Hopkins University. Professor Walter spoke to *Strategy &*

Business in July 1996 during a visit to Washington, D.C.

S&B *A decade ago, economists talked about "Eurosclerosis." By that, they meant that the continent was unable to solve its high unemployment and slow-growth problems. Now they are using that term once again to refer to the continent and specifically to Germany. Is Germany losing its competitiveness?*

NORBERT WALTER A cynic would say that in Germany, nothing is as cyclical or as predictable as the debate over the country's decline. The topic comes up about every ten years. But this time the debate has taken only three years to reemerge.

S&B *Why has the debate been rekindled so soon?*

NORBERT WALTER Part of it has to do with the Maastricht Treaty. Complying with the treaty's criteria has produced a fiscal drag on the economy. This has created a dampening effect on demand in the short to medium term and has extended the cyclical downturn of the economy. This has brought to light some of the deep structural deficiencies in the German economy in general.

S&B *What deficiencies are you referring to?*

NORBERT WALTER Most of Germany's economic wounds are self-inflicted. It has a social welfare system that is extremely costly and is clearly not sustainable at its present level. It has a system of supporting old economic structures through subsidies and government guarantees. These are supported by the taxpayers. As a result, the tax and contribution system in Germany is actually taking money away from productivity. Price increases versus value-added are lower than they should be. This has very negative effects on productivity, since the result of the subsidy system is that we are producing services and goods that are not really very much in demand on global markets.

Let me give you an example of what I mean. In Germany we are subsidizing coal mining, shipbuilding, and agriculture rather than helping build up the service sector in general or those segments of industry where we are really competitive, like pharmaceuticals, high-tech products, cars, machinery, and capital goods and products oriented toward the protection of the environment.

S&B *These subsidies contribute to Germany's cost and productivity problems?*

NORBERT WALTER Yes, but that is not all. There are other areas where Germany's costs are simply too high. Some of these result from overregulation, which has a limiting effect on productivity. For example, the construction sector is very expensive in Germany. The government demands fire doors in houses and offices that could probably withstand a nuclear blast. Now, that is just not necessary. It is what I call "unnecessary quality." Engineers come up with standards, and then there are government regulations put in place, and the consumer is never asked. That adds to the overall cost structure in Germany.

S&B *The government, as service provider and tax collector, accounts for a large share of gross domestic product in Germany. Is its share too high?*

NORBERT WALTER Yes, it is. In the United States, the government's stake in the economy is about 40 percent of GDP. In Germany, 52 percent of GDP is accounted for by the government. That is too high.

S&B *What about the cost of labor in Germany?*

NORBERT WALTER Fringe benefits equal 80 percent of wage costs. In some companies, fringe benefits are even greater than the regular wage costs. Germany is in the top tier of countries in Europe when it comes to these costs. Denmark and Sweden have trimmed their costs. Switzerland has higher wage costs but lower fringe benefits. Other countries are beginning to move in the right direction, but Germany is on the top if you add the cost of fringe benefits and wages together. I don't have to tell you what that does to competitiveness.

S&B *Are you advocating trimming wages?*

NORBERT WALTER No. The wage component is not something I worry too much about. You can defend the present wage level. But you cannot defend the present wage and fringe benefit levels if you take them together.

S&B *So you are satisfied with the present wage levels in Germany?*

NORBERT WALTER Well, I would argue that the wage system for skilled workers is not sufficiently bonus oriented. The way people are paid is part of the problem.

S&B *Unions are powerful in Germany. Would they go along with a new emphasis on bonuses?*

NORBERT WALTER Unions don't have a say over bonuses. They have power that transcends wage-level discussion, because they are part of the political debate and the overall decision-making process. They are also part of business's decision making through codetermination. It is very much of a consensus-oriented system and, as a result, there are few strikes and a very low level of labor unpredictability. Unions also have a say in what government does. They have an important say in what the Social Democratic Party is going to do and with some factions in the Christian Democratic Party. They are listened to and they form one of the best lobbying bodies with respect to Parliament. They are very influential. But they don't have a say over bonuses.

S&B *With the strength of the unions, can German companies trim their workforces?*

NORBERT WALTER There has been a shift because of the extreme economic pressure that is on Germany. For the first time, companies are exposed to international pressure and, as a result, considerable downsizing is now possible. We have also had a series of big experiments in eastern Germany so we now have experience in downsizing and in cutting off some production lines altogether. The production of the Trabant [a small-sized car made in the east] was discontinued, for example. The chemical industry in the east was slashed to something like 20 percent of its former size over the last five years. We have downsized the lignite coal industry to one-third of its size.

So there is the possibility to downsize under very clearly defined circumstances. But if a problem is regionally concentrated—like coal, shipbuilding, and steel—we will have difficulty. We will have much greater success where the industries are spread over the country.

> The government demands fire doors that could probably withstand a nuclear blast. It is what I call "unnecessary quality."

S&B *Change is always difficult.*

NORBERT WALTER It is. Take, for example, retailing. There is a marvelous coalition between the trade union and the employers in this area. They lobby together to defend the shop-closing rules that limit the hours a shop can be open. This is clearly not in the interest of the consumer. But Germany is still—in some ways—very guild oriented. There is a guild structure in retail trade, and there is a guild structure with respect to doctors and lawyers. The guilds determine the number of students allowed to study medicine, for example. This keeps prices high.

S&B *You have described a very rigid system. Are there any challenges to the system?*

NORBERT WALTER There are several challenges to the system.

First, the EU is increasingly the provider of something that I believe is very good—competition. Without the EU and the courts, there would be even more protection than there is today. There would be no open-skies policy for

European airlines, for example. Without the EU, there would be no allowances for competition with regard to electrical utilities. Without the EU, the level of subsidies would be far greater, I believe. Without the EU, entrance into the European telecom, government procurement, and defense sectors would be even more limited. Since all politics is local, it is impossible for a German politician to speak out against coal subsidies. But the EU can do it. So it is important to have Brussels's influence in the economy.

Next, there is pressure for privatization of public services, which is coming from eastern Germany. Let me give you an example. There is still a huge job to do in eastern Germany with respect to the infrastructure. Our politicians have lots of work ahead of them. But they have limited tax revenue, because the economy there is not fully functional yet. So they are unable to do their job without going in the direction of privatization, which is good. They must create public-private partnerships to repair the sewage system, for example. Because there is not much of a tax base yet, they must resort to public-private partnerships to rebuild the reservoirs and water system. Privatization in eastern Germany will come, and it will be positive. Now, if western Germany examines what is happening in the east and realizes that private firms can provide public goods, western firms will copy that model. I think that will be very good.

Finally, I think there is hope for a new political coalition in Germany. This will happen because many people are in fact being kept out of the system. You can't really fire people, and there is also a need to downsize many industries because of labor costs. All of this comes at the expense of the young. This is true in Europe in general, and it is also true of Germany. In Germany, there is a very long and inefficient apprenticeship program. The program really serves to park people rather than to give them the appropriate skills. Because of this program, youth unemployment is not as high in Germany as it is in France or Italy. Even so, young people find jobs only with great difficulty. These young people understand that the older generation is not taking care of their interests. My hope is that they will enter into the parties and unions and change things. They have no interest in preserving the present, rigid structure.

S&B *Will some of these young people become entrepreneurs?*

NORBERT WALTER Some, but not many. It is still rare in Germany. When I was young, anyone considering becoming an entrepreneur was considered crazy. About the only entrepreneurial occupation at the time was to become a dentist. It has changed, but not by much. I mean, you are not considered an outlaw anymore if you start your own business. But the numbers are small. It's not yet in the German mentality. I am in favor of it, however.

S&B *What has to be done to create an environment more conducive to entrepreneurship?*

NORBERT WALTER There are a number of obstacles in our society. As I said, there is the overregulation of society, and there is also the notion that if you failed once, you are basically dead. As a society, we are very risk averse. In addition, the infrastructure of entrepreneurship is not there. Venture capital, for example, hardly exists. And the concept of risk-related investments is not a German concept. In Germany, investors try to have absolute guarantees for their investments. In addition, parents are not willing to give their children a start. So entrepreneurship is not very common. That stands in the way of a more vigorous economy.

S&B *What other forces will propel the German economy into the future?*

NORBERT WALTER Germany has a real competitive spirit. We don't appreciate losers, and if it is demonstrated that what we are doing will make us losers, we will change. We have the "Boris Becker" mentality, and we are very competitive. When you are down, you try much harder.

You know, the problems at Daimler-Benz with its big losses really shocked people. People in Germany just don't believe it yet. What I wonder about is whether this company's example will create the spirit of a new beginning. I don't feel it yet. But I think there will be very positive reactions.

S&B *Are there examples of adversity's bringing out the country's competitive spirit?*

NORBERT WALTER Daimler is building a new sports roadster in Alabama. The project team in Alabama is not just important for its own sake; it is having a major impact on the company internally. For example, there is the perception that the people in Alabama are having a lot of fun. They are very forward-looking, they are working like hell, but they have the sense that they are doing something that is very promising, very successful, very attractive for the company as a whole. They have a real spirit and everyone is watching them.

S&B *Are there other examples of change?*

NORBERT WALTER Yes. BMW shocked people by setting up production in South

Carolina. In fact, I remember in 1990, the chief executive of BMW said that he thought that you could not build a BMW elsewhere in Germany—only in Bavaria! Now they are building them in North America. That is quite a changed perspective from one of our flagship industries.

Of course, there is also negative fallout from these activities, and there are conservative elements in the churches and in the Social Democratic Party that argue that these firms should not be allowed to close down at home and open up elsewhere. These elements have a lot of emotional support.

When I was young, an entrepreneur was considered crazy. You are not considered an outlaw anymore if you start your own business.

S&B *For decades, Germany was the economic engine of Europe. Is that still true?*

NORBERT WALTER

Germany was the locomotive of Europe, but now it is a drag on Europe. It is dragging Europe down and probably will continue to drag it down for some time. The risk is that Germany's problems will endanger Europe's dynamism and integration efforts. It may endanger the enlargement of the institutional setup in Europe, such as the creation of the monetary union and other institutions, like security arrangements and trade functions.

Therefore, I fear that the problems of the German economy may cause a call for renationalization that will spread throughout Europe. If that happens, and Europe loses its momentum, we could be on a dangerous course.

People now openly speculate whether Germany and France will make the Maastricht targets in 1997. If they do not, what will other countries think? Will they keep their currencies strong if France and Germany don't? I don't think so. A great deal of progress will unravel. If that happens, we will lose a decade, I am afraid, before the momentum of integration will resume.

S&B *What will enable Germany and Europe to regain their momentum?*

NORBERT WALTER I don't think that Europe will recover its momentum without external help. If the dollar remains strong, it will allow Europe to recover and that will put us back on track. Only then will we achieve the Maastricht criteria. The only scenario in which the European countries achieve convergence is if the dollar is high and Europe gets its act together.

So you asked if Germany is Europe's locomotive. The answer is no. The United States is Europe's locomotive.

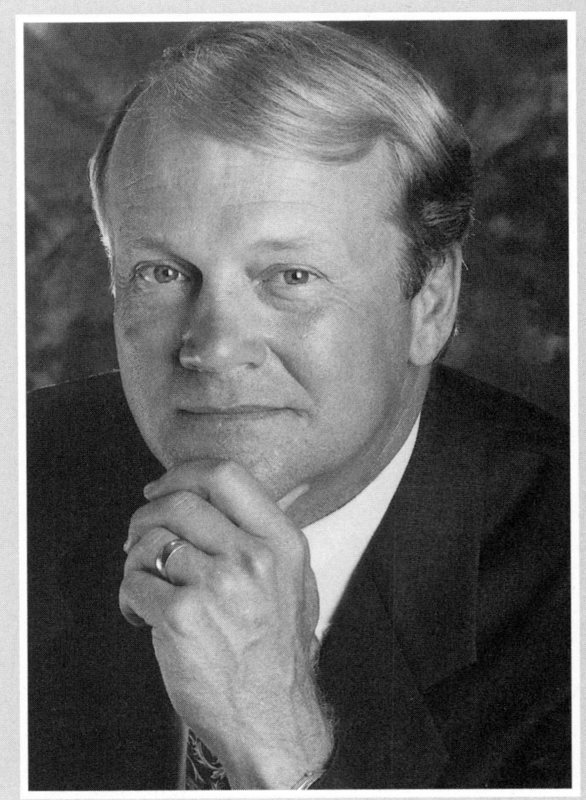

An Interview with

JOHN T. CHAMBERS

CEO, Cisco Systems

John T. Chambers, a forty-seven-year-old native of West Virginia and a former IBM and Wang Laboratories marketing veteran, joined Cisco Systems, Inc., in 1991. He came in as the heir apparent to the chief executive, John P. Morgridge, and fashioned the company's aggressive growth strategy, which included plans for Cisco to be a partner, create joint ventures, and, most of all, acquire its way to a dominant position in the data networking marketplace. Mr. Chambers, who became chief executive in January 1995, spoke with *Strategy & Business* from Cisco headquarters in San Jose, California, in February 1997.

S&B *From its founding in 1984, Cisco seemed content to compete in the marketplace in traditional ways. Then in 1993, the company changed its strategy and put a premium on speed as well as growth. Why did you adopt the new approach?*

We now have a chance to acquire everybody.

JOHN CHAMBERS We decided to become more aggressive as a company and to look at the market more in Internet years, as opposed to calendar years. Things are changing so fast with regard to the Internet that each regular business calendar year equals seven Internet business years. So instead of looking at a one-year plan, we began looking at every quarter and adjusting our plan up or down.

S&B *Prior to the shift in strategy, you were growing pretty fast. Why did you feel the need to change?*

JOHN CHAMBERS Without realizing it, we actually had stifled our growth. Even though the growth rate was off the charts, we probably could have gotten another 20 percent per year by moving a little bit faster. Our conservatism was also one of our strengths—we're more than a bit paranoid. But you always want to balance this paranoia with the confidence and ability to move forward, and in 1993 we decided it was time to make some major philosophical changes.

S&B *Such as?*

JOHN CHAMBERS We got very bold. We made the conscious decision, for example, that we were going to attempt to shape the future of the entire industry. We decided to play very aggressively and truly attempt in the networking industry what Microsoft did with PCs and IBM did with mainframes. If you think of networking as the fourth evolution of computers—the first being mainframes, where IBM dominated; the second, minicomputers, where there was no clear leader; and the third, personal computers and local area networks, which was the era of Intel and Microsoft—and if you understand that each evolution is bigger than the prior generation, you begin to get an idea of what we saw in front of us.

S&B *How does one set out to achieve such world domination?*

JOHN CHAMBERS We moved out of our "religious" technology mind-set, first of all. We were router bigots. [The hardware device known as a *router* forwards packets of data from one computer to another. Switches are faster and more intelligent "internetworking" devices that link local area and wide area networks of computers.] We thought routers were the future, switching was wrong.

So we moved out of that into a nonreligious view about the technology. We also began to think a couple of years out about what could happen. Before that, we never thought beyond a year. We began to set stretch goals that many people would have thought impossible, and we made those goals part of our culture.

Rather than trying to do the impossible just by working harder—if that's all it took, it would have already been done—we asked, What are we going to do uniquely to accomplish our stretch goals? The first thing was to really empower teams. We went through an evolution from a very tight central management group, with the top four or five people making all the decisions, to the empowerment of groups. Our aim was to drive our strategy down through the company.

S&B *You mentioned operating in Internet time. Even though you have internalized that new time frame, do you ever get surprised by unexpected turns in the market?*

JOHN CHAMBERS We have a philosophy that we will eat our own young before somebody else does. In Internet years, things change at a much faster pace than you realize and we get surprised periodically.

Here's an example. We acquired a company called Lightstream in 1995 for its high-end ATM [asynchronous transfer mode] capability. When we acquired it, it had only about $1.5 million in hardware revenue. We paid $120 million for it. One year later, its run rate was $45 million. It was well on the path to being a success, perhaps even a home run.

But then we began to notice that wide area networking and local area networking were coming together more rapidly than we had thought. Customers were telling us they were going to make buying decisions that were going to be implemented in the next year or two based on technology that was available today. In essence, they were telling us that while they liked our direction with Lightstream and liked our next-generation product, we were not going to have the market share that they needed to feel comfortable with in the next twelve to eighteen months.

So even though Lightstream was on a tremendously successful run rate, we literally ate our own young and acquired Stratacom for $4.5 billion—getting a much bigger player in the ATM business—because the market changed more quickly than we thought.

When something changes more quickly than we anticipated, or we make some other mistake, then we adjust very quickly and don't spend a lot of time with the "not invented here" syndrome, trying to protect our political decisions of two years ago.

S&B *How do your acquisitions fit into your strategy?*

JOHN CHAMBERS During 1993, we decided to play across the entire internetworking marketplace, and we began to prioritize which areas we wanted to move into. Remember, this was an era when people thought partnerships and acquisitions did not work. It was a much different philosophy than exists today. Today everyone says acquisitions are an effective way to grow.

Let me tell you, when we did our first acquisition in 1993, we caught unbelievable heat in the press. We paid $89 million for a company called Crescendo that had only $10 million in revenues. A lot of people thought we had lost our frugality and direction. Now that company contributes more than $500 million in revenues to Cisco. In terms of our market capitalization, selling for eight times sales, it's worth $4 billion to our shareholders. And our acquisitions in local area network switching cost us $500 million and now contribute more than $1 billion in revenues—or more than $8 billion to our market cap. So the strategy has worked out well. But at the time, it was not so obvious.

S&B *Since acquisitions were not generally in favor then, what made you decide to adopt an acquisition-led growth strategy?*

JOHN CHAMBERS We had a board meeting in August 1993 when we were trying to decide whether to merge with another large company—either Synoptics or Cabletron. Both companies were about the same size as we were, so it would have been a merger of equals.

But there was another alternative. It was to adopt a different philosophy. That philosophy was based on what we had learned from Hewlett-Packard—about breaking up markets into segments—combined with what we knew about the General Electric mentality of being either the Number 1 or Number 2 player in each segment. When we adopted that new philosophy, we had these choices: achieve it by ourselves by a combination with an equal or by partnering or acquiring other companies.

> In our industry, you are acquiring people. And if you don't keep those people, you have made a terrible, terrible investment.

Our board was equally divided about what we should do. A merger of equals had a lot of appeal. If you combine the Number 1 and Number 2 players in an industry, by definition you're Number 1 in terms of size. That much was obvious and positive. And when you are growing that fast, you have a number of key management openings you have to fill. By combining two companies with good management teams, you automatically build up the strength of your management and you do it quickly. You can also overlap your customer sets, which automatically widens your customer base and gives you more distribution channels.

In addition, a merger of equals that creates the Number 1 player in a market automatically makes your remaining competition second tier. As a result, your competition must rethink its strategy, because if you are able to successfully execute your strategy, they are in deep trouble. In the end, you force a period of mergers and acquisitions on your competition. They have no choice but to respond to the changes you initiated.

S&B *That argument sounds compelling. What kept you from pursuing it?*

JOHN CHAMBERS When we looked more closely, our concerns were raised. For example, the statistics indicate that 50 percent of large-scale mergers fail. It is important to go into them realizing your odds of failure are that high. Mergers can fail on a number of levels. They can fail in terms of their benefit to the shareholders, customers, employees, and business partners. Those are the four constituencies we use to evaluate decisions. A decision has to be right with each of those constituencies, or we would not go forward with it.

S&B *What made you believe you could not overcome those challenges?*

JOHN CHAMBERS If you merge two companies that are growing at 80 percent rates, you stand a very good chance of stalling both of them out. That's a fact. When you combine companies, for a period of time, no matter how smoothly they operate, you lose momentum. Even today, as good as we are at acquisitions—and I think we really know how to do them today—when you make the acquisition, there is a period when you lose business momentum. Our industry is not like the banking industry, where you are acquiring branch banks and customers. In our industry, you are acquiring people. And if you don't keep those people, you have made a terrible, terrible investment. We pay between $500,000 and $2 million per person in an acquisition, which is a lot. So you can understand that if you don't keep the people, you've done a tremendous disservice to your shareholders and customers.

So we focus first on the people and how we incorporate them into our company, and then we focus on how to drive the business. That takes time. But as I said, in a merger of equals, you stand a very good chance of stalling out both companies when you take that time. It can be a major distraction to both.

S&B *What else was involved in your decision to avoid a merger of equals?*

JOHN CHAMBERS When we looked at the visions of our potential partners, as well as where both those companies were going, we found that their direction was different from ours. That was crucial.

If you look at the troubled merger of Bay Networks [a major Cisco competitor that was created in 1994 by the combination of Synoptics Communications, which had been one of Cisco's potential partners, and Wellfleet Communications], you would see that the corporate presentation of Wellfleet and the corporate presentation of Synoptics existed in different universes from each other.

As for us, we are a very customer-driven company. We don't get involved in the religion of the technology. But Cabletron, the other company we looked at, was very technology-driven. The people there believed that ATM, for example, was the future, and they were very much technology bigots. It does not mean one was right and the other wrong. It just demonstrated that our visions were dramatically different.

And while we thought the distribution channels might overlap and actually help us, we came to see a lot of potential contention that would overlap negatively.

We felt, for example, that as much as 60 percent of the channels might actually be driven to another vendor if we combined our two companies. That was the analysis behind our decision not to merge.

S&B *You had the advantage of having done joint projects with both your potential merger partners. What impact did that have on your strategy?*

JOHN CHAMBERS The fact that we had worked with both before made a huge difference in our deliberations. The smaller projects worked fine. But the big joint projects did not work well at all. That did not bode well for a merger. And in terms of future alliances, what would happen to our relationships with other companies in the industry if we did this merger with one of them? We felt there would be negatives.

If you really look at it, mergers of two equal cultures, where you divide the management team—one from company A, one from company B—all the way through, do not seem to work. You try to blend cultures in order to make a single, strong culture. But, in fact, you've got to have one culture that really survives and there has got to be a clear leader, in terms of who is going to lead the combined companies and which culture is going to be the one you stick with.

In the end, when we went back and looked at our strengths and looked at how they fit into a potential merger between equals, we saw it didn't match up.

S&B *How did you persuade your board to follow an acquisition strategy, whereby you buy smaller companies? That strategy has its pitfalls as well.*

JOHN CHAMBERS Our recommendation to the board went like this. Let's go back and build upon our strengths. Let's segment the market much like HP did. Let's break the market into four segments. Let's draw a matrix and adopt a GE mentality and target a 50 percent market share in each area you go into. [You need to do all this] or you don't compete.

Then we said, "Let's determine the product, services, and distribution needs for each segment and combine the way of getting these products developed and sold—whether internally, through joint development, or through acquisition." In essence, we drew a matrix for the board of directors and said, "Here are the market segments we are going into." We said that 70 percent of our products would continue to come from our internal development, but 30 percent would come from other segments. Our chairman asked us to put the concept in graphical form, so we drew the matrix. The only thing we filled in was Crescendo, which was our first acquisition. Then we said that during the course of the next several years, we would fill in all of the matrix.

After that, we filled in the matrix with our overlying objectives: to be Number 1, Number 2, or not to compete; to have a 50 percent share in every market; and never to enter a market where we can't get at least a 20 percent share right off the bat. As basic as that sounds, that is what we put in place.

S&B *The Crescendo acquisition set the tone for the rest of your strategy. At the time, however, you did not have a battle-tested acquisition plan or the structures in place to create one. How did you develop your plan?*

JOHN CHAMBERS What we set out to do at the time of that acquisition was to change our organizational structure. But we did not even tell our internal people what we were doing. In essence, we made the conscious decision to break our company into business units and follow the HP model. We chose not to announce that, though. All we did was to make Crescendo a separate business unit when it came in and to keep our central engineering capabilities on the side. The Crescendo acquisition was successful for a simple reason. This industry had been dominated by small companies. The reason for its fragmentation was time-to-market. Having the fastest time-to-market is such an overriding factor.

When I came to Cisco six years ago, I thought that IBM would be our toughest competitor. But IBM has never really been able to challenge us. The reason is that it just cannot move fast enough. The IBM culture doesn't allow it to. It can't make decisions fast enough. And without realizing it, we were becoming a big company.

When we made the decision to make our first acquisition, we were on a 60-percent-a-year growth curve. At that time, our competitors—3Com, Bay Networks, and Cabletron—were growing at [a rate of] 35 to 45 percent. Most companies would have been ecstatic at 60 percent, because they would be growing almost 50 percent faster than their key competitors.

But guess what? Companies like Fore, Ascend, and Cascade were growing even faster than we were. As a result, we realized that they were going to do to us what we were doing to IBM if we were not able to move even more quickly. We realized that we had to have some way to have the advantages of a big company while acting like a small company from a product development point of view. That's the point when we decided to break ourselves into business units for development while retaining big-company influence by leveraging our strengths in manufacturing and distribution and finance across the entire company.

Let me give you an example. We took a device like Crescendo's networking product, and within eighteen months, we had a $500 million run rate. No small company could go from $10 million to $500 million in eighteen months. They just can't scale.

But we could scale because of our distribution, financial, and manufacturing strengths.

S&B *What are the key criteria for a successful acquisition?*

JOHN CHAMBERS There are really four key issues, and for big acquisitions, there is a fifth. We do not do mergers or acquisitions or partnerships when there is not alignment around these issues.

First, if your visions are not the same—about where the industry is going, what role each company wants to play in the industry—you are constantly going to be at war. There can be differences in technology visions or industry visions. So you have to look at the visions of both companies, and if they are dramatically different, you should back away.

Second, you have to produce quick wins for your shareholders. If we did not produce a win with Crescendo in the first year, our shareholders would have been all over us. And if it is only short-term, then it is not strategic. Shareholders have to benefit from any acquisition.

Third, you have to have long-term wins for all four constituencies—shareholders, employees, customers, and business partners. I know that sounds corny, but it is true.

Finally, the chemistry has to be right, which is hard to define.

The fifth element—for large mergers and acquisitions—is geographic proximity. Geography is key. If you are doing a large acquisition, the minute you get on an airplane, you've got a problem. It is different if you are doing an engineering or technology acquisition, because those can be remote. But if you are combining two large companies and the center of manufacturing or marketing is in San Jose, California, and you are in Boston, what future do you have? It is very limited.

S&B *How disciplined are you in your approach to those five criteria? If they are not all in place, will you still buy a company if the technology is great or the people are very good?*

JOHN CHAMBERS No. We don't do it. We've killed nearly as many acquisitions as we've made. We killed acquisitions for those reasons even when they were very tempting. I believe it takes courage to walk away from a deal. It really does. You can get quite caught up in winning the acquisition and lose sight of what will make it successful. That's why we take such a disciplined approach.

S&B *You've acquired fourteen companies already, with a stated goal of another ten to twelve in 1997. Is there a single thread that weaves through your strategy?*

JOHN CHAMBERS The first thing is you make a decision about what role you want to play in the industry and then what role you can play. Those are two separate issues. Once you do that, you have to ask, What do you have to do to achieve your goal? And you can't get off track on that. One part is to do mergers and acquisitions. So you've got to build a culture that accepts that.

As simple as it sounds, it's like marriage. If you are selecting a partner for life, your ability to select that partner after one date isn't very good. Lots of people in the financial press say once Cisco does an acquisition, it is a matter of management execution as to whether the acquisition works or not.

I argue with that. I think the most important decision in your acquisition is your selection process. If you select right, with the criteria we set, your probabilities of success are extremely high. It's tough enough to make a marriage work. If you don't spend a fair amount of time on the evaluation of what the key ingredients are for that, your probability of having a successful marriage after one date is pretty small. We spend a lot of time on the up-front.

> You try to blend cultures. But you've got to have one culture that really survives, and there has got to be a clear leader.

S&B *At $4.5 billion, Stratacom was the largest acquisition you have made so far. Do you think you could absorb anything bigger?*

JOHN CHAMBERS Our ideal acquisition is a small start-up that has a great technology product on the drawing board that is going to come out six to twelve months from now. When we do that, we are buying the engineers and the next-generation product. Then we blow the product through our distribution channels and leverage our manufacturing and financial strengths. However, we would not rule out larger acquisitions if the industry changes faster than we expected or where there is more of an integration than we expected.

Do we have anything larger in mind at the present? No. Our more typical acquisitions will continue to be smaller engineering organizations. We will continue to go after private companies. You can acquire them much more quickly and with far fewer legal nightmares. There is also a lot less risk in those types of deals.

S&B *Is there something in your model that is unique to high-tech industries?*

JOHN CHAMBERS I think so. As I mentioned, we are in the business of acquiring people. That is different from the automotive or financial industries, where you are acquiring process, customer base, and distribution. So when we acquire something, we are not acquiring distribution capabilities or manufacturing expertise. We—Cisco—are very good at that. We are acquiring technology. In this business, if you are acquiring technology, you are acquiring people.

That is the reason large companies that have acquired technology companies have failed. If you look at AT&T and NCR, or IBM with Rolm, the acquirer did not understand that it was acquiring people and a culture. If you don't have a culture that quickly embraces the new acquisition, if you are not careful in the selection process, then the odds are high that your acquisition will fail.

Two years ago, we used to worry about what would happen if an IBM, HP, AT&T, or other large company acquired one of our key competitors. But the odds are very high that it would have failed. The reason it would have failed is that the culture required to make a company like Cisco or 3Com or Crescendo successful is not the same as the culture that is needed to make IBM or AT&T successful.

As I said, if you pay $500,000 to $2 million per person for the people you acquire, and you lose 30 to 40 percent of those people in the first two years, you've made a terrible decision for your investors. If you go back and look at how many companies in this kind of acquisition deal lose 30 to 40 percent of their people in that period, it will shock you. That is why acquisitions in our industry fail.

S&B *What is special about your culture that allows you to integrate the acquisitions so fast?*

JOHN CHAMBERS Again, you have to look at why many acquisitions fail. It's because the companies are left too independent for too long. Or worse, they know they are eventually going to combine, but you leave them alone and the politics begin and people begin to jockey over who is going to get which positions. We've learned that to make it successful, you have to tell the employees of the companies up front what you are going to do, because trust is everything in this business. You have got to tell them early so you don't betray their trust later.

To move quickly, you want to find the advantages and disadvantages of scale. Usually, we keep engineering independent. We combine marketing and manufacturing and the information systems. We empower very talented people and then hold them accountable for the results. But we are also there to help them from making the wrong turns.

Stratacom is already integrated. The largest acquisition in terms of dollars that the industry had ever seen is something we integrated into our business in four months.

S&B *Out of the fourteen companies you have acquired, how many of the founders' CEOs stayed with Cisco?*

JOHN CHAMBERS About half.

S&B *Is that important? Do you try to get those people to stay, or is it better if they leave?*

JOHN CHAMBERS I missed one acquisition that I should have gotten because of a chemistry issue with the company's president. His was not a chemistry that would have fit into Cisco. The mistake I made was that the chemistry of the company's other leaders and employees would have fit in fine with ours. I should have bought the company, told the president up front that he wouldn't be part of the future, and he would probably have left.

But the real issue is that I want to retain the majority of an acquired company's employees.

S&B *How do you do that?*

JOHN CHAMBERS You understand what is important to them, what motivates them. And you empower them. Take Andy Bechtolsheim, the founder of Granite, one of the companies we wound up acquiring. The first thing I asked Andy, who was also a cofounder of Sun Microsystems, was, "What's important to you? What do you want to do in life?" He said, "I want to take care of my employees here, make sure they are successful, and my customers. But I like to build products that sell billions of dollars." I said, "We're going to get along great." Once I understood how to motivate him, we were off and running.

S&B *The genesis of your acquisition strategy took place when Cisco was essentially invisible. People in your industry knew about you, but it is really only in the past year that the general business community has learned about you. What, other than size, prompted you to raise your profile?*

JOHN CHAMBERS Early on, we had no desire to be visible. Part of the reason was that there was no business advantage to publicity, because most of our sales to our customers were direct. For our customers to hear about us in the press gave us no advantage. In addition, as a company, we never had the ego-need to be visible.

However, we realized about eighteen months ago that we did have to become much more visible because our business was going to become more of a marketing game, in addition to being a product-technology game. To find out what to do, we watched what Microsoft does in marketing. Microsoft is really awesome. We realized that it gets most of its marketing for free. Since we're a frugal company, that really appealed to us. As a result, we made the decision as a team that we wanted to become much more visible.

S&B *Has your increased visibility changed anything in the acquisitions area?*

JOHN CHAMBERS It allows us to move more quickly. When people realize what we do and how good we are at it and how good we are at keeping the people we acquire, it makes it much easier to acquire a company. As a result, we now have a chance to acquire everybody. There's almost no acquisition that goes down, even if one of our competitors is doing the buying, that does not come to us first to see if we are interested.

> You have to tell the employees up front what you are going to do so you don't betray their trust later.

Unless the company is public, the decision is rarely simply a financial one. For example, there were several companies that would have paid a lot more money for Granite than we did. Andy Bechtolsheim knew the company he wanted to be acquired by. He knew the culture he wanted to become part of. He knew his customers and that his products would come to market through us and that his people not only would not be stifled but would have a chance to play a much larger role.

S&B *How do you measure the success of your acquisitions?*

JOHN CHAMBERS The way we measure the success of small-to-medium-sized acquisitions is straightforward. Within three years, we would like to generate in revenue what we paid for the company. If we do that, then the acquisition was a good, solid base hit. If we do more than that—say we do it in two years or even in one year—then the acquisition was a home run or a grand slam. Crescendo was a grand slam.

S&B *With acquisitions fueling incredible growth, are you getting so big that you face the same issues that hammered the hardware giants in the late 1980s?*

JOHN CHAMBERS You know, there's no doubt that running at this pace is a challenge. At the top of the list is, How do you manage the growth? How do you really create the culture of mergers and acquisitions and new ideas and keep your basic strengths? How do you avoid missing the major technology changes that occur? How do you avoid creating the hierarchy where an overhead structure supporting your salespeople and engineers becomes your bottleneck as you drive through it? How do you avoid getting too far away from your customers? Do I think we could trip in the future? Absolutely.

S&B *Yet you have said there will be ten or twelve more acquisitions this year. Is this going to go on forever?*

JOHN CHAMBERS If the industry is going to be as big as some people project it to be, and if it continues to grow as fast as people are projecting it to grow, then acquisitions will stay an integral part of our strategy for the next five years.

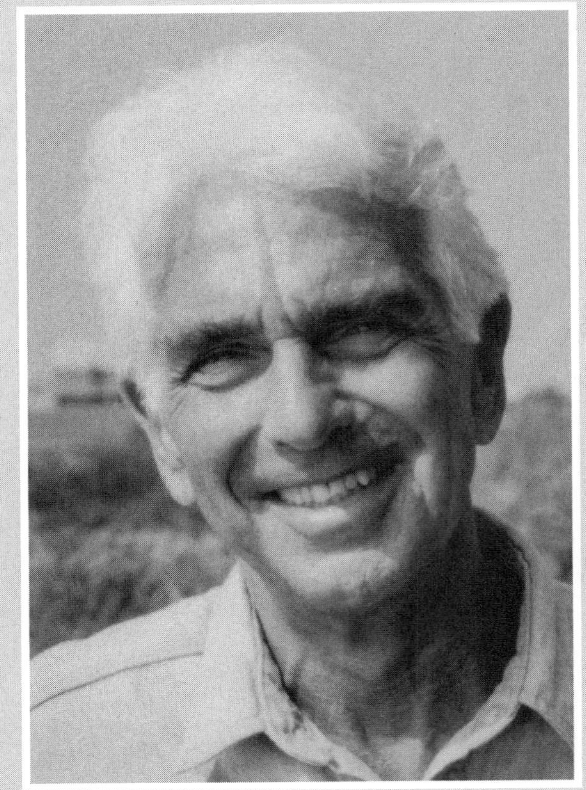

An
Interview
with

WARREN BENNIS

Distinguished Professor of Business Administration,
University of Southern California,
Marshall School of Business

During his long and fruitful career, Warren Bennis has been a student, soldier, scholar, university provost, university president, student of leadership and group dynamics, and distinguished professor.

Mr. Bennis first came to prominence in the early 1960s when he taught social sciences at the Massachusetts Institute of Technology. In 1964, in the midst of the cold war, Mr. Bennis and a coauthor, Philip Slater, who was also a social scientist, published a seminal article in the *Harvard Business Review*—"Is Democracy Inevitable?"—in which they argued that democracy was an unstoppable force. Although the article proved to be correct, it was considered radical at the time, given the formidable power of the Soviet Union.

Even more radical—and timely now—is the reasoning upon which the argument was based. The premise of the piece is that democracy is a system of values superior to and more functional than the values of other systems. Values, in the view of Mr. Bennis, are not simply a collection of a group's mores and attitudes. Rather, they determine which things a group will do and how well it will do them. As such, values are vital to a group's chances of reaching its goals.

Great Groups are a snapshot of the way organizations ought to look—a graphic illustration of what's possible.

The logic of Mr. Bennis's thinking as it pertained to government carried through to his later work. As he turned to the study of business, he once again raised the issue of values. Great leaders are able to accomplish great feats and prod their followers into doing the same, he wrote, because they are able to articulate, focus, and even embody the values of the groups they lead. Not only do different types of groups demand different types of leaders but it is often very difficult to determine whether the leader shapes the group or the group offers up the leader.

Some groups are better than others, Mr. Bennis observed, and occasionally, in business and elsewhere, they rise to the level of what he terms "Great Groups." How do Great Groups differ from the ordinary kind? They are able to achieve tremendous successes, often with very limited resources, he notes in his new book, *Organizing Genius: The Secrets of Creative Collaboration* (Addison-Wesley), which he wrote with Patricia Ward Biederman. In short, they are high-commitment, high-performance, high-output organizations.

In some instances, as with the scientists who developed the atomic bomb in the Manhattan Project or the engineers who came together in Lockheed's celebrated Skunk Works, a handful of men and women and their leaders have opened up new technological territories with outcomes that have reshaped the world. In others, as with the Great Group that makes up Disney's feature animation studio, small cadres of people have changed the face of the arts and entertainment.

To succeed, a Great Group usually requires two sharply different leadership roles to be filled. One role—that of the visionary—is necessary if a Great Group is to set a goal and chart a course for it. The other—that of the protector of the vision, often an unsung hero—is needed to keep the harsh realities of the world at bay. Early on at Disney, Walt was the visionary, while brother Roy served as the protector. In the Manhattan Project, J. Robert Oppenheimer, a temperamental but visionary physicist, charted the course, while General Leslie R. Groves, a tough military man, ran interference. Occasionally, but not often, these two qualities can be found in the same person. What follows is a conversation between Warren Bennis and *Strategy & Business* that took place in May 1997 at Mr. Bennis's home in Santa Monica, California.

S&B *Every company and manager is scrambling these days to figure out how to create a Great Group. But it is clearly a very difficult thing to do. I have been in countless meetings where the question being considered was blunt: "What would it take to get our group to be better, to do a better job?" And most people say, "Get rid of the guy who's heading our department." Is that the key? How much does* *the leader inhibit or help? How much is it up to the group itself?*

WARREN BENNIS Without a terrific leader, you're not going to have a Great Group. But it is also true that you're not going to have a great leader without a Great Group.

S&B *The leader makes the group and the group makes the leader?*

WARREN BENNIS Yes. I realized this close to home, when I was a young man in World War II. I was what was called a "replacement officer." It's a macabre name—I was sort of anesthetized to the full meaning of it. It was right after the Battle of the Bulge—in December 1944—and I was a green platoon leader in the infantry. The first few days, the captain of the company said, "Just do everything I do. Just mimic me."

But when I got back to my platoon, the men were laughing at me. It turned out that the captain had been in combat a little too long and he was getting deaf. That meant he wasn't diving for cover until just nanoseconds before the bombs hit. And that wasn't so funny for me.

So these platoon guys—all were experienced veterans, most were twenty-five or older, and some were even college graduates—helped train me, a nineteen-year-old second lieutenant just out of Fort Benning, to become their leader. They taught me everything from how to hit the ground and dig a foxhole to how to make a decent meal out of C rations and direct my scouts. They taught me all the ropes. They wanted me to lead them and they made it possible for me to do that. I was obviously scared to death at what I was thrust into and they were able to make me into something beyond my dreams. That was a Great Group.

S&B *And what did you give to them?*

WARREN BENNIS I knew some things they didn't know. I had just gotten through four months of the best kind of advanced military training, and I was able to impart some things about strategy. With that knowledge, I was able to give them some sense of perspective about where we were and where the war was going—a glimpse of the big picture—and that gave them an idea of when we were going to be relieved, which was very important.

And I gave them a sense of confidence, which in a way is paradoxical, given the fact that I joined the platoon without any real experience. Yet, somehow or other, they gave me the confidence and then later I gave them the confidence. I think we both realized that we were playing for mortal stakes and that in a morbid sense, our fates were correlated.

S&B *How do we take your extraordinary battlefield experience and apply it to the* *everyday office setting and factory floor? Just what is needed to make a group succeed?*

WARREN BENNIS I don't feel altogether comfortable in saying, "Here are the steps to Great Groups." In fact, one of the questions that has perplexed me is, How do you take the experiences and lessons of the extraordinary groups described in my book and apply them to regular, ordinary organizations?

Great Groups are vivid utopias. They are a picture of the way organizations ought to look—sort of like a set of aspirations and a graphic illustration of what's possible. So how do we, in our mundane, quotidian organizations, create these things? I think there are a number of factors that we can look at.

Perhaps the key factor, and it's almost a banal thing to say, is finding a meaning in what you do. That is, How do you make people feel that what they're doing is somewhat equivalent to a search for the Holy Grail?

This is more than just having a vision. You can see the difference in the often-cited way in which Steve Jobs brought in John Sculley to take over Apple. At the time, Sculley was destined to be the head of Pepsico. The clincher came when Jobs asked him, "How many more years of your life do you want to spend making colored water when you can have an opportunity to come here and change the world?"

So the vision must have meaning, a deep meaning. It has to have some connection with changing the world, with a mission from God.

S&B *In your book, you also say that serendipity is involved. A Great Group must not only have a meaningful vision but also the ability to seize opportunities to fulfill that vision. How it pulls that off is something of a mystery. The groups that you describe as great are, in a sense, closed entities, yet they are somehow in touch with the market.*

WARREN BENNIS That's right. I'm not sure it amounts to a paradox, but it certainly is really strange. On the one hand, these groups are self-contained island communities. On the other, they have antennae that extend to the outside.

For example, J. Robert Oppenheimer, the creative force behind the Manhattan Project, knew where to go to find the best young physicists to develop the atomic bomb. So although he was in Los Alamos, and God knows that was a woebegone place, he was able to go around the country to recruit all of the best minds that were available. He had a Rolodex in his head long before the actual device was invented. Put another way, the groups are enclosed and protected, yet also have the networks to know what's going on in the "real" world.

S&B *But how do they do that? After all, many of the great things that emerge from* *these groups are very radical departures. And yet they fit somehow in the context of a market, whether it's the marketplace of ideas or the market for movies or computers.*

WARREN BENNIS That's where another aspect of serendipity comes in, because you could have a group that is isolated, that is doing what it thinks may be a remarkable paradigmatic breakthrough, and, in fact, it has no resonance with the market, has no connection with what the needs or interests of people are. This is where there's a lot of luck involved. It is also where leadership counts.

S&B *Where does the leader fit into the picture?*

WARREN BENNIS To begin with, a leader is needed to protect the group from disruptive outside forces yet to possess a sort of proverbial Rolodex in the sky to know what's going on. Leaders like Bob Taylor and John Seely Brown at the Palo Alto Research Center [PARC], Peter Schneider and Jeffrey Katzenberg at Disney, and Kelly Johnson at Lockheed were all able to recruit their troops and protect them from the "suits," or what they used to call "toner heads" at Xerox, and also have a strong connection with the outside world. In that sense, the leaders are truly protectors. Kelly Johnson, for example, got himself on the Lockheed board so he could keep the bureaucrats away from the creativity going on.

> The leader is rarely the brightest person in the group. Rather, they have extraordinary taste, which makes them more curators than creators.

S&B *Can you go into that role a little bit? A Great Group has a creative leader, but it also has a protector?*

WARREN BENNIS Well, those roles seem to be split in many cases. Let's take the Media Lab at the Massachusetts Institute of Technology. There, it was Jerry Weisner, M.I.T.'s president, who was the protector, who was able to actually get the money to get the building and protect that money from the other departments and deans, who would have liked it to have gone into their particular fiefdoms. But it was people like Nick Negroponte and others who were the creative animators of the place. So you have that split role. It was that same kind of split in the case of Oppenheimer and General Leslie R. Groves, the military's man in charge of the Manhattan Project.

In a Great Group, you always have to have some patrician in the background, whether it's Kelly Johnson or Bob Taylor, who can talk to the suits. The creator-protector roles don't have to be split, but they often are.

S&B *A leader could embody both roles, even though they represent different states of mind and different ways of operating?*

WARREN BENNIS Yes, they can be embodied in the same person, and for a very interesting reason: the leader, whether filling one of these roles or both, is rarely the brightest person in the group. Rather, they have extraordinary taste, which makes them more curators than creators. They are appreciators of talent and nurturers of talent, and they have the ability to recognize valuable ideas. I think it was Ben Rich, who succeeded Kelly Johnson at Lockheed, who said to me, "I always know a good idea when I hear it, because of the feeling of terror that seizes me." He had a great smell for an idea, like a good editor.

The quality of leadership I'm describing comes through in a story I heard about the difference between having dinner with Prime Minister Gladstone and with Prime Minister Disraeli. When you had dinner with Gladstone, you were left feeling that he was the wittiest, the most brilliant, the most charming person you had ever met. But after dinner with Disraeli, you felt that you were the wittiest, the most intelligent, the most charming person.

Leaders of Great Groups are more like Disraeli than Gladstone. My God, they have to be. I mean, Oppenheimer never won the Nobel Prize, but think of the numbers of people in the Manhattan Project who did.

What I'm getting at is that leaders are almost like midwives of ideas. They really understand what is going on. You know when you come to them with an idea, they aren't going to just say, "Well, that's nice, and maybe we can use that."

S&B *So is it the leader's function to find the link to the market? Is the leader the person who makes it all practical and says, "This is a wonderful idea, but if somehow you put it into a spreadsheet, we can sell a million of these"?*

WARREN BENNIS Yes, exactly. He is the guy who goes to the outside world, who can bring to an audience of executives the work of the true creative genius in the group. He is the salesman. But *salesman* is a trivializing word. He is the translator, facilitator, the articulating point between the group's genius—who is doing great things, producing big and innovative ideas—and the public, the market. It is being able to sell the dream to the people who aren't close to it.

S&B *Let's back up a bit to when the group is first coming together. One of the leader's* *primary responsibilities is recruitment. These are very tight-knit teams. How do you find the right people? And how do you keep out those who might break up the team?*

WARREN BENNIS It starts with a need for people who can play together in the sandbox, in the words of Peter Schneider, president of Disney's feature animation studio. That means a sense of compatibility and a willingness to take the work very seriously. It also means that the team ought to have the right to say who's going to join and who isn't, which sometimes means subjecting the recruit to something akin to a grueling hazing experience.

There is also a great deal to be said about self-nomination. People smell out the group that they may want to join. When a certain field gets hot—and right now it is neuroscience—bright young people are drawn almost like iron filings to a magnet.

Still, you'll make mistakes, because it's a very chancy game and you can't always predict well, even with the wisdom of a good group.

S&B *I recall a study about AT&T that found that the people who did best were those who could fill the gaps. They could run around, they had networks, they could create new networks, and they could fill the holes in their own knowledge. And they just had a sense of how to do it. Now, on a bigger level, is that how a team should be managed?*

WARREN BENNIS I think so. One theory I have about these Great Groups is that the leader is a completer, the person who fills the gap that others may not be filling at a particular time. That means having the protean quality of being able to move into different kinds of roles—and having the capacity to abandon his or her ego to the talents of others, which is such a critical thing.

That is one of the reasons I'm rather concerned now about Disney's Michael Eisner. With all of Mike Ovitz's problems, I wish that Eisner had been able to create a space and a role for the best utilization of his talents. I know that the world is down on Ovitz, but my concern is over how Eisner was unable to fully utilize and work Ovitz into the team at Disney. I think that's a primary function of a Great Group. And, frankly, Disney does not have a Great Group at the top at this moment.

S&B *Let's stay with Disney for a moment and talk about the role of Roy E. Disney as the guardian of the company's values in the mid-1980s. The son of Roy O., who was the cofounder of the company and the protector of its values in his day, Roy E. was sometimes cruelly called "the idiot nephew" by Walt Disney. Yet, in 1984, he thwarted a takeover attempt and started to put together the great team of Michael Eisner and Frank Wells. In some way, he was able to take responsibility to recreate the mix at a time when the company had lost its way. How did he do that?*

WARREN BENNIS Roy is one of the easiest people to underestimate. But he's really an extraordinary man—totally unacknowledged by the world but fully acknowledged within Disney. He is a keen, deep listener, and he just had that faith, that conviction about what it was going to take to remake Disney.

S&B *Can you write the specs of a Roy, of someone who could do the same job for other groups?*

WARREN BENNIS He doesn't get in the hair of others. He doesn't hover. Totally supportive. Protector of a dream, guardian of the group's meaning. That would be the main thing.

At Disney right now, the one feature animation film each year brings in roughly 40 percent of the profits. Not the revenue but the profits. It is entirely understandable why Eisner would want to make two or even three a year. But I doubt if they can do that with the same level of creativity.

Roy Disney is simply a beautiful example of a protector, the translator, the presence on the board. And his relationship with Peter Schneider, the head of feature animation, is extremely close. There's got to be a partnership between the two. Kelly Johnson and the people at Lockheed's Skunk Works also had that.

> People in organizations may have vision, but there's zero meaning to what they're doing. They've actually forgotten why they are there.

S&B *But as you have said, being a protector is not enough. Look at what is happening at Apple Computer. After Apple lost its creative force, it brought in Gilbert Amelio to fill the General Groves role. Now Amelio is bringing back the creative force by rehiring Steve Jobs. Is this the makings of a new Great Group?*

WARREN BENNIS That was the smartest thing Amelio has done. Jobs is a great salesman, and he can also use talent. And much like it was with Walt Disney, people desperately want to please him.

Indeed, the variation of these leaders is an interesting thing, because whereas Bob Taylor at PARC would nurture and treasure and cherish, people like Walt Disney and Steve Jobs were also given to moments, almost like a bipolar personality, in which they could be quite mean, humiliating people in public. Katzenberg, too, can be very, very difficult. Still, people want desperately to please them.

S&B *Why do people respond that way?*

WARREN BENNIS These leaders are the incarnation of the dream, of a form of excellence. Jobs and Disney are incarnations of what it was that would make that group great. And you want to live up to that, you want to achieve that.

When I think about the leaders that I've written about, they have certain things in common: they provide direction and meaning, they generate and sustain trust, they are purveyors of hope, they are people who get results. But their personalities vary enormously, and a Walt Disney and a Steve Jobs are not your textbook, Warren Bennis–type leaders whom we've enshrined in the management literature. They've got this incredible sense of spotting talent. Though they have pre-Copernican egos, they are able to get people who can do things that they can't. That means they are able to abandon those huge egos to the talents of others.

S&B *Personalities aside, how do leaders know how far they have led? You certainly know, if you're Disney, whether "Pocahontas" is a success or a flop. And, of course, you know the Manhattan Project got the result it sought. But as for the rest, is it important for a leader to have a sense of measures and milestones?*

WARREN BENNIS Absolutely. Not only must there be a deadline but also some clear metrics—you've got to keep that in front of the group. And with monotonous regularity the leader must keep reminding people of what's important. If the group doesn't produce by a certain date, then "the Germans are going to get it first" or "some other competitor is going to do this new PC before us." There's always got to be that kind of haunting sense of a deadline. These are fiercely competitive groups, and the only way they can be fiercely competitive is knowing there's a date, there are metrics, and there's a product. Great Groups have to really ship.

S&B *By definition, these groups are going into uncharted territory. How do you know what the metrics should be?*

WARREN BENNIS Sometimes you don't. That sense that you could do something that no one else has done is almost unwarranted optimism. How in the hell did they know they could really make an atomic bomb? Until the morning they exploded the first one, they really weren't sure. They had to have an innocence about them—they did not know it couldn't be done. That's why youth is very interesting here, because they don't know what they don't know.

So how do you get a metric? You get it through a product and a deadline. I don't think you can quite get the metrics from the usual sense, a priori.

S&B *Putting all this together, it seems clear that these Great Groups are very special creatures indeed. Which means that you can't run a whole company as a Great Group.*

WARREN BENNIS No, I don't think you can. It would be very difficult to imagine a large organization filled at every moment in time with Great Groups. But it's imperative that line officers and certainly HR people and CEOs be aware of the conditions that can create electrifying groups that make a real difference—and that they strive to provide a home for them.

But how do you make every other group in the organization give that group, and the people in that group, a sense that what they are doing really has meaning to them? The problem is that lots of people in organizations may have vision, but there's absolutely zero meaning to what they're doing. They've actually forgotten why they are there, which is why bureaucracies become stodgy and obsolete and filled with inertia.

So, the lessons from Great Groups are important for every organization, because they encourage us to aspire to be something more than we are. You're never going to quite make it, but you better be damn aware of what can happen when you can create—or be a part of—the kind of group that's going to make a difference, rather than the kind of humdrum, boring, drifting organization we see too often.

So, yes, it's hard for me to imagine one organization, especially a large one, with hundreds of hives of Great Groups. But the lessons here—about leadership, meaning, recruiting, and what bureaucracies have to do to protect, basically, their human capital and their intellectual capital—these lessons are just terribly important for people to be aware of.

S&B *Now, every once in a while, you hear of a Great Group arising spontaneously, so to speak. Within an organization that has lots of excellent people—you might take a pharmaceutical company like Merck—suddenly the neuroscience or the cardio group seems to be just blooming, flourishing beyond what anyone had expected. How does this sort of spontaneous greatness happen? Is this driven by a leader? Is it a matter of the right chemistry, no pun intended?*

WARREN BENNIS That's a combination of all of those things. Part of it may be serendipitous and plain luck that they hit upon a vein, almost like drilling. You notice in the interviews that you do—and I've done a lot—that you sort of drift around and you throw out probes. Especially when interviewing famous people, because they have a script and they've told their famous stories dozens of times. But every once in a while, you can ask a question and, boy, you just hit, like a vein opens up. So that's part of it.

It could be an area, in taking Merck, where they suddenly realize, "Gee, this drug can cure river blindness," and then it has a resonance with the market and there are a lot of by-products that come out of it. And somehow there are a number of very bright people in that venue who are around.

I'm not sure you can create such a group, but you can permit it when you spot it and then say, "OK, you've got that strike and now you have to manage it to bring it in." You can't predict the strike all the time, but you have to be very aware of those marvelous, propitious moments—and not let them off the hook.

S&B *There's a certain intensity in these groups. You can recognize it when you walk into a particular part of the company, whether it's happening there or not. In the absence of a Great Group, can a bureaucratic, humdrum company learn to produce great products, albeit more slowly and methodically?*

WARREN BENNIS Yes. Let's imagine that a company brings me in to talk about the application of Great Groups to its business—it doesn't matter what company or what business. I would tell them, "Look, you've all been, one time in your life, at least, in a terrific group, one in which you've never felt more creative and that you really enjoyed. It could have been a political campaign, it could have been a play you were in. Write down some characteristics of that group."

Let's say there are fifteen or twenty people in the audience, so you then put them at a blackboard or easel. "OK, now let's take the most significant of these characteristics—which are the ones that most of you said? We'll just say there are six or seven of these dimensions."

Now, some of this may be tough to talk about, because the thing they're going to say is that the leader was of a certain kind, that he had this charisma or this sense of letting go, or had the taste to bring in a lot of good people. And then you can start saying, "Well, how do you think you can get to this, and can you sustain it?"

So the real question that is implied in many of your questions is, Can these groups not only be created within your normal Fortune 1000 company but can they also be sustained? We can go a long way toward actually saying, "OK, what the hell are we doing here together? What are we really trying to produce? What is it that has meaning for us, that's going to keep us motivated? Let's take a look at our leadership. Let's take a look at our compatibility. Let's take a look at whether we have any moments of honoring or celebrating our achievements. Let's take a look at our metrics."

In a lot of ways, you can get groups to be reflective about their shortcomings and the things they could do to make themselves, if not great in the sense of the Manhattan Project, a hell of a lot better than they now are. That would be very useful.

S&B *When you were talking earlier about your experience in the war, you stressed the importance of sharing some of your knowledge with the troops, of giving them a sense of the big picture. Whether I'm leading a Great Group or just a humdrum one, how much knowledge should I reveal? How much should I hold back?*

WARREN BENNIS You should reveal as much as possible but without scaring people. What I learned as a university president was that you can't always talk about your own insecurities. You can't talk about all the perceived difficulties that you might see by virtue of your position and that the others can't see. You don't want to share things that will diminish the enthusiasm. People may not believe that their leaders are omniscient, but they have a certain stake in thinking that a leader has enough of a sense of security to guide them through treacherous waters. One of the characteristics of leaders of Great Groups is perspective—providing a sense of destiny and awareness of the conditions they are up against.

S&B *In the interest of openness, should you talk about threats to the group's budget?*

WARREN BENNIS It would depend. If you ever make an enemy of the bureaucrats, you can, and that would create a lot more cohesiveness within the group. Every Great Group invents or creates an enemy to preserve that kind of cohesiveness and sense of élan and "We can do it!"

If you have a budget shortage, and you're not getting the kind of help you need, you may want to indicate, "Well, we're going to have to do the best we can, given the budgets we're getting from headquarters," and just go with it that way.

I'd always rather err on the side of openness. But there's a difference between optimum and maximum openness, and fixing that boundary is a judgment call. The art of leadership is knowing how much information you're going to pass on—to keep people motivated and to be as honest, as up-front, as you can. But, boy, there really are limits to that.

S&B *We have been focusing on the Great Groups as models for success. What about groups that fail? Does that happen because the troops lose faith in the leader? Is the chemistry all wrong?*

WARREN BENNIS Certainly, there is a loss of confidence in the leader and the leader's ability to be coached back to the right track. We need look no further than Bob Dole's recent presidential campaign to see some of the common faces of failure. Three or four people from his campaign were speaking with different voices, people were quitting in droves before the campaign was over, there was a reduction in the number of sources for getting information, and real dissent wasn't openly addressed.

> You should reveal as much as possible but without scaring people. You don't want to share things that will diminish enthusiasm.

S&B *Can you explain what you mean regarding dissent?*

WARREN BENNIS The best example I can think of is a political one, from Lyndon Johnson's White House during the difficult days of Vietnam. George Ball would tell the president and his advisers, "Well, we've got to pull out." And they would all dutifully listen and relieve their guilt that they weren't listening to us, but it made no difference. They didn't really want to hear dissent, and they would make a feeble show of it by bringing in the one guy who was saying something different. Pretty soon, though, Ball was no longer invited to the meetings. So you're hearing only one voice.

All of these factors happen in consequential failures. You circle the wagons. You stop listening to as many sources as you can. You get dissent that is public and not internal, because you domesticate it.

And the beauty of Great Groups is that they encourage dissent. They are the most verbal, argumentative entities. It is sort of like playing Frisbee with ideas, tossing ideas all over the place. If there is one word to characterize these groups, it is *logorrhea*—these are people who can't shut up.

Disney has a summit meeting once a year in Aspen, and I've been to a couple of those. My God, the wisecracks and the motormouths. The culture of these groups is noisy. Their people feel free. They're outrageous.

S&B *What about groups that fail?*

WARREN BENNIS They are just the opposite. They cover up. They don't encourage different ideas, they don't reward them.

S&B *Now, Eisner says he wants to create an organization in which failure is tolerated. If everyone is spouting off, if everyone has this high intensity, trying out new ideas, some are going to bite the dust. So does a Great Group have to tolerate either a wrong turn or an out-and-out failure?*

WARREN BENNIS By and large, yes. Obviously, you can't fail forever. But that doesn't mean you go into anything thinking it will fail. There's a producer-director for whom I have the greatest respect—Sidney Pollack. He can get just about anyone to work for him, because they know they will be in a terrific movie, one that hums and sings. He has the capacity to create these Great Groups every time he goes out, because he really does say, quoting Susan B. Anthony, "Failure is impossible."

One marvelous story that he told me was about the filming of *The Way We Were* with Barbra Streisand and Robert Redford. Barbra claimed that she couldn't cry and would need ammonia to get the tears flowing. But Pollack wanted tears without a prop. He knew that anyone capable of singing with her emotion could cry. So at the moment she was supposed to cry, he told his assistant director not to shoot until after he hugged her. When he did, the tears just burst forth, buckets of them. It was a "blessed impulse," as he called it, that did the trick.

Well, when you work with Pollack, one thing you know is that you're in the hands of a very competent person. And that makes you—and the rest of the group—do more, perhaps, than you thought you could. It is the same kind of give-and-take that I experienced when I was the novice platoon leader, first getting confidence from the troops and then giving them confidence in return.

S&B *Are there examples of very direct, top-down, hierarchical Great Groups? Or is there always this give-and-take?*

WARREN BENNIS Always. I don't think you can have it without an incredible amount of rejoicing and celebrating and the freedom to express different ideas, crazy ideas, without being cut down. I'm not saying there always has to be a wise, sweet, touchy-feely leader. But there must always be a sense that a good idea really pays off. Even if you're facing the quintessential, most highly acclaimed CEO in America right now, Jack Welch, you know that as tough as he is, if you really produce a terrific idea, the light bulbs will go off in his head.

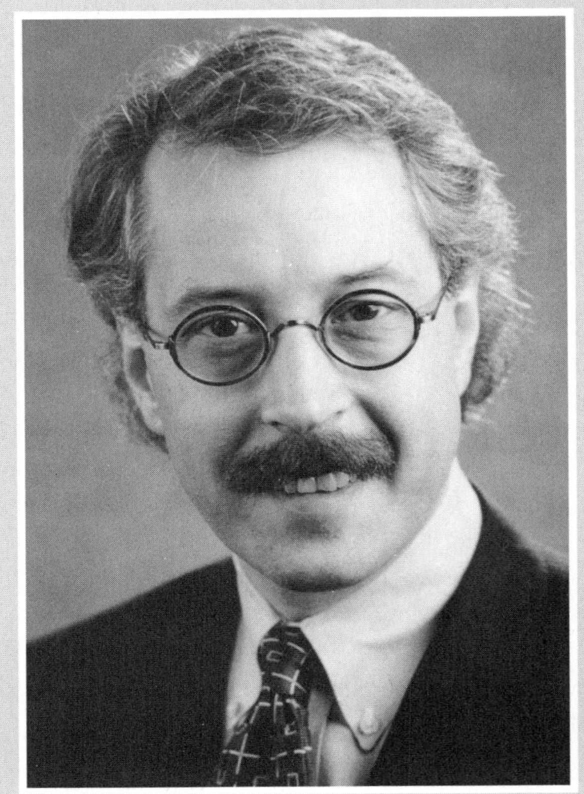

An
Interview
with

GARY HAMEL

Visiting Professor, London Business School, and Coauthor of *Competing for the Future*

In 1994, when Gary Hamel coauthored *Competing for the Future* (Harvard Business School Press) with his longtime friend, collaborator, and former professor, C. K. Prahalad, it was something of a publishing event. The book not only sold briskly and was named one of the best of the year in business, but it also changed much of the debate about how to set strategy. Instead of advocating a top-down approach, Mr. Hamel, who is a visiting professor at the London Business School, and Mr. Prahalad, a professor at the University of Michigan, proposed that strategy should be set in a dialogue involving all levels of a company. Moreover, they argued that when companies set their strategic course, they ought to include younger employees and even dissidents in the process.

Challenging the status quo has to be the starting point for anything that goes under the label of strategy.

In the years since the book appeared, Mr. Hamel, who is 43 years old, has continued his writing and speaking activities and has also founded a consulting firm called Strategos. Whereas the focus of his earlier work was on core competencies, strategic intent, and "stretch," his most recent efforts have concentrated on innovation and creating a "new sense of self" within a business. What does this new sense of self enable a company to do? "It empowers people within the company to stare down their orthodoxies and say that they are not going to be bound by them anymore," Mr. Hamel says. The aim is to help companies create revolutionary strategies to keep them permanently ahead of the competition, he explains.

Staying ahead by being revolutionary is easier said than done. It requires a depth of insight that most companies depend on when they are young but lose when they age. In Mr. Hamel's view, even highly competitive companies can develop blind spots. When that happens, they can lose out to newer challengers. In industries as diverse as retailing, soft drinks, computers, and airlines, successful, old-line companies have watched helplessly as younger ones have moved onto the scene and built up markets. The reason for a company's blindness, Mr. Hamel argues, "is an unwillingness or inability to look outside of current experiences." Helping companies cure that type of blindness has been the latest focus of his work.

What follows are excerpts from a recent conversation with Mr. Hamel that took place at his office in Menlo Park, California.

S&B *You have developed an approach to future growth that you call "next step strategy" or "revolutionary strategy." What does it mean and why is it needed? And how does one become a revolutionary strategist?*

GARY HAMEL In an increasingly nonlinear economy, incremental change is not enough—you have to build a capacity for strategy innovation, one that increases your ability to recognize new opportunities. And the opportunities for future growth are everywhere. Seeing the future has nothing to do with speculating about what might happen. Rather, you must understand the revolutionary potential of what is already happening. And to do that, you must yourself become a revolutionary, embracing three fundamental and related perspectives.

The first is to systematically deconstruct the orthodoxies and dogmas that rule a business. When people sit down and think about strategy, too often they take 90 or 95 percent of industry orthodoxies as a given and as a constraint. Instead, they must stare down their orthodoxies and determine that they are not going to be bound by them anymore. In effect, in looking for new directions, they are simply not going to start with the same old starting point.

The second perspective is to develop a deeper sense of self, one that frees a company to do something that it would not have conceived of doing or making before, because it was imprisoned within a narrow definition of its product market domain.

What is the knowledge or the core competence that we have, and what else can we do with it? How do I get it out of the prison where it may be languishing?

And the third fundamental lens is understanding the discontinuities in the environment that can be leveraged for remaking the structure of an industry to our advantage. As I said, the goal is to understand what has already changed and to identify the revolutionary portent in those changes.

S&B *Why don't we start at your starting point, with the attack on dogmas?*

GARY HAMEL You know, the definition of a *revolutionary* is someone who challenges the prejudices and the dogmas of the incumbent. So in that sense, the future is more often created by heretics than it is by prophets. It is very much about seeing what is already there and being willing to turn around and say, now what?

For example, look at what the companies did that led the HMO revolution in health care. They took what was regarded as the critical success factors in the hospital industry—maximizing the number of patient days and procedures—and turned them upside down. From now on, they said, winning means minimizing those things. And clearly all the big, fat, happy teaching hospitals had enormous trouble responding to that.

Or look at Anita Roddick, the founder of the Body Shop. She watched which way the cosmetics industry was going and walked in the other direction. In packaging, positioning, branding, pricing, promotion, literally everything got changed.

So challenging the status quo has to be the starting point for anything that goes under the label of strategy.

S&B *But do you challenge the dogmas if they are working? Suppose you're United Airlines or Southwest and you're doing just fine, thank you?*

GARY HAMEL It's a bigger point. What you're constantly asking is, What part of this is orthodoxy, and what part of this is gravity? We're not going to reverse the laws of gravity right away. In the airline industry, you still have to put the passengers in a metal tube to get them from A to B. We don't yet know how to overcome that particular orthodoxy.

So you do have to make that distinction. Interestingly, though, when you look at the history of industry revolutionaries, they typically challenge what most people in the business would have thought of as gravity. For example, one of the basic assumptions in the banking industry for years and years was that we, as individuals, were savers, not investors. There was a deep assumption about whether we were willing to take risks or not. And obviously, as we now see from the mutual fund industry, there are a lot of people out there who at some level are willing to take risks.

On the question of being an industry revolutionary, there is another distinction to be made. The goal is to create a movement in your company—a movement that unleashes strategy innovation while creating a revolution in your industry. And there's quite a difference between movements and revolutions.

When you look at movements, you see the women's movement, you see civil rights, you see the quality movement in companies, and what is usually the case is that everybody wins. It is not about "We're going to win, you're going to lose." As women have more rights and have more opportunities, we are winners as human beings, and the same with civil rights. So in that sense, a movement is about involvement and getting people excited about the chance to create the future.

But in a revolution, there are winners and losers. The British lost in the American Revolution. As competitors, we hope that everyone else is going to lose. That is an important distinction. Because while you want some revolutionary goals, you are also going to have to take some evolutionary steps. Particularly in a successful organization, you can't simply turn over everything that you might want to. The challenge is always to distinguish between the part of what we know that we must jettison and the part of what we know that is the path to the future.

S&B *When it comes to understanding the effect on an industry, how can you tell the difference between a change that is a revolution and one that is just an evolution?*

GARY HAMEL At what point does it stop being evolutionary and start becoming revolutionary? I'll give an example.

Clorox has been one of the highest-performing companies in the consumer packaged goods industry over the last decade. One of the things it did that might seem unimportant to an outsider was to figure out how to put fragrances into bleach so the bleach didn't stink anymore. Before that, using bleach was a pretty unpleasant experience. So the change has driven category growth—something that had been absolutely flat has been growing very, very strongly.

To an outsider, that's evolutionary. But the assumption in that industry for years and years and years was that bleach was bleach and you couldn't change it. What Clorox did was very revolutionary within that product framework.

S&B *If you were trying to coach another commodity producer to follow in Clorox's footsteps, what would you say?*

GARY HAMEL One of the fundamental things is to distinguish between function and form. Products typically have a familiar form and function, but what are the other forms in which they could be delivered? Must bleach come in a plastic container, making it stink? Can it be taken home in a box, in ultraconcentrated form, or whatever? Does music have to be purchased via CDs, or can it be pulled off the Internet?

The way you get people to think about orthodoxies is you look at things like the value chain. Does it have to be structured in that way? You look at basic product features and attributes. Do these have to be delivered in the way we're delivering them? You look at the bases that people have chosen to segment the industry. Is there a different way of doing that? You look at the basis of competitive differentiation that is being used. Are there other parameters? You look at the assumptions people have made about who is and who isn't the customer.

For example, one of the assumptions at most car companies is that you are not a customer until you have a driver's license. But why aren't these companies offering driver's education for fifteen-year-olds and winning their loyalty early on?

A revolutionary challenges the prejudices and dogmas of the incumbent. The future is more often created by heretics than by prophets.

S&B *In terms of developing a new product or market, the Japanese often rely on customer feel, the sort of passive or implicit relationship between a product and a person. Is that an element in this?*

GARY HAMEL No. Being customer-led in that sense is very dangerous. Think of a simple two-by-two matrix in which existing kinds of customers and new kinds of customers are on one dimension, and articulated needs and unarticulated needs are on the other. Simply put, when we say we need to be customer-led, what we are trying to do is to better understand the articulated needs of existing customers. In other words, that person driving the minivan would like two sliding doors, or whatever.

Whereas the future-oriented challenge is to understand the unarticulated needs, especially of new kinds of customers. Indeed, creating the future is very seldom about responding to articulated needs. It's understanding deep-down frustrations and anxieties that people have and creating new alternatives for them.

The marketing function is about the worst possible conduit for bringing insight to this process because marketing—particularly through the use of market research—tends to be a prisoner of the existing product concept. And it tends to focus on existing kinds of customers.

The only solution here is to put development people right up against customers, to live with them, breathe with them, understand their frustrations. Then you have the chance of developing deeper insights. You have to take off the blinders, as it were. The problem with most companies today is not that they're fat and inefficient or that they're lazy, because most of them, as we all know, are downsizing and working on reengineering. So the fat and the laziness are being addressed.

My argument is that companies are often blind, and that it is a genetic problem, making blinders a bigger challenge than mere inefficiency. Blindness can even affect an entire industry because most companies are blind in some way.

Coca-Cola is a fine company, but it didn't latch on to the opportunity for either sports drinks or adult teas. That's not because the company is fat and lazy. So you can't really be creative until you begin to remove those scales.

S&B *What causes the blindness?*

GARY HAMEL The deepest reason is an unwillingness or inability to look outside of current experiences. It's the whole set of definitions that grew up over time in a company about what business we're in, what customers we serve, what the bases for differentiation are, where we take value out of the value chain, who our competitors are. And over time in an industry, you get convergence around those things. Why? Because everyone is going to the same trade shows, reading the same industry magazines, talking to the same consultants, and trading mid-level to lower-level managers back and forth. People are spending all of their time focused on somebody else—watching IBM or, if they are at IBM, watching Microsoft—rather than sharpening their own view of the world. And traditional consulting companies, that often transfer the same basic lessons across many companies in an industry, substantially increase the tendency toward strategy convergence, driving companies to price competition. So while consumers may benefit in the short run, they lose benefits of innovation. It may be these consulting firms, more than companies like Wal-Mart, that consumers should thank for brutal price competition.

A lot of this is not simply blindness—a lot of this is denial. Yes, we see it, but it is so uncomfortable that we can't admit to it. And typically, that denial is strongest at the top of the company. I have talked in the past about the need for gene replacement therapy for top management.

S&B *And dealing with the blindness involves the second perspective, of looking deeply within to find hidden knowledge?*

GARY HAMEL Yes. Deconstructing the orthodoxies provides a means of escaping the myopia of a product market definition of a company. Escaping that myopia puts you in touch with the deeper capabilities that I call "core competencies." For example, if you ask the managers of an accounting company about their core competencies, they will tell you about the relationships they manage with CFOs and their understanding of the rules of the Federal Accounting Standards Board and of the tax code.

And I would say to them, "Wait a minute. The deep thing you know how to do is to attest to the accuracy of numerate information, particularly in cases where more than one party has an interest in that information and where these parties have asymmetric access." Classically, the parties were management and shareholders. They both want to know the truth, but they have very different kinds of access and that is why we have auditors.

Where else does this skill come into play? J. D. Power attests to auto reliability, where auto buyers and auto producers are the interested parties. And A. C. Nielsen keeps busy counting how many people are watching *Seinfeld.* Those opportunities would have been open to accounting companies if they had had this deeper self-concept.

S&B *How do you identify core competencies?*

GARY HAMEL A lot of companies try to build the picture bottom up, by looking at the capabilities of individuals, at the specific skills of those in the workforce. But it can't be done that way. If you build up from the individuals, it's extremely difficult to escape the narrow view of product market, because if you started as an accounting company, you say, "Well, what do our people know? They know accounting rules. They don't understand anything else."

Core competence identification has to be top-down. That doesn't mean that top management must do it. It has to be top-down in the sense that you are looking for encompassing things, not simply building up from existing hills.

Put another way, the goal is to discover transcendent capabilities, not generate a laundry list of technologies and functions. You are trying to find capabilities that transcend the traditional boundaries in an organization. When you talk about wireless at Motorola, or miniaturization at Sony, or logistics at FedEx, these are things that you can't put in one function or one category.

The problem is that a lot of companies have done this work, but from the bottom up. And they have ended up restating their business in only a slightly different way. They have missed the payoff that comes from a true definition of core competencies, which should produce a deep conception of who we are as a company.

S&B *So, simply by labeling and identifying what we are and who we are changes what and who we are? If you put your finger on the capabilities within the company, you by definition are changing what the company is?*

GARY HAMEL You're certainly changing your perception of who you are. Searching for the essence of competence is always a redefinition of the deepest sense of self in a corporation.

S&B *Have you observed that? Do you know of a company that has dug inside itself from the top down to find out what its competencies are? And by that fact redefined itself?*

GARY HAMEL Let me give you a couple of examples. I just came back from Australia, where someone told me a very interesting story about a company that had been in the transportation business and understands logistics, moving goods, packaging them, and managing that whole flow. That company moved into the hospital business, where it is the most successful operator of hospitals in the country. It was a good fit because a big part of making a hospital run successfully is logistics—moving patients, moving all the materials and supplies in and out, tracking that in real time, and minimizing the cost of all those flows. And people from the company came up to me and said that they had done this internal core competence exercise and that this is what had come out and it had worked for them.

Another example is EDS. When we started doing work there, their definition of *competence* was all wrapped up in information technology. More specifically, in computers. One of the groups that was looking at competence said, "Wait a minute. We have this competency called 'outsourcing data.' But if you scrape that away and try to get down to the essence, what you find is that we are extremely good at building organizational bridges. When we come in and take over the data center in a company, suddenly it's EDS people sitting in the client's facilities."

So, there is this whole capability to blend two organizations together as you help them manage a part of their operations. Then you say, "Gee, why does that have to be limited to running data centers? Why can't we run the 800 number customer support line? Or why can't we run something else for them?" Getting to that deeper essence gets EDS beyond computer outsourcing. It's maybe not even outsourcing in a traditional sense in that you have to take their assets on your books, or whatever. It is an ability to manage these deep relationships across organizational boundaries.

Essentially, what you're trying to do is search for the deep knowledge that underlies the superficial thing you do.

Look at the assumptions people have made about who is and who isn't the customer. Is there another way to slice the pie?

S&B *I'm glad you brought up knowledge. There's an increasing focus on knowledge these days. And yet the role that it should play in fashioning strategy is not very clear.*

GARY HAMEL Most of the stuff that's been written about knowledge falls into one of two categories.

There's quite a bit that's about the process of knowledge accumulation, but it tends to focus on gains that are incremental, that occur along existing trajectories of knowledge creation. A steel mill learns how to make steel even cheaper or even faster or whatever. And that's very closely related to continuous improvement and *kaizen* and those kinds of things.

Secondly, there's a lot of work on how you make knowledge more codifiable and more mobile inside a company. It's knowledge management: codifying knowledge and making it accessible. The big assumption is that the most important knowledge can be codified, which is an interesting assumption. But the big knowledge problems today are somewhat different. If the goal is to create fundamentally new wealth with knowledge, then there are three additional, very thorny problems that I don't think we have yet wrestled to the ground.

The first is, How do I access and internalize nontraditional knowledge? The examples are everywhere: a chemical company having to come to grips with biotechnology, a traditional computer company having to come to grips with the Internet.

In many, many industries, the fundamental knowledge base is shifting. As we move from mainframe computing to distributed computing, as an example, and as we move from computing to the merger of computing and entertainment, there is a displacement of foundational knowledge. That's a huge challenge for a company: How do you incorporate and understand and bring in fundamental new sources of knowledge?

What makes this even more difficult is that the new knowledge is not only of a different sort but is often in a very different location. Even in our highly mobile world, knowledge tends to be geographically bounded. Every East Coast computer company—Wang, Digital Equipment, Unisys, IBM, Control Data—has gotten into huge trouble over the last ten years. Why? Because the whole geography of knowledge in that industry shifted from the East Coast to the West Coast.

S&B *What is the second thorny problem with knowledge?*

GARY HAMEL That has to do with the ability to integrate very disparate kinds of knowledge. You create value when you apply fundamentally new knowledge to old problems and, in the process, displace the existing knowledge foundation. But the second way of creating value comes from synthesizing discrete kinds of existing knowledge.

You see this happening today in the automobile industry, where we're marrying electronics and communications in products that are ever more complex and systemic. One of the German automakers now has a plan to link air bag deployment to a locator signal and to an automatic call to 911. Not too long ago, the company had to worry only about mechanics. Now it has to worry about advances in electronics and other fields and how to synthesize these changes into new, higher-order solutions.

When you think about synthesizing discrete kinds of knowledge, one simple example that everybody can relate to is Swatch, which successfully rebuilt the Swiss watch industry with inexpensive products. What do you know how to do in Switzerland? You know how to make expensive things out of jewelry and market them. You have a reputation for quality.

Swatch embraced fashion as a new piece of knowledge in the industry. Fashion formerly had meant a very expensive piece of jewelry. Now it meant very clever, compelling design. And it meant synthesizing a number of things in a number of different places. With all due respect to the Swiss, if you want to build a fashion competence, you don't start in Switzerland. The Swiss are not known for their fashion sense. So you import skills from Milan.

To make these new watches out of plastic is an interesting challenge, because you know all about metal bending but you don't know about injection molding and ultrasonic welding. So you form a relationship with Lego in Denmark to learn about that. So you take fashion from Italy, plastic injection molding from Denmark, the Swiss reputation for quality, and you put those things together in a product that nobody could have done on the basis of home country knowledge only.

This is *knowledge synthesis,* and it is becoming more important as products and services become more complex and more systemlike. It is a kind of hybridization. The process of putting things together creates, in itself, a new knowledge. And so the process goes on. But it's not simply stitching together preexisting components. This is not plug and play. It's trying to meld very different kinds of knowledge and capabilities, and therefore typically very different kinds of people and values.

S&B *And the third thorny problem?*

GARY HAMEL Harnessing the great potential in globalizing local knowledge. Being global has meant transferring knowledge in the form of products that are easily moved around the globe. Examples would be Coca-Cola or cellular telephones, where most of the knowledge you need to move is embodied in the thing itself.

Now we're getting to the point where we're beginning to see the globalization of service industries, where knowledge is not embodied in a kind of universal thing, and this makes the problem of globalizing knowledge much, much more subtle. All you have to look at is the trauma that Disney went through in Europe. Or the huge losses of Federal Express, also in Europe. In other words, what you sometimes see are local heroes and global losers—because what they're trying to move globally is very subtle systemic knowledge.

If I have operated in the United States for fifty years, how can I really understand what part of my rules, my procedures, and my approaches are universally applicable and what part is wrapped up in my own domestic culture? What you saw with Disney was the painful process of trying to separate what is universal from what is idiosyncratically American. How do I know the difference when my cultural understanding stops at the Atlantic Ocean?

You can argue there is no simple, easy way to do that. It is always going to be painful. You can probably reduce the risk by starting with a bit of humility, but nevertheless it's going to be difficult. You have to build some very sophisticated cultural bridges, and most bridges take a decade or more to build.

S&B *Besides mastering these three knowledge processes, there is still the matter of freeing up the knowledge we already have that is buried deeply inside something else. Once we* *have freed it and found our core competencies, how do we use it?*

GARY HAMEL That brings us back to where we started. If you look at the companies that have created a revolution in their industries, they are often not the incumbents. If you look at the grocery industry, it was not just Kroger and P&G and so on that were creating the new value. It was Peapod and Starbucks and Petco and Boston Market. If you look at the automobile industry, it has not necessarily been Ford and Chrysler, but Auto-By-Tel or CarMax or AutoNation.

The reason that so many incumbents are being left behind goes beyond a failure to overcome orthodoxies and to develop a deeper sense of self. A company must also understand the discontinuities in the environment that offer new opportunities—and that is a perception that comes more easily to an outsider.

Look at CNN and its creation of global news. It saw at least three things that had already changed in our world that others had not yet put together. One was that you could put a satellite uplink in a suitcase and you could send teams out anywhere in the world to get the story out quickly and globally, as Peter Arnett did in Iraq. It also saw a change in lifestyles—we don't all get home at 6:30—which meant that a different type of scheduling was required to meet the needs of the customers. And finally, it saw changes in the regulatory environment, allowing cable operators to undermine the monopoly of regional broadcasters.

Those were all discontinuities. Those were the things that were already changing. They just needed someone to come along and recognize how these discontinuities could be shaped into something new. Seeing the future is not all forecasting and it is not all scenario planning. It is not about waiting to see if environmental legislation goes this way or technology goes that way. It is imagining what you can make happen, given what is already changing.

S&B *That means everyone has access to the future, doesn't it? That we view it today from the same level playing field?*

GARY HAMEL There is nothing proprietary about the future. By all means, listen to what Nick Negroponte and others have to say, but you must recognize that every one of your competitors is hearing the same thing. So the fundamental question becomes, How do I build proprietary foresight out of public data?

Now, I can't go into all the ways of doing that here. But one way of building private foresight out of public data is looking where others aren't. It's not that the data don't exist. It's that people in an industry are all blind in the same kind of way. So if you want to see the future, go to an industry confab and get the list of what was talked about. Then ask, "What did people never talk about?" That's where you're going to find opportunity.

I talked recently to two hundred utility executives, and I started out by saying, "You guys have nothing to teach each other. You've been reading the same journals and going to the same industry shows forever. So what are you going to learn from each other?" Now, if I could draw a third of this group from financial services, a third from utilities, and a third from telecommunications, then we could have an interesting conversation. That's because the utilities industry needs to understand how to price and manage risk, which is what they have learned how to do in financial services. And the telecommunications industry has already been confronting the issues of deregulation—splitting the network from the distribution—that the utilities are now dealing with.

My fundamental belief is that if a company wants to see the future, 80 percent of what it is going to have to learn will be from outside its own industry.

> How do I know the difference between what is universal and what is American if my cultural understanding stops at the Atlantic?

S&B *How would you organize that effort?*

GARY HAMEL What you might want to do is to organize it around major classes of discontinuities. Who really understands where technology is going? Who understands new work styles or regulation or whatever else? We live in a world where industry boundaries are like borders in the Balkans. So *industry* has become a trivial and unimportant word for the most part.

I would argue that if you look through the three lenses we have been talking about—debunking orthodoxy, defining competency, exploiting discontinuity—you will illuminate opportunities for industry revolution. Now, I'm sure there are other lenses. Those are the ones that I work with and I'm familiar with. If you get some reasonable percentage of an organization looking at themselves and their world through those kinds of lenses, you will dramatically increase the odds of seeing the potential for creating new wealth.

S&B *Now the big question. What we have been talking about are the lenses, not the process. How does all this relate to the strategy process?*

GARY HAMEL Over the last ten or fifteen years, we've had a lot of innovation in the concepts of strategy, an endless barrage of different things to worry about, almost concept overload. What we have not seen is any appreciable innovation in the process of strategy in twenty-five years. The planning approaches that most companies use have not changed at all.

We are working in organizations now where we are creating strategy with five thousand people. We believe deeply in the democratization of strategy, in every employee's right to have a share in the destiny of the organization. But we do not believe for a minute that every employee has the same value to add. Creativity is widely and randomly distributed, but it isn't evenly distributed.

So we know for sure that top management has some tiny proportion of the creative potential of the organization, and therefore top management must give up its monopoly on strategy creation. But not every voice deserves to be heard. That's why we use the metaphor of democracy. The powerful idea in democracy is not "one person, one vote." There are a whole lot of people out there who are not well enough informed to deserve the vote.

Rather, the power of democracy is that you can have an influence that is all out of proportion to your vote. And that is how social systems get changed. Martin Luther King had one vote. Susan B. Anthony probably had no vote when she started. Jesse Jackson has one vote, as does Rush Limbaugh.

In the same way, strategy has to be driven by activists in an organization, because we know that is how great institutions change. They do not change from the top down. This extraordinary arrogance that change must start at the top is a way of guaranteeing that change will not happen in most companies. If you begin to play that out, it leads inevitably to a very different kind of strategy process than we've had.

S&B *Well, the people at the top are generally the last to know how sick the organization is. If you go down a couple of levels and talk to people deeper in the organization, you find it out on day one.*

GARY HAMEL The best-selling management book in history is not *In Search of Excellence* or *Computing for the Future.* It's *The Dilbert Principle.* If you read it, you see enormous cynicism.

To me, the Number 1 management problem in America today is that we have a workforce that has to pay a disproportionate price for the strategic mistakes of top management. And the challenge is, How do you reconnect these people emotionally and intellectually to the company? One of the ways you do that is you tell them, "Guys, we're going to put the future in your hands. We're going to ask you to get involved."

I was inside a company recently that had a reengineering project. About 20 percent of the people were facing the ax. Management said to those individuals, "You have a choice here. You could sit here and this project will play itself out and 20 percent of you will lose your jobs. Or you could pick up the challenge of creating new opportunities for this company. And if you succeed in that, we'll take all the efficiency savings that come out of the reengineering and we'll invest it in your future. But it's your choice." And you know, most people are eager to take up that challenge.

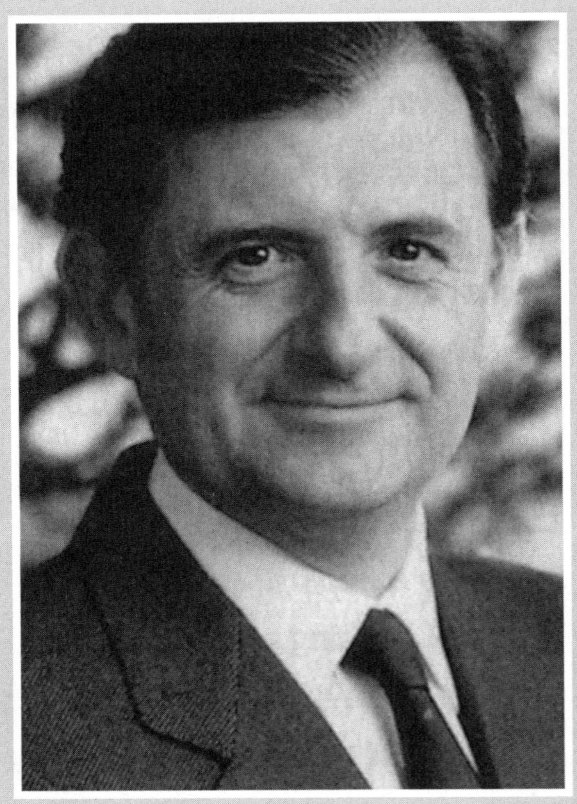

An Interview with

JEAN-RENÉ FOURTOU

Chairman and CEO, Rhône-Poulenc

Jean-René Fourtou, chairman and chief executive of Rhône-Poulenc S.A., one of France's biggest companies, spent the first twenty years of his career at Bossard, a large French consultancy, where he specialized in the chemical and pharmaceutical industries. In the early 1980s, he wrote a report on the chemical industry's future in France that caught the attention of the government, which controlled Rhône-Poulenc at the time. Because of Mr. Fourtou's expertise and because of his report, the government asked him to run Rhône-Poulenc. He became its chairman and chief executive in 1986.

Soon after taking over, Mr. Fourtou, who is now fifty-seven years old, began to transform the company. Not only did he revamp and decentralize the management system, but he also worked to change the culture and make the company more global. Mr. Fourtou

If you meet too often, you take away people's power. You do their work for them. You make their decisions for them.

quickly began selling off poorly performing businesses while buying new businesses that matched his growth-oriented global strategy.

Before his first year in office had ended, Mr. Fourtou launched his American initiative. In rapid succession, Rhône-Poulenc bought Union Carbide's agricultural chemical operations and Stauffer Chemical's industrial chemical business. Then, at a cost of $2 billion, Rhône-Poulenc merged its pharmaceutical operations in the United States with Rorer, the American drug company, to form a new business; Rhône-Poulenc had a 68 percent equity position. Mr. Fourtou also created a partnership between Merck & Company in Europe and Rhône-Poulenc's Pasteur Merieux vaccine business, and he invested heavily in Asia. In 1993, Rhône-Poulenc was privatized. It now has revenues of about $17.3 billion.

Mr. Fourtou's global strategy has worked well, particularly in the United States. During his tenure, revenues from Rhône-Poulenc's American operations have increased from just 3 percent to more than 24 percent of the company's total. Overall revenues from outside France now account for the bulk of the company's business—a full 75 percent, compared with less than 25 percent when Mr. Fourtou took over. Indeed, under his leadership, Rhône-Poulenc has become one of France's most global companies.

Mr. Fourtou, who was educated at France's prestigious—and traditional—L'École Polytechnique, is anything but a conventional leader. He believes in people over systems, in the acceptance of tension within a company, and in individual initiative. Mr. Fourtou—who reads philosophy and once had a philosopher on the staff of his consulting firm—was creating an "empowered" workforce at Rhône-Poulenc long before the term became popular. What follows is a conversation with *Strategy & Business* that took place in June 1996 in Mr. Fourtou's office in Paris.

S&B *A few years ago, you coauthored a book about business called "La passion d'entreprendre," which translates as "the passion of enterprise" or "the passion of entrepreneurship." It is unusual to use the word "passion" in a book about business, at least in the English-speaking world, where business is thought of as analytical, precise, and managerial. For the benefit of us stodgy English speakers, why the word "passion"?*

JEAN-RENÉ FOURTOU To explain, let me first provide a bit of background. Before becoming chairman of Rhône-Poulenc, I was head of the largest consultancy in France. I was only thirty-two years old, and I was running the firm. Now, most people thought the reason I was so successful was that I was a very good salesman. But that was not really the reason. In the entire time, I never lost a client. I kept relationships going.

Now, it is true that as a consultant, I was always selling—new processes, new ideas, new strategies, new approaches, new management methods, new vocabularies, new reengineering ideas, and so on. This is what we were paid to do. But I knew that my clients were not really keeping me because of that. They were keeping me because of something else—something additional—that I was bringing them. Something of which I was not even aware at the time.

S&B *What were you bringing them?*

JEAN-RENÉ FOURTOU I was making the people I worked with happier, which made them much more active. You know, not all of my implementations were big successes. I remember once, when computers were first coming on the scene, there was an assignment with many problems. The computers did not work. But in spite of that, the client kept me. Why? Because even though we had an initial setback, they were happy, and as a result, they were more active, more competitive, more energized.

You see, I have always put a lot of pressure on people not simply to obey but instead to be active, to make decisions, to be empowered, to have life. So as a result, as a consultant I got some really enormous results. And afterward, the clients would say, "My goodness, how this guy works!" So I realized that as a consultant, what I was really bringing to a company was a new sense of vitality—a sense of passion—and that this was what was changing people. I believe very strongly that good management cannot compensate for a lack of vitality.

S&B *How do you create that passion?*

JEAN-RENÉ FOURTOU First, you have to empower people, and you do that by sharing. You have to share vision, share values, and share objectives. You have to bring people together, which I would do. For example, I used to go to football or rugby games with my client, and I used to succeed in bringing both the chairman and the workers to the games. We would sit together and eat together. I mean, I would just go up to them and say, "Are you coming with me to see Scotland versus France?" I would say that to the worker and to the chairman alike. In my opinion, problems started in companies when the workers and the CEOs stopped sitting together, stopped eating together, stopped sharing.

But I must tell you, you cannot have empowered people without also having tensions. You have to live with tensions, you have to accept tensions. But it is more important to have people empowered and sharing visions and objectives than it is to have tranquility.

S&B *So a certain measure of conflict is acceptable within companies?*

JEAN-RENÉ FOURTOU Oh, yes. When there is conflict, there is vitality. But conflicts must be managed and there must be procedures for managing them—even for measuring them—inside the company. This is needed so that the conflict is creative.

When I was a consultant, we invented a way of looking at degrees of conflict and harmony and of plotting them on a grid that has synergy on one axis and antagonism on the other. We separated the matrix-grid into sixteen different boxes, each of which represented a type of relationship between these two extremes. Using this grid, we were able to explain to people the kinds of relationships they were having inside their organizations, and we were also able to train people.

With that knowledge, you can help people to move from one kind of relationship into another and to manage the tensions and conflicts. As a result, we were able to create conditions where there was more vitality and where people take responsibility. We trained more than five thousand people in these techniques.

S&B *Is passion enough?*

JEAN-RENÉ FOURTOU You must be skillful, you must be organized, you must have a system—a system that is really perfectly suited for your company—and, of course, you need management and computer systems and concepts. But, by the same token, if all you have are procedures and concepts and computer systems, then you kill the organization and you kill the spirit of the people who work there. You need a balance between order and disorder. But there must also be a tension between them—a creative, vibrant tension.

S&B *Have you brought these techniques to Rhône-Poulenc?*

JEAN-RENÉ FOURTOU Well, many of these ideas were developed for the consulting firm, where people are partners, where they have to be consulted, where they need to be regarded for their ideas. That place, I thought at first, was a different environment from an industrial firm with manufacturing plants, huge budgets, and a large scale.

But I decided to try anyway to bring a sense of empowerment into this big company. I decided to make the top managers feel like partners, like a community of shareholders. So in my second year here, I proposed to the senior managers that they all buy shares. And they did. These managers all agreed to buy shares equal to one year's worth of compensation. It was a huge commitment, which we were able to help by offering financing. But I wanted them to reach, to change, to feel like partners.

Almost immediately, I noticed a change in the relationships between the people in this group. I noticed it more internally than I did in their relationships with the outside. The goodwill was huge, the community feeling grew, the exchanges between people intensified and became more creative.

But while feelings changed, the funny thing was that not that much changed with respect to having people focus on profits and the value of their shares. They grew closer, but surprisingly, they did not focus more on profits.

S&B *Why was that? A number of important studies suggest that if people have a stake in the enterprise, they will focus their work on pursuits that increase their rewards.*

JEAN-RENÉ FOURTOU Well, that is the case, I suspect, in some other countries. Perhaps in the Anglo-Saxon world. The reason it did not work here, I believe, is that the French are more sensitive to issues of status, while people in other countries might be more sensitive to issues of compensation.

But while people's attention to profit did not change, what was different was that there was a new sense of community, a feeling that it was worthwhile to work together, a search for synergies, and so on. They did begin to feel like partners, and that was very good.

> Problems started in companies when the workers and the CEOs stopped sitting together, stopped eating together, stopped sharing.

S&B *What else have you done to create that sense of community?*

JEAN-RENÉ FOURTOU Three times a year, the sixty-five most senior managers in the company meet for two days. That is the right frequency for a meeting like this, since if you meet more often, you take away people's power. You do their work for them. You make their decisions for them. That is something I do not want to do.

Now, when we all meet, I try to leave enough free time for these people to get together so that they get to know each other informally. I want them to meet informally so that they will create linkages between them, so that they will feel they are part of something. I want to do this—enhance these feelings—rather than work them too hard at these meetings.

One of the ways I try to build these links is over meals, which we take together. During the meals, since I am from the Bordeaux region of France, I take time to educate these managers about the wines of that region. We do that at every meal. That enables me to create a time to share and to create a sense of conviviality among these people. We want them to consult with each other on their own. To ask questions on their own when they are making decisions.

S&B *What if some of the decisions they make are wrong? What are the consequences?*

JEAN-RENÉ FOURTOU Well, everybody makes errors. I mean, we don't want to make errors, we don't like to make errors, but everybody makes them. Within our company, people must be able to learn from their mistakes, which means they must be very determined not to make the same error the next time.

Let me give you an example. We have made some errors in some of our early acquisitions. We have had some huge and successful acquisitions, such as those in the United States from Union Carbide. We have also had some failures. For example, in Germany, our business processes were not working properly. We have set about to analyze these errors and understand how we came to make them, so that we will not repeat them. But we understand that no one is immune from making mistakes.

S&B *Is this analysis formalized, as are analyses carried out after an airplane accident?*

JEAN-RENÉ FOURTOU They are systematic, but only up to a point. And we have learned a great deal from them. I think if these analyses were too formalized and too systematic, they would scare people.

S&B *What else did you do to create a sense of empowerment and community?*

JEAN-RENÉ FOURTOU One of the first things I did when I arrived was to create a small executive committee of the most senior managers. One of its functions is to conduct an ongoing assessment of the company. In that assessment, we ask, What is the state of the company, what are the opportunities, what should we be doing? The aim is to find out what people want to do and then to help them do it. The purpose of this committee is not to do things. That would take away initiative from other people. It would take away the ability of other people to act, which would take away their energy. So we assess the company and set priorities. That is all.

You see, my philosophy is that, to get things done, you have to build common understanding, objectives, and vision so that initiatives are undertaken naturally, rather than imposed.

This executive committee also ensures that I am not alone, that I am sharing with other people in the company, that I have my own linkages. This committee meets once a month.

S&B *You mentioned "linkages." What do you mean by that term?*

JEAN-RENÉ FOURTOU One of those linkages is what we call *family linkages.* For example, all of our scientists within all of our businesses are in one family. All the lawyers are in a family, the finance people are in a family, and so on. All of the families meet at least once a year. They come together. We want people spread through all the businesses so that there is a richness of competencies throughout each of the businesses. But we also want them to have links to one another.

S&B *"Communities of practice" is how this is beginning to be referred to in the academic literature.*

JEAN-RENÉ FOURTOU I would rather call it "communities of people sharing practices." What is important here—more than the practices—is the people, their feeling of empowerment, and their vibrancy. The sharing of understanding, of vision. These are as important as the unity of the group and its cohesion. And, of course, it is important that there is unity and a sense of sharing and that this comes naturally from feeling that one is an individual but also a member of a group. This cannot be imposed from some central authority in the organization. It is a matter of feeling deep linkages between people.

People also come together as members of specific businesses and as members of businesses in particular countries. These are also links. So people come together as members of the ethical pharmaceutical businesses, the vaccine businesses, the agro-chemical businesses, the environmental businesses, the chemical businesses, the food additives businesses, and so on. This is key, because each business has certain factors of success. Since we are in worldwide businesses, where innovation is key, we need to know exactly what is emerging around the world, what our competitors are doing. This is all done vertically, along the lines of the particular business structure.

S&B *What you are saying sounds very well suited to operating in a global environment. But how do you know whether you are succeeding? How do you measure success?*

JEAN-RENÉ FOURTOU We have two types of measures. First, we have financial measures, which are needed in a decentralized, empowered organization. Good numbers and good information are needed by the person who leads the business in a country and whose performance is going to be judged in the end. Everyone shares the same concepts by which we make our financial consolidation.

We try to measure innovation, which is different from business to business. We measure market share. In some businesses, we measure the costs of raw materials. We measure capital employed and profit. We are also beginning to measure economic value-added—EVA—worldwide. Right now, we only do it in our agricultural products businesses. But that measure is used globally. If you go to the agriculture business in Bolivia, everyone understands EVA. If you go to France, they know it. Eventually, when EVA is rolled out around the world for all the businesses, there will be a single, unified set of economic definitions.

These economic objectives are very important, but we also have other priorities.

I try to push everybody to prioritize and to make an evaluation and recommendation regarding their own priorities. If you have too many priorities, you are not effective, but it is the job of management to help people define their priorities and then help them see how they measure up against them.

S&B *Do you use a scorecard to chart these priorities?*

JEAN-RENÉ FOURTOU No. There can be no single set of priorities. You cannot have one single scorecard, because you cannot talk to people everywhere the same way. You cannot, for example, talk to the Americans the way you talk to the Japanese. So you cannot have the same priorities for all.

Now, having people set their own priorities for their work requires that these people have a strong sense of virtue. That they are responsible, active citizens, in a way. Unfortunately, this is tiring for some people. Many people still prefer to obey directions rather than set their own course. It takes energy to set your own course. It takes freedom. It takes a tolerance for ambiguity. Not everyone has these qualities.

> If all you have are procedures and computer systems, you kill the organization and you kill the spirit of the people who work there.

S&B *Does this system work as well everywhere?*

JEAN-RENÉ FOURTOU No. It works differently inside each business and inside each country. It also depends on whether a market is new or old. The priorities and ways you manage a business in China are different from the way you do it in the United States or Germany.

S&B *Is there a single culture at Rhône-Poulenc?*

JEAN-RENÉ FOURTOU We try to have respect for people and their contributions. That is part of our culture. And people have a sense of security working here, though it differs in each country. But most of all, there is a sense that when they work in this company, they are members of a community. As members of a community, they have leverage to do things they could not do on their own. They can get things accomplished here. Within that community, people feel—or they should feel—responsible and empowered and respectful of each other as individuals.

Here is one example of our culture. In our organization, we don't say that "at a meeting it was decided." Meetings don't decide. People decide. Here it is always a person, an individual, who makes a decision and who is responsible for that decision. That person, of course, makes the decision by asking other people and by seeking their consultation. That person has to inform everyone of the decision. Here, people are responsible, not groups. We are a company of individuals first, who all feel that they are part of the group.

Index

D

E

F

Booz·Allen & Hamilton

Booz·Allen & Hamilton is one of the world's leading international management and technology consulting firms, providing services in strategy, systems, operations, and technology to clients in more than seventy-five countries around the globe.

Founded in 1914, Booz·Allen & Hamilton pioneered the business of management consulting. Today, Booz·Allen has more than seven thousand employees in ninety offices on six continents and revenues of $1.3 billion. Its clients comprise a majority of the world's largest industrial and service corporations, as well as major institutions and government bodies around the world, including most U.S. federal departments and agencies.

Booz·Allen is a private corporation organized into two major business sectors: the Worldwide Commercial Business (WCB) and the Worldwide Technology Business (WTB). WCB clients are primarily major international corporations; WTB generally serves governmental clients both in the United States and abroad.

Booz·Allen helps senior management solve complex problems through its expertise in more than two dozen industries as well as information technology, operations management, and strategic leadership.

Consistent with its position as a business thought leader, Booz·Allen publishes the quarterly journal, *Strategy & Business,* which reports on the latest developments in global management techniques, competitive tactics, and strategic thinking.

Booz·Allen & Hamilton is a founding cosponsor of the annual Global Business Book Awards. GBBA recognizes the most innovative contributions to business literature and promotes worldwide readership of business books.

For more information, please visit Booz·Allen's Web site at www.bah.com. Or contact the company at:

Booz·Allen & Hamilton
101 Park Ave.
New York, NY 10178
(212) 697–1900

This *Strategy & Business* book is an excellent business relationship-building tool. By giving this book to your clients, partners, and prospects, you can contribute to their knowledge in a business world where staying current is the only lasting competitive edge. Receive substantial quantity discounts when you place bulk orders. Let us personalize the books with your message.

For quantity discounts and customized orders, contact:

Bernadette Walter
Corporate Sales Manager
Jossey-Bass Publishers
350 Sansome Street
San Francisco, CA 94104–1342
phone: (415) 782–3122
fax: (415) 433–0499
e-mail: bwalter@jbp.com